To the memory of m

Sapper Henry Dadsv

'Bluey the Sig'

for Gillian, Philippa and Fiona

"Justice in a Hurry" is a novel based on the diaries kept by Sapper Dadswell during his service with the Australian Army in WW1. It is a fictional story of mateship and love but includes tales of those who use their power in the Army for personal financial gain, for prestige and promotion and even to execute a vendetta.

"Justice in a Hurry" is a follow on to the book, "The Two Days in Your Life" published in 2015. Originally it was intended to publish "Justice in a Hurry" as a stand alone book, but as it was a continuation of the first book, it was decided that the two books should be combined into one publication.

No doubt there were men serving in the 1st Australian Imperial Force who had names similar to those who appear in the novel but the names of the fictitious characters were chosen at random and that is what they are; fictitious.

First Self Published in Australia 2022
107 The Avenue Armidale NSW 2350 Australia
Email: tozdadswell@westnet.com.au
Website: www.tozdadswell.com

National Library of Australia Cataloguing-in-Publication data:

Author: Toz Dadswell
Title: 'Justice In A Hurry'
ISBN: 978 0 646 86886 8 (pbk)
ISBN: 978 0 646 86887 5 (ebook)

FIC 014040: Fiction/Historical/WWI
HIS 027090: History/Wars and Conflicts/WWI
HIS 004000: History/Australia and New Zealand

Cover image of Henry 'Bluey' Dadswell provided by Toz Dadswell
Cover images have expired Copyright - public domain
Cover and design Marlene Knight
Printed and bound in Australia by IngramSpark

TOZ DADSWELL

JUSTICE IN A HURRY

Toz Dadswell

UNDISGUISED HATRED

Sapper Harold Dowson, lying in the shattered remains of a concrete pillbox, clearly remembered the words of Corporal Alan Wilson, 'There are only two days in a man's life. One day is the day he is going to die. The other, death does not claim him.' The section was huddled in the signaller's dugout having just moved up to the frontline for the first time. The next day they would be in action and they were nervous, each asking himself – 'How'll I go?' Al Wilson was young in years, but a seasoned veteran, having survived a year in France and, before that, the Gallipoli campaign. The newcomers looked to him for reassurance. They had all been there that evening, crowded around the brazier, the light from the flames dancing on their faces. Preacher, Mick, Darkie, Mac, Sam, Jacko, Swede, Skip and himself. Now they were all gone, even the indestructible corporal. The Prince of Darkness had come and claimed them all. Only he, known throughout the Division as 'Bluey' because of his red hair, had survived; and now it was his turn. Marooned in the man-made wasteland that separated the trenches, he awaited his fate.

In the early morning light, he could make out the parapets of the Australian lines, but the safety of the sand-bag walls was denied to him. He knew he was being watched by his own side and it would only be a matter of time before the Germans became aware of his presence on their side of the battlefield. A smile crossed his face. “Well Al, my old friend, I don’t have to ask what day it is today, I know,” he said to himself. “But those bastards will have to blast me out of here and with a bit of luck, I’ll take some with me.” Strange, he thought, I’m not afraid, just plain bloody angry. Angry with everyone and everything. He eased his rifle up into the space he had created between two large chunks of concrete. “Come on, Fritz, come on. Let’s get this over.” And as he waited for the shouts of alarm that would follow his discovery, his mind wandered back. So many good things to remember, so many bad times. What was a boy from the Australian bush doing here, lying in a heap of rubble, in France, waiting to die? Why?

* * *

The muzzle of the rifle never faltered. Slowly, unaware of the danger, the intended victim moved into the sights, stopped and looked around. It was a fatal error and the bullet found its mark. The victim flopped to the ground, gave an involuntary twitch, and lay still.

Without moving the rifle, the marksman worked the bolt, inserted a shell and closed the breech. Another possible victim approached the clearing and, ignoring the dead body, moved into the open. Again, the rifle spat its message of death.

“That’s enough,” said the man standing to the rear of the hunter. The boy emptied the firing chamber, stood up, and handed the rifle to his father. “I’ll get them Dad,” he said as he eased himself over the fence and ran down the slope to where the two rabbits lay. His father watched him go with pride. Those two shots had been at a fairly long range, and only a skilled marksman could accomplish the two kills from two shots. The boy collected his trophies and returned up the hillside.

"Nice shooting, son. We'll get off home now. You can clean and skin them before dinner."

"Pity they weren't Germans" replied the boy.

The old man frowned. "I don't think you would find it quite so easy to shoot German soldiers. For one thing they would be armed, so you might get some of your own medicine back. Tell me Harold, do you really want to kill people?"

"The vicar said on Sunday that the Germans are beasts, not people, so it's all right to kill them."

"The vicar said that?"

"Well not quite that, but that's what he meant."

They walked on, each thinking about the vicar's attitude and about the war. As they approached the small farm house, a younger boy appeared carrying a milk bucket. "Any luck?"

"Your brother doesn't need luck when he's got that gun in his hands, Richard. Don't worry, you'll get fed tonight. By the way, be careful when you're milking Brownie. She has a scratch and it looks sore. Handle her gently."

"I'll be careful, Dad. Mr and Mrs Willis are inside having a cup of tea with Mum. I think they want to talk to you."

"Is Lucy with them?" asked the elder son.

"No, Harold, she's not. I guess she's at home slaving over a milk bucket like me."

"Enough talking, there are chores to be done. Off you go."

The boys departed in the direction of the barn while the old man removed his boots before entering the house. He pulled on a pair of worn out shoes and then joined his wife and their visitors in the parlour. The Willis family lived some three miles away and were the closest neighbours of the Dowson family. The three Dowson children used to ride to the Willis' farm, and from there, the six children together rode the remaining seven miles to school. But now Harold Dowson and the three Willis children, having reached the highest grade at the small country school, had left and sought work. Harold and the Willis' twin sons were the same age, while Lucy, the centre of Harold's world, was a year younger.

After the usual pleasantries, an odd silence came over the group. "I have the feeling, Dave, that you and Muriel have come over for some special reason, and not just a neighbourly chat."

"You're right, Bill. We have something to discuss with you and Joan. No, that's not quite true. We have something to tell you."

Bill and Joan Dowson exchanged looks, feeling they knew what that something was, and they feared how it would impact on their lives. "Well, let's have it. What's so important that you take time off from the farm to visit us during the week in your Sunday clothes?"

Dave Willis looked down at his shining boots. "You don't miss a trick do you, Bill? It's about the twins. Ever since they turned eighteen, they've been at us to let them join the Army. Now they're nineteen they've become even more persistent. And although they haven't said as much, Muriel and I are worried that they may scamper off to the city, change their names, lie about their ages, and join up."

He looked for a reaction, but none was forthcoming. "I know, Bill, from other people, that the Army is not asking too many questions about the age of volunteers, and we don't want the boys running off to enlist under another name. They're determined to go to this crazy war, and I don't think we can stop them. So, if they're to go, then we want them to enlist under the name of Willis. We don't want them to go, but this madness to enlist is dominating our lives, twenty-four hours a day."

"We have the same problem here, Dave. Going off and killing Germans is all Harold can talk about. He's even quoting the vicar at me now."

"Well, the point of our visit is to let you know that Muriel and I have decided to give John and Len our permission to join up. We haven't told them yet but we will tonight. Our reason for coming over, is because we know how close the boys are, and our decision is going to put more pressure on you. I guess Muriel and I have been holding out in the hope that this war would end, but that doesn't seem likely to happen, at least not in the near future. With any luck, it might be over before the boys get to France, at least that's what we'll be praying for."

Bill Dowson reached forward and placed his empty cup on the table. "Dave, Joan and I thank you and Muriel for coming and telling us in person about your decision. It says a lot about our friendship. I would appreciate it if you would ask your children to keep this to themselves for a day or so. We'll have to discuss the matter of Harold's enlistment, and I want to do it at our pace, and not with the outburst of emotion that is sure to come when Harold finds out about the twins. I don't know what we'll do, eh Joan?"

"No, we'll talk about it later." Although Joan Dowson knew perfectly well what they'd have to do.

Dave Willis stood up and his wife followed his movement. "We'll be off, then. I suspect there'll be some sort of celebrating at our place this evening, but I really can't see what there is to celebrate. The casualty lists in the papers are frightening. How could God allow this sort of thing to go on?"

"A good question, Dave, and one I intend to put to the vicar next Sunday. Thanks again for calling. We'll see you at church on Sunday no doubt."

The women embraced, and the men shook hands. From the barn Harold and Richard watched the visitors drive away in the horse-drawn jinker. "I wonder what that was all about?" mused Richard. "You and Lucy haven't been up to any high jinks, have you?"

"Don't be stupid, Dick, and you've got a dirty mind. Lucy and I are just good friends. Still, I'd like to know what went on in the parlour. They all look very serious."

"Oh well, no doubt we'll hear about it tonight at dinner. You finished with the bunnies?"

"Yes. I'd better get them to Mum. Maybe she'll tell me what's going on."

* * *

Harold was more than surprised when his father suggested at breakfast the following morning that it looked like a good day to try for a fish or two in the nearby river. Harold quickly agreed. Fishing was much preferred to mending fences. When the animals were tended, and the two younger children had left for school, Bill Dowson and his son set off. The great red gums, the stringy bark and grey box trees seemed in their towering silence to know the importance of the occasion. Neither man spoke as they walked, each immersed in his own thoughts. Harold recognised that this trip was something special and he felt sure it had something to do with the visit of Mr and Mrs Willis the previous day, but what the problem was he could not fathom.

When the lines were baited and cast, the pair settled down to wait. "Don't think we'll do much good, Dad. It's too late in the morning."

"You're probably right, Harold, but maybe there's a perch or two who missed breakfast. Let's be patient."

For a while both men sat staring at the water, their fingers lightly holding the fishing lines, feeling for that small tug that would indicate a possible victim was testing the food on offer. "Your mother and I had a long talk last night after you'd gone to bed."

"I know Dad. I had to get up around midnight and I could see the light still on in the kitchen. What's wrong? What's going on? Is someone sick?"

"I suppose you could say the whole world is sick at the moment and it was that sickness we were talking about. You see, Dave and Muriel Willis came over yesterday to tell us that they'd agreed to John and Len enlisting in the Army."

"What! They're going into the Army? What about me?"

"Calm down, that's what I want to talk about. That's why we're here. Your mother and I know how keen you are to join up. And now that John and Len have been given permission, we feel we can't stand in your way any longer."

"Oh boy. The Army. Thanks, Dad. I'll make you proud of me. Just wait and see."

"Son, I'm proud of you now. You're the best shot in the district, one of the best horsemen, and you know the bush better than most men twice your age. I don't need you to go off to the other side of the world killing people to make me proud of you."

"But, Dad, it's my duty. All fit men should join up to defend our country."

"Really? Do you think that by fighting the Germans in France you're defending Australia?"

"Dad, you don't understand. This is a war to guarantee freedom to those who want to be free."

The father stared at the slowly moving water and did not reply.

"Well. Isn't that what the war is all about?"

The old man turned and looked into the face of the excited boy. "No, son, that's not what the war's about. War is about two things - power and greed. This war is no different from all the wars that have gone on before. Governments don't ever admit the truth about war, so they drum up good heart-rending phrases such as freedom, the Lord's will, etc. It's all rubbish, and men, thousands of men, and women and children, will die in a stupid struggle for power."

The young man frowned. “Well if you and Mum feel that way about the war, then why are you giving your consent to me joining up?”

“Because not letting you enlist could destroy your life. That’s how stupid this world is. Your mother and I agree to let you join the Army for a stupid cause, knowing that there’s a real danger that you’ll be maimed or killed. A life that shows so much promise, so much talent, put at risk. But if we don’t let you go, there’s the real possibility of you being branded a coward, and that would destroy you. You’re too proud to live with that stigma.”

“I certainly couldn’t face John and Len if they went and I stayed at home. And how would I explain it to Lucy? Dad, there’s no choice, I must go.”

His father shook his head. “I’m the one who should go Hal. You’re old enough to run the farm in my absence, but I wouldn’t get past the medical with this gammy leg. God has a lot to answer for in my book.”

“God? What’s he got to do with it?”

“I believe in God Harold, but I must confess that his ways of operating sometimes confuse me. If he is the God of Peace, then why did he allow this war to start? If he is the God of Love, why did he give me such a wonderful son, and now forces me to send him off to risk death faraway? I thank God every day for our many blessings, but now my faith is being severely tested.”

“Dad you really are looking on the dark side. I can look after myself. I’ll be all right, and when I come home you’ll be pleased you let me go.”

“I wonder how many of those brave men who died at Gallopoli last year said just that. And look at the casualty lists for this year. Son, from this moment, all I’ll be praying for, is that you do return. Now that’s enough talk for the moment. Why don’t you nip off home and saddle up a horse and visit the Willis family. You’ll probably have to go into town to get the necessary papers.”

"Wrong Dad. I've had the forms at home for six months. So, have John and Len. But we do have to find out when and where we have to go for our medicals. See you later. The boy left his line in the water and quickly climbed the bank. He turned to the figure sitting below. "Thanks Dad. Thanks." He then set off at a brisk pace in the direction of the farm.

The old man sat staring at his reflection in the water. "Can we have a pact God? You bring him home safe and sound, and take me instead? Surely that's a reasonable exchange?" The line in his hand quivered, but it was not from the actions of a hungry fish.

THIS MOB HAVE GOT IT

The sun-tanned face of the Sergeant showed no emotion as he surveyed the group of uniformed men lined up in front of him. They had just arrived from the quartermaster's store where they had exchanged civilian clothes for khaki uniforms. At their feet were folded blankets and kit-bags containing all their possessions. Sergeant Davis wasn't too depressed, he had seen such a scene many times. To him it was a challenge to turn this undisciplined gathering into a military formation, ready to fight and, if necessary, to die. To Sergeant Davis they were not people but potential soldiers, a greatly needed commodity.

"Pay attention you lot. My name is Sergeant Davies, your training Sergeant. The Army has given me the heavy responsibility of turning you into soldiers, and believe me I will. Behind you are twelve tents. Each accommodates eight men. When I dismiss you, proceed to the tent that has your name on the slate hanging from the ridge pole. Select a bed and make it up with the blankets provided. The rest of the day is yours to settle in and get to know your mates, because in any army it's mates that count. In the army the first rule is, don't let your mates down, and they won't let you down. One day that piece of advice might save your life."

The Sergeant gazed over the assembled group looking for someone not paying attention. "And one last thing. Your boots. I know the quartermasters store has been dishing out your kit in great haste, and it might be, that some things don't fit properly. I don't give a damn if your tunics are too loose or your hat falls over your eyes, those small problems can be ironed out. But one problem which could arise tomorrow and have a far-reaching effect on you, is the fit of your boots. Tomorrow we'll be doing a five-mile march, to see how fit you are. Five miles is nothing, unless you happen to have ill-fitting boots. Make sure right now that your boots are a comfortable fit. If not, go back to the QM and change them. I don't intend to change my plans because someone has blistered feet. Right, you have been warned. Attention. Dismissed."

The men shuffled around, unsure what to do. They picked up their gear and searched for their tents. Harold's name was on the slate suspended on the second tent. He stepped inside and placed his gear on the first bed to the right.

"And just what do you think you're doing?" The high-pitched voice belonged to a smartly dressed soldier who had just entered. Harold turned and looked at a small, dapper man, with jet black hair, held down by a liberal application of grease. The man's narrow eyes peered at the young recruit. "You have put your gear on my bed, you idiot."

Harold frowned. "Why is it your bed?"

"If you read the notice outside the tent, you would have seen I am in charge of tent number two, and the person in charge always sleeps in the front right hand bed so that training staff can easily contact him."

"Sorry, I'll shift."

"You certainly will you country bumpkin. My God, where does the Army find them?"

Others had now entered and were watching the confrontation. A tall blond man spoke, "Vu have somethink against country peoples?"

The little man spun around to confront the person who had questioned his statement. The words that were about to be spat out didn't arrive. The questioner stood some six feet three inches high and his penetrating blue eyes seemed to light up as if in anticipation of trouble.

The little man meekly asked, "Who are you?"

"Erik Pettersen. I yam from the bush, and ya, I yam proud of it. So vot is it that vu don't like about us? And who are vu, little man?"

"Ronald Johnson. I served in school cadets, and because of my army experience I have been put in charge of this tent. That means what I say, goes. I hope you all understand that."

By now Ronald Johnson had regained his confidence in the belief that no one else had any knowledge of Army procedures and would accept his word. But Erik Pettersen persisted: "Vu called that man a country bumpkin. Why?"

"It's just a term we city people use when referring to people from the country. It's not meant as an insult, it's just a common phrase."

The big man frowned as if the smooth talk didn't ring true. "I think you had better not use this talk when referring to my friend. He doesn't like it."

"Now wait a minute." said Harold. "Thanks for your help but I can look after myself. I don't need a nursemaid. I made a mistake and said I was sorry, so why don't we leave it at that."

"Come on Swede, let's get the bloody beds sorted out and then we can nick off to the canteen for a pint or two." The speaker was obviously a friend of the big man.

"Oh no you won't. I have volunteered this tent for guard duty tonight so no one will be going to the canteen." All eyes returned to Ronald Johnson.

"You fucking what?" stammered Pettersen's friend.

"Each tent takes turns to do guard duty. I told the Sergeant that number two tent would provide the guard detail tonight and that I would instruct you men in guard duties."

"You little prick. Who gave you the right to volunteer us for anything?" Erik Pettersen's companion, a small wiry man with dark complexion, pushed Harold aside to confront Johnson.

"Watch your language soldier. Remember I have been put in charge, and the Army does not take kindly to having orders questioned."

"Balls to that, you little shit. I know your type. You're trying to curry favour with the fucking Sergeant. We poor mugs will do all the work, and you'll get all the glory."

Ronald Johnson looked around the circle of angry faces and decided on discretion. "Each tent has to do its turn at guard duty. Tonight will be the easiest because everyone is excited and tired, so not many will be venturing out from the camp. In the days ahead, guard duty will be more arduous, so I am really doing us all a favour." None of the seven could challenge his arguments and his smooth patter won the day. The men began to settle in, making their beds and getting acquainted.

The small wiry recruit with the mop of black hair was a New Zealander by birth; what he was doing in Australia or why he had chosen to join the Australian Army was unclear. His swarthy complexion instantly won him the nickname of Darkie. The big man, Erik Pettersen was of Swedish descent, hence the nick-name, Swede. The liaison between Darkie and Swede stemmed from a chance meeting the previous night, and over numerous beers they had become firm friends.

The other four men in the tent came from different backgrounds. One was a shop assistant, one a trainee solicitor, one a railway worker and the other, a clerk. It was inevitable that the red-headed Harold would rapidly become known throughout the camp as Bluey.

As predicted by Johnson, the guard duty was uneventful, and the animosity towards him diminished. The five-mile march was followed by several hours of squad drill and there was no mention of a visit to the canteen that evening. Most of the men were young and fit, and the drilling was relatively easy, but some of the older men, and those who were unfit, suffered. Despite the Sergeant's warning, blistered feet were a problem, but no excuses were accepted for absence from the drills.

The third day was similar except the march became seven miles. Day four was a repeat, but the march reached the nine mile mark. The pattern had been set. The only changes were the distance marched and the improvement in drill standards. By the end of the week the squads were able to step off as one man, and nearly all had discovered the difference between their right foot and their left.

Saturday was no different and it was with relief that the men heard Sergeant Davis say, "Tomorrow is the Sabbath. I therefore have to turn you over to God for the day, although I doubt if even the Almighty could make soldiers out of you lot. You may have leave from after the church parade until 9.00pm, but for those of you planning to play up I advise you to be temperate in your conduct. Starting Monday, you'll be marching with your packs plus a rifle. Believe me, it'll make a difference. Don't say I didn't warn you. Fall out."

The men from tent number two had formed into three groups. Ronald Johnson did not fraternise with any of the occupants and at times was able to dodge drill sessions. This seemingly favoured treatment, plus his aloof attitude towards his tent mates, excluded him from their discussions. Bluey, Swede and Darkie were drawn together as a result of their encounter with Johnson on day one. The other four formed another group. However, in the canteen after the church parade on the Sunday, most tents sat together at the same table and drank Victoria's famous beers. As a non-drinker Bluey soon left and sought the company of the Willis twins. Like him, they had found the transition to army life easy. Their fitness made the marches more like a pleasant stroll.

"It's amazing Harold. Sometimes we get back and some blokes just fall into bed exhausted. They even miss the evening meal because they are too tired to get up. Len and I try to help by smuggling some bread and jam back, but it's risky."

"Yeah, don't let the cooks catch you. The chaps in my tent aren't that bad. But what really annoys me is that damn Johnson. I don't know if he's fit or not, he dodges most of the drilling. He said it's because he has done all the drills and he's just waiting for us to catch up."

"Which is he?"

"He's not here, Len. His mummy came to collect him in a big chauffeured car immediately after church parade. In fact, she collects him most evenings, so we really don't see a lot of him."

"Isn't he a recruit like the rest of us?"

"A recruit, yes. Like the rest of us, no. He apparently went to some lah-di-dah school here in Melbourne and was in the school cadets. On the strength of his so-called previous experience, he seems to be able to dodge anything that looks energetic. Darkie says he's a poof."

"A what?"

"A poof. A homosexual. A queer. I don't know, but I don't like him. He's not pulling his weight in keeping the tent tidy. His bed and belongings are always in a mess. I think he's always had someone pick up his things and put them away. Anyhow, he says his mother knows a General and he is just filling in time until he's sent to do an officers course. The sooner the better, as far as I'm concerned."

"You really don't like him, do you Harold? Has he tried any funny business with you?"

"No and he'd better not try. I guess I don't like him because I don't trust him. The others feel the same. He's always volunteering our tent to do extra duties, like cutting firewood for the cook house. But when we tackle him, he always has a plausible reason why we should do it. Of course, he never gets his hands dirty, but he gets all the kudos from the officers and the Sergeants."

"Our tent is pretty dull compared with yours. Come on, let's go over to the YMCA and write some letters."

"I'll come with you John," replied Bluey. "There's not much news to tell but I promised Mother I would write every week."

"And you also promised Lucy," chided Len. "You're going to be a busy boy with all that letter writing. I'm staying here to see if things liven up. Some of the blokes are hitting the grog pretty hard."

"Just make sure that you stay out of trouble." advised his brother. "You're a bit too fond of trying to prove what a tough guy you are, and some of these blokes have been around a bit."

* * *

The second week saw more and longer marches. This time rifles bounced up and down on shoulders, and arms ached from carrying the weapons. Squad drill now involved the rifle and the men learned how to shoulder, slope and present arms. Slowly the group began to act as a coordinated unit. They would return from a twelve mile march still in step, rifles at the correct slope and arms swinging high, causing Sergeant Davis to remark to one of his colleagues, "Pride. That's what makes the difference. You can teach them all you know, but unless they are proud of what they're doing, they'll always be a rabble. This mob have got it. They believe in themselves, and it shows. Mind you, they don't know, no-one knows, how they'll perform when Jerry starts to knock them down, but I reckon they'll be all right."

At the end of week three came the time to actually fire the rifles. Until now it had all been drill, drill and more drill. Four tents were detailed off for the trip to the rifle range where they spent time being lectured on the .303 rifle and safety precautions. Finally, the men from number two tent lay on the firing mound. The Range Sergeant walked along the line and laid five shells alongside each rifle.

"We'll start with five single shots. At the order, load a shell in the breech, close the breech and assume the firing position. Do not place your finger on the trigger. Load."

Eight shells were loaded but not before several men had been severely admonished for allowing the muzzle of the rifle to waver.

"Take your time. Line up your sights and fire when ready. When you have fired, open the bolt and lay the rifle on the ground."

All had been warned that the .303 Lee Enfield would kick on discharge. But some, unfamiliar with guns, failed to hold the butt tightly against their shoulder, and cries of pain identified the victims. Sympathy was absent, but abuse from the Range Sergeant was plentiful.

"Now let's see how you went. Watch your target and the markers will indicate the position of your shot."

The results for number two tent were poor. Only three of the eight had managed to hit the target at a range of 100 yards. Bluey could not believe his eyes. "You could throw a stone from here and get a bull," he remarked to Darkie.

"Don't worry about throwing stones Bluey. Let's see how you did before you sling off at the others."

Bluey had Johnson on his left and Darkie on his right. The marker indicated a miss for Johnson, an inner for Bluey and outer for Darkie.

"Well Bluey, you didn't hit the bull after all."

"Yeah Darkie. I need to adjust to this gun, it fires a little high. What about you, Ronald? You should've done some shooting in the cadets."

"It seems Dowson, I've been given a misaligned rifle. Typical of the slovenly organisation around here."

Further conversation was halted by the Range Sergeant ordering the second round to be loaded. The results were slightly better all round, with both Bluey and Darkie scoring bulls. The firing continued until all five rounds had been expended. Ronald Johnson still had a clear target, while Bluey had scored four bulls and one inner, against Darkie's three bulls, one inner and one outer.

The Range Sergeant went along the line laying a clip with five shells loaded alongside each soldier. He stopped alongside Johnson. "Not good Johnson. In fact, bloody awful. I expected you to do better."

"Not my fault Sergeant, this rifle is totally out of alignment. It's a useless piece of equipment and should be thrown on the scrap heap." Johnson's face was red with anger and embarrassment.

The Sergeant's attitude dramatically changed with the unexpected criticism of one of his beloved weapons but, before he could respond, Bluey spoke. "Sergeant, this rifle is fine. What about I give it to Mr Johnson in exchange for his. Pity if he doesn't get a chance to show us what he learned in the cadets."

"Don't push it Bluey," muttered Darkie from the side of his mouth.

Bluey turned to look at his companion and gave a long wink.

The Sergeant paused as if debating with himself what he should do about the outspoken Johnson. He nodded. "Yes Dowson, that seems a reasonable thing to do." Satisfied the weapons were safe, the Sergeant exchanged the rifles and then continued along the line distributing the remainder of the loaded clips.

Realising that he'd been out-foxed by the red-headed recruit, Johnson stared across the hundred yards separating him from the target as if willing the marking team to give him a good score.

The Range Sergeant continued. "Right men. When I give the command, load the clip and bring the rifle to the shooting position. Do not wave it around like a sailor's wooden leg. Keep the muzzle pointed at the target at all times. When you're ready and comfortable, discharge five shots at the target. It's not a race. Take your time but keep the rifle in the sighting position as you work the bolt. Right, in your own time, load and commence firing."

Bluey and Darkie smoothly executed the exercise, while others had problems, with the odd shot discharged towards the sky overhead. The Range Sergeant's language was colourful. On completion of the shoot, the Sergeant again recorded the scores. "Well, what have we got now Johnson?" The signals went up. One inner, two outers and two misses. "Better, much better." observed the Sergeant. He turned to Bluey. "Now lad, how did you go with that rifle?" The score was signalled. Four bulls, one inner. "Not bad seeing you had a misaligned rifle. You've used a gun before haven't you?"

"Yes Sergeant. My family depends on the gun for a fair number of meals, so I need to know how to use one."

"Thought so. I'll be keeping an eye on you, you might be a candidate for the sniping team. Now what about you, number three?" Darkie also had four bulls and one inner. "You a bushie too?" asked the Sergeant. "No Sergeant, I learned to shoot in New Zealand, mainly hunting for sport."

"Right. I'll put you down also as a possible for the sniping team, but both of you'll need to prove yourselves over longer distances." He moved on.

Bluey turned to his left to find Ronald Johnson staring with undisguised hatred. "You'll pay for this Dowson. You deliberately set out to embarrass me in front of everyone. My God I'll make you pay."

Bluey started to answer but Johnson turned away.

Darkie shook his head. "You're a bloody fool Bluey. I told you to lay off. You've made a real enemy now. I've seen that look on a man's face before. Total hate. He'll do anything to get even. You watch your back."

Bluey gazed down the range. He had gone out of his way to put Johnson down and now he felt guilty. He had never had an enemy before. Back home everyone was friendly and open, but this man was evil. It showed in his eyes and in his actions. Bluey shrugged. "Too late now to say sorry. I guess you're right Darkie. I did that on purpose and I don't really know why. It's going to be a bit hard to keep out of his way seeing we are in the same tent."

"Just stay close to the rest of us and watch your step. Come on, we have to let the next group have a go. I'll tell the others what happened. They'll enjoy the story but I don't think they'll realise the danger you are in."

* * *

For the next three weeks, Johnson completely ignored the young redhead unless there was some unpleasant duty to be allocated, and then it was inevitable the task would go to Bluey. The others watched and sympathised but could do nothing about the situation.

The men found themselves spending more time at the range with the distances ever increasing. Bluey continued to be above average and his inclusion in the sniping team was accepted as certain. Darkie was clearly the second best shot but his performances usually related to the amount of rum consumed the previous evening.

"God Darkie, you'd better watch it. If Johnson finds you have a bottle of rum in the tent, you'll be paraded," warned Bluey.

"No chance Bluey. I'm at the far end of the tent and he never ventures past his own bed. No, it's you and Erik he's after, and I reckon he'll make his move soon. Training is nearly over. Just keep out of his way and you'll soon be off to sniper's school."

"What about you Darkie? You don't seem interested in being a sniper."

"No Bluey. Erik and I are going to be signallers. We've looked at the options and reckon the sigs have got it made. None of this rushing across no-man's land to be shot down by some Jerry machine gun. No, the sigs stay back in cosy little dugouts. No danger, and that appeals to me."

"And Erik thinks the same?"

"Yeah. We met the night before we marched into camp and had a real party. We decided then we would stick together."

"I've noticed that Darkie. He'll do anything you ask. It's almost as if you were his elder brother. He hangs on your every word."

"He's had it tough, Bluey. Lives out in the sticks, only child, no friends. He needs someone to look after him. He believes everything anyone tells him, so the boys tend to string him along. I keep pretty close to him, and if they go too far, then they have me to deal with. Erik's a good man, but too trusting."

The conversation was interrupted by the arrival of Ronald Johnson.

"Ah Dowson. Tent six has a couple of men sick and I've agreed to provide a couple of men from our tent to help with guard duty tonight. Find Pettersen and the pair of you report to the Sergeant of the Guard."

"But we had extra guard duty only two days ago. Why can't someone else do it?"

"Yeah, I'll find one of the others and we'll do it." said Darkie.

"No you won't. I make the decisions. If you want to disobey me Dowson, then say so." It was an open challenge to Bluey, and he saw it as such.

"All right, I'll find the Swede. He won't like it any more than I do, but we'll be there."

"You'd better be Dowson. You had better be." And with that threat, the little man strode off.

"Little bastard," muttered Darkie. "Be careful Bluey, he's all fired up and I reckon he's had the odd sherry. He's up to no fucking good. Keep an eye on Erik. He's too gullible to cope with Johnson's cunning."

"Don't fuss Darkie. It's only piquet duty and we've done it plenty of times. There's the Swede now. I'll break the news to him gently, as I would hate to upset him. I reckon if he hit you, you'd stay down for the count."

"You can bet on that Bluey. See you in the morning."

* * *

Guard duty at the camp had changed drastically over the past two months. The guards now patrolled sections of the camp perimeter with rifles at the slope. Each day a new password was introduced and everyone who entered the camp was challenged with the cry of 'Halt. Who goes there? Friend or Foe?' The correct reply was 'Friend.' The sentry would then say 'Advance friend, and give the password.' Most men took the duty seriously, others regarded it as a bit of a joke.

Bluey complained to the Sergeant of the Guard one night that the routine was all wrong. "By standing there and calling out, the sentry is giving his position away. An enemy would surely shoot him rather than stand and reply, 'Foe'."

"Soldier we've been doing it this way since Julius Caesar crossed the Channel, and I doubt if it'll ever change," was the only explanation given.

Bluey and Erik found themselves rostered for duty at the main entrance from 10:00 to 12:00pm. In the main, it was quiet as there were few men returning to camp. Knowing they were under some sort of scrutiny, both men marched up and down diligently. About half an hour before midnight, a large car pulled up and Ronald Johnson got out. He stumbled slightly as he approached the gate.

“Halt. Vu goes there. Friend or Foe.” The challenge came from the big Swede. Johnson continued to approach. “You know who I am Pettersen,” he said in a slurred voice.

“No, vu must stop and give the password,” Erik said uncertainly. “Vu must obey the rules.”

“No Pettersen, I don’t have to. Anyhow I’ve forgotten the password so you’ll have to let me pass.”

The Swede was unsure what to do. Even the officers followed the set routine.

“Look Pettersen, you’ve got something stuck in the muzzle of your rifle. Let me see what it is. To have a dirty rifle is a serious offence.” Johnson had stopped directly in front of the confused recruit. With a sudden movement, he snatched the rifle from Pettersen’s hands.

“Now you great oafish fool, you’re in big trouble. You have lost your rifle when on guard duty. You’re finished.”

“No. No,” the Swede cried out. “Not finished,” and before Johnson could move the big man’s right fist thundered into his face. There was a sickening thud and Johnson hit the ground. Erik picked up his rifle and stood over the fallen man. “I yam sorry Ronald, I yam really sorry, but vu made me do it.”

Bluey, who had witnessed the whole incident from some twenty yards away, ran towards the two men shouting, “Sergeant of the Guard wanted at the main gate.”

“No Bluey. Ve don’t want the Sergeant. I must help Ronald. I have hurt him.”

"Leave it to me Erik. Just leave it to me," replied Bluey. "I'll explain to the Sergeant what happened. It'll be all right."

"Help me. Oh God someone help me. I'm bleeding to death," screamed the man on the ground.

The Sergeant appeared from the nearby guardhouse. Arriving at the scene he stopped. "What in blazes is going on here? Johnson, what the hell happened to you?"

"Arrest this idiot Sergeant. He attacked me. I'm going to bring charges against him. Lock him up, he's a maniac."

The Sergeant looked at the confused Pettersen. "You do this?" he asked, pointing at the fallen man. Eric nodded.

The Sergeant pointed to Bluey. "Take Petterson's rifle and escort him to the guardhouse." He then turned to the fallen man. "You'd better see a doctor Johnson. That looks nasty."

"A moment Sergeant," all eyes turned towards Bluey. "Don't you want to hear what happened?"

"Not at the moment soldier. Johnson says Pettersen hit him, and Pettersen hasn't denied it. You'll be required to give evidence at the parade tomorrow but for now, you can escort Pettersen to the brig. I'll detail a new piquet. Be at the Major's office at 08:45am tomorrow. Come on Johnson, I'll see if I can round up a medico to have a look at your pretty face."

* * *

Bluey watched next morning as the Swede was marched into the administration building. He wasn't called in to the hearing until Ronald Johnson had given his account of the incident, but Bluey did not expect the Swede to put up much of a defence.

The call came. "Private Dowson." Bluey came to attention, marched into the hearing room and saluted the officer. "Private Dowson," the Major was not in a good mood, "I've heard from Private Johnson that he was violently struck by Private Pettersen last evening while returning from leave. Did you see Private Pettersen strike Private Johnson?"

"Yes Sir. In the execution of his duties, he was compelled to use force to prevent an unauthorised entry into the camp."

The Major's eyebrows rose slightly. "In the execution of his duties? Since when do guards hit people who are trying to return to the camp?"

"Sir, everyone I have ever challenged to stop and give the password has complied with my challenge. You yourself have done so. Last night, Private Pettersen challenged Private Johnson. Johnson didn't stop, and didn't know the password. I would say that Private Johnson was trying to make an unauthorised entry to the camp."

"Johnson. Is this true?"

"Not exactly Sir, I didn't forget the password. I was well aware of the normal procedures but I wanted to test the sentry to see how he would react should an unauthorised person approach."

"Really? Now Private Dowson what part did you play in this incident? Did you go to the assistance of Private Pettersen?"

"No Sir. I was about twenty yards away and it was all over before I could reach the men."

"So you did nothing?"

"I took aim at the intruder Sir. In a real-life situation, where I would have had ammunition, I would have dropped Private Johnson before Private Pettersen had reacted."

The Major suppressed his surprise at the answer. "Really? Just like that, eh?"

"Yes Sir. I wouldn't have missed at that range."

The Major studied the face of the young man to see if he was being sincere. Satisfied that he was, he turned to Johnson. "So Johnson, as I see the situation, you, on your own initiative, decided to test the camp security. As a result, Private Pettersen struck you in order to regain his rifle. A reasonable reaction in the circumstances. And if you'd been foolish enough to test the guard in a war-time situation, you'd have been shot. I don't know why you took it upon yourself to conduct a security check of the camp, but in such circumstances, you must be prepared to accept the results. I dismiss the charges. I trust Private Pettersen you won't give up your rifle to friend or foe in future."

Erik stood looking at the Major, confused by the events of the past few hours.

"Well Pettersen, do you have anything to say?" asked the Major.

"Ya," said Erik. "Next time I yam to shoot him before I hit him."

"Something like that Private Pettersen. Something like that. Dismiss the parade Sergeant."

The two privates saluted and marched from the room.

"One moment Johnson," the Major said as the injured man saluted and prepared to leave. The officer shuffled through some papers on his desk. "I was going to send for you this morning but you saved me the trouble. I don't think you'll be popular in your tent today, tomorrow, or ever, for that matter. What you did was damn stupid, although I couldn't say that in front of those men." Johnson stared at the floor.

"However, fate, or some other authority, has stepped in. You're to report to Victoria Barracks for further orders which I'm told will include a posting to officers training school. You're not due there for a few days, so I suggest you take yourself off on leave and see if you can get your face back into better shape before fronting your fellow officer cadets. I suppose congratulations are in order. Off you go. Clear out your gear and report to the orderly room for your papers."

Ronald Johnson saluted and left. His appointment to the officer training school was to have been a great victory over the idiots in his tent, but he felt cheated. The men would be on the parade ground and he would not get the opportunity to boast. His face ached, Dowson and Pettersen had gone free, and he could sense the contempt in the Major's voice. "Cheated by those bumpkins from the bush. Well they'd better hope and pray our paths don't cross once I have my commission, because if we meet again, my God I'll make them pay."

* * *

As the angry Johnson walked towards the tent lines, he was watched by the Major and the Sergeant.

"You look unhappy Sergeant."

"I am Sir. I would've thought someone would've asked me for a report on Johnson's progress before posting him to officer training."

"Yes. I agree that someone might have sought your opinion. However, I also suspect you wouldn't have recommended him."

"He's no soldier, never will be, and he's no leader. God help any men who have to serve under him."

"Interesting. I wondered about the lack of a request for a fitness report, so I think we can assume he has friends in high places. Well it's done and we can't stop it. My God, that Pettersen certainly laid one on him."

"A sort of farewell present Sir. I doubt if anyone will ever try to play silly buggers with the guard in future, especially when Pettersen's on duty."

* * *

The news that Ronald Johnson had departed the recruit camp was well received in the tent that evening. Erik Pettersen had overnight become something of a folk hero and his newfound status embarrassed him. His close mate Darkie embellished the story each time until it became clear that Erik was a distinct possibility of being released from the army to fight for the world heavyweight championship.

"Tone it down Darkie," advised Bluey. "Soon you'll have everyone wanting to take the Swede on in the ring just to prove how good they are at boxing."

"Don't worry Bluey, Erik can look after himself in or out of the ring. You know we could line up a few bouts for him and place a few bets on the side. We could make a little extra for ourselves."

"Darkie. I thought you said he was your mate. And if he really is your mate then you won't use him for such a purpose. It's immoral."

"No Bluey, it's not immoral, it's business. But don't worry, I won't let him get hurt. You're right, we're mates. By the way, aren't those two over there your mates from back home."

Bluey saw the Willis twins approaching and it was obvious that something was wrong.

"Thank goodness we've found you Harold. You have to help us." John blurted out.

"What's wrong?"

"Len has just been told that he's going to be detailed off to join the signallers. They haven't enough volunteers, so they picked out some names at random and Len's name came up."

"That's bad luck, but how can I help?"

"Harold, we can't be separated. We must stay together. We have never been apart from each other, ever."

"Yes I know John, but what can I do?"

"Remember at the railway station when we were leaving for camp you said to our mother, 'Don't worry Mrs Willis, I'll look after them'."

"Yes Harold, and you told Lucy the same thing," added Len.

"I know I did, and I meant it, but how can I help?"

"We have talked to the Signaller Sergeant, and he said if Len can find someone to take his place, then he can stay in the infantry."

Bluey stopped smiling. "You mean you want me to volunteer as a signaller? You're asking me to do that?"

Bluey was in a corner. The twins knew he would never go back on his word, especially his word to Lucy.

"Look fellas, I'd really like to help, but I think I've a good chance of going to the sniper's school. It's quite an honour to be selected."

The twins gazed at Bluey's face as he sought to extract himself from his predicament. It was as if the twins were calling up all the IOU's from their childhood days. Only they could release him from his promise, and they were not about to do that.

"I'll not be going back on my word, but it's not fair, and you both know it. You can tell the Sergeant I'll take your place Len, but I think we all should understand that from now on, I won't be taking care of you as I promised. I won't be able to. You're on your own."

"Harold, you know, and we know, it was an idle boast you made at the railway station as there isn't any way you could look after us. From what we've heard, once we get over there, everyone will be too busy looking after themselves to worry about others, but we knew you wouldn't refuse if we asked this great favour of you, even if it meant giving up sniper school. So, what I'm saying is that John and I are now in your debt, and one day, somewhere, somehow we'll repay you."

"Such as?" asked Bluey.

"Such as letting you marry our sister. How about that?"

Bluey smiled. "Not yours to grant Len. Yes, I'm disappointed at missing out on sniper school, but I guess it's important you two stay together. Come on, let's find this sergeant from the Signallers and tell him to change the names."

* * *

The next morning was the final parade of the recruits. They formed up in front of the other squads. A General arrived and painstakingly inspected the ranks. He stopped from time to time to speak to a man. The well-fitting uniforms, the highly polished boots and brass work passed his keen inspection. The General returned to the saluting dais where he delivered words of encouragement. The parade then marched past the reviewing officer and off the parade ground. Basic training was over. The great adventure was about to begin.

STILL THINK IT'S A BREEZE

Bluey walked towards the transport pick-up area where Darkie and Erik were standing with six other soldiers. He was still smarting from the sarcastic tongue lashing he had received from Sergeant Davis. "I picked you wrong young fellow," snarled the Sergeant. "I thought you were made of the right stuff to become a first-class sniper, but I was wrong. I hear you have volunteered for a soft job with the signallers. Well I hope you enjoy your cushy job while your mates do all the fighting. On your way and good riddance." The words had hurt the young redhead, but he saw no reason to explain the circumstances to the angry Sergeant.

He reached the group and although he vaguely recognised some of the faces, he didn't know their names. Darkie seemed to have taken charge of the group.

"Fellows, this here is Bluey Dowson. Best bloody shot in the Army, and I talked him into becoming a signaller so he could protect us. That right Bluey?"

Bluey blushed at Darkie's introduction. "Don't take any notice of Darkie fellows, he talks a lot when he's been drinking, and that's fairly often."

"Now then Bluey me old mate, that's no way to talk about your old pal. Now, this long lanky bag of bones is Tom Lacey, and he hails from South Australia. His dad grows grapes over there, so he can't be all bad."

The tall man with blue piercing eyes shook hands with Bluey. "I suspect your boon companion has a few too many of father's grapes in him at the moment."

"Rubbish Preacher," laughed Darkie. "They call him Preacher 'cos he's always reading the Bible and going off to church, but we'll win him round."

"Perhaps Darkie, or maybe he'll win you round."

"Fat chance of that happening." Darkie continued with the introductions. "Now this is Robert McKenzie, known for some reason as Mac. His old man owns a sheep station down in the Western District. He must have a sense of humour somewhere but I've yet to find it. Come on Mac, give us a smile."

The athletically built man stepped forward and thrust out his hand. "I'm pleased to meet you," he said with a hint of a Scottish brogue. "We're hoping you kin control this man."

"No I can't," laughed Bluey, "no one can, but I do try to keep him out of trouble."

Darkie considered this remark for a short while and then decided to ignore it. "Next is Skipper. His real name is Max Walters and his dad owns a fishing boat down Gippsland way. Skip should've joined the Navy but he doesn't like the sea. Right Skip?"

The solidly built man with a weather-beaten face and a shock of fair wavy hair, thrust out his hand. Bluey could feel the roughness of the skin as they shook hands.

"Pleased to meet you, Bluey. He's right you know. I couldn't see any point in sailing around the ocean cleaning brass work for the Navy. I reckon I'll see some action in the Army."

"You may get a bit too much Skip, if the papers are anything to go by," answered Bluey.

Darkie interrupted. "Come on Bluey that's enough of that sort of talk. This here little fellow is Sam Ralston, a bank teller by trade, but the cash box was a little light on one day so he left and joined up."

Sam put forward his hand. "I hope you don't believe any of the nonsense your partner carries on with."

"No Sam I don't. Pleased to meet you."

"Next is someone you'll understand Bluey." Before Darkie could say any more, a tall rangy man in his late twenties stepped forward to shake hands.

"I'm Ken Jackson. Spent most of my working life as a shearer. Most folks call me Jacko."

"Pleased to meet you Ken. Tried my hand at shearing a couple of times. My back still aches when I think of it." The final member of the group was small, with a sallow complexion. He too didn't wait for Darkie's introduction: "Mick O'Brien," he said with a strong Irish accent, "pleased I am to meet with you."

"Likewise Mick. You from around here?"

"Lived all my life in Melbourne, out Collingwood way. Been working in a shoe factory since I was fourteen. You follow the footy?"

"Not really," replied Bluey, "but I wouldn't have to be a genius to work out who you barrack for."

"You're right. The mighty magpies. Pity the footy season's finished or I could've taken you all along to see a real team in action."

"Before you all get involved in football, I suggest we collect our gear and climb aboard that truck." Tom Lacey spoke in a quiet tone of voice but the authority was evident. Without question the men moved towards the vehicle.

"How come you know this truck's going to Broadmeadows, Preacher?"

"It's no great mystery Darkie. While you were acting as the official receptionist for the group I walked over and asked the driver. He said he was here to collect nine signallers bound for the sig school at Broadmeadows. Someone had to do something, or we'd be here all day listening to your jokes."

Darkie scoffed. "Well I've heard your stories and they mostly come from the Bible. That's not my scene."

"We'll see, but for now I suggest you dump that bottle in the garbage bin over there or the MPs at the camp will have you as their guest for the evening."

Darkie looked around the group. "Anyone want a swig before I ditch it?" There were no acceptances, and so with great ceremony, Darkie lowered the bottle carefully into the bin.

"Why didn't you smash it?" asked Mac.

Darkie looked aghast. "Blimey Mac, you're a cruel one. Somewhere out there," he waved his arms in the direction of the city centre," there's a bloke dying for a drink, and in due course he'll look in this bin, and lo and behold, his wishes will come true."

"You're all heart Darkie," said Bluey. "I doubt if a fly could get a sip out of what was left in that bottle."

"It's the thought that counts mate. Give me a leg up into this heap of nuts and bolts. Why couldn't they have sent a bus for us? These trucks are bloody murder on the old bones."

With all nine men on board, the truck set off on the trip to the north. Conversation was impossible above the noise and each man settled down with his own thoughts.

Bluey eyed the group, nine men of a variety of ages and backgrounds. He wondered what had motivated each man to join the signallers. He wondered how they'd get on. At least there was no Ronald Johnson and that must be a plus he thought.

* * *

The truck delivered the nine would-be signallers to a hut inside the boundary of Broadmeadows Camp. As they sorted out their kit-bags, a Sergeant appeared in the doorway. "Pay attention men, I'm Sergeant Reynolds." he said quietly. "I have twelve weeks to turn you lot into a highly professional section of signallers. There is much to learn, and as my reputation is at stake, I can promise you that you'll learn everything. It's as simple as that. Now get yourselves settled into your quarters and then I'll show you around the camp. You'll not have time for guard or cookhouse duties as you'll be busy every evening. Oh yes, just in case you're wondering, you'll have Sunday afternoons and evenings free, but you won't leave the camp. Welcome to the Signal Corps."

The Sergeant turned smartly and marched away, leaving his charges in a state of shock.

"So, the sigs have got it made eh, Darkie?" Bluey took pleasure in the look of shock on the New Zealander's face.

"Twelve bloody weeks without leave. He's got to be joking." The words stumbled out of Darkie's mouth.

"I don't think he was. Come on, let's get settled in."

As the men selected sleeping spaces it was evident that tentative liaisons had already been formed. Erik and Darkie moved to a corner at the far end of the hut. Opposite them were Skipper and Mac. Sam Ralston and Ken Jackson had shared a tent at recruit camp and had gravitated into a close duo. Preacher Lacey, Mick O'Brien and Bluey selected beds near the entrance.

"How old are you Mick?" asked Preacher.

"Old enough. What's it to you anyhow?"

"Whoa, don't get on your high horse. It was just a remark to start a conversation. I hope we can all get off on the right foot because I feel our stamina and patience will be sorely tested in the next twelve weeks."

"Sorry, I didn't mean to jump on you. I'm twenty, or will be next month. You're a lot older, aren't you?"

"Oh dear, am I showing my age? I'm twenty-nine which I suspect makes me an old man in your eyes." Preacher laughed at himself. "An old man at twenty-nine!"

"What did you do back home Preacher?" asked Bluey. "I mean, you're not a real preacher are you?"

"No, I was a school teacher, but my family are serious about our religion and so am I."

"So am I Preacher," interjected Mick. "But I reckon we're on different sides of the fence."

Preacher turned. "I'd like to think there is no fence Mick. Perhaps we see things differently but after all, we do believe in the same God."

Mick frowned. "My mother warned me there'd be people who'd try to confuse me, but you won't fool Michael O'Brien."

Preacher sighed. "I'm not trying to confuse or convert you away from your beliefs, Mick. You follow Him in your way, I follow Him in my way. That's the difference."

"Preacher's right Mick, and it's best we respect one another's views, as we can't be sure who has got it right." Bluey was surprised to find himself taking part in a religious discussion. "Perhaps in the future we'll find out more about our God. From the look of the casualty lists, we may have a great need of protection from above."

Mick looked at Bluey. "Yeah. Let's drop it for now."

"We haven't got any choice," said Preacher. "Here comes Sergeant Reynolds. Here we go again."

The men formed a squad of two ranks and marched around the camp. At various locations Sergeant Reynolds explained the purpose of a building.

"This is the Morse training classroom. Morse code is your bread and butter for the next four weeks. You'll eat, sleep and dream in dots and dashes. If you don't keep up with the pace, you'll get back-classed to the next entry, and if you fail that, then it's back to the infantry. I can't think of a worse fate for anyone."

A bell rang. "Chow time. You, do you remember where the mess hall is located?"

"Yes Sergeant," Preacher replied.

"Right. Take charge of the squad and march the men to the mess hall. Have them back here in exactly one hour to start work. Got that?"

"Yes Sergeant." Preacher took up his position. "Squad quick march."

"Bluey, did you hear that?" The voice of Darkie was incredulous.

"Keep silence in the ranks," thundered Sergeant Reynolds. The order held an unspoken threat of what might happen if silence wasn't observed. The men marched on in silence.

* * *

After the meal, the group lolled about on their beds discussing their first impressions.

"Still think it's a breeze Darkie?" asked Bluey.

"Yeah, of course it is. You heard the man. All we have to do is learn about these fucking dots and dashes and then we get to sit in a nice warm shelter sending messages while the poor bloody infantry goes out and gets killed."

"Come on," called Preacher. "Get formed up. This sergeant might look meek and mild, but I've got a feeling he's not the sort of man to upset. Remember no talking and march smartly."

Preacher was enjoying his new-found position of authority.

Sergeant Reynolds was waiting at the hut door. He had watched the approach of the men with studied interest but said nothing as they filed into the lecture room.

With each man at a desk, Bluey thought how similar the setting was to the old schoolhouse at home. Only the faces were different.

Sergeant Reynolds was tall with close-cropped greying hair. His voice was soft and his words were well chosen and few. He continually shifted his gaze as if taking stock of his new charges.

"It is my task to mould you into an efficient squad of sappers in the Signal Corps. To accomplish this challenge, I have been given twelve weeks. I will need every one of those eighty-four days if I am to succeed. This room will become like a second home to you. You will always sit at the same desk. Take no notes or material from this room without my permission. Each week one of you will be designated as the soldier in charge, and he will hold a key to this room. The man in charge will open the room as and when required, and will be responsible for locking it when it's not required. The room must never be unlocked when it is unoccupied. Any questions so far?" The Sergeant didn't wait for any possible interruption.

"You men have been selected to serve in the elite branch of the army. Any fool can be taught how to fire a gun, or how to charge across the land waving a bayonet, but only the signaller can tell him where to charge, when to fire, what to fire at, and what his friends and foes are doing. Without intelligence, the gunners and infantry would be operating in the dark, and it is we, the signallers, who convey and distribute the intelligence to them. Here in the training camp, you may find at times the ignorant infantry passing derogatory remarks about the sigs. Ignore them. Once in action, they will be begging you to mend their telephone lines, get messages back to HQ and so on. In action, they will depend on you, and you must never, never, let the infantry down." The Sergeant paused and again studied the nine faces.

"Now, first and foremost is the magic called Morse code. It may be magic to others, but to you it will be bread and butter. You will learn to read and transmit Morse by flag, light and buzzer. Twice a day I will run tests to monitor your progress. The mastering of the code is the biggest problem for the trainees. There is no easy way, no short cuts. It's a matter of concentrating and practising."

For the next half hour, the Sergeant explained the basics of Morse code. The time taken for a dot was one unit, the time for a dash, three units. The interval between one or more dots or dashes was equal to one unit and these time ratios remained unchanged regardless of the speed of the signalling. Rhythm was the key to success in both sending and reading. The Sergeant used a flashing lamp on the desk to demonstrate.

"That's probably enough for now. On your desk is a card which sets out the code. This is the one piece of paper you can take from this room. It fits into your top pocket, and I suggest that you look at it and learn something new every time you sit down. If you start to lag behind with Morse, it will be most difficult to catch up. If you think you are falling behind, get the key and come and practise. Tomorrow morning, I will expect you to know the first five letters of the alphabet and I'll be testing you. The course is now up and running and so are you. Right Lacey, you're in charge this week. Here's the key. Lock up and march the squad back to your barracks."

The Sergeant departed but the men remained seated.

"Twelve bloody weeks just to learn these stupid dots and dashes." snorted Darkie. "Twelve days should be more like it, then we could have some leave."

"Don't be fooled Darkie." Skipper spoke. "I've had to learn Morse so I could work the wireless on our boat, and it's one of those funny things to learn. Some people pick it up right away, comes natural to them. But others find it a slog. I wonder what speed we have to reach."

"Speed? What are you talking about? You saw the man. Dot wait dash wait dot. It's so slow anyone with half a brain could read it."

Skipper moved to the desk and connected the battery to the lamp box. "Right Darkie, let me show you what I mean." Skipper slowly clicked the Morse key. "I don't expect you to have read that, but what I said was, 'Darkie is mistaken and will soon know it.' Now let me increase the speed, and remember I'm no expert."

The light flashed at a much quicker tempo and the watching men had trouble in sorting out the dots from the dashes.

"You see, that's what I mean by speed, Darkie?"

"That's rubbish, no one could count the dots and dashes at that speed."

"Correct. You can't. You don't count dots and dashes, you learn to recognise the letters as a whole. For instance, the letter A is not a dot and dash, it's the combination of a dot and dash."

"Come on, time to get back to our hut. Skip, we might need your help in the weeks ahead." Preacher was looking as worried as the rest.

"If I can help I will, but as I said before, some will take to morse without any trouble, but some may find it hard work."

Preacher locked up and marched the squad to the barracks. From the shadow of the building opposite Sergeant Reynolds emerged. He watched the backs of the retreating men. "You boys just might do. The first signs are good but we'll soon know for sure."

* * *

The squad went for a brisk two mile run next morning before settling down in the classroom. They were impressed that the grey-haired Sergeant Reynolds accompanied them on the run and showed no sign of fatigue although he ran and walked with a limp.

The Sergeant, using the signalling apparatus, took them slowly through the first five letters of the alphabet.

"I will spell some three letter words which I want you to write down. Try to memorise the letters and so the words will flow. I will pause between words so you can write them down."

The lamp flickered. After ten minutes, the Sergeant moved around the group to scan the results. He made no comment on what he saw.

"Right, we'll move to the next five letters and tomorrow I'll test you on those."

On completion of the Morse session the Sergeant gave the class a short break to clear their minds.

"How did you go Darkie?" asked Skipper.

"Easy mate, easy. Nothing to it."

Skipper smiled. "We'll see. What about you Erik?"

"I got mixed up Skipper. I would be working out one vord, and ven I vos writing it down, he would start sending another. It's hard, very hard."

"Don't give up Erik. It's always difficult, especially when we start with the buzzer. But suddenly it will all come out right. You'll see."

"I hope so Skipper. I don't vant to go back to the infantry."

The Sergeant re-entered the room and the men fell silent.

"You may have got the impression from yesterday's chat that all you have to learn is how to send and receive Morse code. Let me assure you that there's more to it than that. Hands up those who can ride a horse."

Bluey, Darkie, Jacko and Mac raised their hands. The Sergeant noted their names in the book he always carried.

"Who can ride a motorcycle?"

Mac and Sam Ralston raised their hands. Again, the Sergeant made an entry into his notebook.

"Who can swing a shovel?"

The group hesitated, it seemed a trick question and to raise one's hand might be interpreted as volunteering for some hard labour.

Sergeant Reynolds smiled. "It doesn't matter whether you can use a shovel or not at this stage. However, next to your signalling gear, the shovel is going to become your most important piece of equipment. War comes down to four things. Eating, sleeping, shooting and digging."

"Digging? Digging what?" asked Sam.

"Dirt my boy. Dirt. The world is full of it and there are times when it has to be moved."

"Such as?"

"If you want to build a latrine, you dig. If you want to fill a sandbag, you dig. If you want to protect a cable, you dig a trench for it. If you want to protect yourself, you dig a funk-hole. If you want to bury your mate, you dig. There's no end of opportunities to use a shovel. Now let's talk about other activities you'll become engaged in. I've already touched on the basics of signalling, but to put your Morse code to use you'll have to learn how to set up, operate and maintain signalling lamps, heliographs, signalling telescopes, buzzer sets as well as operating Morse and Semaphore flags."

The grey-haired man paused, but there was no reaction. "You'll learn how to set up, operate and maintain telephone sets and the cables that go with them. You'll learn how to lay telephone lines on the ground, above the ground and under the ground. You'll learn how to repair the lines by day and by night. It'll all become second nature. You'll learn how to map read, to pass messages both in plain language and in code, and for the really clever ones, there is the wireless. Now all this I can, and will, teach you, except the wireless course. What I can't teach you is, how to do it in safety when some Jerry sniper or machine gunner has you in his sights. You'll learn that over there. But if you mess up, you won't last as a signaller and they'll send you back to the infantry. Any questions?"

"Why the questions about horses and motorcycles?" Bluey asked.

"Because, young man, signalling is about passing messages. The best way to pass a written message is to hand deliver it. You can take that message and walk or run with it, or you may be able to ride a cycle, a motorcycle, a horse or even catch a taxi cab, but the message must get through. If you can't walk or run or hitch a ride, then you must use flags, the lamp, the buzzer or the telephone. So you, the signallers, must be able to use whatever system is available to get the message through. Right, now you know what's expected, let's get cracking and learn how to do it."

* * *

The next weeks became a nightmare. Each day started with a run, each time a little longer. Each morning the dreaded Morse code test. They struggled with the theory of electric current, armatures, transformers, condensers, batteries, circuits, receivers and transmitters. Every day they practised finding breaks in field cables and mending them. It was go, go, go, from morning until night, and it was an exhausted group who climbed into bed each evening. Then just as they seemed to be coping with the flashing light, Sergeant Reynolds introduced them to the Morse buzzer.

"You must now train your ears the same way as you have trained your eyes. You must hear the letter, not the dots and dashes." The men tried desperately to heed his advice.

Erik was having more difficulty than any of his counterparts and Skipper gave the Swede extra tuition.

"It's strange isn't it." Skipper was talking to Preacher and Bluey over the lunch table. "Erik is very good at Semaphore. He's probably as quick as any of us. But he has this hang-up with Morse. The Semaphore shows he has the co-ordination between brain and hand to read the messages, but with Morse, that co-ordination seems to falter. I'm sure it's a fear of failure that's stopping his progress. It's a mental block and I don't know how to overcome it."

"Will he pass the final test?" asked Bluey. It was a question that was often asked by the men when out of Erik's hearing.

"Probably not, unless there is a sudden breakthrough. Hell, I'd hate to see the Swede fail. He tries so hard and is a great team man."

"No doubt about that Skip." replied Preacher. "But there's not much we can do except hope, and in your case, continue with the extra tuition."

* * *

After ten weeks, they felt they were beginning to master their newly chosen trade. In the field, they became proficient at running out cables, repairing breaks and reeling in the cables. They could pass messages by flags, lights and buzzer. They wondered if Sergeant Reynolds had any surprises for them over the final two weeks.

"I've taught you about all I can, and now we must see if you have taken it in. Tomorrow morning you'll move to a field training area near Castlemaine. There will be two infantry companies exercising in the area, with each company representing a battalion. One company will have its own signallers and you'll act as the signal section for the other. This is not a competition. You are not out there to compete against the other section. You'll be judged on how you perform your various tasks. As you know, the infantry can be very difficult at times, but you are there to provide a service to them."

The Sergeant's dislike of the infantry was well known and he made no secret of his belief that they were the servants of the signallers. The infantry merely carried out instructions carried to them by signallers.

"Tomorrow you'll go by train to a small town just south of Castlemaine and from there by truck to the exercise area. You'll be shown the battle area and you'll have to decide where you're going to set up your quarters, and then build them. You may decide to set up tents or you may decide to build a dugout, something a little more substantial, a little more protective, than a sheet of canvas. Remember you'll be in a war situation and in some instances real ammunition will be used. You need to elect a leader who will, for this exercise, act as corporal of the section."

The men looked at each other. It was Mick who broke the silence. "I reckon Preacher is the bloke for the job. He's always got plenty to say, so let's see if he can now put what he preaches into practice."

"Mick, I think your proposal is a way of getting back at Preacher because he usually beats you in your debates, but I'll second the proposal." Bluey felt that Preacher had the respect of all. "No problem for me," remarked Darkie. The others nodded.

"Right. Lacey, it's now up to you to organise this group into an effective working section." Sergeant Reynolds looked into each face to make sure his words were being recorded.

"By your own choice, you have made Lacey your leader. As from now, you will do without question, without complaint, whatever he tells you. When you get to France, you'll most probably be allotted a corporal with battle experience to be your section leader. As with any chain of command in a battle zone, total obedience is required. That's what you must learn and learn well. Right Lacey, they're all yours. The train departs at 8:00am. You only need to take your personal gear as everything else will be available. I'll be around, but only as an observer. Good luck." The Sergeant strode from the room. The group turned to Preacher.

"What about a leave pass General?" Darkie never let an opportunity pass.

"Sorry Darkie. No leave, no canteen. We're going to do this properly and show we're ready for the trip overseas. Sergeant Reynolds has put a lot of time and effort into our training and we're not about to let him down. Right, fall in and we'll get back to our hut. We'll have breakfast at 6:30am and I'll arrange a truck to pick us up at 07:15 to take us, and our kit, to the station."

The squad marched off. Each man knew the exercise was really the final test to see if they were ready to join in the battle overseas. Each wondered if he was ready.

A NASTY PIECE OF WORK

As the squad stood on the small railway station platform, two army trucks rumbled around the corner. At the same time two infantry Sergeants, accompanied by two military policemen, emerged from a nearby building and approached the men.

"Who's in charge of this scruffy lot?"

"I am in charge Sergeant but I don't think your description of my men is apt." Preacher was riled by the coarse greeting.

The Sergeant was short and overweight, and from his unshaven appearance, Preacher suspected that the previous night had been spent propping up one of the local bars. He ignored Preacher's remark.

"Right, pay attention. You are here to show us what you can do under simulated battle conditions. I'm Sergeant O'Connor and this here is Sergeant Redman. We are part of the supervising staff. You can recognise members of the exercise staff by these here red bands on our arms. What we say goes without question. Got that?"

"Yes Sergeant. I think we understand that."

"Just don't forget it. We are now going to take you out to the exercise area. You will be operating in the southern section of the area with the enemy to the north. To get to your area we take you south a couple of miles on the main road then head east for four miles to your camp. To reach his lines, the enemy exits the town to the north for a mile or so, before turning east. The two lines are about five miles apart, but more of that later. This town is the Exercise HQ and none of you will come into the town unless you have written authority from a member of the exercise staff. If you do enter the town without authority, the military police will arrest you and you will be considered to have become a prisoner of war. Understood?"

"Yes Sergeant."

"Right, get your gear and yourselves into the trucks."

The trucks set off and the men braced themselves against the constant bumping and lurching.

"Bluey, didn't you say you had relations living in these parts?" asked Preacher.

"Yes, in fact I think their farm must be on the corner where we leave this road. They are a couple of miles south of the town. I've got a feeling I know the valley that the Sergeant was talking about. I've spent a few holidays up here with my cousins."

"That local knowledge might be useful. Looks like we're turning off the main road now."

"I was right. See, there's the farm. What a pity we'll be so close and I can't say hello to them."

"These cousins Bluey, they wouldn't be female by any chance would they?" asked Darkie.

"Oh God you are hopeless, Darkie. Booze or women. Do you ever think of anything else?" The others laughed. "Yes, there are two young ladies in the family but they also have two brothers and a protective father. I wouldn't advise dropping in with evil intent.

They are tough and everyone in the family can use a shotgun to good effect. You may well end up with a tail full of buckshot if you upset them."

"Nice people your relatives."

"They are, but they are also quiet country folk who keep to themselves. As a guest you are most welcome, but intrude into their personal lives and they can get very upset."

"Well, you won't have to worry about upsetting them Darkie because I have a suspicion that you won't have any time to be making social calls. I can't say I'm too impressed with O'Connor and Redman. They both seem to have a distinct dislike of signallers." Preacher looked around for confirmation of his suspicions.

"I think you're right Preacher." Ken Jackson was a man of few words. "It's strange isn't it, this hatred or rivalry between infantry and signallers. At times, I wonder if we're all on the same side." Several of the men nodded.

"Recognise any of this country Bluey?"

"Yes Preacher. I've been out here shooting rabbits. You should all be taking in the scenery and picking out landmarks which might come in useful."

"Landmarks? What the hell are you talking about? What sort of landmarks?" Skipper was confused.

"Sorry Skip, perhaps they're not the sort of landmarks you sailors are used to, but landmarks all the same, and one day they may come in handy in helping you to find your way home. See that outcrop of rocks. Very unusual, distinctive. If you were to see that in the daytime, it would help to orientate yourself, or if you stumbled onto it at night you would then know you were a quarter of a mile north of this road. There's no signposts out here."

The men started to take a keener interest in the passing scenery. Several good reference points on both sides of the road were identified.

"Why not stick to the road?" asked Mick.

"If you are in the bush you need pointers to show you where the road is. There are no signposts out here and getting lost in the bush is not wise. And secondly, the road may not be safe to take as an enemy would expect you to travel that way. So, it might be best to avoid the road and travel across country using the landmarks."

"What about snakes Bluey?"

"What about them Mick? The country's swarming with them. Tiger, brown, black. Take your pick."

"Bloody hell. I'm going to stick to the road. I don't care if I do get captured. I'm not going to tangle with a snake. I've seen them in the zoo. Horrible creatures."

Bluey laughed. "If you see one Mick, stand still and give him a chance to get away. Don't get a stick and try to kill him. Just leave him alone." Bluey could see that Mick was not convinced but there wasn't time for more discussion as the two trucks came to a halt.

"Gather round men, 'cos I'm only saying this once and you had better listen and get it right." Sergeant O'Connor was plainly looking forward to finding a quiet spot where he could sleep off his hangover. "For this exercise, the old hut to your right is Battalion HQ. On that hill, a mile away is our frontline. There you will find three trenches running along the hill top. That's where the infantry will take up their positions in three days time. So, what you have to do is set up your living area and a Battalion communication site. I don't care where you live or how you live, but the communication tent or bunker is to be adjacent to this hut. From the communication centre, you will run lines to each trench and also a line to Exercise HQ back in town. The route you take with the lines is up to you. Any questions?"

"Yes Sergeant. Food. What are the arrangements for eating?"

"You'll find boxes of tinned food plus fresh food in the second truck. Once you have eaten the fresh food you will have to exist on the tinned goods, just as you would in a real battle. Now instead of standing around gawking, I suggest you get cracking. As the infantry doesn't arrive for three days, running lines to the trenches is not a high priority. Sergeant Redman and I have to return to town but we'll be back tomorrow to review your progress. Now get those trucks unloaded."

Soon the contents of both trucks were on the ground and the Sergeants and the trucks departed. The squad felt alone and unprepared.

Preacher looked around his charges. "What I propose is that we concentrate on setting up our camp. Tomorrow we'll establish the communications centre, and on day three we will run out the lines to the trenches and the town. How does that sound to you blokes?"

"Sounds fine Preacher, but it's way past lunch time."

"Right, let's sort out this gear. Put the food over there, tents and ropes over there and the signalling gear over here. Darkie, you and Mick get a fire going so we can have a brew and sort out something for lunch."

Pleased to have something to do the men fell about their allotted tasks. A call from Mick brought them to the camp-fire where a billy was on the boil.

"Sandwiches for lunch. This bread won't keep fresh for long so we had better use it up."

"Preacher, there's not a lot of tucker here," said Darkie. "I suppose we'll get daily deliveries seeing we have eight days here."

"Sure to Darkie. It's obvious nine men wouldn't be able to survive on what we brought out here today." Preacher spoke with a confidence he did not feel. "Now, any suggestions for where we should set up camp? Bluey you know the country, let's hear from you first."

"I think we should heed the warning Sergeant Reynolds gave us about being exposed to enemy fire. I think he was trying to tell us something. So, I reckon we should tunnel into that bank over there."

"Tunnel? Where the hell are we going to tunnel to?" Darkie could immediately see that Bluey's suggestion meant hard labour.

"Not a tunnel really, but a dugout into the side of the bank. There are heaps of empty sandbags here, so as we remove the dirt, we fill the bags, and they can be used in the building of the signal centre. I suggest we make two dugouts, so if one gets hit the other will still be available."

"What do you mean, if one gets hit?" asked Mick.

"Well, for exercise purposes. You know, a pretend shell. If we divide ourselves into two parties we can't all be put out of action by one incident."

Preacher looked at his men. "Well, any other suggestions?"

The men shook their heads. The unfamiliar environment had made them feel vulnerable and they welcomed leadership and direction. Preacher divided the squad into two and they set about carving havens into the side of the steep bank. Two men using picks and shovels dug the earth while the other two filled sandbags. It was hard work and they remembered the words of Sergeant Reynolds; "Can you use a shovel?"

"Where the hell is Preacher?" asked Jacko. "You don't think this acting corporal business has gone to his head and he's nicked off for a quiet snooze, do you?"

"Not Preacher. I guess he's doing a recce of the area or something like that." Bluey looked around. "I hope he doesn't go too far away. It would be a disaster if our leader got lost on the first day."

"Come on Bluey, Preacher's not that stupid. Anyhow, here he comes."

Preacher walked to the fire and filled the billy. "Right fellows, take a break and have a cuppa." He called out. They dropped the tools and settled around the fire.

"Well Bluey you're the construction foreman, how is it going?"

"Slower than I thought but we'll get there. I suggest Erik and Mac take a couple of axes and fell a few of those smaller gums. The straight ones about six to nine inches in diameter. We can build an entrance or porch in front of the dugouts using sandbags as walls and then lay the poles across the top. We then put a canvas fly or tent over the poles and cover it with earth. That way we can double the area of the dugout but still have protection."

"What about the sandbags for the signal centre? Won't we use up all our bags on the dugout?" Sam was looking ahead.

"We have plenty of bags Sam. I'm suggesting we finish our accommodation quickly and without reducing the protection. Tomorrow we can fill the remainder of the sandbags with the sand from the creek bed. It's easier to manage than this hard rocky stuff."

"Right, that's what we'll do. Now while you have been building barracks, I've been building a latrine. It's just beyond that clump of trees. I need to go a bit deeper but it should be operational by nightfall. Please use it."

"And what about dinner tonight Preacher? Who's the cook?" Darkie's questions were predictable.

"You and Mick did such a good job with lunch Darkie, you can be cooks for today. Knock off digging around five and see what sort of meal you can rustle up. I haven't drawn up a list of duties but I will tonight and we'll all take turns at them. Let's go, there's a lot to do."

As darkness approached, the order came to down tools and scrub up before dinner. The men stripped to the waist and used the creek to wash off the layers of dirt. The water was clear and cool and they joked about the hardships of war as they splashed around.

Preacher and Sam walked up the bank together. "Hell Preacher, there's something wrong."

"Wrong? What's wrong Sam?"

"The fire's gone out, and where's Darkie and Mick?"

As if in answer, Mick appeared at the door of the hut.

"Ah Preacher. Hurry those other blokes up will you. Dinner's ready and good chefs don't like to be kept waiting." The others heard the invitation and quickly assembled in the kitchen of the crudely built hut.

"Darkie, who gave you permission to use this building?"

"Permission Preacher? Who needs permission? This is Battalion HQ of the southern army and at this moment we are the southern army, so why do we need permission?"

"I'm sure Sergeant O'Connor did not intend that we use it."

"Perhaps Preacher. But then he didn't say we couldn't use it. I mean, we're not disobeying any instructions."

"I guess not, so let's eat and then sort out the sleeping arrangements for the dugouts. They look good Bluey. You chaps have done a good day's work."

"They're coming along just fine, but as we seemed to have taken over HQ, why don't we sleep in here for tonight? It looks like rain, so I suggest we put all our gear, especially the signalling gear, in the dugouts for tonight, and get a good night's sleep."

"Well?" said Darkie. "What about it General?" Darkie felt that it was really his idea but Bluey had argued it better.

"All right, you win. Let's get the gear under cover and grab a good night's rest. Bluey, you and Skip will be cooks tomorrow, so make sure breakfast is ready by 7:00am. The rest of you will be washed and shaved by that time and work will start at 07:30. Once we are out of the hut, Bluey and Skip will clean it so there is no trace of our visit. Understood?"

"Yes Preacher. Don't worry. Those Sergeants will never know."

With the gear stowed in the dugouts, the men selected their sleeping spots and soon the hut resonated to snoring. Preacher sat at the table drawing up duty lists. He was pleased with Day One. The team had worked hard, shown initiative and enthusiasm. Perhaps a soldier's life wasn't so hard after all.

* * *

The call of magpies woke Bluey. He quickly got the fire going in the wood stove and put the kettle on. No morning activity could begin until the first cup of tea. He rattled a couple of pots and pans and slowly his companions awoke. One by one they filled their mugs with hot black tea and then moved out to gaze at the countryside.

"It's so bloody quiet," remarked Sam. "And so beautiful. One day I'm going to buy a farm and settle down to the easy life."

"You think a farmer's life is easy do you Sam?" Mac had joined him on a fallen log outside the hut. "Let me tell you, it's bloody hard work all the year round. No holidays. The damn cows don't recognise them, no weekends off. And then nature plays games with your life. She either holds back the rain or sends it down in buckets so you have a flood. And then she dries it all up and sets fire to it. Easy? No, that's not a word I'd use to describe life on the land."

"Mac, look around you. Listen to those birds. I've dreamed about being a farmer and one day I will. It's so beautiful. However, I suppose that nasty O'Connor will soon be along to spoil everything."

"Sure to, but I hope he doesn't arrive until we have cleaned that hut. I agree with Preacher. I don't think we were supposed to be using it. Come on breakfast is ready."

After eating with an appetite created by hard work and fresh air, the men returned to the dugouts and set about making them habitable. Floors were levelled and bracken spread over the innermost floor area. The men were pleased with their creations.

Attention then turned to erecting a signal centre. It was built adjacent to the bark hut and as the sandbags were filled, the structure grew. The exercise staff remained absent much to the relief of Preacher. Bluey and Skip had removed any trace of the previous night's occupation, even to the extent of scattering fine dust on the furniture and floors. A new campfire was created close to the food dugout. Bluey and Skip carried stones and rocks from the creek to make a bushman's oven and grilling plate. A cauldron of water was kept close to the boil at all times so a man could make a billy of tea in quick time.

After lunch Preacher took Bluey and Skip aside. "What do you think about the food situation?"

"Well Preacher," replied Skip, "I wouldn't plan on putting to sea for very long with the provisions we have left. I suppose Sergeant O'Connor will bring rations, if and when he comes."

"I hope so Skip. You two have done a good job setting up the campfire and eating area, but now I have another job. Bluey, you know this country and I can trust you not to get lost, and Skip, you are our expert on visual signalling. I want you to go up to the trenches O'Connor spoke about and have a look around. Try to find the best paths for the telephone lines. And Skip, see if you can find sites near the trenches that'll give us line of sight for visual signalling. The routes may be obvious, but then again, we may gain something in the way of surprise if we stay away from the obvious."

"Right Preacher." Bluey welcomed the opportunity to walk through the bushland. "Come on Skip, I could do with some exercise."

Preacher watched the men depart. Although he was becoming more confident in himself and his squad, he also had a feeling that things were going too easily. The noise of an approaching truck snapped him out of his pondering. Sergeant O'Connor stepped down from the cabin followed by an officer, a grey-haired man with a pronounced limp.

"Lacey, this is Major Wiltshire, the officer conducting this exercise. This Sir, is Private Lacey. He is in charge of this motley group."

Preacher saluted. "With respect Sir, the men may look somewhat dishevelled at the moment, but they have been working, and were unaware of your impending visit."

"You don't have to apologise for men who have been working." The Major looked around him. "I can see these men all kissed a razor this morning which is good enough for me. What do you think Sergeant?"

"I agree Sir. Personal hygiene is very important."

The Major hesitated and then turned back to Preacher. "Right, show me this hard work you mentioned."

Preacher led the small party to the dugouts and explained the layout. The Major, who wore the insignia of an engineer, surveyed the work. "I'm impressed soldier. I can see that you are taking this exercise seriously, not like some others who seem to think it's all a bit of a skylark. Now, how do you intend to run your lines?"

"I have two men out at this moment surveying the routes to the trenches and later today we'll do a survey run to the exercise HQ in town. We need some supplies so the survey team can pick them up while they're in the town."

"I'm not sure you're allowed to do that," replied the Major.

"No Sir, they're not," chimed in Sergeant O'Connor. "Town is strictly out of bounds except for the exercise staff, and anyone found there will be arrested and for exercise purposes be declared a prisoner of war."

"What do we do about supplies if we can't go into town to get them?" inquired Preacher.

"Once you have established a land line between here and exercise HQ, you send in a requisition via the line and the supplies will be sent out. That's how it works in real life." The Sergeant looked pleased with himself.

"Well Private Lacey, it looks as if the line to the exercise HQ has some sort of priority. However, I feel sure Sergeant O'Connor could take a requisition back to town with us and send out some supplies. Now, what else have you got to show me?"

The inspection continued and again the Major expressed his satisfaction. As the visitors took their leave, Preacher handed the Sergeant a piece of paper on which he had scribbled an order for rations.

"Not good enough, Lacey. Not good enough. Requests for rations must be submitted in the correct terminology on the correct ordering form. Best you get that line to exercise HQ going like the Major said." With that, he stuffed the piece of paper in his pocket and boarded the truck. The men came to attention and Preacher saluted as it drove off.

"Bloody hell, Preacher. What do we do now?" Darkie was more than slightly upset. "We are almost out of food and he won't send us any. What sort of a caper is he up to?"

"I don't know Darkie but we'll have to make do with what we've got until tomorrow. However, the line between here and exercise HQ is our first priority. Mac, you take Darkie and look for a route over that hill to the west and into town. Mark the route as you go and remember we have to bowl this drum of wire along to lay the wire, so make sure the route is as flat as you can find. Go around any really steep parts."

"Why not go around the road, Preacher?" Sam asked.

"I suspect that our so-called friends have thought of that and made sure that there isn't enough wire on the drum to reach town via the road. No, it's up and over that hill, so let's have a brew and then get started. It's not going to be easy, but then we didn't expect things to be easy out here."

After a mug of tea Mac and Darkie set off. The others watched until they were hidden by trees. "Right, we have to devise a way of trundling this drum along, paying out the wire as we go." Preacher was under no illusions about the size of the task. "Any suggestions?"

Sam, who had a methodical approach to all problems, spoke: "On flat ground, two men can roll the drum along without much trouble. On rough ground, you'll need four men and for the inclines, six, perhaps eight. Two men can push on the rims of the drum, any others will need some sort of a harness attached to the axle. Some sort of rope apparatus, like they use to pull sledges across the ice."

"Sam that makes sense but we don't have any apparatus or harness."

"We do Preacher. Or at least we have the material to make some harness. Because we made dugouts we didn't use all the tent ropes. We can make the harness out of those."

"Right Sam, it's your idea, you organise it." Preacher was happy to hand over responsibility for this particular problem.

Sam looked around. "Erik, you and Jacko get the drum moving along the route marked by Mac and Darkie. Preacher can you get Bluey and Skip back here in a hurry? I need Skip to help with the ropes. He's an expert on knots. We need all hands right now."

"Right. Mick, race off along that track towards the trenches and yell as loud as you can. Once they hear you, I'm sure they'll turn back. Get them back here as quick as you can. Sam, you and I'll lay out the ropes and see if we can make a rough model for Skip to copy. Let's go men, we're not beaten yet."

Erik and Jacko set off with the large drum. It bounced along the uneven ground but they kept it upright and moving. Mick disappeared along the northern track stopping occasionally to call

"Cooee", the call he had learnt from Bluey. He soon saw the two men hurrying back. On the way to the camp he briefed them on what had happened. When they reached the campsite, Preacher and Sam had all the ropes laid out and had designed a harness of two loops, one for each shoulder, and these were then joined to a central rope which in turn would be connected to the protruding axle of the drum.

"Clever stuff, eh Skip?" said Sam. "I saw a picture once and the men crossing the ice had a harness something like this."

"I hate to think what our shoulders will look like Sam, but it might work. What do you think Bluey?"

"It's worth a try Skip. Once we get to the top of that hill it will be downhill all the way so we may have to use the ropes as brakes."

"At least you are thinking of reaching the top," said Preacher. "I'm not convinced we can get that far."

"Come on," said Skip, "let's get the Ralston harness ready. As I see it, we need to make four sets. Two men will have to push on the rims and keep the drum steady with four men pulling." He started to knot the ropes together.

"Sam, you and Mick go after Erik and Jacko and give them a hand. I'll stay here as I don't trust our Sergeant O'Connor. I have a fear that if we leave the camp unattended some disaster may befall it."

"Right Preacher. Come on Mick, those two are probably looking for some help by now." The trail was easy to follow as the rims of the drum had left a distinctive furrow and the wire lay between the two ruts.

"Thank your lucky stars Preacher, that it didn't rain last night. We would never move that drum across wet ground."

"You're right Bluey. Didn't Sergeant Reynolds talk about mounting a drum of wire on the back of a horse drawn wagon?"

"Yes he did. Perhaps we can order a wagon and team of horses for when we have to reel the wire up."

Skip soon had the four pulling ropes ready. "I've made them in pairs," he said, "so the four men are not bumping against each other as they pull. The leaders will be about fifteen feet from the axles and the other two about ten feet. I hope it works."

"So do I. By the way, did you survey the routes to the trenches or didn't you have time?"

"There's no problem there Preacher. The routes are easy to follow and we'll be able to run lines up there in quick time. There's even a small dugout to the rear of each trench which I take to be the company command post, so all we have to do is run the wire. Ready Bluey, we'd better be off."

Gathering up the ropes, the two men set off watched by a worried Preacher. Bluey and Skip soon caught up with the other four and the drum of wire.

"I think the easy ride is over," said Jacko as the six men surveyed the ground before them. "It hasn't been too hard up to now but four men can't really get a purchase on the drum, there's not enough space. We tend to get in each other's way."

"Well that's why we have Sam Ralston's all singing, all dancing, rope harness, fresh off the production line. Sam, you invented it, you take charge."

"If you say so Skip, but you made the gear, shouldn't you be in charge?"

"Oh for God's sake Sam, take charge," urged Bluey. "We can't stand around here talking. How do you want to play it?"

"Right. Erik and Jacko take the lead, Bluey and Skipper be the number twos and Mick and I'll push. Jacko, you be the lead horse," called Sam. "Pick the best path. All ready? Move it."

To their delight the drum ran fairly easily and their spirits rose as they made good progress. However, as the gradient increased and the men tired, the rate of progress fell. Stops became more frequent and the ropes bit into their shoulders. The pairs changed at each stop, but still the summit appeared beyond their reach.

"I don't think we'll make it, at least not today." observed Sam. He and Mick were not used to manual labour and were suffering.

"Ve must make it," said Erik. "If ve don't, then ve starve. Come on, ve must get going." The big man got to his feet and single-handedly started hauling on a rope.

"Hang on Swede. You can't do it on your own, and if you pull like that the drum will topple."

"No it von't. See. I have the leaders ropes and I can move it." The big man hauled and the drum moved forward.

"Wait Erik," Bluey held up his hand, "you have proved your point. What we'll do is let you lead with the two ropes until you need a spell. Two of us will pull in the number two positions as before, letting one man rest. Now Erik don't kill yourself. We'll get there."

"Ya. Ve'll get there. My mate Darkie, he vill have food for us ven ve get there."

"What do you mean? He'll have food?" asked Bluey.

"Darkie tells me before he vent off vith Mac, he vould find some food for us in town."

"Bloody hell," said Mick, "town's out of bounds and they'll nab him for sure. Those MPs' looked nasty."

"Maybe," replied Bluey. "But Darkie's been around. He can take care of himself. Our worry at the moment is this damn drum. Come on, let's move it."

The procession continued. Despite pleas to Erik to take his turn at having a spell, the Swede would have none of it. The blood oozing from the rope marks began to stain his shirt but he still refused to rest. The hours went by and progress was painfully slow. The men were close to exhaustion when a shout revived them.

"It's Mac." said Sam. "But where's Darkie?"

"I shudder to think," replied Mick, "but we'll soon know."

Mac approached and from a bag he was carrying fished out some apples. "Here try these." The men dropped the ropes and sat down munching on the apples.

"Christ Swede, what have you done to your shoulders?" exclaimed Mac.

"It's nothing. Vot have you done vith Darkie?" replied Erik.

"Darkie's in jail." He looked around at their looks of disbelief. "I'm serious. We reached the HQ and were met by Sergeant O'Connor. I think he and his mate Redman had us under surveillance from the time we came over the hill until we reached the HQ. You can't miss it. It's a boarding house next to the pub. It has a flag and an army sign up. We were allowed to examine the room they called the signal centre and then told to return to camp. Darkie started off with me but then turned back. He said he was going to get some food. I waited for him, but the silly bugger went into the pub and of course the MPs were waiting. They marched him back to the HQ and I guess that's where he is now."

"So, no food and no Darkie?"

"Well no Darkie, Sam, but I did swipe some apples from the orchard on the way out. The apples were in a shed, so I helped myself. But that's all I got. O'Connor was on his hobby horse about no supplies unless ordered on the correct form in duplicate. He's a nasty piece of work."

"Sam, you're in charge. What now?" Skipper was already on his feet.

"What to do is easy Skip. We have to get this wire to HQ and get it connected. How to do it? That's the problem. Mac, what's ahead of us?"

"You're only a hundred yards or so from the summit Sam but it's pretty steep going. After that it's downhill all the way. A gentle slope through the bush to the orchard. It's not too far, once you reach the crest of the hill you can see the town."

"And they can see us."

"So what. They know you are coming with the wire."

"Come on Sam, take charge. We are wasting valuable time."

"All right Bluey, be patient. Erik, come back here and help Mick and me push. The rest of you grab a rope. Let's go."

It was hard work but the men persisted and finally the drum was resting on the crest of the hill. After a brief pause the expedition continued, the drum rolling easily towards its destination.

The team crossed the orchard and approached the building designated as the Exercise HQ. Sergeants O'Connor and Redman came to meet them. The surprised looks on their faces indicated that they had not expected to see the drum of wire that day.

"That's far enough for you men." said O'Connor.

Sam walked towards him. "No, it's not Sergeant. Our job as signallers will be completed when this line is connected to the receiving panel in the signal centre and that's where we're going now."

"Well two men may advance with the wire and connect it. The rest can return to your camp or wait here till the line's tested. Then you can all go back the way you came."

"We need supplies Sergeant. You know we're out of food and I don't want any of this nonsense about forms in duplicate. I want to speak with Major Wiltshire." Sam was tired, angry and hungry. The Sergeants conferred and Redman departed in the direction of the hotel.

"As I said before, two can advance and connect the line. Two, and two only. Sergeant Redman has gone to get rations. Anything else you want soldier?"

"Yes Sergeant. Where is Private Fleming? We want to take him back with us. We need every man we have for this exercise." Sam was adamant.

"Fleming? Oh yes. The renegade New Zealander. He's quite comfortable in custody. He won't be taking any further part in this exercise. He is a prisoner of war. The rules for this exercise were clearly spelt out to you, and Fleming chose to break the rules. Fleming is no longer part of your team. Come on, I'm not going to stand around here all day yapping to you lot. Get that wire into the signal centre and be quick about it."

"Come on Mick, give me a hand. The rest of you take a spell. You might find a water tap or some shade over there by that shed in the corner of the orchard."

The Sergeant hesitated, as if he was going to say something, but then walked away followed by Sam and Mick pushing the drum of wire.

"A real little Napoleon our Sam has turned out to be." observed Bluey.

"Yeah," smiled Skip, "he's plenty mad and rather hungry, but he'd better be careful or O'Connor will make something unpleasant happen to him."

"Maybe we should go back and give him some support."

Skip shook his head. "No Bluey, don't fuss. Mick's with him, and Mick is a street fighter. He mightn't say much but then he doesn't miss much. If O'Connor tries something on Sam, Mick will cut him down to size, and I mean cut."

"Come on, let's grab a drink of water and some apples before that Sergeant wakes up to what we're doing."

The men settled down in the shade of the shed and watched the boarding house. After twenty minutes Sam and Mick appeared with Sam carrying a hessian bag. The others stood up and moved forward.

"Sorry blokes, but that bastard Redman only gave us half a dozen tins of bully beef for rations. Said it was all he could spare." Sam was despondent.

For some reason Mick was smiling. "Cheer up Sam, let's get out of here before they find out."

"Find out what, Mick?"

"Find out what I added to that sack when I went to the bathroom. There's a ham, some sausages and a couple of loaves of bread in there with the tins. I was going to grab some eggs but they would've got smashed. It's only a matter of time before someone realises the ham is gone, so let's move."

Sam looked bewildered. "But how did you get into the kitchen?"

"Through the window. And I can do it again if I have to. In quick, grab the stuff and out. I've had a bit of practice."

Skip looked at Bluey and winked. With their pockets bulging with apples, the group followed the telephone line back towards camp.

"I bet O'Connor and Redman are still scratching their heads as to how we got the drum into town so quickly. Hell, I'm dreading what Preacher is going to say when he hears about Darkie."

"He already knows Mac. After we connected the line O'Connor put through a test call to the camp and Preacher answered. O'Connor took great delight in telling him that Darkie was a POW for the duration of the exercise."

"Poor bloody Darkie. I wouldn't like to be in his shoes right now."

"Sam, vot say ve go back and rescue him?" Erik was upset.

"No Swede. That's what they probably expect us to do. Anyhow in war, we wouldn't be charging around the countryside trying to rescue POWs. No, Darkie broke the rules and he'll pay for it. How he'll pay, I'm not sure."

They reached the camp and Sam related to Preacher the events of the day.

"Well at least we can have our evening meal, thanks to Mick. We'll keep the bully beef for tomorrow. We have a busy day ahead. One man will have to man the phone to HQ and the rest will have to run lines to the trenches. We must have everything in place before the infantry arrives."

"Perhaps they are meant to feed us?"

“Perhaps Sam, we’ll see. You did well today.”

“Everyone did well Preacher, except Darkie. Erik, I think you had better let Preacher have a look at your shoulders. Those cuts need some sort of treatment.”

“Sorry Erik, I should’ve tended to those wounds earlier. The rest of you turn in. We’ll keep one hour shifts during the night so that the telephone is manned and the fire kept going. It’s been a long day but a good day. Thank you.”

YOU'LL GET YOUR RATIONS

The birdlife of the bush made sure the men didn't oversleep.

"Hell Bluey, is it always so noisy out here?" asked Sam.

"Fancy a city bloke complaining about noise. It's only in the bush that you get woken up by such music. I bet the birds are even better at singing in the Gippsland forest where Erik hails from."

"Ya Bluey, it's true. They are vunderful."

Preacher walked over. "Here's the plan for today. Erik, you're to stay in camp and rest those shoulders. We'll take it in turns to man the telephone. Bluey, you and Mick run a line to the most eastern of the trenches. Sam, you and Jacko run the line to the centre trench and Mac, you and Skip do the western trench. Any questions? Good. Off you go and be careful. We don't want any broken legs or arms. Take it easy, there's plenty of time."

Bluey and Mick picked up one of the smaller drums and set off, paying out wire as they went. The route was clearly visible but they took the precaution of stringing the line through the branches of trees so no one would trip over and break it during the exercise. They reached the eastern trench and quickly connected the wire to the portable phone they were carrying. Bluey called into the battalion signal centre and was relieved to hear Erik answer.

"Well that's fixed we can go back now." As he said the words the crack of a rifle reached their ears.

"Hell Mick, that bloke's not too far away from here."

Mick walked to the crest of the ridge. "Let's have a look."

"Shit Mick, keep your head down." Bluey seldom swore and the tone of his voice had an instant impact on Mick.

"You think he's shooting at us?"

"My guess is that he's a sniper of some sort put there to keep us on our toes. I don't think he's seen us as I didn't hear any bullet. Hang on, let's ask the Swede."

Bluey turned the handle. An excited Erik came on the line. "Bluey, they try to kill Sam and Jacko. Yust missed them, there's a madman out there. Be careful."

"Relax Erik, we're all right, and I don't think the sniper is out to hurt anyone. He just wants to scare us."

"Vell he certainly scared Sam and Jacko."

Another shot rang out. Bluey looked at the ridge ahead. "You know Mick, we haven't got much to do for the next hour or so, how would you like to go hunting?"

"Hunting? You mean go after that bloke with the gun? Are you sure we should?"

"No, I'm not sure. If we had infantry up here they would take care of him." Another shot rang out. "But, as we haven't got the protection of the infantry, I think we should take some sort of action to defend ourselves."

"I'm with you. Got any ideas?"

"Let's head along this ridge. We'll keep well below the skyline. See those rocks up there, that's where we'll head for. Come on this should be fun."

“Fun? The bloke’s got a rifle and you call it fun?”

They traversed the slope and arrived at the outcrop. “Mick, here’s your first lesson in stalking. Never stick your head up over the top, always move slowly and look around the side. A sudden movement can catch someone’s attention, but in the main people look at the top of things.”

From different sides of the rocks each man peered out. Soon another shot rang out. “See him?” whispered Bluey.

“Not a bloody thing.”

“See that clump of trees about 200 yards away? There is one very tall gum and half a dozen smaller trees.”

“Yeah. The big tree with a real lean to the left. Is that the one?”

“That’s it. Our man is lying behind a fallen log just ahead of the big tree. He’s got glasses and is watching the western trenches. Good, that suits us. Follow me.”

Mick shook his head in disbelief as they headed further eastward into the scrub. After a while, Bluey turned north and hurried along. He didn’t bother to crouch as Mick thought he should.

“Hell Bluey, what do we do if he sees us?” he panted.

Bluey stopped and looked at his companion. “If he sees us, we’re dead ducks, but this is only pretend war so I guess he’ll let us off with a warning. Got your breath back? Good. From here on we crawl, slither, and in general stay low, very low. I’ll lead. You just look at the soles of my boots. Don’t lift your head to see where you’re going. Trust me. Here we go mate.”

For the next half hour, the two men wormed their way forward. Mick had no idea how close they were to their quarry until he saw Bluey’s boots disappear and heard him say, “This is a bayonet sticking in the back of your neck, and if this was for real you would be dead.”

Mick got to his feet and saw Bluey bending over the sniper. “Get his rifle Mick. Good. Now give it to me.” With a quick action, Bluey cleared the breech. “Now my friend, you may sit up.”

The sniper rolled over and sat up with his back resting against the fallen log. "Who the bloody hell are you, and what sort of game do you think you're playing at?" Indignation had replaced shock, and the young blonde man was very upset.

"We're the enemy you've been taking pot shots at and we don't like it. So, you're now our prisoner."

"Prisoner? You can't take me prisoner. That's not part of the exercise. Hell, you're not even infantry."

"Sorry about that. By the way, what's your name?"

"Collins, Jock Collins, and I suggest you give me back my rifle and hightail it out of here before the exercise staff finds out what you've done."

"Sorry Jock, it's too late for that. You won't do anything stupid like trying to run away, will you?" Bluey looked serious.

"No mate, I'm not running away. It's only a game. But what's your name? You look familiar."

"Dowson, Harold Dowson, and my friend is Mick O'Brien."

"Dowson. Of course. I used to shoot for the North Ballarat Club and you shot against us last year."

Bluey frowned. "Well I did shoot against that club last year, but I'm sorry, I don't remember you."

"Not surprised, I was just one of the mob but you took the cup that day. It's a small world."

Bluey looked at the sniper with interest. "You know your way around this area pretty well I guess."

"Yeah, I've done this job for a few exercises now. Why?"

Bluey ignored the question. "Tell me. Are there any burrows around here? I've seen signs of rabbits but no burrows, at least not on our side of the ridge."

"Rabbits! They're here in their thousands. There are masses of burrows over that ridge. There's a creek over there and the rabbits have taken over. What have you got in mind?"

"Pick up your gear. We're going hunting."

"Hunting? My God you blokes really are mad." Jock looked at Mick. "Are you sure your mate's not suffering from a touch of the sun?"

"Don't ask me," replied Mick, "these country boys are a strange lot at the best of times. I don't try to understand them. I just came along for the ride."

"Let's go," snapped Bluey and set off at a quick pace with the others following.

"You know, I could tell you both to bugger off and leave me, except I need my rifle back." the sniper complained.

"I know," said Bluey. "That's why I've got it. Where it goes you'll follow. Now hurry up, there's a lot to be done and our side will be getting worried about us."

They crested the hill and moved down the slope towards the creek. Jock had been right. Rabbits could be seen moving about even though it was mid-morning.

"You'll make an awful mess of a rabbit with that rifle Bluey." advised Jock.

"Not if I knock his head off. Let's get a bit closer and no more talking."

The rabbits seemed unaware of their approach or had decided to ignore them. Bluey selected a fallen log to use as a rest for the rifle. He whispered to Jock, "Does this thing shoot straight?"

"It's about two inches high at one o'clock at two hundred yards but at this range it'll be straight enough, if you're good enough."

Bluey settled over the rifle. The noise shattered the stillness of the bush and a rabbit catapulted into the air, fell and lay still. The men waited. Soon the animals began to re-emerge from their burrows. A second shot found its target. Four more shots and four more rabbits lay dead.

"That's enough." said Bluey. "Mick, gallop over there and pick up our dinner. Six rabbits should fill our bellies."

The men set off for the southern lines. Jock and Bluey walking together, Mick bringing up the rear with the six rabbits suspended from a stick resting on his shoulder. As they walked Jock briefed Bluey about the exercise set-up.

"You see Bluey, it's the southerners who are being tested, if that's the right word. The northern camp provides token opposition, and at night sends out raiding parties to infiltrate the southern lines. It gets quite rough at times. But the idea is to keep the southern group under pressure for the five days, that applies to you signallers as well."

"What's your job? I mean where do you fit in?"

"Oh, I sit out there in the daytime, and if a man shows himself above the skyline I let off a shot to indicate that in the real war, he would be a casualty. That's what I was doing today. Your blokes on the west side were walking about in full view, but I didn't see hide nor hair of you two. Now I know why."

"What do you know about Sergeants O'Connor and Redman?"

Jock shook his head. "Bad news. I hear that they're running rackets in the town like selling army supplies, petrol, etc. They were out at the northern camp last night selling beer to the chaps at a high price. Stay clear of them. They have the MPs on their payroll."

"Too late for that. They really have it in for us as a group. It's as though they've a score to settle with someone and they can do it through hurting us. But thanks for the warning."

"I think I'd better warn the northern camp about you lot. Their raiding parties will try to cut your lines but I wouldn't like to run into you or your mate out here on a dark night. Hell, I've been around, but you crept up on me in broad daylight."

"Oh, we were lucky, you weren't expecting us. But we may have to arrange a few surprises for these raiding parties. I find city blokes don't like snakes so I think I'll plant a few along the lines."

The sniper stopped and looked at the redhead. “Plant snakes? What the hell are you talking about, you some sort of snake charmer?”

“No. I get along with snakes, so I catch them and keep them in bags as pets.”

Jock shuddered. “What a creepy idea.” Bluey looked back to see Mick’s face turning white. He winked and Mick got the message. By the time Jock returned to his camp the snake story would have been embellished and expanded. The northern raiding parties would give any bags left along the line a wide berth.

Preacher saw the group approaching and came to meet them. He’d been worried about them as they couldn’t be raised on the telephone. The shots had been heard and the group feared the worst.

Bluey waved to the one-time shearer, “Jacko, could you do the honours, and skin and clean these bunnies? At least we’ll have a good lunch.”

Preacher shook his head. “No Bluey, let’s keep them for dinner. We can have the bully beef for lunch. It’s quicker and ready to be served.”

“Fine by me, Preacher. By the way this is Jock Collins, he’s the fellow who scared Sam and Jacko. I could do with a mug of tea and I suspect Jock wouldn’t say no.”

Jock nodded. “You blokes have set up a fine camp. The previous groups have thrown up a few tents and of course the raiding parties knocked them down. Total chaos most nights. I think this exercise is going to be different somehow.”

“That bloke over there is our permanent guard,” said Bluey pointing to Erik. “God help anyone he catches snooping around here. We haven’t got guns so the Swede prowls around with a pick handle. He’s really mean. In fact, back in recruit camp he flattened a bloke for not knowing the password.”

“Yeah, I heard about him. Everyone did. God, he looks mean.”

"Well," said Bluey, looking very serious, "pass the word will you? We're dead scared he'll kill someone one night."

Jock nodded. "Yeah I wouldn't like to tangle with him. Oh, here comes the trucks and I suspect your favourite Sergeants."

The men watched the infantry climb down from the trucks. They quickly unloaded their gear and marched off in the direction of the trenches. The signallers were completely ignored.

"Not a friendly, happy bunch." observed Preacher. "Ah, there's Sergeant O'Connor. I want a word with him."

"More likely the other way around Preacher. He has just spotted Jock Collins and I don't think he's too happy. Stand by everyone here comes trouble."

Sergeant O'Connor followed by Sergeant Redman approached the signallers. He pointed at Bluey. "What is that man doing with a rifle, Private Lacey?"

"He's guarding our prisoner Sergeant. We're not sure what we should do with prisoners but we have his rifle so he's harmless."

"What the hell are you talking about, you moron. Prisoner? That man is an exercise sniper. You can't take him prisoner. Collins, what the hell is going on?"

"They jumped me Sergeant. I guess I'm dead, as I doubt if anyone in the field would take a sniper prisoner."

O'Connor pointed at Bluey. "You, give that man back his rifle."

"Why can't we keep it Sergeant? We captured him and it'd be useful to have a weapon here to defend ourselves with."

"I just gave you an order soldier. Return that rifle or I'll have you on a charge."

Bluey looked at Preacher who nodded. Bluey opened the breech and handed it to the sniper.

"Right Collins, get your arse onto one of those trucks returning to town and from there get yourself out to the northern camp. I'll talk to you later."

“Thanks for the brew, fellas.” Jock said as he shouldered the rifle.

“Move it Collins. This is no tea party. Get out of my sight and stay out of it.” Jock waved to the group and walked towards the trucks.

“Sergeant O’Connor, are our rations in those trucks?” asked Preacher. “I sent in an order this morning as directed.”

“No, the rations aren’t in one of those trucks. The message you sent was garbled and we couldn’t make out what you wanted. Fill in the appropriate forms and I’ll send them out tomorrow.”

“Garbled? How could my message be garbled. I sent it in clear language. I told the operator at the other end exactly what I wanted in plain, simple English.”

“Well, he got it all mixed up and that’s that. Have you got all the lines set up as directed?”

“Yes, all three company command posts are connected. We’ve the switchboard in the Battalion HQ manned so they can call in at any time.”

“We’ll soon see. Oh yes, another thing. You lot can forget about visiting the shed in the orchard. I’ve told the local police about some men stealing apples and they’re not very happy about it. Come on Bill, let’s walk up and see if these clod-footed soldiers have got themselves organised in the trenches.”

The two Sergeants set off in the direction of the frontline leaving the signallers to fume.

Preacher watched them disappear in the direction of the trenches. “Thank goodness for your rabbits, Bluey. At least we’ll eat tonight. Who’s that going into the hut?”

“It’s Corporal Sweeney, the Sergeant’s driver, cook and general hand. Jock Collins said to be careful of him. He’s O’Connor’s hit-man and into all sorts of rackets. If someone welshes on a deal, it’s Sweeney who teaches them a lesson. He’s a real toady.” Mick was staring at the corporal who was unloading supplies.

"We do seem to have fallen into bad company. Bluey what's this about snakes in bags and Erik being a maniac with a pick handle?"

"As I understand it Preacher, there'll be small bands of raiders attacking the trenches and when possible, they'll try to get in behind the trenches to cut the wires and even attack battalion headquarters. Now Jock is convinced we're different. Capturing him was a shock to his system, then he saw the dugouts and that impressed him. So, I just put a couple of ideas into his head and no doubt he'll pass them on. Mind you he has to explain how he got caught, so that story will be embellished as will the snakes in the bags and the stories of the mad Swede."

"An interesting thought."

Bluey continued, "All this will impress the enemy. We'll leave empty sandbags tied around the top with twine along the lines. Make-believe booby traps. A bloke crawling around in the dark won't be too happy if he touches a bag. His imagination will take over. As for Erik, everyone in the army has heard about the mad Swede and Ronald Johnson. I think they'll leave this camp alone, but of course, we can't be certain."

Sam shook his head. "It won't work Bluey. Not that sandbag stunt anyhow. I'd give it a day, perhaps two at the most, before someone twigs that it's a fake."

"Right Sam, I'd have to agree. So, we need to make sure that one, perhaps two bags, do contain a snake, then it becomes a raffle. Which bag is dangerous, which is harmless." By now the group was hanging on every word.

"Bluey, you really scare me at times. I suppose you're now going to suggest we go on a snake hunt."

"Mick, I'll do the hunting. I've grown up in the bush and snakes don't worry me. I certainly respect a snake, but you can catch them. Once you have them by the tail, they can't strike at you. Of course, getting hold of them by the tail is the clever bit. However, I'll need someone to hold the bag." He looked around.

"I'll help, Bluey."

"Thanks Jacko. I figure you'd have seen your share of snakes while working the sheds. We'll wander down to the creek later and see what we can find."

Preacher looked worried. "But what if someone does open a bag and there's a snake inside? He might be bitten, he might even die."

"Possibly Preacher. However, it's my theory that Jock Collins will spread the story around. They'll check with O'Connor or Redman. The Sergeants will then confront us. We'll then produce a couple of loaded booby traps for the Sergeants. After that, no one will go near any of the bags, especially at night."

Mick's fear of snakes was now becoming a total phobia. "Don't you dare bring one of those loaded bags into my dugout. I'll go bloody mad if you do."

"Don't worry Mick, It's the enemy I want to scare."

"You mightn't be trying to scare me, but you have bloody well succeeded. Just to talk about those slimy creatures sends me into shivers."

Preacher looked worried. "Bluey, I don't like it, but if the group agrees with your plan I'll go with it. What do you blokes say? Hands up those in favour."

All men raised their hands, including Mick.

"Fair enough. Go to it snake charmer, but don't get bitten, we've enough problems at the moment."

Bluey and Jacko stood up and gathered a couple of sandbags. "Be back soon" called Bluey. "Keep the billy boiling"

Preacher wondered where all this would end.

* * *

The two Sergeants arrived back at the battalion HQ late in the afternoon just as Sam and Jacko had started to cook the rabbits.

"Well, what do we have here?" sneered O'Connor. "Rabbit for dinner. My favourite. Ralston, put three of those onto a dish and take them over to the hut. Sweeney can make us a decent stew out of them."

Sam turned and stared at the Sergeants. "Get your own rabbits, this is all we have to eat."

"Soldier you have pushed my patience about as far as it can be pushed with safety."

Sam's fists were clenched for a show-down but Sergeant Redman intervened. "He's got a point there, Pat. We should do a swap. One rabbit for one tin of bully beef. That seems a fair arrangement to me."

"Well soldier, what say you to that?" O'Connor was relieved that Redman had found a way out of the situation. "It's more than fair in my book. We could order you to hand all six rabbits over to us but my friend here has a soft heart."

Sam hesitated and looked at Jacko. "Don't think you have a choice Sam," the ex-shearer said. "Three bunnies are better than none, and we can mix up some sort of a stew with the bully beef."

Sam hesitated before replying. "Tell Sweeney to bring us the bully and then I'll give him the three animals. We also need some tea and sugar."

"You're pushing your luck soldier." snarled the Sergeant before striding off in the direction of the hut.

"I'll send Sweeney over with the tins and some tea and sugar," Sergeant Redman seemed keen to keep some sort of harmony. "Pat's just had a bad day and he's not in the best of moods."

"I've yet to see him in anything but a bad mood." replied Sam. "And while we're on the subject of food, how does the infantry expect to exist? Are they going to starve too?"

"No one's starving. You'll get your rations once you get organised. You seem a bit slow on working out the local rules. As for the infantry, they've established a field kitchen to the rear of the trenches and they'll be supplied on a daily basis from Exercise HQ."

"How come that the infantry gets it's rations without fuss, while we're scraping to put together one meal a day?"

"As I said before, rations are available but we have local rules. A request in the correct form will work wonders. Think about it."

Sergeant Redman walked away before Sam could continue with his questions. Soon Corporal Sweeney appeared with the promised tins of bully beef, a bag of tea, a bag of sugar plus some potatoes. He selected three rabbits from the baking dish and departed without saying a word.

"Not very talkative?" remarked Sam.

"No, but I bet he doesn't miss much." replied Jacko.

"Come on, let's try and turn this lot into some sort of stew. I guess the potatoes were Redman's idea. That other bastard would see us starve before he gave us a sniff of rations. Here comes Preacher and the others. Now there'll be hell to pay."

The group gathered around the fire while Sam and Jacko recounted what had taken place. Preacher shook his head. "I should've been here. I should've put up a fight for our food."

"Don't fret about that Preacher. Sam stood up to O'Connor just like he did yesterday. The strange thing is that remark by Redman. What did he mean when he said a request in the correct form will work wonders?"

"I suspect Jacko, that if we knew the gist of that remark, we would know what this is all about. However, you two have done a good job to get some more tea and sugar out of O'Connor, and with the bully beef and potatoes, I'm sure we can have a feast of sorts."

* * *

Bluey was up, washed and shaved, and had the billy boiling before the others stirred. He had just finished stoking the fire when Corporal Sweeney appeared carrying a box. Placing it beside the fire he muttered, “Some grub for your breakfast,” and with that he walked away. Bluey watched his retreating back, a look of wonderment on his face.

“What’s up Bluey?” Skipper asked as he approached from the signal centre.

“Damned if I know. Sweeney just came over with a box of rations which he said was for our breakfast. Everything is in it. Eggs, bacon, bread, jam, the works. Why the sudden change of heart?”

“I think I can answer that,” said Skip. “About 10:00pm last night, I took a message from exercise HQ saying an inspection party would be here at 9:00am. I suspect O’Connor doesn’t want any complaints aired.”

“Give the others a call while I get this breakfast under way. We’d better have this place cleaned up before the officers arrive.”

The thought of a good breakfast was an incentive to get the group busy. By 9:00am, the camp was ready for inspection, and the men smartly dressed.

“Funny,” said Preacher, “you can usually hear the trucks approaching for quite a while before they arrive, but I can’t hear a thing.”

“That’s because horses are quieter than trucks,” said Bluey. “Look over there.”

Four officers and a Sergeant appeared on horseback from the tree-line to the west.

“Light horsemen. God, don’t they look smart,” observed Mac.

“They certainly do, and one of them is Major Wiltshire. Here come our dear chums O’Connor and Redman. My, don’t they look smart today.” Skipper’s voice revealed his contempt.

“You lot, get fallen in. Look smart about it.” Sergeant O’Connor was determined this visit would more than compensate for the previous visit by Major Wiltshire.

The party of horsemen arrived at the camp site, but only Major Wiltshire dismounted.

"Here Sergeant O'Connor. Take my horse and escort these officers to the trenches. Sergeant Redman will escort me on an inspection of the communications set up."

"Perhaps Sir, it would be better if Sergeant Redman escorted the mounted party, and I stayed here to brief you on the communications." It was more of a plea than a suggestion.

"No O'Connor. Off you go. He's a quiet animal but don't give him too much rein or he'll take himself and you home via the shortest route."

A bewildered Sergeant O'Connor was settled in the saddle before he could think of any further reasons why he should not be.

A tall man wearing the insignia of a Lieutenant-Colonel looked down from his horse and spoke, "Right Sergeant, lead on. Oh, one other thing Major Wiltshire, I think we should be back by 11.30am. Will you be finished by then?"

"Yes Sir. Do you want to lunch out here or back at HQ?"

"HQ. These men have work to do and laying on luncheon parties is not part of their training."

The mounted party disappeared along the track leading to the trenches.

"There's going to be trouble." said Bluey as the party disappeared from sight.

"What sort of trouble?' asked Major Wiltshire.

"Well Sir, Sergeant O'Connor appears to be more concerned about staying in the saddle than he does about guiding the horse and I doubt if the horse knows the way to the trenches."

"Not my worry soldier. Now Lacey, show me what you have done in preparation for the exercise, or would you prefer to show me around Sergeant Redman?"

"I'll accompany you Sir, but Lacey can explain how we're set up."

The three set off for the communications centre.

"You reckon O'Connor's in trouble Bluey? I mean, you can hurt yourself if you fall off a horse." Mick was hoping that Bluey's reply would confirm his hopes.

"Oh, anyone can fall off a horse. Everyone does at some time or another. Whether you get hurt or not depends on how you fall, and I don't think Sergeant O'Connor has had much experience at falling off horses."

The group sat around the camp-fire each hoping Sergeant O'Connor would suffer the indignity of falling and suffer an injury that would require him to be medically evacuated to Melbourne. Major Wiltshire, Sergeant Redman and Preacher reappeared, and the Major accepted the offered cup of tea.

"I congratulate you men on the way you have established the communications. The real test starts at midday when Exercise HQ and the phantom battalions will start sending messages. These messages are designed to test the men at the front and of course, the communications. Messages will be sent constantly over the next 72 hours. The enemy will try to disrupt communications by getting behind the trenches and cutting the lines. You must use every trick you know to keep those lines open and operating. They might even try to capture Battalion HQ in which case you should call for help from the infantry. Should the enemy destroy your base, then you must rebuild it and get the lines open again as quickly as possible. Any questions?"

"Sir," as usual Sam had a question. "As we don't have rifles it'll be difficult to put up a fight against an enemy raiding party."

"True, but you are not expected to fight. That is the job of the infantry. Your task is to keep those lines open. As I said before, you must use cunning and deception to fool the enemy."

"Such as?" Sam was confused.

"Well, I'm not here to give away any secrets but I'll give you a hint." The Major smiled. "Should the enemy cut a line that wasn't in use, then he wouldn't do any damage to your organisation would he?"

"I think we get the message Sir," Preacher answered.

"Here comes the mounted party. Well, most of them." observed Bluey.

"Oh dear," said the Major, "my horse seems to have lost his rider. I do hope that Sergeant O'Connor is all right."

The mounted Sergeant who was leading the Major's horse came over. "I'm afraid Sir, Sergeant O'Connor wasn't prepared to remount after his second tumble. He is unhurt but prefers to find his way back on foot."

"Thank you Sergeant, for bringing Blackmore back. It's a wonder he didn't make for home once he had unloaded Sergeant O'Connor."

"I think the horse was surprised that anyone would fall off while he was walking along so he just stood quietly until I came up."

From the saddle the Major looked down. "Good luck men. The next three days won't be easy, but then, that's what it's all about." He turned his horse and cantered after the others.

* * *

At midday, the operator's panel in the communications centre came to life. Messages flowed between the trenches and the Exercise HQ. Preacher had detailed the men to work in pairs. One pair would work in the communications centre for four hours before being relieved. Those not manning the communications centre were free to do whatever they liked within the confines of the camp. The plan was that in the event of a line failure, a pair would be called to trace the fault and mend it. For the first few hours, the lines operated without interruption.

It was just going on dark when the two sergeants accompanied by Corporal Sweeney stormed into the camp-fire area. Preacher rose to greet them.

"I suppose you have brought us some rations Sergeant."

"Rations? Rations? No, and there won't be any fucking rations for you lot until this exercise is over." Sergeant O'Connor was in an uncontrolled rage.

"Sergeant we can't operate without..."

"Shut up Lacey." It had not been a good day. "I've just received a message that you stupid idiots have put snakes in sandbags and left them along the lines where some poor fool is likely to get bitten. Is this true?"

"Yes Sergeant, we have booby trapped our lines."

"What a stupid fucking idea Lacey. What if someone gets bitten and dies?"

"Wait a minute Pat." Sergeant Redman had been trying to come to grips with this unexpected turn of events. He turned to Preacher. "How many of these booby traps have you laid, Lacey?"

Preacher turned to Bluey.

"About six on each line, so that's eighteen, and of course we have a couple in reserve here in the dugout."

"Hear that Pat? This mob of lying bastards expect us to believe they've caught twenty snakes and popped them into bags. What are they, soldiers or professional snake charmers?"

"Shit Bill you're right. Nice try Lacey. You nearly had me fooled, but not anymore."

"Sergeant O'Connor, I'm telling the truth. We do have snakes in bags."

"Rubbish Lacey. It was a good try but it's not going to work. If you have a snake in a bag I'd like to see it."

"Bluey?" asked Preacher.

Bluey disappeared into one of the dugouts and came out holding a bag tied at the opening with twine.

"Sweeney, take a peep in that bloody bag." Sergeant O'Connor believed that he was now in charge of the situation.

"But what if there is a snake in there Sergeant?" Corporal Sweeney was not as confident as his leader.

"What the hell are you talking about Sweeney? It's a sham. If you don't want to stick your nose in the bag then just up-end it and let's see what falls out."

"Steady Sergeant, I wouldn't advise that. That snake will be pretty mad when he drops out and someone may well get hurt." Bluey looked concerned.

"You won't give up will you? Go on Sweeney untie the bag and let's see this fearsome viper." Sergeant O'Connor was now enjoying the situation.

Gingerly Corporal Sweeney accepted the bag from Bluey. Bluey stepped back and picked up a stick from the wood pile. The remainder of the group retreated some paces back.

"Go on Sweeney, let's see this dangerous booby trap." urged the irate Sergeant.

Realising that it was futile to protest any further, Sweeney released the twine and up-ended the bag. His shriek of fear filled the air as a four-foot black snake fell to the ground. The snake arched into a striking pose and at the same time Bluey swung the stick he was holding, breaking the snake's back.

"You bastard, I'll fix you." screamed Sweeney, producing a large hunting knife.

"You make one move towards me with that stick-pin, corporal, and you'll be as dead as that snake." The stance and the tone of Bluey's voice halted Sweeney in his tracks. "I warned the Sergeant not to let that snake out but he wouldn't listen. So, if you have a beef, it's with him, not me. I just saved your miserable life, perhaps that was a mistake on my part."

"Sweeney, put that knife away." Sergeant O'Connor realised the situation was in grave danger of getting out of control. Sweeney returned the knife to its sheath. The look of fear on his face was now replaced by a look of hatred.

"I'll remember you Dowson. One day I'll get you, I promise."

"Enough Sweeney. There are other matters to attend to right now." The fat Sergeant was slowly regaining his composure. "Lacey, you're to send out parties immediately and retrieve all your so-called booby traps. You're to kill all your pet snakes and report to me when this has been done."

All eyes turned to where Preacher stood, apart from the others. The flames of the camp-fire reflected on his features giving him a strange appearance. Even his voice had altered. Normally Preacher spoke in a soft reasoning tone but now the words came out with a harsh ring.

"The booby traps will remain where they are, and more will be laid around the camp-site. It is obvious the enemy knows about their presence, and if he acts as foolishly as you, then you are right, someone will get hurt. As for Corporal Sweeney and his threats, I expect you to take appropriate action. This man has threatened to take the life of Private Dowson. You along with everyone else here, are a witness to those threats. Now, as we are supposed to be in a war-like situation, I suggest we get back to our duties, or do you wish to call Exercise HQ and report the matter. They may even call the exercise off. Perhaps you would like to call it off?"

"Nothing could make me call off this exercise Private Lacey, nothing. However, I can guarantee the next three days will be the worst three days any of you have ever, or will ever, experience."

The words came slowly from O'Connor's mouth. The hatred was undisguised. The two Sergeants and the corporal turned and walked back to their quarters.

* * *

The six men were seated around the fire awaiting directions from Preacher when they were joined by Skipper and Mac.

"What are you two doing here?" asked Preacher. "The operator's switchboard is to be manned constantly."

"O'Connor told us to push off while he sent some confidential messages. Said he would call us when he was finished."

"Confidential my arse! I bet he's talking to the enemy and relating the events of the past hour." Sam didn't usually resort to strong language.

"I hope he is Sam. He'll be telling them the booby traps are real and that we won't move them. That should make them a little more cautious in their raiding."

"Agreed Preacher, but only for tonight. Tomorrow O'Connor will have men out there beating the daylights out of every sandbag in sight. It was only a temporary thing. We can expect a fairly easy time tonight but tomorrow night will be different."

"You're right Bluey, but thanks to your snakes we'll have some time to reorganise. Can you catch more snakes? Remember I promised O'Connor we would lay more booby traps and I would like to have some in reserve so I can carry out my threat."

Bluey smiled. "You know Preacher, a lot of people can be frightened by a dead snake, especially if it's in the dark and they don't know it's dead. We used to play all sorts of tricks on our friends by putting dead snakes in their rooms, even in their beds."

Mick looked at Bluey with horror. "My God you red-headed bastard, you really are weird."

"Stay close to me Mick and you'll be all right. I'll see you don't get bitten."

"Bluey there's something you should know. I thought I recognised that creep Sweeney when first I laid eyes on him, and now I know. When he pulled that knife it all came back. He used to run with a mob working the Carlton area. A bunch of mean bastards. Bluey, I think you should stay close to one of us while we're out here. Sweeney will be watching you and if he can get you on your own he'll fix you. Take my word, he's very bad news and he can use that knife."

"Thanks Mick, but I can handle a sneak like Sweeney."

"No Bluey, you can't. He's a street fighter. He doesn't work the way you do. He doesn't know the meaning of rules and you've dented his professional pride. Imagine what the boys back in Carlton will say when they hear he was scared of a little snake. Take care, especially if he can get his hands on a rifle."

Preacher looked at Mick. It was hard to see his face in the firelight. "How come you know so much about this mob in Carlton, Mick? You ever run with them?"

"No Preacher. I'm a Collingwood boy and we stayed on our side of the fence. There's only trouble between the mobs if one crosses into another's territory, and the usual reason is a girl. I've seen Sweeney once or twice, but he has a bad reputation. What baffles me is, why he's in the army. He can only be in it for what he can get out of it for himself."

Preacher stood up. "We haven't time to sit around talking. There are things to be done. Firstly, we need to settle on the pairings. Bluey, I'm putting Erik with you. That should act as a deterrent to Sweeney, with your bush skills and Erik's strength, you should be a good team. Skipper, you and Mac can continue together, Sam, that puts you with Jacko, and Mick will partner me. Any questions?"

"Fine by me Preacher. Jacko is teaching me about farming so I can go on the land when this war is over."

"Ya, me and Bluey is gud, but ven Darkie comes back I vont to be vith him." said Erik.

"Darkie. I'd almost forgotten about him. Sorry Erik, but I don't think your New Zealand mate will be rejoining us, certainly not for this exercise. I don't know how the brass will view his performance seeing he is spending most of it as a prisoner of war."

Erik looked devastated. "Vat? Darkie von't be a signaller? Yust because he vent looking for food for us?"

"Food. That's another thing Preacher." Sam's stomach was already telling him how long it had been since breakfast.

"Well Sam, a funny thing happened during the inspection by Major Wiltshire. We were out of earshot of Redman, and I asked the Major about Darkie. He said he was helping around HQ as a cleaner, but the military police kept a close eye on him, and he was locked up at night in a room next to the MPs. I said to the Major, 'Well I hope he's being well fed.' Wiltshire looked at me in a strange sort of way and said, 'I'll tell him about your concern'."

"Do you think the Major knows about our food situation?"

"Don't know Sam, but I suspect the Major knows a lot more about what is going on than he openly admits. Think back. Remember he said to use every trick you know. It was almost as if he knew about our booby traps and was telling us that it was all right to use them. At least that's what I think he meant, so that's why I told Sergeant O'Connor we wouldn't move them, and you notice he didn't press the point. Now Bluey what were you saying about dead snakes?"

"Just a thought Preacher. I'm not all that keen on catching snakes. Muck around with them long enough and sooner or later you get bitten. But dead snakes don't bite so there's no danger. But if you tread on a dead snake or one happens to fall on you as you sneak through the scrub, it's a very brave, very cool man, who doesn't react."

Mick shuddered. "Good God Bluey, how's a snake going to drop onto you, especially a dead one?"

"I'll take Erik down to the creek at first light and with a bit of luck we should be able to kill a couple, perhaps more. And we still have the remains of Sweeney's one over there. And I still have one live one in a bag in the dugout. I want to keep him for an emergency."

"Emergency? What the hell are you talking about?" Mick was convinced that Bluey had taken leave his senses.

"Just that Mick. We may need to convince someone, at sometime, that we still have a supply of angry live snakes. And I might even present it to O'Connor and company as a farewell present when we leave."

"We won't be leaving here if we don't get food." Sam was back on his favourite subject.

"You know Sam you can eat snake, it doesn't taste all that bad."

"Have you eaten snake?"

"I've tried it. If you're starving then snake steak just might save your life, but then the bush is full of tucker. Don't fret Sammy we won't starve."

Before any further discussion Preacher spoke.

"Right, remember the Major's advice about confusing the enemy. I want you to run dummy lines to the trenches tomorrow. Try and conceal the real lines. Put them up in trees or bury them under rocks, rubbish, anything to make them harder to find than the dummy lines which we'll leave out in the open. Also, each pair is to take three sandbags to imitate booby traps. Don't make them too obvious. Put sticks in them so they look as if something is inside them. At night, a patrol won't be spending too much time crawling around looking for a line. Once they find and cut a line, they will reckon they've done their job."

The snarling voice of Sergeant O'Connor broke in, "You signallers, back in the signal centre. Hurry up. There's a war on."

Skipper and Mac ran off in the direction of the hut.

"I'd give a lot to know what that bastard O'Connor is up to."

"Perhaps it's best you don't know Jacko. It might only upset you more. I think we've done enough talking. We may have a quiet night thanks to Bluey's pets, but then again, we may not, so let's try and get some sleep. If they call for linesmen, Sam, you and Jacko take the first call. Mick and I will take the second and hopefully that will leave Bluey and Erik free to take over from Skip and Mac at midnight. After your turn in the signal centre, Bluey, you can go snake hunting. But remember what Mick said, keep Erik near you at all times. That's all for now. Tomorrow should be an interesting day."

SNAKES, SNAKES, BLOODY SNAKES

It was a quiet night on the lines. Messages flowed without disruption. It was a good start but the team felt it was only a short time before life would become difficult.

The sun was chasing away the shadows of the night when Bluey and Erik appeared from the direction of the creek. Preacher and Mick were stirring life into the fire and the billy was warming up.

"Any luck Bluey?"

"Two very nice brown snakes. I just got Erik to lift a few logs and there they were, hiding underneath. Erik doesn't seem at all worried by the possibility that they may strike at whoever disturbs their shelter."

The Swede looked pleased with these words of praise. "Vu vouldn't let me get bitten Bluey. Vu are too quick vith that stick. Tell Preacher vot happened last night."

"Happened? What's he talking about?"

"It was about 2:00am and Erik was manning the operator board when he let out a shout."

"Ya, I couldn't help it Preacher. It vos Darkie on the line."

"Darkie? But how? I mean, how would they let him use the line?"

Bluey shook his head. "They didn't let him use it Preacher. He could only speak for a minute or so. Said he'd been waiting for the operator to go out for a piss and then he ducked in and called us."

"But he's supposed to be locked up at night." Mick stopped stirring the billy.

Bluey smiled. "I imagine Darkie has been locked up before and knows how to get around such problems."

"Well, what did he say? Come on Bluey. Why did he call?" Preacher questioned.

"He could only speak for a minute. He said not to worry about the tucker, that would be fixed soon. Then he said he was more useful where he was, rather than being out here. That's all he had time for."

No one spoke for a while as each pondered Bluey's words.

"Don't worry about the tucker. He said that?"

"Yes Preacher. Don't ask me how, when or why, that's all he said."

"Darkie vill fix it. Vu see." Erik would hear no criticism of his mate.

"I doubt if Darkie will drive up here with a truck load of rations in daylight, so I guess we must get through today on empty stomachs although we do have plenty of tea and sugar remaining." Mick was looking towards the hut where a spiral of smoke was escaping from the chimney. "Well we do at the moment but I suggest we keep it safe."

Bluey nodded. "Good thinking Mick and I know a very safe place. Let's put it in an empty sandbag and leave it at the back of one of the dugouts. There's no way Sweeney would touch another sandbag."

Mick looked at the bushman. "You're right Bluey but then none of us would either, so we'll have to go without a brew unless you're around to dish it out."

"Mick, the snakes go into the left-hand dugout, the tea and sugar into the other one. Trust me. Sweeney won't know that but he'll not be going into any dugout inspecting sandbags."

The tea was brewed and poured. "Right fellas, soon as you're washed and shaved, I want dummy lines run to the trenches and the fake booby traps placed. Mick and I will relieve Sam and Jacko. I don't want to be away from the camp in case something develops as a result of last night's confrontation. O'Connor has a personal score to settle with me and I want to keep an eye on him." Preacher was enjoying his taste of command. "We can get through a day without food. I'm sure in real war the troops don't get three meals a day, so it's all part of the training. Come on, let's get cracking. Don't let O'Connor and his cronies get you down. We'll fight them and the enemy."

* * *

Except for the non-stop flow of messages, the day passed quietly. Exercise HQ would issue lengthy orders to the infantry, then amend the messages and finally cancel them. Each message required an acknowledgment from the infantry and in this way the HQ staff could determine if the communications net was fully operational. For the two signallers in the centre, each message had to be written down, repeated back to check for accuracy, then relayed to the infantry using the same lengthy process. The men soon realised that the work in the field was preferable to the four hour stint manning the switchboard. Sergeant O'Connor and Corporal Sweeney departed from the camp mid-morning and didn't arrive back until just before dusk, with O'Connor showing signs of drink. Sergeant Redman made numerous visits to the signal centre to check that it was operating as required, but there was no other supervision. As darkness fell Preacher called for a council of war.

"We should expect things are going to start happening tonight. We've done a good job on the lines and Bluey was right, someone has been making an awful mess of the sandbags along the track. So, we can expect the lines to be cut and perhaps an attack on this site. The cut lines don't worry me, but an attack on the camp, is another thing. What do you think, Bluey?"

All eyes turned to Bluey. They knew he'd killed the snakes for a reason and somehow that reason was linked to a possible raid on the camp. But they didn't know what Bluey had in mind.

Bluey picked up a stick and brushed away the twigs and leaves to make a clear patch of ground in front of him. He drew a map in the dirt with the stick.

"I could be wrong, but if this war game is even remotely real, then a raiding party won't come through the trenches. So, we can expect the party to scout around the eastern or western flanks of the trench line. To the east is the creek. It's a natural barrier and although you could wade or swim across, my guess is that a raiding party would opt for the easiest crossing, and that's the ford used by vehicles. From there, they'd come along the side of the road to the camp."

"And to the west?"

"Not so simple Preacher. It would depend upon how far west of the left-hand trench they go before turning towards the camp. However, in the end, they have to arrive here at the camp, and so my guess is that they'll come along the fence line and then move up this small gully to the south west of the hut. It may even be that O'Connor and his mates have some sort of method of signalling to them, such as a light in the window. So, we have two possibilities, and we should decide whether or not we cover both avenues, or take a punt and concentrate on one."

"And if we pick the wrong one?" questioned Mac.

"Then our camp will be wrecked and we'll have to start all over again."

"What about some help from our infantry?"

"I thought of that Mac," answered Preacher. "I sent a message to them this afternoon to see if they'd provide us with protection. They replied that they were unable to help. So, we're on our own."

"Ve vill fight them." Erik was not about to concede defeat.

"We can't fight them Erik. They will be armed, and we don't know how many there will be." Preacher was gazing at Bluey's rough map. "Go on Bluey, you obviously have some sort of plan."

"My snake theory Preacher. Remember what I said about people being frightened of snakes, especially in the dark when the snake has you at a disadvantage? Even seasoned bushmen don't like being up against a snake in the dark. It's a no contest, all the odds are in the snake's favour."

"So?"

"My plan is simple. If the raiding party was made up of tough, bush-wise men then it would only create a minor hiccup. But if the party consists of normal citizens pretending to be soldiers, then I think we may be able to cause enough panic to break up the attack."

"Go on."

"We have four dead snakes, so we can use two snakes at each ambush, or if we decide to go for one approach, we have four available."

Preacher intervened. "Bluey we can't take the risk of putting all our eggs into one basket. We must cover both approaches. At least that's how I see it?"

There were no dissenting voices.

"Right that means two men for each ambush, two in the signal centre and two in camp to relieve them. If the pair in the signal centre aren't relieved on time, O'Connor will smell a rat."

"Bluey, it's your plan and they're your snakes, so you and Erik are obviously one of the ambush parties. Mac, you and Skipper are the other. Any problem with that?"

"Snakes, especially dead ones, don't worry me." Mac looked at his companion.

"Nope. Dead ones don't fuss me."

"The line to Exercise HQ is down." shouted Sam from the communication dugout.

"Right Sam we're on our way. Bluey you take charge of things here and get your ambushes set up. Mick grab the gear and let's get the line to HQ fixed. We can only hope the break is not too far along the line." Preacher and Mick set off along the main line, and the others turned to Bluey.

"Right fellas, here's what I have in mind, but you'll have to be flexible. Make up your own plan if things don't work out the way I'm hoping."

* * *

Soon after midnight, Bluey and Erik heard the approaching patrol. The moon was up and the bush had a ghostly dappled appearance.

"Bloody hell, they're noisy. They must be a good half mile away. You happy Erik? You clear on what to do?"

"Ya Bluey. Ve vill give them something to make a noise about."

"Hell, I hope so. They obviously don't expect any resistance or trouble. Time to get into position. Remember, pull the string firmly so the snake moves quickly across the path. We'll be in trouble if they don't walk under this red gum but after you do your act, I think they'll come over here. Good luck, and Erik, if things do go wrong, don't start a one-man war. If they get past us then we'll have to try something else."

The big man crossed the small clearing and took up his position in a clump of bushes. Bluey waited a while longer to make certain that the rowdy soldiers were following the expected path, then climbed the old tree and eased his way out on one of its huge branches.

The enemy raiding party believed that this was a routine patrol. The unarmed signallers would either flee at their approach or surrender. If they surrendered, so much the better. Sergeant O'Connor had hinted he had a few scores to settle and that could be worth watching. The Corporal leading the party had brought a bottle of rum and from time to time, this was passed down the line. All in all, life in the army wasn't all that bad.

"Shit." The cry from the Corporal brought the column to a sudden halt.

"What's up?" The men closed upon their leader.

"A bloody snake just crawled across the track and disappeared into those bushes on the right." The Corporal pointed towards the bushes where Erik was hiding.

"Leave him be, Corp. We're not here to chase snakes, and I for one am not going looking for him."

"Yeah Smokie, but the buggers give you a fright when they pop up and you're not expecting them."

The Corporal started to move forward once more but by instinct, he veered to the left leading his men under a large red gum tree. As the third man passed beneath his perch, Bluey dropped his surprise weapon. The scream as the snake fell across the man's shoulders was electrifying. The patrol froze, then quickly backed away from the stricken man.

"It's a snake. It's bitten me Corporal. Jesus I'm going to die." The man fell to the ground, the snake alongside him. One soldier moved forward and struck the reptile with the butt of his rifle.

"The bastard won't bite anyone else." he roared. The men gathered around the sobbing victim.

"Christ what a mess. Andrews, get off to the southern camp as fast as you can. Tell Sergeant O'Connor what has happened. We need a doctor. Get going man, time is precious." Corporal Lane was at last showing some signs of leadership. "Now, you two get his coat off and then shove your rifles through the sleeves and make a sort of seat, a platform for him to sit on. You two help support him. Shut up Rixon, we're doing all we can to help you. Pull yourself together. Shit you're a soldier not a baby."

"It's all right for you, you're not dying. Oh Christ, why did I ever join this outfit." The men settled him on the makeshift seat. "Hurry, please hurry. I might make it if I can get to a doctor in time."

The procession set off hurrying as best it could. They failed to notice the two shadowy figures that appeared from either side of the track and followed them. Bluey had been correct. Darkness and fear, plus a vivid imagination, make a formidable enemy.

* * *

The shouts and screams from the raiding party had been heard in Battalion HQ and the signallers camp. The two Sergeants and Corporal Sweeney strained their eyes to detect signs of the approaching patrol. A man came running up the path.

"Sergeant, Private Rixon has been bitten by a snake. He's in a bad way. He needs help."

Sergeant O'Connor swore. "Damn. What a bloody stupid thing to do. Bill, get on the line to HQ. Tell them what's happened. Sweeney, get the truck ready. You may have to drive into town. Perhaps they can find a doctor and he can meet the truck halfway. What's your name, soldier?"

"Andrews, Private Andrews." the exhausted man gasped.

"Right Andrews, you'll find a stretcher by the side of the hut. Grab it and get back to Lane. Shit what a mess."

The three men left leaving Sergeant O'Connor to stare at the flickering campfire and the figures of the signallers.

"A bloody snake. I don't know how you did it you bunch of bastards, but I bet you arranged this. Holy Moses are you going to suffer if this bloke dies. The whole bloody army will settle with you." The words were softly spoken but the venom they carried could be felt by the men by the fire.

"Hell Preacher," muttered Mick, "Bluey and Erik have whipped up a storm. I can feel Sergeant O'Connor looking straight through me. What a racket."

Skipper and Mac joined Preacher and Mick at the fire. "We heard the commotion and decided the raid was not coming along our path, so we came back. What have Bluey and Erik done?"

"Don't know, but you can be sure there's going to be hell to pay shortly." Preacher was clearly worried. "It's obvious someone is hurt, hence the stretcher."

"Maybe Erik hit someone." suggested Mick.

"Well if he did, they sure would be hurt. Preacher, why don't Mac and I sort of get around to the rear of the mob and see if we can link up with Bluey and Erik? They might need help."

"Good idea Skipper. Keep clear of the enemy, but see if you can make contact with the others. I need to know what happened."

"Right Preacher. See you soon."

"Probably in jail Skip. Keep your head down." The two men disappeared into the darkness.

* * *

The position of the raiding party could be easily determined by the noise as Sergeant Redman rejoined his colleague. "Major Wiltshire was in the signal centre when I got through. He and the light horse Sergeant are coming out on horses. He's sent a car to collect the local doctor."

"Right Bill, that's about all we can do for the present. Here they come. What a fucking mess."

Corporal Lane advanced to meet the two Sergeants.

"It's bad Pat. Real bad. A bloody snake jumped out of a tree right onto him." Lane was very excited.

Sergeant O'Connor snarled. "A snake jumped out of a tree? What the hell are you talking about? You're pissed, you little shit.

The snake more than likely came out of a rum bottle. Christ Lane, what is going on?"

"It's true Pat. A snake jumped, fell, I don't know how. It landed on Private Rixon and bit him on the neck."

The stretcher party arrived and set the stretcher down on the ground.

"Shut up man," O'Connor snarled. "Where did this snake bite you? Bill, bring that lantern over here."

By the light, the Sergeant examined the victim's neck. "There's no sign of a bite. Not even a scratch. You haven't been bitten by a snake, not even a bloody mosquito. Lane what the hell is going on? Are you all pissed?" The rage in the Sergeant's voice was uncontrolled. Suddenly he remembered the activities he had initiated.

"Bill. The Major. The doctor. Quick get on the line again. Cancel everything." Sergeant Redman departed for the signal centre at the run. "Lane, you really are in the shit this time."

Sergeant O'Connor was almost speechless with rage. "You dare to call yourselves soldiers. You were supposed to sneak up on this camp and attack it. Now look at you. A rabble. A complete bloody rabble, all because of some cock and bull story about a snake jumping out of a tree."

"But it did Sergeant. We all saw it." The shaken Corporal was convinced. "Smokie killed it. It was a snake. A real snake."

"Bullshit Lane. I reckon you've all been on the bottle and concocted this snake story. Why I don't know, but by God I'm going to find out."

"No Sergeant. It's all true, except we didn't know that Rixon hadn't been bitten. There was a snake. Two in fact. One slid across the path right in front of me, and then there was the one that fell out of the tree onto Rixon. Sarge, you have to believe me." Lane was pleading.

"Snakes, snakes. That's all I've heard about for the past two days. How come snakes are suddenly so bloody prominent in this neck of the woods?" Sergeant O'Connor stopped and reflected on what he had just said. "Snake? Of course. It's so bloody obvious, Lacey and his bloody snake charmer. Lacey, come here." he roared.

Preacher appeared from the darkness.

"You want me Sergeant?" he politely enquired.

"No, I don't bloody want you. What I want is an explanation. You and that damn snake charmer Dowson started all this nonsense, and now you have stuffed up the whole exercise. Well man, I'm waiting for an answer."

Before Preacher could answer, Sergeant Redman and Corporal Sweeney rejoined the group from the signal centre. "Bad news Pat. All hell is about to break loose. Major Wiltshire and the Sergeant are on their way by horse and can't be reached. They should be here soon. HQ is sending out a runner by bike to tell the doctor he's not required. The Colonel has blown his top and I reckon Wiltshire will roast us all when he gets here and finds out what's happened. Heads are going to roll."

"It's all Lane's fucking fault." O'Connor turned to the frightened corporal. "You're in the shit, well and truly. When Wiltshire's finished with you I reckon he'll book you a passage on the next boat to France. You deserve all you get you useless toad."

"Careful Sergeant O'Connor." Lane had decided that under the circumstances attack would be the best method of defence. "There are a lot of things I know that Major Wiltshire would be interested to hear. You drop me in the shit for this, and I'll make sure you are on that boat with me, probably as Private O'Connor."

Sweeney moved swiftly to Lane's side. "You don't really mean that do you?" His quiet voice held a sinister threat. Lane realised that he'd overstepped the mark and more than his career was now in danger. "Yeah Sweeney. You're right. I was just mouthing off. I wouldn't blab. No way. Not me." Lane was very frightened.

O'Connor turned to Preacher. "It's all your bloody fault. You damn signallers. Well, seeing the raiding party is here, they may as well do what they came for. Lane, get your men cracking. Destroy this camp."

"Hold it Pat." Sergeant Redman raised his hand as if to stop traffic. "When I called into HQ, the exercise was put on hold. The order said all exercise-related activities are to cease until further notice. With Wiltshire due to arrive, I don't think it would be wise to let Lane's mob loose."

"And Sergeant O'Connor." All eyes turned towards the Preacher. "We're not about to allow anyone wreck our camp. If they try, they'll have a fight on their hands, that much I promise you."

The warning given by Redman had registered with the angry O'Connor. There was enough trouble brewing without creating more.

"Lane, you and your men go with Sweeney. Wait outside the hut. Lacey, you and your men return to your camp. No further action by anyone, but the signal centre is to continue to be manned. Now get out of my sight."

The signallers made their way to the camp-fire where Mick had the water on the boil.

"Right you blokes. Sit over there while I get you dinner." Mick looked very pleased with himself.

"Dinner? Vot dinner?" asked Erik.

Mick dipped a ladle into a cauldron and dished out large helpings of stew onto the plates.

Preacher explained. "Just before you left the camp, the line to HQ was reported as being down and Mick and I went off to mend it. We found the break about half a mile along and we also found the culprits who had cut it."

"More of O'Connor's henchmen."

"No Bluey, a young man and a young woman. Relatives of yours, I believe, Paul and Jessie Taylor."

Bluey nearly choked. "What? Why would Paul and Jessie cut a telephone line?"

"Stop asking questions and eat. We don't want any of that mob coming over and discovering our secret. They cut the line because that's what Darkie told them to do. No questions, just eat and listen. Jessie works part-time as a cleaning lady at the boarding house, which is also Exercise HQ. She met Darkie while he was doing his cleaning duties and they got talking. When Darkie found out she was related to you, he told her about our problems. Jessie told her family and they decided to help us. Seems O'Connor and company have been operating out of this town for some time and are not popular with the locals. Anyhow, Paul and Jessie rode out with that stew and some grub for breakfast. They'll be back again tomorrow night. So, as Darkie said, don't worry about the tucker."

"Darkie, he's a great man." Erik's admiration for his friend had reached new heights.

"Quite so Erik, but I wouldn't want to be in his shoes if O'Connor finds out what he's been up to."

"Don't vorry about Darkie. He can take care of himself." Erik would not accept any criticism of his mate.

"Here comes trouble." Bluey had detected the sound of approaching horses.

The men stood up as two horsemen trotted by. The mounted men looked down but said nothing.

"Best we stay here for the moment." said Preacher. "O'Connor suspects we had a hand in this but he can't prove anything."

Major Wiltshire and the Sergeant entered the hut. Corporal Lane was summoned. Shortly after, the listeners could hear the angry voice of Major Wiltshire. The words and tone left no doubt about his opinion of Corporal Lane and his men. The tirade lasted for several minutes before Lane emerged. The chastened Corporal called his men together and they formed up as a squad on parade. With heads bowed they marched off towards the northern lines, passing the signallers' camp in silence.

"Now what Preacher?" asked Mick. "Is the war over?"

"We shall soon know what is to happen. Very soon I expect, as here comes the Major now."

The men stood up and Preacher saluted the officer as he neared the camp-fire. The Major stood close to the group and looked into each face as if seeking some clue, some indication, some explanation about the events of the night.

"Private Lacey, isn't someone going to offer me a brew? Seems I've ridden all this way on a wild goose chase."

"Sorry Sir, how rude of us. Mick, a cup of tea for the Major. Like to sit down Sir?"

"Thank you but no. I just want a brew then I'm off back to HQ to try and explain to the Colonel just what is, or has been, going on out here."

"We've been working hard to keep all the lines open as ordered Sir, and so far, I think we've managed fairly well."

"Oh yes you've managed well, and HQ has no gripes about the lines being kept open. It's the strange happenings that have occurred around the area that interest me."

"Sorry Sir. I don't follow you."

Major Wiltshire stared at Preacher. "No, I didn't think you would Lacey, and then again it might have been a real snake. Who knows?" The Major paused. "Well, snakes or no snakes, the exercise has to proceed, and no doubt will, as soon as I get back to HQ and advise the Colonel. I don't think you will get any more trouble from the enemy but the message traffic will be increased considerably. As I have said before, your job is to see the messages get through. The exercise will finish at noon the day after tomorrow so you have a bit over thirty hours to go."

"That shouldn't be a problem Sir. We're in good shape and the routine we've established seems to be working."

"Right for tucker are you?" It was a loaded question.

"We can cope Sir. It's been a challenge in many ways, but we'll survive."

The Major seemed to ponder the answer, as if he'd expected to hear something different. "Right then, let's get on with the business we are here for. Thanks for the cup of tea."

The men rose and Preacher saluted.

"I bet O'Connor is in a foul mood after that roasting," observed Mick. "I wonder what he'll try now."

"Who knows and who cares," said Preacher. "Let's get back to the schedule. Remember, no one goes anywhere on his own. Always work as a pair, and keep on your toes. We've come this far and done all right. Another thirty-three hours and it'll all be over." He looked at the roster he'd drawn up. "If all goes according to plan, Bluey and Erik should be on line repair duty at 9:30pm, so you two can make the meet with the Taylors and collect the food. If you're busy, we'll have to work out some other arrangement. I suggest we grab some shut-eye. It's been a long night but a successful one, thanks to Bluey."

"And Erik. Don't forget Erik played a big role. He did well."

"Of course Bluey. Thanks Erik. Darkie will be proud of you."

Erik beamed. It was the greatest reward he could have.

* * *

The next day was extremely busy. Corporal Sweeney departed in the truck immediately after breakfast and didn't return until sundown. The two Sergeants spent the day checking the messages without comment. Twice during the day Sergeant O'Connor ordered the operators out of the signal centre so he could make confidential calls to HQ. No food was offered to the signallers and none was requested, something that puzzled the two Sergeants.

At the pre-arranged time, Bluey and Erik met with the Taylors and took delivery of the food. Jessie also carried a scribbled note from Darkie asking for information of the events of the previous night, saying that all he knew was that all hell had broken loose. Bluey related the sequence of events which caused Jessie and Paul to break out in laughter. By noon, the whole town would know about the tree-hopping snake and the brave soldiers. As the exercise was to end at midday the following day, they agreed that further resupply trips would be unnecessary, but Jessie invited the squad to dine at the Taylor farm the following evening, if their commitments would allow.

Next morning Sergeant O'Connor sent for Preacher. "The exercise will finish at midday. Immediately we receive the message to stand down, you and your bunch of snivelling rats are to commence reeling up all the wire you have laid out, including the line to HQ. That should keep you busy for the afternoon and half the night. Corporal Sweeney will bring the truck out to collect you lot tomorrow morning to take you to the train. Do you think you can handle that?"

"We seem to have managed so far Sergeant so I guess we can dismantle the camp without too much trouble. Am I to understand that we won't be seeing any more of you and Sergeant Redman once you leave here?"

"You're right Private Lacey. You won't be, and for that, you should count yourselves lucky. But let me tell you this, if I ever come across any one of your scheming squad again, his life won't be worth a penny. That's a promise."

"Thank you Sergeant. I'll pass on your good wishes to the men, but I doubt if they'll be anxious to renew your acquaintance." Preacher walked back to the camp-fire where all but Bluey and Erik were seated.

"O'Connor has confirmed all activities will cease at 12:00pm, and that he and his friends are taking off in the truck, just as soon as they can after that. We have to reel up our wires and Corporal Sweeney will pick us up tomorrow morning."

"Where are they off to, Preacher?" asked Mick.

"I don't know, O'Connor just said they had business to attend to. I was happy to hear that they were leaving."

"It's funny though. Very odd." Mick said.

"Something bothering you, Mick?"

"It's the truck Preacher. Last night I went for a stroll, and as I was passing the truck I decided to have a peep in the back. It's loaded to the hilt with all sorts of gear, cans of petrol, reels of wire, cases of tinned food, all sorts of stuff. Now why would they load up at the end of an exercise?"

"I don't particularly care, Mick, and I advise you to keep clear of them and their truck. They're not very pleased with us. Time we relieved Bluey and Erik and do our last stint on the phones."

The two walked to the signal centre and took over the operators' duties from a weary Bluey and Erik.

"Plenty of traffic Preacher, but it's easing off. Reckon everyone's getting ready to go home."

"Thanks Bluey. You and Erik better wash up and have breakfast. We have a lot to do this afternoon."

"Oh yes. Got a message to say Darkie is to be released from POW prison as soon as the exercise finishes. At least that's another pair of hands to help dismantle the camp."

Bluey and Erik left the other two with the talkative telephone. By late morning, a convoy of trucks had arrived to pick up the infantry from the trenches and traffic on the telephone lines ceased. An hour later, the long awaited message signalling the end of the exercise arrived. Sergeant O'Connor and his two companions quickly boarded their truck. As it was about to depart, O'Connor called out to Preacher. "Make sure you scrub the hut and leave it spotless." He laughed. "Sweeney will inspect it tomorrow so it had better be shining. Drive on Corporal, and a bloody good riddance to this useless mob."

"Bloody hell Preacher, have you seen inside that hut? It's a pigsty. I don't know how they could live in it." Mac was furious.

"I've seen it Mac. I can't understand how those two made the rank of Sergeant. Surely someone in authority can see what is going on? However, for now we have to do what we're told. Mick and I'll clean up the hut. Straight after lunch, the rest of you start reeling up the lines to the trenches as per the roster. Now who's this coming through the bush at a gallop?"

A wild yell from the approaching horseman quickly identified the rider as Darkie. He pulled the horse up close to the camp-fire and ran from man to man shaking their hands.

"You're all bloody famous. Christ why wasn't I here? The whole town, the whole bloody army, is talking about the Signals Snake Squad. What a hoot."

All started talking at once but Darkie held up his hand for silence. "Where are those bastards O'Connor, Redman and Sweeney?" he asked.

"Don't fret about them. They've packed up and gone. Sweeney is to come back tomorrow to collect us after we've dismantled the camp."

"Gone? Gone where? What the hell's going on?"

"Calm down Darkie. It's all under control. We have a roster and we'll be ready by morning although we'll have to get cracking. Now you're here you can help, but be assured friend, that we were most grateful for you organising the food. We were in big trouble until you fixed that."

Darkie scowled, "It's all wrong Preacher. Those fucking useless bastards moving out like that. They and their military policemen mates are up to no good. They kept talking about the deal, the end of the 'exercise deal' they called it. From the room where I was locked up, I could hear them talking on the phone. They kept referring to Robbo, but there's no Robbo that I know of on the exercise staff."

"Robbo. You sure Darkie? That was the name?"

"Yes Mick. They said Robbo was waiting for the delivery, but damned if I know who Robbo is, but he is obviously a big wheeler dealer."

"Think Darkie. Anything about a time, a place?" Mick was persistent.

"Well there was a panic when Major Wiltshire suggested that the exercise should be extended because of the time lost in the snake attack. One MP said something about an 6:00pm deadline."

Mick turned to his leader. "Preacher could that truck reach Melbourne by 6:00pm?"

"Barring any accident, they should reach the city between 5:00 and 6:00pm. The roads aren't too bad."

"Preacher I'm not sure, but I have my suspicions about those three and what they're up to. You remember I said Sweeney ran, or used to run, with the Carlton mob."

Preacher nodded.

"Well the boss of the Carlton mob is a bloke they call Robbo. A real nasty type. He would've put you in the river in concrete boots as quick as a flash if he thought you'd crossed him. He's as bad as they come in Melbourne. My guess is that these bastards have been ripping off the Army and selling the stores to Robbo. Those telephone wires would be worth a packet and all that petrol. It's my guess that they're on the way to deliver that stuff to Robbo."

"The lousy bastards. Well Preacher what are we going to do?" asked Darkie.

"I don't know Darkie. What can we do? Tell the Military Police?"

"Hell no Preacher. Remember I overheard those rats talking about this caper. They're in it up to their scrawny necks. Well the two in town are. Mick, you got any ideas?"

Mick thought before speaking. “Listen, you don’t know what it’s like to mess with these people. They have ways of finding out about people who cross them, and they have ways of dealing with such people. This is another world to the one you live in. Stay away from them.”

“You mean ignore what has happened? Turn a blind eye to what we know is going on?” Bluey was stunned by Mick’s suggestion.

“Bluey, it’s all very well to get on your high horse, but that doesn’t help when a bunch of thugs have chopped off a couple of your fingers or smashed your legs with a pick handle. I should’ve kept my mouth shut.”

“No Mick, I can’t go along with that.” The anger in Bluey was rising. “These scabs are sabotaging the war effort, and we know about it. We can’t just sit here and forget it. And what about the way O’Connor and Co have treated us? If we do nothing, then the next squad will get the same treatment. I say we do something.”

The men sat in silence. It was Darkie who spoke first.

“Mick, you know the situation in Melbourne, so we must be guided by you.” The others nodded in agreement. “What about an anonymous phone call to the police in Melbourne, tipping them off that a delivery of stolen goods is being made in Melbourne tonight?”

“And just where is this delivery going to take place Darkie?” Preacher had trouble with the practical side of the suggestion.

“I think I can answer that, Preacher.” Mick spoke slowly. “Robbo has a garage, well, more of a warehouse. I reckon the truck is headed there.”

“And what do you think of Darkie’s suggestion Mick?” Preacher asked.

Again, Mick took his time before answering.

“We’re out here in the sticks, so if we’re to do anything, it’ll mean going into town to make a phone call. The MPs are in town, so that could be a problem, and a phone call from the country could easily be traced through the local operator. So, we can't risk going into town and phoning. However, there may be a way. I could go to the Taylors and ring a friend in Melbourne. Someone who has a score to settle with Robbo. I pass the information on, and they use it as they see fit. My friend would also know cops who would welcome a chance to nail him."

"It's a great idea Mick. Preacher, let's get on with it instead of sitting around here talking." Bluey was angry and impatient. The others nodded in assent.

Preacher looked relieved. "Mick can you ride?" he asked.

"Me? On a horse. You must be joking."

"Right. Bluey you take Mick on the horse Darkie rode. It can easily carry two and time is slipping by. When you reach the Taylors, you must make the decision on how much they should be told, but keep it as little as possible. They mustn't become involved."

Willing hands hoisted Mick up behind the saddle.

"Preacher, I could run there just as quickly."

"Get a good grip of Bluey's belt and hang on. Off you go and good luck."

Bluey nudged the horse with his heels and the animal started forward. The horse, sensing that it was heading for home, broke into a smart trot although Mick's protests could be heard long after they'd disappeared from view.

"Come on you lot, there's work to be done here." Preacher was happiest when organising his team. The men set about their tasks with enthusiasm.

* * *

Working with a will, the men had the lines reeled up, the hut cleaned and all their gear packed ready for uplift by late afternoon.

"Want us to start on the main line to town Preacher?" asked Sam.

"No, it's too late and besides we have to reel up that line from the town end where the drum is." He paused. "Look."

A large hay wagon pulled by four horses was approaching the camp.

"It's Jessie Taylor." Darkie ran forward to meet the young girl. "Jessie, what are you doing here?"

"What do you think I'm doing here, Mr Fleming? Harold sent me out to pick up you men and your gear." She tied the reins and climbed down from the driver's seat.

Preacher walked forward and shook her hand. "I'm delighted to see you again Miss Taylor. Surprised, but delighted. We can offer you a cup of tea, if you would like it?"

"I certainly would, I never say no to a cup of tea."

One by one the men introduced themselves. A tree stump was produced to serve as a makeshift chair and the group settled around the fire to hear what news Jessie had brought.

"Harold and his friend Mick arrived at home about two hours ago, but I don't think Mick will ever get on a horse again."

"Where are Bluey and Mick now?"

"Harold explained how you had to break camp and get ready for a pick-up in the morning so we, that is the family, had a talk and decided to help. I'm here to pick you up and to take you back to the farm. You'll be sleeping in the barn tonight but it's not too bad. Mum's got Dad to put a sheep on the spit so we won't be eating till fairly late."

"Sounds great Jessie but the main line between here and town has to be reeled up. It's a big job, and we need to be onto it first thing in the morning."

"Oh, I forgot. Harold said to tell you to disconnect the main line and bring the switchboard and all the other stuff from the signal centre to the farm. He and my two brothers have taken another wagon into town and they're going to put the drum on the wagon and reel it in."

"Quick Sam, you and Jacko disconnect the line before any weight comes on it. The rest of you start loading the wagon. Men, we're leaving this neck of the woods to Bluey's snakes."

The men needed no second bidding to set about dismantling the camp and soon the wagon was loaded.

"Look Preacher the wire to town is moving."

"You're right Sam. Bluey and his friends haven't wasted any time. You and Jacko had better follow the line to make sure it doesn't snag. Somewhere along the way you'll meet up with Bluey and his mates. We'll see you all back at the farm. Now Jessie, let's get going. I can't say that I'll be sorry to see the last of this place."

* * *

The next morning, after a very hearty breakfast at the farm, the soldiers said their farewells to their hosts and climbed aboard the hay wagon. With Jessie and Paul as drivers, the wagon headed for the railway station.

"What happens now Preacher?" asked Sam.

"Firstly, we return all this gear to the quartermaster store near the station. Once that's done, we wait for the train at 10:00am, which will take us to Melbourne. From there, I guess we'll have to make our way to Broadmeadows, but I'll try to ring Sergeant Reynolds from town and let him know what train we'll be on. I doubt if anyone else is interested in us or our whereabouts."

"Wrong Preacher." said Bluey who was standing up in the wagon alongside the driver's seat. "We have a reception committee waiting for us at the railway station. Major Wiltshire, the local policeman and the two MPs."

Preacher got to his feet. "Well men, it's nice to know that someone cares about us. Leave the talking to me. When we pull up at the QM store, make yourselves busy with unloading the stores."

Preacher jumped down, approached the officer and saluted. "South camp secure Sir. We have all the stores here except the large drum which is over by the old Exercise HQ. If you want it brought over, we can soon do that."

"Thank you Lacey. It can stay where it is for the moment. Where are Sergeants O'Connor and Redman and Corporal Sweeney?"

"Don't know Sir. They left the camp just after the exercise finished. Said they had some business to attend to while we struck camp. Corporal Sweeney was to come back and collect us this morning, but as we had packed everything up, and the Taylors offered us use of their barn for the night, and it being closer to town, we moved there."

"And where was Sergeant O'Connor going?"

"He didn't say Sir. Just said they were off to attend to something. I wouldn't expect Sergeant O'Connor to confide in me where he was going."

"Perhaps Corporal Sweeney is out at the camp wondering where you are. Or didn't you expect him to return?" The loaded question came from the MP Sergeant.

"Oh no, he's not out there Sergeant."

"So you didn't expect him to return?"

"Yes we did Sergeant. But to get to the camp, the only road leads past the Taylors' farm and we were ready to hail him. Mr Taylor is still keeping an eye on the road to stop him when he turns up. As we had all our gear on this wagon, Mr Taylor suggested we bring it in here to the store rather than transfer it to the truck to save double handling."

Major Wiltshire's eyes never left Preacher's face. "Do you know what happened last night in Melbourne?"

"In Melbourne Sir? No Sir."

"Tell me Lacey, what was in the truck when they left you yesterday?"

Preacher frowned. "In the truck Sir. Couldn't say. The covers were tied down and I didn't look inside. Sir, may I ask what all this is about?"

"You'll hear soon enough Lacey. That truck, with O'Connor, Redman and Sweeney on board, was stopped by police unloading stores in a warehouse in Carlton. A search of the warehouse revealed a considerable amount of Army stores. A serious offence at any time, but in wartime, it's unforgivable."

"You don't think we had anything to do with it do you Sir?"

"No Lacey, I don't. I suspect that trio has been running a racket up here for some time. You chaps want to ask Lacey any questions?" He turned to the two MPs and the constable. They all shook their heads.

"Right Lacey. Get the large cable drum from the Exercise HQ and once the quartermaster has cleared your stores list, you can fill in time until the train arrives. I'll ring Sergeant Reynolds and tell him you're on your way back."

Preacher saluted and turned to leave.

"One moment Lacey." Preacher turned to face the Major. "Sergeant Reynolds will want a complete report of this exercise and I mean complete. Do you understand?"

"I think so Sir."

"Complete Lacey. Warts and all, or should I say, snakes and all."

"Yes Sir." Preacher saluted and moved over to the squad.

"Everything in order Preacher?" Sam asked.

"Yes Sam. Everything is in order. Say your farewells to Jessie and Paul. We have to move the wire drum to the QM store. Once that's done, the exercise is over. I can't say I'm sorry to be leaving but you all did well, even Darkie."

SEE WHAT YOU'RE LOOKING AT

Back at Broadmeadows Camp, the squad marched to the instruction hut. Sergeant Reynolds was at the blackboard as they filed in, his piercing eyes going from face to face as if seeking some clue as to what had occurred during the exercise, and why.

"When I sent this squad to the exercise area, I had great hopes for each and every one of you. I have had a long talk with my ex CO from Gallipoli days, Major Wiltshire, who has given me a detailed report of your behaviour." He paused.

"His report states that from a technical point of view, you performed extremely well. He also reported you showed admirable initiative, a high standard of personal qualities, good judgement and dogged determination. In summary, you all passed."

This was the moment they should've broken out in smiles, even cheering, but the manner of Sergeant Reynolds restrained them.

"Normally, the next two days would be taken up with your final tests, but as Major Wiltshire has already passed you, such tests won't be necessary. So, I move onto another matter, a matter which has cast a slur on the Australian Army. The matter of someone frightening our brave infantry men with snakes. The infantry is most upset, so upset that I believe retribution will be taken against you men, probably at the weekend. I have discussed the matter with the Camp Commandant and we have agreed that it would be in everyone's interest if you were not here at the weekend."

"You'll leave here this afternoon and move to a billet at the Port Melbourne Transit Depot. Tomorrow, each of you will be interviewed by the civil and military police concerning alleged thefts of Army stores. Once the interviews are completed, and I imagine that would be sometime tomorrow, I'll arrange leave passes for you all to go home for Christmas. Your leave will expire at 9:00am 7th January. At that time, you'll return to the depot at Port Melbourne to await further orders. Lacey, you will remain behind now to brief me on everything that happened during the exercise. Major Wiltshire will be joining us, as he is interested in what you have to say. You will rejoin the squad later this evening."

Sam stood up. "Sergeant, if we're to return to Port Melbourne after our leave, does that mean we're on our way overseas?"

"I can't answer that Ralston as such information is confidential. But two more things. As you successfully completed the course you are no longer privates, but sappers in the Signal Division of the Australian Army Engineering Corps. Congratulations. And the other piece of news is that on Major Wiltshire's recommendation, Sapper Lacey is now Lance Corporal Lacey. Well done Lacey."

The men broke out into cheering, slapping Preacher on the back and shaking his hand.

"Settle down." called the Sergeant. "You'll find in the Army you are always saying goodbye to people, to friends. Some you'll meet again, some you won't. So it is today. In the time available, I've tried to pass on as much technical knowledge as I could, but you still have much to learn. Don't ever think you know it all. When you get over there, remember other people's lives will depend on you. In this world, there is no greater responsibility. Let that be the standard you work to. Good bye and good luck."

Preacher got to his feet. "Sergeant Reynolds, I know I speak for all the squad when I say thank you. Should we ever be found wanting, it won't be any fault of yours. We shall do our best not to let you down."

The men stood up. Bluey walked forward and held out his hand to Sergeant Reynolds who shook it firmly. The other men followed his lead; no words were spoken, the gesture said it all.

* * *

The next evening the nine men gathered in the canteen at the Port Melbourne barracks.

The conversation quickly turned to the forthcoming leave and beyond. Their leave passes were ominously stamped 'pre-embarkation leave' and each felt a sense of excitement as he read them.

"Ve are really going, Darkie. It's our turn. Ve are off to see the vorld."

"Calm down Erik. It's not a holiday tour we're going on. There's a war going on, remember?"

"Oh that vill be over soon. Everyone says so. Just as long as ve can reach Europe before the var ends. My parents vant me to visit my relations in Sweden." Erik's excitement was unstoppable.

"Preacher. Do you think the war will be over soon?"

"Why should it Darkie? Everyone said it would be over by Christmas 1914, then they said Christmas 1915, now it's Christmas 1916. And look at the list of casualties. No, I don't think we are going to miss out." The room was quiet. All had read a familiar name in the casualty lists published in the newspaper.

"Hell, let's not start thinking about the war till we get there." Mac tried to rekindle the cheery atmosphere that had prevailed in the gathering before Preacher's words.

"You're right Mac. Why don't we turn in and get some sleep? Tomorrow it's home. No more reveilles, no more guard duties, no more marching."

"No more Sergeants."

"No Darkie, but we must all remember not all Sergeants are like O'Connor and Redman. Let's turn in."

"Yes Sir, Lance Corporal." Darkie saluted Preacher.

They laughed and headed for bed.

* * *

Bill Dowson was waiting at the railway station with the horse and gig as the train pulled in. Bluey sprang onto the platform. With his kit-bag slung nonchalantly on his shoulder, he moved quickly to greet his father.

"Where's everybody? It's not every day a soldier comes home on leave."

"Dick and Betty are at school and I'm afraid your mother's not well."

"Not well. Why wasn't I told?"

"It's nothing to fuss about. She didn't want you worrying while you had so much to do. She sometimes gets pain and the doctor says the best care is rest, so we've been nursing her. She'll be all right, you'll see. Let's get home so you can see her for yourself. She's very excited about you coming home for Christmas."

"Not half as excited as I am. Can I drive?" Without waiting, Bluey leapt onto the driver's seat and waited as his father settled himself. "Let's go," he called to the horse, giving it a slap with the reins.

"Steady son, we've aways to go and I'd rather get there in one piece than end up in a ditch."

"Sorry Dad. Easy boy, easy." Bluey pulled gently on the reins and the horse slowed its gait.

"Peter Taylor was on the phone yesterday. Said you and your mates had been over their way stirring up a hornet's nest."

"Not really. We had a couple of Sergeants who made life difficult for us, but we worked as a team, and in the end, came out on top. I'm lucky to be part of such a great team, we all get on so well."

"That's good to hear, but what's all this talk about snakes? I didn't believe half of what Peter was telling me."

"Oh that. Well, what really happened was..." Bluey told his father about the training exercise and how he'd used the snakes to put their opponents off balance.

His father found the story very amusing. Suddenly he turned to his son.

"Harold, did you notice that horse back there standing by the fence?"

Bluey smiled. It was an old game. "Yes Dad I saw it. It was a black stallion with a white blaze on its forehead and two white socks on its front legs. Its tail had been cut and because it didn't smile, I couldn't count its teeth, so I don't know how old it is."

"Good, very good. You haven't forgotten."

"No, I haven't forgotten. I never will."

Bill Dowson had always played games with his children. In reality, they were his way of teaching them to take an interest in what lay around them. In the evenings, he would make up trays of objects and cover them with a cloth. It was a version of Kim's game, made famous by Rudyard Kipling. Each child would be given a set time to observe the contents of the tray, the tray would then be covered and the child had to write down what they'd seen. As they grew older, the game was moved to the outside world. Bill Dowson would have been most disappointed if Bluey had merely seen a black horse. All the Dowson children lived by his teachings.

"Make use of the great gifts God gave to you," he would say. "See what you're looking at, understand what you're hearing, and if you don't know, then find out."

Bluey steered the horse into the stable yard, passed the reins to his father, and jumped from the gig. He ran to the house and to the door of his parents' bedroom. He knocked and entered.

His mother was propped up in bed with arms outstretched. "Harold, it's so wonderful to see you. Give me a hug."

Bluey threw himself into her arms, not daring to speak for fear his faltering words would give him away. Big boys don't cry, and certainly not soldiers. They held each other tightly.

"Pull up a chair young man, and tell me all about the Army. Your father can make us a cup of tea."

"How are you Mum? Dad said you've been ill and have to take it easy."

"I am taking it easy, but you're the best medicine I could have. I want to hear everything, especially about what happened at the Taylors. I suppose you've already told your father but now you'll have to tell me, and I suspect when Richard and Betty get home, you'll have to do it all over again. And then again when Lucy gets here, I've invited her over for dinner. I would have asked all the Willis family but I'm not really up to being a hostess just now. Lucy won't mind Betty's cooking."

Bluey heaved a sigh of relief. It already had occurred to him that, with his mother unwell, it would be difficult for him to leave the house on his first night at home.

"I thought that might please you son."

Bluey looked up to see his mother had been watching his face and had detected the pleasure at the news of Lucy's visit. "Thank you Mum. Now where shall I begin?"

"I thought your father had drummed into all you children that the beginning is always a good place to start."

"Hang on son," came a voice from the doorway, "I want to hear all this as well as your mother. Let's get some tea served and then you can tell us both."

* * *

Dinner was a happy occasion. Mrs Dowson sat at the table for the meal, but then retired to bed. Bluey dominated the conversation, mainly answering questions.

"Uh. Fancy being so scared of a snake, and a dead one at that," scoffed Richard, "what sort of soldiers are they?"

Bill Dowson looked at his youngest son. "Tell me Richard, how many snakes have you encountered at night?"

"None Dad. You never see them in the dark. You always said make a noise and they'll get out of your way."

"Exactly. You've never seen a snake at night, but you pour scorn on soldiers who did. Until you've tangled with a snake at night, especially when you're least expecting it, don't judge too harshly their reactions. And remember they were probably city folk."

"Still Mr Dowson, you must admit it was a brilliant idea of Harold's." Lucy's eyes seldom strayed from the young man sitting opposite her.

"Oh yes Lucy. It was a clever idea, and it worked. Now then, that's enough talk for this evening. You two youngsters help me clear up the table and get these dishes washed. Harold, you had better walk Lucy home."

"Lucky you Harold. Be careful you don't run into any snakes." Richard ducked as his elder brother let fly with a playful punch.

"I'll say goodbye to Mrs Dowson," Lucy said. She quickly returned. "She's asleep, Mr Dowson."

"Fine Lucy. That's the best medicine. Off you two go while I try and prevent these two breaking all our good china."

The two young people set off for the lengthy walk through the bush.

"Here, hang onto me Lucy."

"I intend to Harold. And I intend to talk loudly just in case any of your slippery friends are out and about. That story of yours was spooky."

"Rubbish Lucy. But talk away, I'm listening."

They strolled along arm in arm, totally oblivious to anything but the company of each other. At the gateway to the Willis house, they stopped.

"Are you coming in to say hello to Mum and Dad?"

"No Lucy, it's rather late. I'll come over tomorrow to see them. You haven't mentioned the twins except to say they're all right. Where are they?"

"Dad will tell you all about that. They're in Belgium somewhere. They've been in action, but that's all we know. Letters take so long and tell so little. Dad reads every word in every paper and keeps a map on which he marks where he thinks they are. I guess they'll be having a white Christmas this year."

"I don't know about white Lucy, but I bet it's cold and miserable. I wish I was with them."

"Oh really, what's wrong with my company Sapper Dowson?"

"Sorry Lucy, it was just an expression. You know I want to be with you."

"Well show me Harold Dowson."

Harold wrapped his arms around the young girl and their lips met. Slowly their embrace became tighter and their mouths sought each other with a growing sense of urgency.

"Phew! Wait on soldier. I'm convinced." Lucy placed her hands on Harold's chest. "Where did you learn that?"

"Learn what?"

"How to kiss like that. Just what have you been up to in Melbourne?"

"Nothing. Nothing like that. Surely you can't think that?" Harold was confused and defensive.

"No my darling. I don't think that of you. Now give me a nice kiss and off you go. We'll expect you about three o'clock for afternoon tea." They kissed again and Lucy had to disengage herself from Bluey's strong hold. "Slow down Harold, we've got two weeks to go. Don't break my ribs on the first day."

"Sorry Lucy, I'm really sorry, but I've dreamt of this moment for so long." Bluey stammered.

"So have I my darling." She moved away and blew him a kiss. "See you tomorrow. Be careful of snakes on the way back."

She disappeared in the direction of the house and Bluey watched her go. He set off, but time and distance meant nothing. He was totally, completely, happy.

* * *

The December days passed quickly. Bluey helped his father working on the property and threw himself into each task with vigour and enthusiasm.

"Dad. I must keep fit. Once we're over there, fitness will be very important. What with all these huge meals, I would soon turn into a dumpling if I didn't work it off. And strangely, I find the chores I used to dislike are now almost a pleasure."

"Well your brother is certainly enjoying your leave. I haven't seen him touch an axe or clean out the barn since you've been home. I think you've chopped enough wood to last until next Christmas!"

"Next Christmas. I wonder if the war will be over by then."

"For two years, people have been saying that it'll soon be over, but I can't see that happening unless the leaders in Europe are suddenly struck with a severe bout of common sense." He paused. "You and Lucy are pretty thick these days aren't you? Are you planning to get engaged?"

Bluey was silent for a moment. "We've discussed it Dad. Some days we think it would be a good idea, and then others we're not sure. She's my girl Dad and when I get back from the war we'll get married. There's no question about that. It's just this formal thing of announcing our engagement. It's like putting my brand on her so no one else will steal her while I'm away. And of course, there is always the chance my luck might run out and I won't come back. Should that happen, I'd want Lucy to marry someone else, not waste her life pining for me."

His father leant on his shovel and gazed at the youthful face. "Do you ever think about what might happen over there?"

Bluey gazed across the field. "At times we do. Sometimes when we're sitting around a table someone will read out a name from the papers, the name of someone they knew and then the subject seems to get around to other names, other casualties. We all believe that if we stick together, support each other, look after each other, then we'll all come through. They're a great bunch of mates. We're so close, I'd trust my life to any one of them."

"It's good to hear you talking like that Harold. I suspect that where you're going you'll need friends you can trust."

* * *

Christmas Day passed and the next big event was a party to see the new year in. It was held in the school which doubled as a church and community centre.

"I guess there's not one family here that hasn't got a man overseas this year."

"Not quite correct Lucy, but I'm about to put that right," replied Bluey.

"Oh yes Harold, I wasn't thinking straight, but then I have this forlorn hope it'll all end before you leave and I can have you here safe and sound."

Bluey looked into the upturned face. "It's not going to end Lucy, well, not for a while. But when I come back, you'll be so proud to have an ex-soldier as your husband. It's the men who don't go to war that'll be at a disadvantage."

"Perhaps Harold, perhaps. But there are a lot of men who aren't coming back, and what is their reward?"

Harold stopped dancing. "Lucy I have to go, and I'll be coming back, and then life will be wonderful for us. Think, next new year's eve, we could all be here having a great time. The twins and all the other men. It's going to be all right. You must believe that."

"Let's dance and not talk about the war any more. If my prayers are answered, you and the twins will come back safe and sound, but for now, I have you here and I don't want to spoil our happiness."

They continued to dance watched by the elders of the district. The Dowson and Willis families were pioneers and it was right and good that Lucy and Harold should be courting.

Bill Dowson had stayed at home to look after his wife and Bluey had driven the family gig to the party. Dave and Muriel Willis had thoughtfully called in to pay their respects to Joan Dowson on their way and had offered a lift to the two younger Dowsons; an offer Bluey had readily accepted on their behalf. This arrangement meant that he had Lucy as his sole companion for the drive home after 1917 had been suitably welcomed.

Lucy snuggled up to her man as the horse slowly walked along the road towards the farm. Bluey's arm held her tightly to his side and, as if by accident, his hand cupped her breast.

"And just what do you think you're doing with that hand, Harold Dowson?"

"Sorry Lucy, it just seemed to end up there." said an embarrassed Harold moving his hand to her waist.

"I didn't say I didn't like it." The hand quickly returned.

"You're so beautiful Lucy. So beautiful. At night, you're in my every dream."

"I had better be Harold."

"Oh but you are. There is no one else, never has been for me and never will be."

"I believe you my dearest. Do you think the horse knows his way home?"

"Of course he does. Why?"

"Well if he can find his way home on his own, you don't need to use that other hand to hold the reins, and instead of looking at the road you could kiss me."

They embraced and stayed locked together for a long time. Bluey's fingers were now teasing the erect nipple and the other hand started searching for an opening in Lucy's dress.

"Easy Harold, easy." Lucy pulled away from the excited young soldier. "We both know where this can lead, and that's an area we should not trespass."

"Lucy, look at me. I'm so much in love with you it's hurting."

"I can see that Harold, but that's something you'll have to cope with. You know that one thing can lead to another, and so on, until we lose control and then it's the girl who gets hurt."

"Oh come on Lucy, take pity on me."

"Pity Harold? Why should I? You're off to the war, you're going overseas, a great and exciting new adventure. And I'll stay here and wait, dreading every letter in case it's bad news. Why should I pity you? But that's how it will be. It always has been for the womenfolk. Stay at home and wait."

"You make it sound as if you're the one facing the danger, not me."

Lucy smiled. "Yes Harold, at this moment, it is I who am facing danger. If we should lose our heads, there is the danger of me becoming pregnant. All your mates would pat you on the back and say well done, but what would happen to me? Oh yes Harold Dowson, I'm the one in danger at the moment, not you."

"I wouldn't let you get pregnant Lucy. I'd be careful."

"I wonder how many other girls in Australia are hearing those same words tonight. And I wonder how many will give in because they feel it's the greatest gift they can give to a soldier soon to leave for overseas. No Harold, not me. I love you and want you in every way, and when you come back from your war, I'll still be here, and still in love with you."

There was a long silence broken only by the sound of the horse's hooves striking the ground. "I'm sorry Lucy. I was being selfish and you're right. I'll come back. I'll marry you. That's the dream that'll carry me through the war." Bluey turned to her and kissed her lightly.

"Harold Dowson, that's not what I call a kiss. Come on, we're nearly home." Lucy took his hand and placed it on her breast. "I didn't say no to that, did I?"

* * *

The final days of leave raced by. People from all over the district dropped in to have a traditional cup of tea and to wish Harold well. Evenings were spent with Lucy, either at the Willis home or at the Dowson's. Their embraces were passionate and exhausting. It was as if the two young people wanted to prove to each other, that the bonds holding them together, could be made even stronger by the strength and length of their embraces.

There was little conversation at the Dowson breakfast table on the departure day. Richard attempted a couple of jokes but these received only polite laughter. Mrs Dowson was not well enough to travel to the station, and despite pleas from Richard and Betty, their father packed them off to school. Bluey waited until the last minute to enter his mother's bedroom to say his farewell. Few words were said.

"Please write son. I know you'll be busy, but do try and write. Your letters will sustain us while we wait and pray."

"I'll write every week Mother, I promise. Please get well and don't worry about me." They hugged each other and the young man turned and quickly left the room. His father was waiting in the gig.

"Seems you have acquired some extra baggage, Harold."

"Yes Dad, all the ladies have been giving me presents of knitted socks and scarves. I guess I'll appreciate them when I get to

France but I don't know how I'm going to get them all into my kitbag. I'll probably share them around."

"Sounds like a good idea to me son." He flicked the reins. "Come on fellow, we don't want to miss that train." They rode on in silence for a while and then Bill Dowson put his hand in his pocket and produced a small parcel. "Your mother and I wanted to give you something special as a going away gift, and this is what we decided on." He handed over the packet. Bluey looked at it, turning it over and over. "Go on, open it. It won't bite."

Bluey tore off the wrapping to reveal a small cardboard box. He lifted the lid. "Oh Dad, I can't take this, it's yours. It's so very special." Bluey's protest was over a tooled leather fob watch holder. He knew that inside was a magnificent gold watch, presented to Bill Dowson in recognition of outstanding bravery one day at the sawmill. Normally excess steam would have escaped via the safety valve, but on this occasion the needle on the gauge had passed the blow-off mark and continued to climb. A cry of alarm alerted nearby workers that the boiler was about to explode. While most ran for cover, Bill Dowson seized a sledge hammer and carried a ladder to the boiler. He climbed the ladder and swung a heavy blow against the valve. The valve broke and the steam erupted into the atmosphere. The force of the escaping steam knocked Bill Dowson from the ladder. His face and arms still carried the scars from the burns and his limp was a constant reminder of his injuries.

"Dad, it's too much. I couldn't take it."

"Son, it was given to me by the logging company and I can do what I choose with it. Your mother and I want you to have it as something special to remember us by."

Bluey continued to stare at the watch. It was a ritual in the household that the watch was wound at exactly seven o'clock each evening. The children took it in turns to carry out this most important chore.

"Remember Harold, it'll go two days without being wound but you should try to remember to wind it each day, preferably at the same time."

"Yes Dad, I've learned that over the years. It really is a wonderful watch."

"More than just a watch son. Sure, it'll tell you the time, and I would think accurate time is important in the Army. But it's also useful as a compass or a heliograph if you can see the sun."

"Open the cover Harold. See the mirror on the inside. You can use that for shaving. A bit small, but it's functional. And there is another trick you can use the mirror for."

"What sort of a trick?"

"Well if you want to see something or someone without them knowing you're looking at them, you just turn your back and pretend to look at the time. You then use the mirror to see what you want to see. Young men use that trick often when they want to study a young lady without her knowing."

"Dad this is the most wonderful gift. Don't worry, I'll look after it and when the war is over, I'll put it back on the mantelpiece in its old position."

"That'll be a great day Harold," replied his father, "one your mother and I'll be looking forward to."

"Mum's going to get better isn't she Dad? She looked so white and drawn this morning."

"Oh, I think that's because you were leaving. Don't worry about your mother, Harold, we'll look after her. You concentrate on looking after yourself."

"I told her I'll write every week, and I will. I also told Lucy that I'd write every week, so you'll know all my news."

"Good boy. But number your letters so we'll know if one has gone astray. The mail route from France must be a trifle difficult for the postman."

Bill Dowson had the gig outside the station only a few minutes before the train's arrival. There was no time for long drawn out farewells. Lucy and her parents were there with a few other old friends. Father and son shook hands awkwardly, neither able to find the right words. One last kiss for Lucy, and Bluey was on his way to war. He leant out of the train window for as long as the group on the platform could be seen. He then slumped back into his seat. He looked at, but never saw, the beautiful gum trees, the stream that flowed alongside the railway, and the hills in the distance.

There was no sense of excitement, just a dull ache in his heart, and more than a hint of tears in his eyes.

BASTARD FIRST CLASS

On the designated Monday, the section gathered at the transit depot to await their orders. They didn't have to wait long. An officer arrived with a sheaf of papers, checked off their names, and gave them the news they'd been waiting to hear.

"Tomorrow you will go to the medical centre for a final medical check-up. Once you have your medical clearance, you will report to the quartermaster for an issue of new clothing. Remember, you can only take one kit-bag so everything has to go in it. Don't take civilian clothing. You are soldiers, and your uniform will be the only clothing you will wear. Once you have all your gear, return here and clearly mark every piece of clothing with your name and number. There are metal stamps to mark your boots and leather items."

"At 9:00am the day after tomorrow, a truck will collect your gear and transport it to Station Pier. At 9:30am, you will fall in with the other troops billeted here and march to the pier. Your ship is the Military Transport AGENOR. On arrival at the wharf alongside the ship, you will be fallen out. Should friends be on the wharf, say goodbye, but make it quick. Collect your gear and embark. Once on board, the ship's crew will direct you to your accommodation. Any questions?"

The men remained silent.

The Lieutenant looked around the circle of beaming faces. "I know you are all anxious to get over there to do your bit for your country, but I meet the returning ships as well as those departing, and I know how tough it is over there. So, keep your heads down and good luck."

"We did it Preacher. We're on our way. Whacko!"

"Steady Darkie. You heard the man. The way things are over there we could be heading for more trouble than we bargained for."

"Come off it Preacher. This is why we joined, to get overseas. See all those famous places like London and Paris and to meet some French girls."

"Speak for yourself Darkie. I'm going to fight for my country." Sam was appalled at Darkie's attitude.

"Sure Sam, that too. But we're going to see the world as well. Come on, cheer up. All that hard work has paid off. Let's have a party tonight." Darkie looked for support for his suggestion.

"Maybe tomorrow night Darkie." Bluey said. "That'll be our last night. Tonight, I want to write a few letters."

"Letters Bluey? How can you be writing letters when you only left home yesterday? What is there to tell them?"

"All the things I should've said when I was there and either forgot, or couldn't find the right words. There'll be plenty of time for celebrating on the ship going over. Anyone else coming over to the YMCA?"

* * *

Next morning the group had their final medicals and collected their new clothing. They no longer accepted what the quarter-master storemen put in front of them, tunics, hats and boots were tried on for size and comfort. Second best was no longer good enough.

The party that evening was not the ribald gathering that Darkie expected. They sat in small groups, trying to crack jokes which had mostly been heard previously. The night was still young when they started to drift off to their sleeping quarters. There they packed and repacked their kitbags. Items were left out during one packing and then included in the next. It was a very subdued gathering. When they finally did turn in, few slept well. Tomorrow they would be sleeping in a ship's bunk, after that, who could guess. For some, it may have been their last night in a proper bed, their last night in Australia.

As they marched out of the barrack gates the next morning the men were surprised to find crowds had gathered to cheer and clap as they marched past.

They marched with heads held high, chests out and arms swinging as one. They were proud to be there and it showed. The march to the pier at Port Melbourne was little more than a mile and as they approached, they got their first glimpse of the ship that was to be their home for the next six weeks. His Majesty's Transport AGENOR was an impressive sight. She had been a passenger liner on the England to Australia run, and she appeared enormous.

"Well Skip, you're the expert. Is it safe?"

"Hell Sam, that ship's twenty times bigger than anything I've been in. Of course she's safe. Looks like we've got ourselves an armchair ride."

"Come on, stop gawking and collect your gear." Preacher was anxious to get the party on board. Those with friends and relatives gathered on the wharf took their last farewells, then hurried after their companions, hiding their emotions as best they could.

Without a conscious decision, Skipper became their natural leader on the ship. The group found it had been allocated one four-berth and one six-berth cabin. They quickly stowed their gear and returned to the upper deck to watch. At 11:00pm, the lines were slipped, and the AGENOR moved slowly away from the wharf. A few streamers were thrown and held by the soldiers, but there was little gaiety. A few calls of 'good luck', a few 'cooees', a few waves, but that was all. It was as if those departing and those farewelling them, recognised the solemnity of the occasion. All knew the odds were heavily stacked against many of them returning.

As the ship moved steadily down Port Phillip Bay, the men mustered in the dining room to receive a briefing on the ship's routines. After lunch, all the troops were mustered on the upper deck for lectures on lifeboat drills, where to muster if the alarms sounded, and where to find and how to wear a life-jacket.

"Hell Skip. Aren't we a bit too close to the land?" The exclamation from Mac caused all heads to turn to look at the nearby shore.

"No Mac. We're passing through the Rip. It's the narrow entrance to Port Phillip Bay, very narrow, but we're all right. The thing now is to look at the water outside the Bay and see if we're all going to be at dinner tonight."

"What do you mean? Why won't we all get dinner tonight?"

"I think Sam, that it's going to get fairly rough tonight, and for some it won't be a very happy time. Getting sea-sick is a real curse, but if you do, just remember it will pass once your body adapts to the motion. Try to keep warm and stay in the fresh air as much as possible. If you do get sick, just remember, you will get better."

The ship turned south westerly, and the gentle movement became more pronounced. A little later, when a westerly course was set, the long low swell induced a corkscrew action into the ship's movements. Skipper had been accurate with his assessment that not all would make the dining room that evening.

The next day, the row of men lining the leeward rail had noticeably decreased, but for some, the wretched agony of severe sea-sickness continued. Skipper, Darkie and Jacko seemed indifferent to the awkward motion and Erik, Preacher and Mac were soon over the worst of the malaise. But Bluey, Sam and Mick continued to suffer. Despite the sympathetic attention Skipper paid to the victims, the three failed to shake off the effects of the ship's motion and their lives were total misery. On the night before arriving at Fremantle the nine sat down to dinner, the first meal all had eaten together since lunch six days previously.

Two rows of large boxes on the upper deck amidships had been a source of much speculation ever since the men had boarded the ship. They were strangely constructed and empty. It was Skipper who discovered their purpose.

"It seems that in Fremantle, we're to take on twenty-four remounts for the Light Horse in Egypt."

"The poor animals, they'll die long before we get to Egypt." Bluey was horrified that his beloved animal friends could be subjected to the horrors of a sea passage.

"I don't think so Bluey. The Light Horse have taken thousands of horses over, and apparently, they've survived rather well. Anyhow, you'll be pleased to know the Indian Ocean is usually far more friendly than the waters we just passed through."

"Thank God for small mercies." breathed Bluey.

"So, it's Fremantle tomorrow for a twenty-hour visit and unless any of you have made plans, I suggest we go ashore as a group and take the train to Perth." Preacher looked around the group.

"Why Preacher? Aren't there any pubs in Fremantle?"

"I'm sure they have pubs in Fremantle, Darkie, but we don't want you and Erik getting into trouble. It'd be sad if we sailed with you two in jail as guests of the West Australian police."

"Really, Preacher? And how do you propose to ensure that we all stick together? It's a free country, so I'm told, and what we do on our leave is our own business."

"Normally Darkie I would agree, but since we're the only signallers on board, the officer in charge of the detachment of Engineers says that we have to look after ourselves, and as the Lance Corporal in charge, I'm responsible."

"Oh God Preacher you should hear yourself talking. You sound just like that oily bastard Ronald Johnson. So, you're in charge. So?"

Preacher was no longer smiling. "So indeed. You see Darkie, I have the leave passes, and unless you agree to stick with the group, you won't be going ashore. So, what's it to be?"

Darkie looked around as if to seek some support for a show of defiance to the dictatorial style of Preacher. There was no support. "Not got much choice, have I?" muttered Darkie.

After Preacher left, the others sat around talking, except for Bluey who started to write a letter.

"Bloody hell Bluey, what can you be writing about?" demanded Mick. "You've been flat on your back for six days, and the only things you've done in all that time is throw up, sit on the toilet and wind that bloody watch."

"Well Mick, at least that's one thing more than you've done in the same amount of time. I have to get these letters off in tomorrow's mail. If I don't get them written, then I won't be able to go to Perth with you chaps."

* * *

A forty-minute train ride brought the men from Fremantle into the beautiful city of Perth. Preacher led the group to the central YMCA where volunteer workers arranged city tours. Young suntanned girls divided them into groups of three and put each group into a car. It was with some trepidation that Preacher watched

Darkie, Erik and Skipper depart in company with a particularly attractive driver.

It was a pleasant and relaxing day. The group sat on the grass in Kings Park to eat the picnic lunch provided by the girls. As the afternoon passed, the three cars made the journey back to the ship at Fremantle where the men said their farewells and thanks. It was the young driver of Darkie's car who brought home the significance of the day.

"You all have the telephone number of the YMCA in Perth and for those of you who return, we would love to duplicate today's farewell party with a welcome home party." She paused as if realising she had made an error. "When I said, those of you who return, I was referring to the fact that not all ships call in here on the way home. My friends and I hope to see you all back here one day."

"I think we all know what she meant," Darkie observed. "Come on chaps, kick the dirt under your feet. Who knows when we'll next be standing on Australian soil."

Each soldier ground the toe of a boot into the gravel. It seemed the proper thing to do before marching up the gangway. It was the only way to say goodbye.

* * *

Next morning the twenty-four horses were coaxed up a special gangway onto the ship.

"Bluey why do they call them 'Walers'?" asked Skip.

"It's just a general term. They are a mixed breed that has been developed here in Australia for use as stockhorses. Australia has been supplying horses to the British Army in India for years. As they originally came from the colony of New South Wales, they called ours 'Walers', and the South African horses 'Capers', short for Cape Colony. They're beautiful animals. Go anywhere, and never let you down."

"I suspect we won't see a lot of you on this leg of the voyage. You'll be helping to look after those animals."

"I hope I can help look after them. To be around horses is like having a link with home. You're lucky in a way. The sea has been your life, and so being on board a ship is natural to you. To me it's just the opposite."

"Bluey, you and I are very alike in one way, but totally opposite in another. We're as one with our environment, but the difference is the environment. I love the sea, I respect its moods, I watch it change, and read from those changes what is happening or about to happen. I know the inhabitants of the waters, their habits and behaviour. I am only happy when I'm at sea or near it. You are the same, but instead of the sea, your love is the bush. I watched you at that training exercise. You knew every tree, every bird call, every animal track. You were totally at home while most of us floundered. I envied you. Come on, looks like we're getting ready to sail."

The wharf was crowded with people. Streamers were thrown. While the departure from Melbourne had been solemn, this time it was more of a celebration, with singing and cheering. Slowly the ship drew away from the wharf. As the tugs turned the ship so the bows pointed towards the harbour entrance, a long piercing note from a bugle rent the air. All onshore and onboard, turned to a lone bugler standing on top of the bridge housing. A strange silence descended. The air was filled with the mournful notes of the 'Last Post', each note drawn out as if to stress the gravity of the moment. As the notes died away the men turned to watch the receding crowd. No longer the cheers and waves. A few arms were raised as if in salute, and there were few dry eyes. It was a moment, a farewell, that they would never forget. For many it was to be the last time they ever saw Australia.

* * *

The next day the signallers mustered in the after saloon which they'd taken over as their own recreational space. On board were detachments of infantry, light horse, medical staff and engineers. The groups tended to keep to themselves and that suited the signallers.

Preacher strode in with a sheaf of papers. "Major Kelty, who is the Senior Army Engineer Officer on board, has virtually given me a free hand to organise our group. He has given me three directives. The first is that we are to keep fit. Once in France, there'll be no time for working off excess poundage, so I'm going to set up a program of physical exercising. We can do our own or join in with the infantry. Personally, I think we can look after ourselves."

"The second directive is that we're to practise and, where possible, improve our professional skills. Really all we can do is practise our Morse and Semaphore. The ship's captain has agreed we can man the signalling lamp when another ship is sighted. They prefer to keep radio transmissions to a minimum, so most traffic will be passed by light. We will not be allowed to sit in on the wireless telegraphy as some of the messages received may be sensitive. Any questions?"

"Yes Preacher, can we use the lamps for signalling practice?" asked Mac.

"We can, but not at night. Each morning one of us will man the lamp on the wing of the bridge and send two messages. The rest will pair off, one man reading a message, the other writing it down. All messages are to be checked by the sender so I can keep a check on how we're going. We'll repeat the exercise after lunch each day, but the man on the bridge will transmit in Semaphore. That should keep us in touch with our signalling."

"Now Erik. You have a special problem. I think you know that your Morse is below standard. Sergeant Reynolds made me promise that I'd personally supervise extra signalling training for you during this voyage."

"Come on Preacher, he's not too bad." Darkie sprang to the defence of his friend.

"Wrong Darkie, and you know it. It's critical to the men we'll be supporting. So Erik, you will do extra signalling each day, and Skipper, I want you to organise those sessions."

"Can do Preacher. And don't worry, Erik will get there. He's keen and that's important."

"What was the third directive, Preacher?"

"The third is the easy one Sam. We're to stay out of trouble."

"What sort of trouble?"

"Any sort Sam." replied Preacher staring straight at Darkie.

"Don't look at me like that Preacher. Didn't I behave in Perth? And with only an occasional bottle of beer to drink on board I won't be causing any trouble."

"Glad to hear it Darkie. Right. You're all in the picture. We start with physical training tomorrow at 6:30am, before it gets too hot, then signalling practice at 8:30. The rest of the day is yours until 1:30pm, when we'll muster for Semaphore practice. Of course, there are the usual mess hall duties to do. I'll see what is required and draw up a roster. That's it fellas."

Most dispersed to advantage points on the upper deck where they could relax. Bluey moved towards the horse stalls and was soon in deep conversation with three of the attendants.

Skipper turned to Preacher. "I bet you Bluey doesn't have another day of sea-sickness this trip. He's found an interest and he'll forget all about his discomfort while he concentrates on looking after the animals. He's lucky in a way, because boredom is going to be one of the dangers of the trip."

Preacher nodded. "I've thought of that. We must keep ourselves busy and entertained. There's a piano in the saloon. Perhaps we could start having evening sing-songs. Sometimes you can be surprised by the hidden talent around you."

* * *

The group settled into a routine. Bluey spent his spare moments either writing letters or helping with the horses. Each day the animals were walked along the deck to ease the strain created by their cramped quarters. All the horses had names and men would line the rails to pass comments about each animal.

The signallers gathered in the after saloon each night to talk or join in a sing-song around the piano. Preacher was a talented pianist. As soon as one of the men started to sing, he would pick up the tune. One evening they had broken into 'Danny Boy' when they became aware of a new voice, a melodious voice that transposed all the off-key notes being offered by the others. The group fell silent and turned towards the tenor with the beautiful voice. It was Mick. With eyes closed, he was obviously singing in another place. Oblivious to his amazed companions, Mick sang on, Preacher matching the highs and lows, the pauses, the moods of the singer. As the song ended, Preacher commenced playing another old Irish favourite, and then another, and then another. Mick did not move, he didn't open his eyes. Wherever his mind had carried him, he wanted to stay. Other men outside came crowding in. It was a concert they'd never forget. Slowly the notes of the piano died away and to a man the onlookers clapped and cheered. Mick, startled from his reverie, blushed and made a quick exit through the crowd.

Preacher found Mick leaning on the guard rail at the stern of the ship watching the wake boil up and then melt away. "You certainly surprised us tonight."

Mick turned quickly. "Oh, Preacher. Yeah, I got carried away. Made a bit of a fool of myself."

"Just the opposite. Mind if I join you?"

The two men stood side by side gazing at the night sky.

"Tell me Mick, where did you learn to sing? That's no ordinary voice. You've been taught."

Mick continued to stare at the sea. "My mother taught me. She was a singer when she met Dad. Things were tough, so they came out to Australia, and I was born on the ship coming out. In fact, I suspect I was one of the reasons they packed up and left Ireland. You know, young girl in the family way. But they were very much in love."

"Did she sing in Australia?"

"No. Dad didn't approve, but she sang with the church and took in pupils. It helped with the housekeeping. We didn't have much, never did, and then Dad was killed."

"Killed! How? No, you don't have to answer that Mick, unless you want to. I'm not prying."

"It's all right Preacher, just as long as it's between you and me."

Mick looked up at the bright stars as he spoke. "There was a rumble."

"A rumble?"

"A brawl. A mob from another suburb came over to our patch and stirred things up one Saturday night. It wasn't uncommon. Dad copped a smack on the head and it fractured his skull."

"This other mob, they didn't come from Carlton did they?"

Mick swung around. "How did you know?"

"It was just a guess Mick, based on what I saw back on the training exercise. The look on your face when Sweeney appeared, and your reaction to the mention of Robbo, made me think that these people had been in your life previously."

Mick turned back to look at the ocean. "Yeah, you guessed right Preacher. It was Robbo's mob that did for me Dad."

"I saw that Robbo, Redman, O'Connor, Sweeney and a few more went to jail for a fairly long stretch. Seems the judge didn't go along with people trying to sabotage the war effort."

Mick nodded. "They got what they deserved. Mum was pleased."

"Was it your mother who tipped off the police Mick?"

"Jesus Preacher, you're a crafty. I told Mrs Taylor I had to ring my mum 'cos she was ill and that's the truth. I didn't say too much on the phone in case someone was listening. But Mum and I don't have to say much to get a message across. To Mum and me, what happened to Robbo and his mates was a great thing, and it was only possible because of the team, but I can't thank them because that would mean telling them the whole story, and sooner or later it would leak out."

"But you can repay them."

"Repay them? How?"

"By singing for them. They loved it. You should've opened your eyes and seen their faces."

"Well if that's all they want, it's no trouble. I actually enjoy singing. It's the only thing I can do well."

"I'm not sure that that's the truth Mick but why did you join the army? I don't think you have a burning passion to fight for an English king."

"Oh, it's all part of mum's plan for me. You see Preacher, we're never going to have enough money for me to travel to Ireland to see my kinfolk, and mother is desperate for me to visit the grandparents and the aunts, uncles and cousins. So here I am. On my way to Europe. I just have to pop over to Ireland when I'm on leave and I'll meet all the relations."

"Just where in Ireland Mick?" murmured Preacher.

"Ennis. It's in the west. Every evening my Mother would tell me about it and the people. I reckon I could describe every house, every road in Ennis."

"Mick, I don't want to spoil things for you, but the way things are in Ireland, I'm not sure the Army would be too happy if you went sightseeing in Ennis. Things are pretty tense over there at the moment. In fact, I'm pretty sure they won't let you visit Ennis, leave or no leave."

"Bugger the Army, Preacher. I'll pull my weight with you guys and I won't let you down, but what I do on my leave is my business. Anyhow I've promised mum that I would go see her folks and that's what I'll do. But you keep that to yourself Preacher."

"You have my word Mick. But I don't like what I'm hearing, and I'll probably try to talk you out of it."

"I expect you will, Preacher. Time to turn in. See you in the morning."

* * *

The evening sessions around the piano in the saloon became a highlight of the ship's activities. The size of the audience at the Sappers' Concert quickly grew until the signallers were forced to move the piano out to the open deck so that all could see and hear. Talent nights were introduced and men came forward, sometimes voluntarily, sometimes pushed, to perform. Singers, instrumentalists, story tellers, comics and jugglers emerged. They all provided an enjoyable diversion from the monotony of ship life. Preacher and Mick spent most of their leisure hours arranging the evening program.

The two were seated in the saloon one morning comparing notes when three men entered. One had a swarthy complexion and wore the stripes of a Sergeant. One of his companions was short and slim with dark eyes that were never still. It was as if he was continuously looking for someone, or something, that he feared. The third was a big, solidly built man. He always stood behind the other two and did not speak. To answer, he either nodded or shook his head. He conveyed a message of unrefined power waiting to be turned loose.

"Well, more volunteers? And what do you three do?" asked Preacher. Mick frowned.

"We're not here to join in your stupid party Lance Corporal. I am here to tell you we've had enough of your fucking concerts."

"Sorry Sergeant, I don't understand. We've had nothing but encouragement from the officers and the men. What is it that you object to?"

"I'm not here to answer your silly bloody questions soldier, I'm here to give you some good advice. No more concerts. Got it? No more fucking concerts."

Preacher was bewildered. "And who are you to even suggest such a thing?"

"Listen you piss-poor excuse for a fighting man, I run things around here, and what I say goes. No more concerts, that's it."

"Sorry Sergeant, but that's not it. We intend to run two more concerts before Colombo and probably three before Aden." Preacher was now on his feet, his anger obvious.

"Well, just remember I offered you a way out, and should anything happen to anyone, it's your fault." The Sergeant turned and left the room with his escort.

Preacher sat down and stared at Mick. "Do you have any idea what that was all about?"

"That Preacher, is Sergeant Adcock, bastard first class. A bit like O'Connor. Somehow, he has access to considerable beer supplies which he sells to the troops at outlandish prices. He also runs a two-up school and a card game. Until we started the concerts, he had a monopoly on the men's spare time and was making a fortune. He's upset because our concerts are costing him money."

Mick paused. "We need to be careful, Preacher. Those two sidekicks are his trump cards. The little one with the nervous tic is a nasty piece of work. His speciality, like Sweeney, is the knife. His name is Borzic. The other one, the big oaf, is Henry Conway. He's about as dumb as he looks and acts. But he's very handy with his fists, and if anyone stands up to Adcock, Henry soon shows them the error of their ways. They are called the alphabet gang because of the initials of their surnames. Very unpleasant people."

"I thought after O'Connor and company we would be rid of such people. Why are they here?"

"Really Preacher, for someone so clever, you do amaze me. You'll always find people like O'Connor and Adcock where there's an easy quid to be made. And they'll always have around them, weak, nasty people to do their dirty work. It's a normal part of life, it happens all the time."

Before Preacher could reply the door opened and the rest of the group filed into the room.

"Where's Bluey?"

"Where do you think Preacher?" Darkie answered. "Cleaning out the horse shit from the stalls or sponging the nags down. He's always there."

"Right, I'll talk to him later. Now pay attention. We have a problem."

They listened in silence to Preacher's story.

"If it's left to me, I'll continue as before. But I see this as a group activity and I'll go along with the Majority vote."

"Don't suppose Bluey can find any snakes on board?" smiled Jacko.

"No Jacko, I don't suppose he can." Preacher failed to see anything to joke about.

"Mick, what do you think this mob might do to carry out their threat?" Darkie asked.

"Who knows. They can be very mean. If we keep together we should be all right, but if you wander around the deck at night looking at the moon, you may have a nasty accident."

"Well Preacher it's nearly lunch-time and I'm hungry, so my vote is that we continue with the concerts but stay on our toes." Mac had risen to his feet.

"Yeah I'll go along with that." said Skipper.

"Me too." added Jacko.

"Erik and I agree, don't we Erik?"

"Ya Darkie. Ve agree."

"All right, we go ahead as planned, but be careful. I don't know what they can do in a confined area such as a ship, but the show will go on. I'll brief Bluey."

* * *

That night, there were noticeably fewer in the audience and two of the performers failed to appear. One of the acts, a juggler, fell down a ladder and broke most of his fingers. A message had been clearly sent. Next morning the sappers gathered after signalling practice.

"There's no need to beat about the bush men. I've spoken to the chaps who didn't turn up for their acts, and it's clear that they were warned off. And the juggler, who supposedly fell down a ladder, suffered very strange injuries from his fall. So, what do we do now?" Preacher was angry and worried.

"Preacher, I don't think this is a problem you can handle." All eyes turned to Darkie. "No, seriously. You're full of laws, rights and wrongs, justice and all that. This needs special attention."

"Darkie I won't allow or condone you or anyone else going outside the law. To do so would make you no better than Adcock."

"You're absolutely right Preacher. But how about leaving things rest for a while, say until this afternoon. I have an idea I want to discuss with Erik and Mick."

Preacher hesitated, but he knew he was at a disadvantage. "All right Darkie, but you do nothing, and I repeat, nothing, until you have our agreement. We're all in this together."

"Fine Preacher, you're the boss."

* * *

The group returned to the saloon on completion of the afternoon signalling session.

"Well Darkie?"

"All's well Preacher. There'll be no more threats to the concerts, or at least not until after Colombo, and if all goes according to plan, there'll be no trouble then."

"Why, what have you done? Come on, out with it." Preacher did not like the smug look on Darkie's face.

"It was easy," answered the swarthy sapper. "You said it had to be legal. Well, all disputes on board have to be settled in the boxing ring, right?"

"Yes, that's the army way."

"Fine. So Erik is going to fight Henry Conway on Saturday evening, the day before we get to Colombo. Adcock has agreed there'll be no disruptions to our concerts until after the fight."

"Why did he agree to that?" asked Sam.

"Because he believes Henry can beat Erik." Darkie was enjoying himself. "And if there is any hint of nastiness before the fight, then the fight is off, and Adcock would miss out on the purse which he thinks is money for old rope."

"Money for what?"

"It's an old saying Sam. Easy pickings. Adcock believes his boy will win easily and he'll collect."

"Collect what?" Sam was totally confused.

"The prize money, Sam. The hundred pounds prize money."

"One hundred pounds!" The words came from almost every mouth.

"Where do you think we're going to get one hundred pounds? Darkie be serious. You didn't make an agreement like that on our behalf did you?" Preacher was horrified.

Darkie laughed. "Preacher we don't have to find one hundred pounds. All I've done is put up an IOU for the amount. Come Saturday evening, we'll be sharing Adcock's money."

"And if Erik doesn't win, just where does the money come from?" asked Sam.

"Sam trust me. I know what I'm doing. Erik won't lose and we'll make a killing. When we were on leave I saw Erik fight. Hell, he flattened four blokes at the pub without any trouble, and they were timber cutters. Erik will murder Conway. He's just a big fat oaf."

"But he's done a bit of fighting in the ring Darkie. He didn't get those flattened features from smelling roses." Mac, like some of the others, was not entirely convinced as to Erik's fighting skills.

"Possibly Mac, but he's way out of shape and Erik's fit. Look the whole ship's buzzing with the news, so if someone offers you a bet, take it. We're on a certainty."

"Darkie I don't like it, but you seem to have committed us, so we don't have much choice. What do you think Erik? I hope you were asked before this bout was arranged." Preacher was worried.

"It's good Preacher. I vill vin. Don't vorry about me."

"I hope you do Erik, and I guess I should say thank you for doing this. But tell me Darkie, after the fight, why won't Adcock continue with his shady business?"

"It's life Preacher. It's a way of life you're slowly being exposed to." Mick spoke. "Adcock is already offering odds to the troops if they want to bet against his man. If Erik wins, then Adcock loses a lot of money, but more importantly, he's no longer seen as top dog. In his game, you must always be on top. Once the men see that Conway can be beaten, they'll start losing their fear of him, and if they don't fear Henry, then Adcock's hold over them is weakened. The men will reason that if Henry comes on at them, then they can call on Erik to repeat the dose. The law of the jungle."

"I hear you Mick, but what if Erik loses?"

"Oh well then we're all in Adcock's grip. He becomes the undisputed supremo on this ship. But don't worry, Erik will win. He has to."

Darkie stood up. “Come on Erik, we’d better start a bit of training, although you don’t really need it.” With that, the meeting broke up and the men went their ways. Mick remained behind with Preacher.

“Like Darkie said Preacher, don’t worry. It’ll all work out.”

“I hope so Mick. Why is it we seem to spend more time worrying about these silly little battles with cheats and bullies, when what we should be concentrating on is the big battle, the war?”

“As I said before Preacher, it’s life. It’s always been this way, always will be. Your big war is just the same as what is going on here, but on a bigger scale.”

“Really Mick? That’s a deep philosophy for one so young.”

“One so young? What you really mean Preacher is for one so uneducated. But my mother and our priest, have often talked about the ways of men, and I learnt a lot from them. Remember O’Connor and company, and you couldn’t work out why they wouldn’t feed us?”

“Yes. Do you know why?”

“Yep. You see, they were used to extracting a levy from men on exercise. In other words, you had to pay for your army food. Remember what Redman said: ‘a request in the correct form will work wonders’. The ‘correct form’ Redman was referring to, was a request with a couple of pound notes attached to it. It was one of the rackets they were running, but we arrived and wouldn’t pay. That upset them, but it wasn’t so much the money that irked them, it was the challenge to their power that worried them. They tried to bring us to heel but failed. It was the beginning of the end for them, just like Erik’s victory will be the beginning of the end for Adcock.”

“Really Mick, you continue to surprise me. Anyhow, O’Connor never asked us to pay, or at least I don’t think he did. Not directly.”

"Hints, Preacher. Remember what Redman said. It was a pretty obvious what he was getting at, or it was to most of us. O'Connor finally did ask and was told what he could do with his food."

"By whom?"

"Darkie told him to piss off. O'Connor could see that Darkie was a problem. He wanted him sent back to Broadmeadows, isolated from the group. Luckily for Darkie, Major Wiltshire was a wakeup and let him stay."

"Why wasn't I told?"

"Because you had enough on your plate at the time. Anyhow I'm off now. And stop worrying Preacher, it'll be all right."

* * *

The ship was alive with talk about the fight. Darkie took his role as a fight trainer seriously, and had Erik running around the deck and working out on a punch bag. Erik's strength was in his youth and physical fitness as he had little knowledge of the finer points of boxing. If Henry Conway trained, it must have been in secret, as no one saw him doing anything other than follow his master.

It was late Friday afternoon, when most of the signallers had gathered in the saloon, that their world was shattered. Wild eyed and gasping for breath, Darkie burst into the room. "Erik's had an accident." he shouted. "He's broken his arm. Those stupid fucking blokes who look after the horses had hosed down the steel deck and it was slippery. Erik went arse over elbow and cracked his arm."

This announcement was met with stunned silence.

"The doctor says he'll be in plaster for about three weeks. My God, what a thing to happen! Now that bastard Adcock will get away with all of his dirty tricks."

"What happens to the purse for the fight?" Sam asked.

Darkie stopped as if this aspect of the tragedy hadn't registered. He looked around for help, for guidance, and it was Skipper who came to his aid.

"If Erik can't fight for a legitimate reason, which he certainly has, then the fight's off and so are all bets."

"Yeah of course, you're right Skip."

"Yeah, I am right about the bets Darkie, but about the purse? What was the challenge? Was it Erik versus Henry or was it us versus Adcock's gang? Think now. How did you put it to Adcock?"

"I can answer that." The voice was soft but full of venom. Sergeant Adcock had entered the saloon unobserved. "I heard the question and you're right about the bets. But the challenge was, and I quote: 'our man will knock the living daylights out of your man.' Those were the exact words. I took the term 'our man', to mean a man representing the signallers. No name was mentioned at that meeting."

"You bastard, you know very well I was talking about Erik." Darkie snapped.

"Not so, Sapper Fleming. That man," Conway pointed to Mick, "I was there. You may have been talking about him. As far as I am concerned, the challenge was from a representative of this scrawny group, and the challenge stands. So, unless one of you cowardly flag wavers is prepared to step into the ring tomorrow evening with Henry, you'd better start counting your pennies, because you're going to need one hundred pounds at 8:00pm tomorrow night."

Bluey stepped forward. "I'll fight him. He's just a great lump of lard anyway." Something resembling a growl escaped from Conway's mouth.

"Steady on Bluey." Mac had risen from his seat. "I think it's time I made a contribution to the cause."

"No Mac, I'll take him."

"No Bluey, Mac's right." Skipper was also on his feet. He walked over to Sergeant Adcock. "Sapper McKenzie will be representing the signallers tomorrow night. All right by you?"

Adcock looked at Mac, then back to Skipper. "Keen to send one of your mates to certain death eh lad? And believe me, Henry will kill him."

"I don't think so Sergeant, and to back up my words, I'm willing to put money on Mac."

"You're not only a coward but a fool. First you volunteer one of your mates, and now you want to throw away money on him." The Sergeant's eyes glistened with greed at the thought.

"You can't rile me Sergeant. What odds will you give me?"

"Two to one. No, three to one."

"What? One minute you're telling me how your man is going to wipe the floor with Mac, and now you're only prepared to give me three to one. Having some doubts are you?"

The Sergeant was clearly annoyed. "No doubts. I'll give you ten to one."

"Taken. Ten pounds at ten to one. Tell your side-kick to write out the bet."

The Sergeant nodded to Borzic. "I hope you know what you're doing soldier. Ten pounds is a lot of money. A lot of money, especially on top of the one hundred you'll have to find."

"I know how much ten pounds is, and I hope you know how much two hundred is, because that's what I'll be around to collect tomorrow night." said Skipper with a smile on his face.

Borzic wrote out the bet on a page of his notebook, tore out the page and handed it to Skipper before following the Sergeant from the saloon.

"You shouldn't have done that, I stood up first." Bluey was still fuming.

"Calm down Bluey. You saved us with your snakes and now it's time for someone else to lend a hand. You're right. Conway is a lump of lard. Mac will handle him."

Darkie shook his head. "No offence Mac, but you'll be giving him a good forty pounds. You'll need to be quick on your toes, 'cos if he hits you, it will be bye-bye for the Scots."

"We'll see Darkie, perhaps I can run faster."

"Perhaps, but there's not many places to hide. And you Skip, what was all that crap about odds for a bet?"

"Just wanted to throw some worries into the enemy camp. Adcock now knows that if Mac wins, he's up for two hundred pounds, maybe more if people let their bets ride. I reckon that's a bit more than he's got in ready cash, and if he welshes on his bets, he'll be shark bait. I bet he doesn't sleep too well tonight."

"Speaking of sleeping, has anyone given some thought to the matter of the one hundred pounds we have to find should Mac not be successful?" Preacher spoke slowly and deliberately. "Now don't start saying he can't lose. I've heard all that before. What I want to sort out so I can sleep soundly is, where is that one hundred pounds coming from?"

They all looked at Darkie. "Yeah I know. I dropped you all in it without asking you, so it's my debt. I'll find some way of raising it."

"Thank you Darkie, that's what I was hoping you'd say. Not the bit about you raising the money, but the acknowledgment that you should have consulted us before you committed us to the deal. The challenge came from the signallers not from an individual, so we're all in it together. By my calculations, each man has to contribute eleven pounds two shillings and threepence. The odd threepence left after paying the debt we'll give to the Red Cross."

Preacher waited but there were no objections. Eleven pounds represented about forty-five day's pay to a soldier on five shillings a day, but there flickered in the heart of each, the hope that a miracle would happen, and that the next night they'd be walking around like millionaires.

* * *

Only those on duty were absent from the ringside. Men packed in around the twelve-foot square and those unable to find a nearby position climbed on top of structures. As the officers had crowded onto the wings of the bridge in contravention of ship's orders, it seemed reasonable not to ban the troops from such vantage points.

The two gladiators entered the ring to much cheering. It seemed to be a terrible mismatch. Conway, tall and powerfully built, towered over Mac as they stood in the centre of the ring receiving instructions from the referee. Three three-minute rounds, with a one-minute interval between each, eleven minutes from start to finish unless the fight ended early.

"If you do your sums Preacher, it's a pound a minute for each of us when you include the breaks."

"Yes Bluey, and I think it's during the breaks that we'll get value for our money. That Conway is a monster."

Bluey was staring at the two men in the ring. "He's big, but there is a lot of fat on him. What we don't know is how good our man is. Quiet as a mouse and yet he stepped forward to take on Henry the Horrible. He certainly looks relaxed."

"I know nothing about fighting, Bluey. I don't like it, never have, and I certainly don't like what I'm seeing or about to see."

"Much better to settle grudges or arguments in the ring Preacher. Fair to both parties."

The bell sounded and Conway rushed across the ring intent on ending the fight there and then. He swung a vicious right hand at the head of Mac who slid to one side and moved along the ropes.

"Phew! Thank God that didn't connect." breathed Bluey.

Conway again rushed at Mac swinging wildly but again the target moved. It was the pattern for the rest of the round. Conway charging, swinging punches, and Mac moving away or swaying to one side. The audience cheered every move but there was also the occasional, "Stand and fight you coward!" As the bell sounded the end of the first round, a great roar went up. While most men supported the signaller, they had expected the fight to be a blood bath, with an early victory to the giant. That Mac had survived the initial onslaught was worthy of recognition.

"Well Bluey. We, or at least Mac, lives to fight another day or should I say another round."

"Yes. The judges will have no problem scoring that round. No one landed a punch, although they might give Henry a point for being aggressive. He's puffing a bit and Mac hasn't even raised a sweat."

"Yes, but he can't run away for all three rounds. Sooner or later Conway is going to catch him in a corner and then it will be trouble."

"You know Preacher, it wasn't just luck that Mac dodged those punches. Some of them missed by a whisker as he swayed out of their reach. I think he knows what he's doing. He's been in a ring before. Anyhow we'll soon know."

This time, Conway approached more cautiously as if briefed by Adcock to try to box Mac, as opposed to the previous strategy of brute force. The big man threw a straight left which sailed over the shoulder of his opponent. Mac seemed to have all the time in the world to rip three left jabs into the ribs of Henry before skipping away. Conway's face showed pain. With a snarl, he lunged, but again the target had shifted, and as his right glove dropped, Mac's left hand made its mark on Henry's nose. Blood appeared and to the spectators this was a mini victory in itself. Conway was in two minds. He had tried fighting and that had failed, and now boxing had been unproductive. He made his decision. He lunged forward throwing punches from every direction. Henry knew that the longer the fight went on the greater the possibility of his defeat. His limited knowledge of the boxing world, told him he was facing one who knew his way around a boxing ring. One punch was all he needed, one good punch and it would be all over, but landing that telling blow was the problem. The sudden onslaught of thrashing arms and fists did not appear to worry Mac. He continued to evade the swinging gloves and from time to time would catch Conway off balance and land a hurtful punch on the big man's face. The crowd, who had no love for Adcock or his side-kicks, were ecstatic. The bell to end the second round came as a welcome relief to Henry, although the black look on Adcock's face was hardly an encouraging welcome when he reached his corner.

"See what you're looking at." muttered Bluey.

"What did you say?" asked Preacher.

"It's a saying my father used to drum into us. See what you're looking at. And I've been looking at Mac for about five months now, and not seen."

"Bluey you're not making sense."

"Consider Preacher. When we went on those long route marches, who always came back fresh as a daisy? Even when he carried Sam's pack as well as his own?"

"Mac?"

"Yes Mac. Who was, and still is, the best at mending lines, getting things to work? Anything to do with head to hand co-ordination. Mac. Who is the same height as me but weighs about twelve to fourteen pounds heavier, and it's not fat? The answer is Mac. He has all the attributes of an athlete; solidly built and very fit, good co-ordination and speed. It was there all the time, but we didn't see it."

Bluey looked across to the corner where Skip was sponging Mac's face. "Skip's bet wasn't a gesture at all. He knew something about Mac that we didn't."

The bell brought the two men out from their corners and a tremendous shout from the crowd. They could smell blood and it was blood they wanted. The pair spent the first few seconds eyeing each other off. Henry had no game plan left and Mac made the running. He moved forward and threw out a tentative left hand. Conway countered by poking out his left and Mac glided under it and a vicious right hit the big man flush in the midriff. Conway's right glove moved away from its protective position alongside his face and Mac's left speared into his chin. Instinctively, Henry moved both gloves to shield his face and Mac beat a tattoo on his midriff. It was now a demonstrative bout with Mac using Henry as he might a punching bag. After a while Mac stepped back and looked at the referee. "Box on!" the referee called and Mac resumed the onslaught. Now the crowd became silent. This was not a contest, this was murder. Still Henry remained on his feet, absorbing the cruel punishment. Finally, in attempting to throw a round arm punch, he tripped and crashed to the canvas. The referee motioned Mac to a neutral corner. After looking down at the fallen man he advanced across the ring and raised Mac's hand in victory. The crowd went wild.

No one from Conway's corner moved to help the stricken fighter and Mac waved to Skip to attend to him. Jacko and Sam also climbed into the ring to assist.

"Another example of man's brotherly love." observed Bluey. "Adcock and Borzic are his mates, or were, and now he's been beaten, they no longer have any use for him. It's those two who should be put in the ring with Mac."

* * *

An hour later, the group again gathered together. "Well Mac?" asked Sam.

"Well what Sam?"

"Come on, you know. We all want to know. Where did you learn to fight like that, and why didn't you tell us you were a champ?"

"A champ? That's a bit rich. I did learn boxing at school and I was pretty good. And after leaving school I boxed in the amateur ranks and did quite well. I wanted to have a go at professional fighting, but my dad wouldn't have a bar of it. He was right of course, but I had an inflated opinion of my ability. He sure fixed that."

"How?" Sam was fascinated.

"Dad got a real pro, he had been welterweight champion of Victoria, to box a few rounds with me. It was a put-up job. I was given a boxing lesson, a hiding and a lesson I won't forget. You see, you have to be better than good, you have to be very good if you're going to get to the top. I was good, but not very good, and this bloke, after knocking the stuffing out of me, pointed out that I would become one of the human punching bags if I turned pro. Yeah, I can look after myself most times, but I'm no champ."

"I bet Conway doesn't think that."

"Conway is stupid. He's had a few bouts and won a few, but he's unfit and overweight. He wasn't a problem, but it would've been an interesting match if Erik had fought him."

Sam turned to Skipper. "You knew didn't you Skip? That's why you took that bet with Adcock."

"I knew Mac could look after himself. I'm surprised that Adcock gave me ten to one. It was a stupid move on his part. And speaking of bets, I had better go and collect."

"No need Skipper. You're trusty agent has done that." Darkie was beaming. "Don't look at me like that, someone had to collect before Adcock ran out of money, which he has. So here you are. Each envelope contains eleven pounds two shillings. A small deduction has been made for expenses. Skip, your envelope contains one hundred and eleven pounds which makes you a very wealthy man. Now Mick, Sam, Erik and I managed to muster four pounds between us for a side bet, and I got Adcock to give me five to one, so there's another fiver for each of us. Now, is everyone happy?"

Preacher threw his arms into the air. "Darkie this time yesterday you were desperate to raise one hundred pounds and if I guess correctly, you only had one pound to your name. Now I find out that you bet your last pound on the fight. What if Mac had lost?"

"Preacher, there you go again, thinking about losing. It makes you lose sleep and you can get ulcers. No, I knew just as soon as Skipper made that wager that Mac was a certainty. Relax Preacher, it's all over. Adcock is finished. Totally wiped out. He couldn't pay all his debts and that's bad news for him. Borzic tried to pull a knife on one bloke who was demanding his money, but the mob took it off him. He won't be doing that again."

"Over until another thug takes over eh Darkie? Isn't that the way it works?"

Darkie beamed. "At last you are learning Preacher. You're right, but as far as the rest of the troops are concerned, you're Mister Big now. It was your boy who cleaned up Henry Conway, and you have this gang of cut-throats around you to do your bidding. And of course, there are vague rumours about how the Snake Section operated back in training. You're really big time Preacher. All you have to do is pass the word and everyone will bow. You've got it made Preacher. Now what do you want us to do?"

Preacher was shocked and angry. He looked at Mick. "Do you believe this rubbish Mick?"

"Yeah Preacher. Darkie passed the word around, and now that Mac has put Conway away, you're top dog. So, what's it to be?"

Preacher sat silently for a while contemplating his new-found power.

"Right, if that's the way you've set it up Darkie, so be it. Mac, do I have your support?"

"All the way Preacher, you're the boss."

"Good. Tomorrow we'll be in Colombo and I've got leave passes for all of us. The same rules as I applied in Perth will also apply tomorrow. We go ashore together and we stay together. After all, I can't go anywhere without my gang to protect me. Right Darkie?"

This sudden turn of events was too much for Darkie. He meekly nodded.

Preacher stood up. "I'm going to bed and I suggest the rest of you do likewise. It's been a long day and a most interesting one. Goodnight gang, and thank you again Mac. We owe you a lot."

LAST LINK WITH AUSTRALIA

All the troops were on deck well before breakfast to catch their first look at Colombo with its strangely rigged fishing smacks and dark-skinned crews. The ship dropped anchor inside the sheltered harbour and immediately coal and cargo barges made fast to the ship's side. The law of the sea required the replenishment of the ship before all else.

The morning's broadcast informed the men that leave would be granted from 10:00am until 7:00pm. Libertymen would disembark by the lighters.

"Where's Bluey?" demanded Preacher. "He'll miss the boat."

"Not coming Preacher." answered Mac. "The heat and the coal dust are playing havoc with the horses. Nothing would get him away from those animals. Skip and I tried to talk him out of staying on board, but it was no use. You know Bluey."

"Yes I do, and I wonder if we'll lose him when those horses go ashore in Suez."

Mac stopped with a look of surprise on his face. "Are you suggesting that he might change over to the Light Horse?"

“I don’t know, but Major Kelty asked me for my opinion as the Remount Section had approached him. I don’t know if anyone has spoken to Bluey, but there’s no rule or regulation to stop him changing. It’s up to him.”

“Bloody hell.” muttered Darkie. “After all we’ve been through, Bluey’s going to desert us.”

“You’re jumping the gun, Darkie. We don’t know what Bluey’s going to do, and he wouldn’t take too kindly to being called a deserter.”

Once ashore the men were surrounded by hundreds of eager locals trying to sell the visitors anything and everything.

“Don’t buy anything yet,” cautioned Skipper, “wait until just before we leave, and they know it’s then or never. The prices will fall dramatically.”

“You been here before Skip?” asked Sam.

“A couple of times. Dad wanted me to get some experience, so he got me a berth on a rusty cargo ship on the India-Australia run. I did three trips.”

“As the experienced traveller, Skip is hereby appointed OIC shore excursion. Right Skip, what do we do?” asked Preacher.

“I reckon we should hire four rickshaws for the day. That way we can stay together and use the local knowledge for sightseeing. I’ll nip off to the end of the wharf with Erik to bargain with the rickshaw drivers. You lot follow up slowly. See what the stalls are selling and what the prices are for comparison later.”

“Why Erik?”

“Because Sam, when you’re bargaining, it’s good to have a show of strength on your side, and Erik is a giant among these people, even with his arm in a sling.”

The group had a relaxing day touring, and about 4:00pm stopped outside the Grand Hotel.

"Time for refreshments." called Skipper. "In about ten minutes the heavens are going to open up, and I mean open up. The storm will probably last an hour, perhaps two."

The section relaxed in the main lounge while a tropical storm took its toll.

"You've done a great job, Skip. My only regret is that Bluey stayed on board."

"Bluey is probably the most contented of all of us Preacher. We'll have time to think about what lies ahead, but not Bluey. His mind is focused on getting those horses safe and sound to Egypt. I bet most of the time he doesn't even think of himself as a soldier. If you ask me, he's the lucky one. I once told him, that on board the ship he would be the stranger in my land. I was wrong. With those horses, he's completely at home."

Preacher nodded. "I hope he stays with us. He's a damned good signaller and a good mate."

"Amen to that Preacher. I guess that's the end of the storm so let's head back to the ship. We'll have some fun fighting our way through those stall holders, but that's part of visiting Colombo."

It was a weary but happy group that climbed the ladder from the lighter to the ship's deck.

* * *

During the night, the ship weighed anchor and left Colombo. When the men came on deck the next morning, they again found themselves alone in the vast expanse of the ocean. Preacher sought out Bluey. He picked up a brush and began grooming a horse. Bluey watched.

"Preacher, I suspect you came up here to talk to me about something, not to brush down a horse?"

"Why do you say that? Aren't I doing it properly?"

"Yeah, you're doing a good job, and the horse really appreciates it, but then he's rather used to it as I've been grooming him for the past hour. The other horses will be getting jealous."

"You're right Bluey, I did come down to have a chat. I'm sorry you missed out on the shore visit. The break would've done you good. You really are spending too much time here."

Bluey rubbed his hands along the animal's shoulders. "Too much time? How could anyone spend too much time with these poor creatures? Can you imagine what an experience it is for them? I worry about us striking rough weather. I don't know how they would cope. Anyhow Preacher, I get to signalling practice each day and have had a couple of stints working the lamp on the bridge. I'm keeping up with the others."

"Bluey, I'm not worried about your work. What I really came over to talk about, are these rumours that you might transfer to a signal company in the Light Horse. Any truth to them?"

Bluey brushed back his hair. "I've been asked to change over by the Remount Section, but Major Kelty has made it clear it'll be my decision. No one is going to make me change over. So, I have a problem. I have to choose between you blokes and these horses."

Preacher searched the young man's face to see if this statement was some sort of a joke. The concerned look on the young redhead's face convinced him that Bluey was serious.

"Bluey, I know I speak for all the section when I say that we'd be very sad if you left us, but as you say, it's your decision."

"Thanks Preacher. Don't worry, I'm not rushing into a quick decision." The horse turned its head and gave a playful nudge. Bluey patted the neck of the animal. "And you can cut that out old fellow. You're not going to push me into a decision any more than Preacher here."

Preacher watched the man and horse. "You know Bluey, I think that horse understood everything we've said."

"Of course he did Preacher, they're not stupid. Maybe they don't know the words but they sure can read moods, tones and gestures."

"Next time I want to discuss something with you, and a horse is around, I'll write a note. That'll fool them. Anyhow I must be off."

"Preacher, do you know our program? When do we arrive at Aden?"

"We'll take eight days to get there. We're to take on coal, and then it's five and a half days to Suez. From then on, it's all a bit vague. But we have to wait for a convoy to make the passage through the Suez Canal. I guess your mates here will be off loaded at Suez or Port Said. I really don't know."

"Ah well, for a change I know something that you don't. The horses are going to be landed at Alexandria, so I have about two weeks in which to make up my mind. When I do Preacher, you'll be the first to know."

"I doubt that Bluey."

Bluey frowned. "What do you mean? I wouldn't blab to anyone else. You'll be the first person to know, that's a promise."

Preacher laughed. "Yes Bluey, I'll be the first person, but I bet you tell your four-legged mate here before you tell me."

Bluey looked into the animal's big brown eyes. "You're right. Rocky here reads my mind. I can't keep any secrets from him." The horse nodded and Preacher understood the dilemma that the young soldier was grappling with.

* * *

Aden, a small town, nestling at the foot of rugged mountains, shimmered in the scorching sun. No leave was granted and the small boats, overloaded with souvenirs of all sorts, were kept away from the ship's side by a flotilla of harbour craft manned by police. Those traders who did manage to slip through the cordon, were doused by fire hoses as they neared the ship's side. It was a one sided battle, and in the end, the men found themselves cheering for the traders who they saw as the unfairly treated underdogs.

However, the heat and the clouds of coal dust were the eventual winners. The traders dispersed, and the men departed the exposed decks to seek what respite they could below. As the sun dipped below the horizon, the anchor was weighed and the AGENOR headed for the straits leading into the Red Sea. A new sense of excitement prevailed. On their right was Asia, to their left, Africa. To most it was their first entry into the old world which, until then, had been accessible only through the pages of books. It was as though they'd been transported from one world to another by the simple action of raising an anchor.

* * *

Five days later, off Port Suez, the men were again mesmerised by the sight and sounds of a new world. The landscape was foreboding and the Arabs selling their wares, were a source of amusement. Tutored in how to speak Australian by the thousands of diggers who had passed this way, or had been stationed in the area, the traders had a grasp of every swear word ever heard beneath the Southern Cross. The men soon realised that those using the words and phrases had no idea of the meaning of what they were saying. Having accepted that this schooling was part of a game, the soldiers immediately started to teach more phrases. When a bright student had mastered a phrase, he was usually rewarded by a coin thrown into the water. This would be followed by a legion of traders diving from their small craft to recover the small treasure. Fights broke out and the troops cheered the contestants, and then rewarded the victor with another coin which inevitably led to more fighting. Eventually the ship weighed anchor and took its place in the convoy for the canal transit.

AGENOR was the fourth of fifteen ships. As the ships ahead negotiated the first curve in the canal, the men saw one of the great wonders of the time. The sand dunes on the banks shielded the waters from the vision of the watchers and it seemed the ships were sailing across a sea of sand. It was spectacular. The sand stretched into the distance, and not a tree was to be seen. All along the banks were groups of soldiers, many of them Australian, and they called out for news of home. Men called out the names of towns they hailed from, and occasionally their call was answered by another from the same town. As the ship slowly glided by, the two men would exchange home town news. Every so often the call would come to the men on the ship. "Are you down-hearted?" "No," would be the roared response from the ship. "Well you bloody will be soon, you poor bastards," was the standard reply.

Preacher and Sam saw Bluey standing apart from the others and moved over to join him. Bluey was looking at the scenery through the eyes of a bushman. "Just look at that country. Not a tree, not a blade of grass. How could any animal live there?"

"I don't know Bluey, but they have for thousands of years. Our boys down there don't seem to be very happy."

"Can you blame them? Fancy being stuck out there guarding this canal when all the action's in France." said Sam.

"Many of them are Light Horse and probably saw all the action they wanted at Gallipoli. Still it's a miserable place to live."

"I agree Preacher, a real hell hole, but if you're fishing for information, I can tell you that I won't be living there. Rocky and I had a long discussion last night and I'm staying with you guys."

"Rocky? Who the hell is Rocky, and how come you didn't talk it over with us Bluey? We're your mates remember." Sam was indignant.

Bluey smiled. "Sam, Rocky is a horse. A special horse, and I had to tell him last night that we were soon to part company. It was a very difficult decision to make, but I'm sure he'll be well looked after once he gets his land legs back."

"You did a great job with those horses Bluey. You can be very proud that you got them here safe and sound, but I'm delighted to hear your news."

"Thanks Preacher, but I was just one of a team. Didn't lose a single animal, but now I look over the countryside I wonder if we did the right thing. That's camel country, not horse country. Poor beggars. To survive that long journey only to find your new home is sand, sand and more bloody sand. I bet Rocky will kick my backside if we ever meet up again, and I wouldn't blame him."

"When do the horses get off?" asked Sam.

"Day after tomorrow, or so I've been told. We reach Port Said tomorrow and then we'll do an overnight trip to Alexandria. After that, who knows? Do you Preacher?"

"No, my information is the same as yours Bluey. Some people say we'll all get off at Alexandria, others say we'll go on to England. It's all a lot of guesswork but we'll know soon enough."

* * *

After berthing at one of the pontoons at Port Said, gangways were put in place and there was a rumour that leave would be granted. These hopes were dashed as military police mounted sentries at each exit and the ship's broadcast announced that no personnel were allowed ashore. From the upper deck, the men could see the rows of white houses crammed together and their nostrils suggested that perhaps it might not be such a good idea to go ashore. The waterside area was teeming with people. On one side the small boats of the traders clustered around and trading was brisk. The traders would throw up a rope to the men above and a basket would be attached to the line. The men would indicate what merchandise they wished to examine and the game of bargaining would commence. The buyers soon realised the trick was to return the item to the basket and commence lowering it back down. This would instantly bring a sharp reduction in the offered price and negotiations would recommence. In the end, both parties would agree on a price and the payment would be sent down in the basket. To the soldiers, each purchase seemed to be a bargain. From the look on the faces of the traders it was obvious that any sale was good business. Again, the coarse foul use of the English language was evident and all bargaining was punctuated with crude descriptive words used without meaning or understanding. But the novelty of trading soon wore off and the men once again sought shelter from the hot sun.

Late in the afternoon the voice of the Officer in Charge of the troops came over the ship's broadcast. "The ship will be sailing sometime tonight. From the time of leaving until advised otherwise, no lights are to be shown outboard. That means no smoking on the upper deck or in exposed spaces. The crew is currently securing portholes and covering them with black material. No one is to attempt to open a porthole or interfere with the blackout material in any way. Your safety depends on these orders being adhered to. If you see anyone attempting to disregard these instructions, it is in your interest and your safety, to report the offence. Offenders will be severely dealt with. That is all for now."

"Well Sam, our war starts tonight."

"Yes Preacher, and now everyone on shore knows that we're sailing tonight. What if there are enemy spies in that crowd? We've given away any chance we might have had of sneaking away."

Preacher nodded. "You could be right Sam. There probably are people out there who are sympathetic to the Germans and the Turks, but all they have to do is sit in their lounge and watch us cast off, they don't need to hear the ship's broadcast. No, the real danger is from the enemy getting a sight of us. Hence the blackout. Anyhow there's nothing we can do about it except keep our fingers crossed."

* * *

AGENOR sailed before midnight and once clear of the entrance to the canal proceeded at full speed towards the west. The thought of the possibility of a torpedo exploding against the thin steel plates of the ships side sent many men up on deck to sleep.

The thought of being trapped below in a sinking ship convinced them that there was much to recommend sleeping on the wooden decks exposed to the cool night breeze. The irony of the blackout was not lost on the men as brightly coloured sparks leapt from the funnel giving any would-be enemy submarine a clear indication of the whereabouts, speed and course of the troopship.

Next morning the ship docked in the inner harbour of Alexandria and the twenty-four horses were gently led ashore. Bluey stood at the head of the long sloping gangway that led from the ship to the wharf. As each animal walked unsteadily past him he spoke to them and patted their flanks. Mac and Jacko watched from nearby.

"Mac, I reckon each of those horses gave Bluey a nod and a wink as they passed."

"You're right Jacko. I thought Bluey would jump at the chance to stay with them, but I was wrong. He's going to be lost for the rest of the trip without Rocky and his mates. Have you heard where we're heading?" All the men were desperate to find out their destination.

Mac shook his head. "Preacher says they'll let us know once we're at sea, so your guess is as good as mine, though I agree with Darkie. I'd rather be going to France than staying in this hell hole."

The ex-shearer nodded in agreement. "Yep. Paris and all those beautiful French girls, look out here we come."

Mac was surprised. "You don't suppose we'll get some leave in Paris before we go to the front do you?"

"Why not? After all this sea time, we need some time to relax and regain our land legs." Jacko was enthusiastic about a visit to the French capital.

With the horses landed, AGENOR moved to the outer harbour, and came to anchor. There were four ships already at anchor in the area.

"Look over there." Skip pointed. "Looks as if we're going to get a Navy escort from here."

The five merchant ships and two destroyers weighed anchor soon after dark. The ship's broadcast again warned of the seriousness of breaking the blackout rules.

The signallers gathered in the saloon after the evening meal to await Preacher, who had gone to the Captain's briefing. His appearance was greeted with calls for news. "You may not be so keen when you hear what I've got to say, but then we're here because we wanted to fight the Germans, and that's where we're going. Barring any mishaps, we'll reach Marseilles in five and a half days' time. Only two of the convoy are going to Marseilles, the others are bound for England. They have British troops on board. Once at Marseilles, we'll have to stay on board until train transport can take us north. No one knows how long we'll be staying on board but the orders are very clear. There'll be no leave in Marseilles. Apparently, there has been some trouble with transiting troops in the past and the authorities don't want a repeat."

"Stuff that Preacher, it's a whole month since we left Fremantle."

"Darkie, the orders are very clear. Anyhow you'll get plenty of shore time once we reach the north of France. I hear the mud is feet deep in places so you'll have all the ground you could ever want, plus a bit more."

Bluey, without his four legged friends to tend, had begun to worry about the possibility of a return of his sea sickness. "What's the weather forecast Preacher?"

"The Captain says it'll be good for the next three days, but once we turn north towards the coast of France, we could run into a storm. And as we get further north, you can expect the weather to get much cooler."

This was it, the last leg of the long trip to Europe. The holiday cruise was coming to an end.

The signallers got a lot of practice with the signalling lamp over the following three days, by passing and receiving messages from the other ships.

"Those navy guys are a bit slick, aren't they?" commented Bluey after a rather lengthy message had been received from the lead destroyer.

"Not surprising, it's all they ever do. Bet you could beat them at milking a cow." replied Jacko.

"Not much chance of finding out while we're here. Look lively, that damn destroyer is off again. I hope he's realised that I'm not as fast as his navy mates." Bluey clicked the lamp in acknowledgment and started to read, with Jacko writing down. Although they worried about their prowess at signalling, compared to the navy professionals, they were all secretly proud of the fact that, within AGENOR, they, along with the ship's officers, were the only ones that could talk across the waves to the other ships. It made them feel a little bit special.

* * *

France. The very name, Marseilles, filled the soldiers with a sense of history and excitement. The greenery of the landscape and the rugged tree-clad mountains, contrasted so vividly with the monotonous bare landscape of Egypt. As soon as the gangway was in place, there was a stream of visitors on board, doctors to check that all had the necessary vaccinations, movement officers to check the numbers for transport, and liaison officers to give briefings on France and its people. The day passed slowly. Although the troops had developed a sense of belonging to AGENOR, they were impatient to be on their way north.

Late in the afternoon the news they'd been waiting for came. "All troops will muster on the wharf at 8:00am tomorrow dressed in full kit and carrying kit-bags. Kit-bags will be taken to the railway station by lorries. Troops will be detailed off into companies and marched to the railway station. Thank you, and good luck to you all." The voice that had played such an important part in their lives over the past six weeks fell silent. AGENOR represented their last tangible link with Australia, and that bond was about to be severed.

Preacher came to the saloon where the men had gathered through habit. "Just a few things to add to all the other information you've been bombarded with. Major Kelty asked me to pass on his thanks to you all for the way you've conducted yourselves during the voyage. You'll be called at 0500, so make sure you pack your kit tonight and don't leave anything behind. It's also suggested you have a good meal tonight and a hearty breakfast tomorrow, as meals on the train may not be as regular, or as filling, as they are on board. Any questions?"

"Preacher, how long will it take us to reach wherever we're going?" Sam always had a question.

"Can't help you Sam. All I know is that we're heading north."

* * *

Sleep did not come easily that last night on board AGENOR. The men had become so accustomed to the ship that the thin steel walls surrounding them represented a barrier against danger. In the ship, they had found a new home. Tomorrow they'd be leaving...for what? That was the troubling thought on every mind.

Breakfast was a quiet affair. The time had come to break the last link with Australia. Questions began crowding into their minds, questions they felt that they should've asked long before, but it was now too late.

Major Kelty, impressed by the signallers' dedication during the voyage, had secured them space in a passenger car on the train, while many of the other troops found themselves herded into enclosed trucks fitted out with wooden seats. It was favoured treatment that the section knew would stop at the end of the train journey.

The signallers found themselves occupying two compartments, each designed to accommodate six passengers. Preacher and Mick, who had become almost inseparable, entered the first compartment.

Darkie, who resented the hold Preacher exercised over the group, entered the other compartment followed by his disciple Erik. It was a classic combination of the quick-thinking operator and the slow-acting devotee.

Skipper and Mac had also developed a great sense of companionship and were rarely separated from each other's company. They were mates in the long accepted sense of that term, as were the other pairings in the group. They joined Darkie and Erik.

The fourth pairing was perhaps the strangest of them all. Jacko by nature was a loner, a man who had battled his way in the hard world of sheep shearing. He showed little inclination to take the lead in any activity, but was a tireless worker who could be relied on to complete any task. His world revolved around work, and he was most contented when fully occupied. He rarely spoke. Sam adopted Jacko as his partner for two reasons. Jacko was the only one who didn't tell him to stop asking questions, and many of the questions asked by the young bank teller were about the land, and the land was one subject Jacko would talk about. Sam's dream of a farm was very strong, very real, and so was his thirst for knowledge.

The odd man out was Bluey who had no designated partner. Bluey was a mate to all of the group. His devotion to the horses, his dedication to letter writing and his meticulous adherence to the ceremony of winding up his watch, were all the subject of light-hearted banter by the others. When asked the time Bluey would make a small production of supplying the answer. He would carefully remove the leather-covered box from his pocket, remove the watch from its protective shield and hold it to his ear. Once he had confirmed that the precious object was still ticking, he would open the cover and gaze at the dial. Then with a flourish he would snap shut the cover, return the watch to its case and return it to its pocket. Then, and only then, would he pronounce his findings. But Bluey never gave an actual time in hours and minutes. He would always announce, “it’s nearly tea time,” or “lunch will be soon,” or “it’s time for lights out.” Bluey reasoned that these were the reasons people asked for the time of the day or night. Hours and minutes were simply numbers, what people wanted to know was the relation of time to an activity, and that is how he handled such questions. At first his companions complained that they did actually want to know the exact time, but Bluey could not be swayed to change his approach to the matter, and they had come to accept the redhead’s philosophy on time.

For the train journey north, Bluey moved into Preacher’s compartment and after a while he managed to secure the window seat facing the direction of travel. The others were content to let him have this premier position and the young bushman used his vantage point to record in his letters his impressions of the people and the passing landscape.

It was still quite cool in the south of France and the temperature fell as the train wended its way north. At times the train would be diverted onto a siding to allow bigger, faster trains to pass, and on such occasions people would gather along the line to wish the men well and to hand up food. Many of the women were dressed in black, a sign of mourning for one who would not return from the front, but almost, without exception, they waved and smiled to the men from a country many of them had never heard about, but who had come to save France. The scenery dazzled the men. It was, even in winter, a green they had never experienced before. The trees were still in their winter nakedness but the grass and the gardens gave the countryside a brilliant carpet of lush green. The fields were small and orderly with their neatly furrowed surfaces awaiting the arrival of spring.

For three days the train progressed north, skirting Paris much to the dismay of its passengers. On the third morning, they arrived at the picturesque town of Abbeville and were ordered to disembark. It was a cold, bleak day, with light rain falling and the men, accustomed to the warmth of the tropics and the Middle East, felt the chill. A tall, stockily built Sergeant approached the group. He looked the men over and on sighting the lone stripe on Preachers coat, walked over to him.

"I'm Sergeant King, Sergeant in charge of the Brigade signallers, and you lot have just joined my team. Get your men to collect their gear and climb aboard that truck and make it snappy. It's too bloody cold to be standing around here."

The truck moved off through narrow streets and eventually turned into a camp. All the men could see was a sea of canvas tents.

"I thought Broadmeadows was big," exclaimed Sam. "Just look at this!" The rows of tents stretched as far as could be seen in all directions.

Darkie was also impressed with the sheer size of the camp. "How the hell can anyone find his billet in this lot?"

"I'm sure there's some sort of orderly arrangement of the various groups and we'll just have to be smart and learn, and learn quickly Darkie." replied Preacher.

"Righto you lot, jump down with your kit." The Sergeant was slapping his arms to his side to keep warm. "Right, single file. Keep on the duckboards and follow me." He led off at a brisk pace. After a short walk, Sergeant King turned off the main walk and entered a tent. Inside were ten stretcher bunks. Without being told, each man selected a bed and placed his kit-bag on it. There was already gear on one bed next to the entrance.

"This is your new home. Make sure you remember the letter and numbers painted on the fly. The letter tells you which sector you're in, the next two figures tell you which walkway to take and the last two figures tell you which tent. Right, let's go and find Al Wilson."

"Who the hell is Al Wilson?" asked Darkie.

"Corporal Wilson. He'll be in charge of your section. You're lucky to have him. He's one of the best. He has a couple of weeks to knock you lot into shape if you're lucky. There are rumours of a big push being mounted soon and I'm only guessing when I say two weeks. It might happen sooner, so listen to him and do what he tells you to do. That way some of you might survive."

"Some of us?" Sam spoke for all the men.

The Sergeant looked at their shocked faces. "Perhaps you'll all come through, perhaps none of you. We've had heavy casualties over the past year. At Fromelles, over 5000 men in one day. No one is invincible. We all want to stay alive, and the better you are at your job, the better the odds are for surviving. I suppose I should be feeding you a line of hope and glory but it's not like that. The best advice I can give you is listen to Al Wilson. He is good, very good. Some say he takes risks but then he has to, it's part of the job. What he does is keep the risks to a minimum. Learn from him, watch how he operates, copy him, and your chances will improve. So, take those surprised looks off your faces. You're now at war. Come on, let's find your corporal."

With the collars of their greatcoats turned up to keep out the icy wind, they trudged along in single file, each thinking about the Sergeant's words.

"Just as I thought. There he is over by the cookhouse." The men looked up to see a slim man standing outside a wooden building, a steaming mug in his hand. "I thought I told you to wait in the tent Corporal Wilson."

"Sorry Sarge but it was too damn cold, and I reckoned you'd all be looking for a hot cuppa so I came over here to organise it." The cheerful young man waved his hand in the direction of the stove. "Grab a mug and fill it up, then come over to the meal hut across the way." The men hurried forward.

The corporal and the Sergeant stopped by the door of the hut.

"Right Al, they're all yours."

"Any word on when we'll be moving up to the line Pete?"

"Nope, but from the hustle and bustle at HQ, it's my bet we'll be there by the first of March, if not before."

"Bloody hell. That doesn't give these blokes much time to settle in."

"Can't be helped Al. You know I would normally split them up and spread them around to the other sections, but Phil Reynolds wrote to the Captain and said he should keep them together as a unit. And the Captain reckons that Phil Reynolds knows what he is talking about. Good luck with them."

"Thanks Pete, I'll need all I can get."

AVEZ-VOUS LOGEMENT?

"Gentlemen, now we all know each other, may I say welcome to the war. I don't want to know your reasons for wanting to be part of this senseless killing, mainly because so far, I haven't been able to work it out for myself. But here we are, so let's make the best of a shitty situation. Now there are a few things you should know before we start on the whys and wherefores of being a frontline signaller."

"The first thing you should know is that you're being treated differently from other reinforcements we've received. You may well ask why. In the past, we've integrated newcomers into the sections by pairing off a new bloke with an old hand. It seemed to be a good way of doing things, but it didn't always work out. Some of the old hands objected to being burdened with a raw recruit, sometimes there was a clash of personalities, and so on. A pair of signallers working the line has to be a team. Each man must know instinctively what his mate will do in any circumstances. That mutual trust takes time to develop. Our Commanding Officer, Captain Solway, Sergeant King and myself have been together since Gallipoli. We understand each other, and we have been aware of the problems of integration for some time."

He paused to see if there were any questions. "There's another player in this game, Sergeant Phil Reynolds. Ah! I see you remember old Phil. It was he who suggested that we take a group who had gone through basic training together, and keep them together as a section here in France. His reasoning was that you would already be familiar with each other's habits, good and bad. He felt that pairing off would be easier to organise. Phil pointed out that we went into Gallipoli as raw recruits, there were no old hands to guide us. He also pointed out that now we had officers and NCOs who know the ropes and can recognise problem areas, something we didn't have at Gallipoli. So, Phil persuaded Captain Solway to give the system a try. It was Phil who recommended that you should be the guinea pigs."

"Shit, and I thought Sergeant Reynolds was a good bloke."

Al Wilson looked at Darkie. "And you were correct soldier. They don't come any better. Anyhow that's what this is all about. If I don't think it's working, all I have to do is pass the word and we'll go back to the old method. So, it's all up to me and, of course, you."

Preacher raised his hand. "I can see merit in what Sergeant Reynolds proposed and you were right in assuming that we've tended to pair off, but when and where are we going to learn how to carry out our duties in combat?"

"Ah yes. When and where. Well, the answer to where, is simple. In the frontline. You can play around here practising for as long as you like, but believe me the only real training ground is up at the front."

"And where's that Corporal?" Sam had to ask.

The young Corporal thought for a moment. "The last time a General spoke to me was in 1915 and it's probably moved by now. But I do seem to recall Peter King saying only the other day that

Jerry was dug in to the west of Peronne. That's about 50 miles from here, or 80 kilometres in French distance. A small point. Always check whenever someone gives you a distance whether he is quoting miles or kilometres. If you have to run a message on foot I can tell you ten miles is a bloody sight further than ten kilometres. Now what was the other question?"

"When do we start?"

"Ah when to begin. Perhaps it's not a good idea for us to rush off today to Peronne, so we'll wait until tomorrow. We'll go by truck, if I can organise one. We'll go to a lovely little town called Corbie where the Brigade is being held in reserve."

"And if you can't organise a truck?" Sam was concerned.

The reply was what everyone expected and dreaded. "Then we walk. It's only about 55 kilometres. But don't fret, there is plenty of transport going at Amiens so I'm sure we'll get a ride that far, then It's only a short hop, skip and a jump to Corbie."

"How big a hop, skip and a jump?"

"Sapper Ralston, you do ask a lot of questions. Corbie's about sixteen kilometres from Amiens. A brisk stroll for soldiers."

Preacher raised his hand. "Why did we come to Abbeville? The train went through Amiens early this morning."

"Indeed it did Lacey. But the Army has a system and we simple soldiers cannot alter or interfere with the system. You're here in Abbeville to fill in forms to prove that you've arrived in France. Then you'll officially be allotted to the Brigade and I'll sign to show that that's where I'm taking you. You'll then draw rifles and any clothing you may need. May I suggest you grab a couple of extra flannel undershirts and a spare blanket, if you can carry it. Also socks. Right, the cooks are just setting up to serve lunch so let's nip out there and be first in the meal line. Bring your meal back here and once we've eaten, we'll get cracking and get the paperwork out of the way. It gets dark pretty early so there won't be much time to exercise those flabby muscles of yours but we should be able to get in an hour or so of doubling and marching. Let's go."

* * *

It was an exhausted group that returned that evening. Al Wilson's idea of an hour or so of drill developed into two hours of non-stop marching and running without a let-up. It was dark and cold before he marched the group back to their accommodation.

"Right. Dump your gear and let's get down to the mess hall. When you've had dinner come back here and repack your gear, ready for an early start. Eat up big because we may be on our way before breakfast."

The men silently followed their leader to the mess hall. The Corporal quickly ate his meal and left.

"Well what do you make of him Preacher?" asked Bluey.

The others leaned forward, eager to hear Preacher's assessment of Corporal Wilson. Preacher gave the question some thought. "Cheerful, very fit, and presumably good at his job. However, I think there's another side to Al Wilson which we haven't seen, and maybe won't see, until someone does something wrong."

"I agree. He couldn't have survived this long unless he was good at his job, and the fact that the captain and the Sergeant have given him a free rein with our frontline training must mean they have confidence in him."

"A good point Mac. I doubt if corporals are normally given such responsibility, so he's obviously something special. Right, everyone finished eating? Let's go back to our tent in company so no one gets lost. Come on, follow me."

* * *

The men were asleep when Corporal Wilson entered the tent and climbed into bed. They were still asleep when he stirred, rolled out of bed and quickly dressed.

"Righto. Everyone up. You have ten minutes to have yourselves and your gear at the pick-up point which is at the end of the tent walk. Come on, move it. I'm off to get the truck. If you miss it, you'll walk to Corbie. That's a promise." Picking up his kit-bag the Corporal departed.

The men scrambled to get ready.

"Shit Skipper, think he means it?"

"Means what Darkie?"

"That crap about leaving us behind to walk." Darkie was worried.

"Yeah, I reckon he meant it, but I'm not going to test his sincerity, I'll be there."

Darkie shook his head. "When does the man sleep? He wasn't here when we turned in and this morning he's up and dressed before anyone else stirred."

"Don't worry about it Darkie. Just do as he says and hurry up. The ten minutes are just about up."

Despite their best endeavours it was closer to fifteen minutes before all had reached the end of the duckboards where Al Wilson was waiting with a truck.

"Come on, move it. When I say ten minutes, I mean ten minutes. Next time you'll be walking. Climb on board."

The men quickly settled in the back of the covered vehicle and the truck moved off. In the centre of Abbeville it stopped and the Corporal ordered the men to climb down.

"This is the YMCA, open twenty-four hours a day. We can get a wash and something for breakfast here. It's a better set-up than tramping for miles to the camp toilets. I want to be on the road in thirty minutes so don't loiter in the showers. Yes, you heard me, I said showers, hot showers. Use them because it might be a long time before you have your next decent wash. Follow me."

The men were back on the road after a thirty-minute stop.

"We're lucky men. The driver is going to Albert and has agreed to drop us on the way. If he's got time in hand he'll take us right to Corbie, if not, he'll drop us at a place called Lahoussoye and we'll march from there. And before you ask me Sam, it's about five kilometres."

"Do we stop at all on the way?" asked Preacher.

"Yeah, we have to for fuel, and the road isn't the best. Mind you these roads weren't built for the kind of traffic that has been racing around the countryside for the past two and a half years. Settle back and relax. We should make Amiens for lunch and then reach Corbie mid afternoon. Anyhow, who's in a hurry? This area, like all of France, is steeped in history. It's a pity we don't have time to stop and look at some of the old churches. However, we'll be stopping near the Amiens Cathedral for lunch. Now that's really something special!"

Al Wilson shut the sliding panel between the cabin and the back of the truck and the men were left to their own thoughts. Every now and then the panel would be opened and the Corporal would talk about the town they were passing. Ten kilometres after leaving Abbeville the truck crossed the Somme and followed the southern bank of the famous river.

"It's awful flat," observed Jacko, "those bare trees won't give a man much cover." The men suddenly ceased admiring the beauty of the countryside and began looking through the eyes of a military man.

"Jacko's right. You can see for miles. No wonder we've had so many casualties."

The panel slid open. "Just entering Amiens fellas. There's a YMCA near the cathedral and that's where we get lunch. The driver has to collect some things to take to the officer's mess in Albert so we'll have a while to look around. You can leave your kit in the truck but take the bolts out of your rifles." The trapdoor slammed shut.

After negotiating narrow crowded streets, the truck arrived at the Square. The men climbed down and stood, faces upturned, to look with awe at the imposing Amiens cathedral.

"Well what do you think? Started in 1220, five years after King John signed Magna Carta. I've seen a few churches and cathedrals but never one to compare with this one. Come on, we'll eat and then I'll give you a tour."

* * *

It was mid afternoon when the truck returned to the Square. Half of the back was stacked with boxes and crates destined for the officer's mess. Darkie's eyes lit up when he saw what the boxes contained but his interest didn't escape the watchful eyes of Al Wilson.

"Forget it Fleming. You so much as smell that cargo, and I'll fix you. We're riding on this truck as a special favour and you'll not be repaying the favour by looting the goods. Got it? Right. Let's go."

* * *

The journey to Corbie was made at a snail's pace as the driver was anxious not to damage the fragile cargo of bottled spirits and wine destined for the officers' mess. The ten miles took over an hour and the shadows were already long when the truck pulled up outside a building flying an Australian flag. Corporal Wilson entered the building as the men climbed down with their gear and rifles. The group waited for their Corporal to reappear, and when he did, he wasn't smiling.

"Problem men. Seems like all accommodation in Corbie is occupied. I've never seen so many men about. The rumour of the big push must be true and pretty soon I'd say. But our first problem is to find somewhere to sleep. We have to find ourselves a billet, the question is where."

"What sort of billet Corporal?" asked Sam.

"For Christ's sake stop calling me Corporal. My name's Al and I prefer you use it. From here on we're a team, so let's start acting as one."

"Fine Al, but where to from here?"

Al frowned. "Bloody soldiers everywhere. That means they've spread into the countryside in all directions. Brigade HQ is in a Château to the north-west of here so the boys will go in every direction but that one. That's where we'll go."

"Just like that. March north till we find an inn with a vacancy sign. Damn, it will be dark in an hour."

"Right you are Darkie. Here's the plan. This road behind me leads to Lahoussoye. About a kilometre out of town there is a split in the road. The one on the left goes to Querrieu, the other to Lahoussoye. When we reach the junction we split up. Preacher, you will take four and keep on towards Querrieu. I'll take the others and head for Lahoussoye. The drill is this. The locals have to provide billets on demand unless of course they already have a house full, and I use the term 'house' rather loosely. The best you can hope for is a good solid barn with clean hay. At the moment, that's all we want for tonight. Anyone speak French?"

Sam raised his hand.

"Oh God, you mean you can ask all those silly questions in two languages?"

"I studied French at school." explained Sam. "I've never had to speak it since, but I was top of my class."

"Fair enough. You go with Preacher's group. Let's go. When one group finds a billet send one of the group to catch up with the other group. Preacher, if you reach Querrieu without finding any accommodation, turn right and proceed along the Amiens-Albert road. Likewise, I'll turn left on the same road if we have no luck, so we should meet somewhere. Let's move. It's going to be a cold night, especially if we have to sleep out."

The party parted at the road junction. They kept to their adopted pairing as usual with Bluey going with Preacher's group to make up the five. It was obvious that Sam's second language was very broken French, so he wrote down a simple question which he presented at each farmhouse.

"Avez-vous logement pour les soldats?" The reply invariably was a curt "Non."

"Sam are you sure that you're asking the right question? The residents don't seem very happy."

"You can't blame them for being a bit put out Jacko. After all, how would you like it if some strangers came knocking at your door looking for a bed for the night?"

"I think Sam is right," declared Preacher. "At some of the places you could hear voices speaking in English, which would tend to suggest that they already had visitors, welcome or not."

"Perhaps Al and the others will have better luck. We can't be all that far from Querrieu." Said Bluey as they stopped outside a door set in a high brick fence. Sam knocked. They waited for a response but none came.

"Perhaps their front door is off the yard." suggested Jacko. "Give another knock Sam, and this time make it a bit louder."

A ray of light appeared through the gap at the bottom of the door. The noise of bolts being drawn was heard and the door swung open. An elderly lady with snow white hair, dressed in black, carried a lantern which she held up so the light fell on the faces of the men.

"Bon soir Madame. Avez-vous logement pour les soldats?"

"Attendez." snapped the old lady, stepping back before closing the door with a bang.

"So much for your smooth tongue Sam. Let's go."

"No Jacko, she didn't say no, she said wait," Sam said.

"You sure Sam? She sure looked like she was saying no."

"Of course I'm sure. She said wait. See, someone is coming."

Again, the door opened. This time the holder of the lantern was a petite woman, much younger. She too held the lantern on high.

"Bon soir Madame..." began Sam but the woman interrupted him.

"According to my mother-in-law you speak French with an awful accent, so why don't we converse in English."

"Of course, thank you Madame," stuttered Sam. Preacher moved forward.

"We're sorry to trouble you Madame, but my companions and I have just arrived in the district and need accommodation for the night. We were hoping that you might have some area out of the cold where we could sleep."

"You have a strange accent monsieur. You are not English?"

"No, we're Australians and we are very cold."

"Well don't stand there, come in. Follow me, and please would the last one bolt the door." The woman led the way across a courtyard. The men followed through another door into a large room without any furniture but with stone benches around the walls and a large tub in the centre. The walls and floor were painted white. The woman explained the room had been the central room for a dairy before the war but it was no longer used.

"You can use this as a wash room and sleep in the barn which is through that door. There is plenty of clean hay. I will get a couple of lanterns, but please be careful, we don't want a fire."

Preacher bowed his head slightly. "Thank you Madame, we are most grateful, but there is something I must tell you. We are ten in number not five. The other five went along the road to Lahoussoye looking for a billet. Is it all right with you if they come here?"

"Five, ten, what does it matter? We once had twenty cows in the barn and now we only have two, so there is plenty of room." The woman looked around. "Who is in charge? Which of you is the officer?"

"Oh, he's with the other group, but I'm in charge until he gets here."

"And what do they call you?"

"Preacher. I mean Tom Lacey, but most people call me Preacher."

"Very well Monsieur Preacher, that's what I will call you. I am Madame Pruvost. How do you intend to tell your friends that you have found accommodation?"

"I'll go Preacher." Bluey started to put on his greatcoat. "Excuse me Madame, we made arrangements to meet on the Amiens-Albert road and I think it's probably quicker for me to go forward rather than retrace our steps."

"Of course it is. Come, I'll point out the road that stays on this side of the Hallue River and joins the Amiens-Albert road. If you go into Querrieu you will probably get lost."

Having set Bluey on the road the woman returned. "Have you had supper?" she asked.

"Oh, we haven't eaten but it's still early. I'm sure Al Wilson will have thought of something."

"Tell me Monsieur Preacher, do Australians like drinking tea like the British?"

"Yes Madame. Probably more so, but we haven't got any tea with us."

"That's not a problem. I'll boil some water and have it ready when the others get here. The kitchen is through that door but I must insist that you knock and wait for permission before you open the door. You agree?"

"Of course we do. It's your house, your home. You make the rules and we'll abide by them. That's a solemn promise."

The woman looked carefully into Preacher's eyes. "Good. I'll get those other lanterns and you can start arranging your sleeping accommodation. There is plenty of hay and it's a well-made barn. The weather doesn't get in. Do you have enough blankets?"

"Plenty thank you."

After the woman had left the room, Jacko started to laugh. "You're really funny Preacher. You should see yourself. Yes ma'am, no ma'am, anything you say ma'am. And you were stuttering and blushing like a young school boy. Hell Preacher, I've heard of love at first sight but this really takes the cake."

"Oh shut up." Preacher might have gone further but for a gentle knock on the kitchen door which he quickly opened.

"Two lanterns as promised. Please let me know when your friends arrive."

"Certainly Madame. And again our sincere thanks for your hospitality."

The woman smiled and closed the door.

"There you go again Preacher. Tongue-tied. You're a hopeless case."

"Ignore him Preacher." advised Mick. "Here give me one of the lanterns and let's inspect the boudoir. I hope cows don't snore."

"I'm betting that the cows are hoping that we don't snore, but wait till they hear Darkie. That'll put them off their milk."

"Speaking of cows Jacko, could you teach me how to milk?"

"I could Sam but I bet Bluey is a better hand at milking than me. Ask him. She didn't mention a horse did she Preacher?"

"No she didn't, but then she probably thought you wouldn't know the difference." Preacher was still upset by Jacko's earlier remarks. Jacko saw something in the look on Preacher's face that made him realise his remarks had struck a chord, a nerve, in the tall man's system. A nerve that until now had been relatively undisturbed.

They heard the outer gate opening and Al Wilson's team came stumbling into the room. Light snow had started to fall and they were cold.

"Welcome to our humble abode." said Preacher, matching his words with a low bow.

"Strewth Preacher, how did you find this place?"

"It's all due to Sam's eloquent grasp of the French language Al. He talked his way in." Preacher replied.

Al turned and looked at Sam. "I guess I owe you an apology. I thought you were kidding when you said you spoke the language. From now on you can give the rest of the men lessons in the basics. It's a valuable asset to be able to make yourself understood in another person's country. I might even put you up for an interpreter's job."

"Whoa, not too fast Al. The lady of the house speaks very good English and I think that helped our cause. She told me to let her know when our Officer arrived so I had better do that." Preacher realised that his joke had gone far enough.

"Sure Preacher. I was only teasing Sam. Bluey filled us in with the details of how you got here. So, where's this lovely lady?"

Preacher walked to the kitchen door and knocked gently. The door swung open and the petite lady stepped into the room.

"Oh dear," she cried. "you all look half frozen. All of you, come into the kitchen and get warm."

She led the way into a large room which served as a combined kitchen-dining room. An open fire blazed at the far end of the room and chairs were arranged so the family could sit in a semicircle to enjoy the warmth. As the men filed into the warm room three young ladies rose from their chairs, the old lady remained seated.

"Gentlemen, my family. Firstly, my mother-in-law, Madame Pruvost." The old lady stopped knitting, looked at the men and nodded. "Mother speaks little English but can understand simple sentences. My daughters, Marie, Nicole and Yvette. They all speak reasonable English. Marie and Nicole work at the Château where your senior officers live. Yvette has just completed her schooling but I keep her home with me for the present."

The men nodded to the three young women.

"We are very pleased to meet you, and most grateful to you for taking us in on such a night." Al then turned to the old lady and repeated the words in French.

Sam shook his head. “I might have known it. I suppose you speak several languages beside playing the violin and painting.”

Al looked at the young bank teller. “Now how did you work all that out? Yeah, you’re right, but I’ve misplaced my fiddle somewhere.”

“Ah Monsieur, perhaps we can get you to play for us one day? My husband played the violin and it’s still here.”

“Called your bluff Al.” laughed Sam.

“I don’t understand that remark, but perhaps you would all be kind enough to introduce yourselves.”

“Of course, I’m Alan Wilson but normally called Al.”

Each man gave his name, followed by the name he wished to be called.

“I’m sure we will get you all confused for a while but soon we will know you by the right name.”

“You seem to have forgotten one person, Madame Pruvost.”

“Who?” she asked.

“Yourself Madame, unless of course you wish us to call you Madame Pruvost, but as there are two Madame Pruvost it could become confusing.”

“Of course. I am Ghislaine and I would be happy for you to call me by that name. We are lucky our table is large and can seat everyone although it might be a little cramped. Would you please join us for supper?”

“Madame. I mean Ghislaine. That is most kind but you can’t feed ten strangers who have just appeared out of the night. We only came looking for a place to sleep out of the weather.”

“Monsieur Preacher you do fuss a lot. I will let you into a secret. Because Marie and Nicole work at the officers’ mess, they are permitted to bring home left-overs from the kitchen. I suspect the cooks who give these presents expect one day for a reward but they will be disappointed. However, a little flirting always seems to produce extra food. Now I have confessed, and tonight I have made a thick soup and we have bread and cheese. I can also offer tea or coffee. Real English tea. So, take your places and the girls will help me serve."

* * *

As soon as the meal was finished and the table cleared, Al thanked the family and indicated that the men should retire to the barn to prepare their sleeping quarters, but it was Bluey who had the last say of the evening. It was a gesture quickly grasped by the young girls.

"Who milks the cows?" he asked.

"We do." chorused the three girls. "We take it in turns. Two of us milk a cow each morning and evening while the other has a day off."

"Well, if you leave a milk bucket in the dairy, I'll milk tomorrow morning, and that will save you coming into the barn."

"Thank you Monsieur Bluey. It was something that had crossed my mind and I am pleased you have solved the problem. The girls have never been keen on getting up early, especially on a cold morning." Ghislaine paused, before turning to Al. "Monsieur Al. How long do you and your men intend staying here?"

"All I can tell you Ghislaine, is that I intend to leave early tomorrow morning to find my commanding officer. He is somewhere in or around Corbie. Once I have spoken with him, then I'll know what we are doing. Would it be asking too much if we remained billeted in the barn for at least another day? We don't expect you to feed us, just let us sleep in the barn."

"Monsieur Al, you can certainly stay. There is no problem with that, especially with Monsieur Bluey doing the milking."

"Thank you Madame. I hope to be able to tell you more tomorrow evening. Till then goodnight ladies, and thank you for a lovely meal."

* * *

The men filed into the barn and set about arranging their beds. "Right fellas, gather around and pay attention. In all my time in France, I've never run into a situation such as this and it worries me."

"What is the problem Al?"

"This place is the problem Preacher. It's a soldier's heaven, but why aren't there queues of soldiers lined up fighting to get this billet? Young ladies, hot food, warm sleeping quarters. I ask you, where are the queues of lonely, hungry soldiers? That's what worries me."

"Well, what do we do?" Preacher asked.

"Do Preacher? We enjoy it while we can, but let me spell out a few rules. No one goes past that kitchen door without permission from a family member. Secondly, no one, and I mean no one, makes any sort of a pass at any of those young girls. Treat them with total respect at all times. Got it?"

They all nodded.

"Good. Let me tell you something. This is as close to heaven on earth as you're going to get, so don't spoil things. Tomorrow morning, I want you Preacher, to come with me. We'll leave at 7:00am. Bluey get your milking done and when you take the milk to the house, see if you can get some tea and toast which will have to do for breakfast. Everyone is to shave so you'll need to get some hot water. Each day one of you will be the duty man. We'll start in alphabetical order, so you'll have the duty tomorrow Bluey, then Darkie and so on. I'll work out a duty list tomorrow."

The Corporal paused while considering his next instruction. "Tomorrow Bluey, you march the squad out of here at 8:30am, and march to Corbie. Stop outside the building you saw me enter today, and ask at the desk if there are any instructions from me. If I haven't left any instructions, have a twenty-minute break in

Corbie. There is a good YMCA where you can get a cup of tea. Then march to Lahoussoye and back to here via Querrieu. And when I say march, I mean march, not shamble along. If you see any officers, salute them, because if you don't, I'll get to hear about it. You should be back here by midday. Preacher will be here with rations for your lunch and with a bit of luck I might be here as well. Take an hour off for lunch and then repeat the morning's routine. Any questions?"

"You mean we're going to spend the whole bloody day marching around the countryside?"

"Yes Darkie, I do, unless of course you prefer to run."

Darkie shook his head.

Al Wilson continued. "Right, from now on whenever you want to get somewhere, you'll march. The Germans are about thirty kilometres east of here. When we go to see them, we'll probably march, and after we've seen them, we'll march back, or if they are chasing us, we'll run. Right let's get some shut-eye. We'll leave one lantern burning through the night in case someone wants to have a pee. Watch where you're walking and be careful with the light. A fire would be nasty for everyone."

* * *

Al and Preacher had left before Bluey called the men to join him for an early morning brew. The men quickly donned their clothing as protection against the cold.

"Hell Bluey, don't country people ever sleep?"

"Yes Sam, but we don't waste half the day lying in bed. Anyhow the cows reckoned it was time for milking so I hopped up. Thought of waking you up for your first lesson but then decided to start your instruction tonight. Hang on fellas and I'll get you some hot water for a shave." He knocked on the kitchen door and entered when Ghislaine called "Entrez." He emerged with two buckets of steaming water. "Right, use your drinking mugs for shaving and then use those basins over there for a wash. Ghislaine said that if you have any clothing that wants washing leave it in a pile over there. How's that for room service?"

"Bloody great Bluey, but what about breakfast?" Darkie had his priorities sorted out.

"Don't worry, the girls are cooking up some sort of tucker and the little one is the toast maker. We won't starve"

Fifteen minutes later Ghislaine knocked on the door and called them to the kitchen. "Where are the other two?"

"Sorry Ghislaine, I should have told you, there's only eight for breakfast. Al and Preacher left earlier to find our Brigade."

"So what will you all do to fill in the day?"

Darkie couldn't resist the opportunity. "March. That's what we will do. March, march and march. At least that's what we have been told to do. It's up to Bluey."

"We'll do what we're told Darkie. I don't fancy trying to put one over Al Wilson. We leave here in fifteen minutes." Turning to Ghislaine, he said, "You really don't have to go to this trouble, we can wash our gear tonight when we get back."

"Just leave the clothing in the dairy room. We use the large vats for the washing and we also use them for baths in the summertime."

Darkie looked at the three young girls. "That should be interesting. When's bath night?"

Ghislaine laughed. "Any night we don't have visitors, but if you want to have a bath tonight I can put la chaudière on the stove late in the afternoon."

"Put what on the stove?" asked Sam.

"Come on Sam, you're our linguist, remember." chided Mac.

Ghislaine came to Sam's rescue. "A cauldron Monsieur Sam. Don't let them upset you. Your French is good. Well, at least what I've heard so far."

"Right fellas, that's it, time to go to work." Bluey turned to the woman. "I think we'll give the bath a miss tonight Ghislaine. We don't know what Al has planned for us."

* * *

Preacher was waiting when the squad halted outside the farm gate shortly after midday.

"What news Preacher?" demanded Darkie.

"Come inside. Wash up and we'll have lunch. Bully beef, jam, cheese and biscuits. We'll eat in the dairy room."

"You mean the bathroom don't you?" chuckled Darkie.

Preacher looked puzzled. "Bathroom? What bathroom?"

"The dairy is now the bathroom, laundry, the mess hall or recreation space. It goes under many names, and has many uses, but let's eat."

The men gathered around a trestle table that had appeared in the dairy room with ten chairs. On the benches, there were plates and eating utensils.

Preacher walked to the table and picked up a piece of paper. "Sorry fellas, no brew. The ladies have gone out. This note was on this table. Ghislaine said your laundry would be dry by this evening. What's that all about?"

Bluey filled Preacher in on the domestic arrangements. "Come on Preacher, what's happening?" Sam spoke for all the men.

"We found Sergeant King and he took us to a briefing room and explained to Al where the frontline is and what is planned for the Brigade."

"Well? What is?" asked Sam.

Preacher threw his hands up in the air. "I tried to follow what they were saying, but honestly they talked in a language I can't understand. They only use initials not names, and if there are too many initials, then they make up a word out of the initials. They even have their own names for the French towns, and then of course there are places which have been given soldiers' names such as Hell's Corner, etc. It was all double dutch to me except Al was right, there's going to be a big push very soon. The Sergeant reckoned it would happen in about a weeks time, and we're part of it."

"Where's Al?"

"Should be here soon Mac. Your afternoon stroll is cancelled. He went off to the Château to find Captain Solway, our boss. Sorry chaps, but that's all I know."

When their meal was over the men settled down to wait. Bluey retired to a corner to write letters while the others played cards. The light was beginning to fade when a truck pulled up. Preacher and Mick went out to meet it. Al climbed down from the back, and the two elder Pruvost girls descended from the cabin.

"Sorry for being so long, but I saw the girls at the Château and decided to offer them a lift home once they had finished work. It's a fair hike to the Château and with all these soldiers around it's probably not a wise thing for two young ladies to be walking the country lanes."

"Rubbish Monsieur Al. We walk to the Château and back each day, except of course when some kind gentlemen offers a ride in his limousine, and we thank you."

"There's no one in the house Marie. I mean none of your family."

"No Monsieur Preacher. It's Tuesday, and mother, Yvette and grandmère have gone to the markets at Corbie. They will be home soon. Grandmère doesn't walk too quickly these days. Perhaps you would like some water boiled for your cups of tea?"

"Yes please, that would be great. Perhaps Mick and I should go along the Corbie road and help the ladies. What do you think Al?"

The Corporal laughed. "Really Preacher, I bet you used to help little old ladies cross the street back home. Go on, off you go. It'll help our noble image. I'll get the others to unload the truck."

It was dark before the women and their escort arrived and Preacher and Mick rejoined the party.

Sam could not contain his impatience any longer. “Are we on the move Al?”

“Yes Sam, we are on the move. Pay attention. First the good news. You can have another night at the Pruvost Inn. That means another good night’s sleep and probably another good meal. The bad news is that the party finishes at 7:00am tomorrow. We’re moving up to the line. A truck will pick us up here and take us as far as Albert. That’s a real bonus as all transport is heavily committed. From Albert, we’ll march along the road towards Bapaume. The frontline is somewhere this side of Bapaume, and somewhere around there is Brigade headquarters. That’s what we have to find.” He paused and looked at his audience.

“Pack into your kit-bags all the stuff you can live without. We’ll leave the kit-bags in the store in Corbie. Into your knapsack goes everything you need. Basically, that’s underwear, socks and toilet gear. Carry your rifles and see that your ammo pouches are full. There is ammo in those bags plus tins of bully beef and fruit. The runners will try to keep the food up to you but when it gets really rough you’ll need some tins in reserve. There are just two rules. Carry only what you need but remember, you have to carry it. Blankets and groundsheets are first priority. Any questions?”

As usual Sam held his hand up. “Why are we taking rifles and ammo? You said yours was back at Gallipoli, so obviously you haven’t found much use for a gun.”

“True Sammy, but the army says you carry them. When we get to Brigade HQ you can stack them in a corner and forget about them. But you never know, one day we may have to forget about communications and hop into the trenches like infantry. Anyhow you’ll carry rifles to the front. Now get packing. If you have any doubts about whether or not you should take something, ask me.”

There was a knock on the door. Preacher sprang to his feet to open it and Ghislaine entered.

"I hope I'm not interrupting you, but I was wondering what time I should serve dinner. You are going to have dinner with us?" She left the question hanging in the air.

"Thank you Madame Pruvost. We will be eating here this evening." Al rose from the table and picked up two bags from the heap in the corner. "I know you get a few hand-outs from the cooks at the Château, but I did a bit of scavenging myself today and these are for you."

"For me? Thank you Monsieur Al. Your kindness is appreciated."

"Not at all. We're entitled to draw rations and I thought the goods available at the Château were probably better than at our cook-house. Oh yes, one other thing." Al handed the bags to Preacher and returned to the heap of bags. He lifted a small box from the pile. "Just a small token of thanks Madame, from the group." he said handing the box to Ghislaine.

"A present?" she beamed. "We don't seem to give or receive presents very often these days. Thank you." She turned to leave. "Oh dear, I nearly forgot what I came here for. Would dinner in an hour be all right?"

"Perfect Madame. Preacher, would you take those bags through to the kitchen for Ghislaine?"

"Yes, right, certainly Al." stuttered Preacher.

When the door had closed the men turned to Al. "A present for the lovely lady? What a charmer! You'd better watch out Al, Preacher will be getting jealous."

"Our Preacher's a bit of a lady's man is he?"

Bluey shook his head. "No Al. My impression is that he's very shy when ladies are around, but he sure as hell has been hit by cupid's arrow here. But don't tease him, he is confused enough. What was the present?"

"Oh, just a couple of bottles of very good wine. Seems our Colonel had a whole heap of presentation packs made up to give to his friends, so I thought we might borrow one. The old boy won't miss it."

"Good one Al. Perhaps Ghislaine will share the wine with us at dinner."

"Perhaps Darkie, but you won't get a lot if it's shared between fifteen."

The door opened and Preacher rejoined the group. "It's all hands to the galley in there. We'll dine like princes tonight."

Al didn't smile. "Enjoy it. God only knows when next you'll be able to sit down at a clean table to have good food. Now get cracking with your packing. I want to see each of you fully booted and spurred with all your gear before we go into dinner."

For the next hour, the men packed and repacked. Al Wilson carefully inspected each man and his load. "Damn it Sam. You won't last five miles with a pack like that. What in the blazes have you got in it?"

Sam removed his back pack and emptied its contents on the floor. Al watched in amazement.

"Sam, I said a couple of tins of food for an emergency, not a full week's supply. Stick a tin in each pocket of your tunic, then they won't dig into your back and cripple you. Now repack that lot and remember it's cold out there."

* * *

The meal was most enjoyable and Ghislaine did offer the wine to her guests. She was surprised when Al, Preacher, Bluey and Sam declined the offer, opting instead for a fruit drink made by the girls.

"You somehow don't fit the image I had of Australians." she said.

"Really Ghislaine. And just what was your image of Australians?" asked Al.

Ghislaine paused as if to conjure an image in her mind. "Strange isn't it. Before the war we knew very little about your country. Even now, all we know is what we have learnt from you and from the Australian officers at the Château. When we were told that the Australians were coming to fight in France, the British told us stories about what a wild lot you were. Real ruffians from a hard country. So, I guess that's what I expected to see when I opened the door. A group of big, unshaven men somewhat the worse for drink. Instead, there was this young baby-faced boy asking for lodgement in French, but with an accent that made him difficult to understand. No wonder Madame Pruvost came in and said there were some strange foreigners at the gate." Everyone looked at Sam who blushed deeply. Ghislaine leant across the table and patted his hand. "It's not true Monsieur Sam. Your French is good. I was teasing."

"So now you know differently Madame?" asked Preacher.

"Oui. Now I know differently. Are you an average cross-section of Australians?"

"You can't count Darkie, Ghislaine. He's a New Zealander. They're different again." said Sam.

"So Monsieur Darkie. You are different. Please tell us about New Zealand and then each of you can tell us about the part of Australia you come from. That way we will learn about both countries."

"Oh hell Ghislaine. There's not much for me to tell."

"I don't believe that Monsieur Darkie, but perhaps I can bribe you with another glass of wine. What do you say?"

"I'd say it was blackmail Ghislaine, but I'm not going to fight it."

And so, for the first time since the men had been together, Darkie spoke of his homeland. The others followed, some spoke briefly, others at length. Each man reaching back into his memories to find the good things that came readily to mind. They spoke of friends and family, of schools, sports, outings and work.

"It all sounds so wonderful, so beautiful." enthused Marie.

"Perhaps Marie but there is always another side to any story and these boys have concentrated on the good side of life back home." Al had not volunteered his story. "I'm sure that everything said tonight is true, but slightly biased. We have our problems back home, problems that seem insignificant when we see what is happening here."

"And you Al? You have said nothing about yourself."

"No Nicole. It's late and we have to be off early tomorrow. My story can wait."

The mood changed, the laughter had gone.

"What time are you leaving Monsieur Al?"

"Transport will be here at seven o'clock."

"Very good. Breakfast will be served at six thirty. I know we can't ask you where you are going but everyone in Corbie is talking about the big battle. May God go with you and take care of you."

"Thank you Ghislaine."

Then from the old lady sitting at the head of the table came a short rapidly spoken sentence in French. The men looked to Ghislaine.

"Mother said good luck and make sure you kill lots of Germans."

The men stood as one and bowed slightly towards the old lady.

"Thank you Madame. That is our intention." Al looked at Ghislaine.

"No translation is necessary Al, she understands."

ONLY TWO DAYS IN YOUR LIFE

The mood at breakfast next morning was in stark contrast to the levity of the previous night. Bluey produced a bundle of letters which Ghislaine promised to mail. The sound of a truck sent the men scurrying to collect their gear. As they climbed onto the back of the truck the three girls handed each man a small parcel of food. "Your lunch," explained Marie. "You won't find many cafes the other side of Albert."

"Merçi beaucoup," chorused the men, and all laughed at their appalling efforts to imitate the French tongue.

Ghislaine took Al's hand and held it. "Monsieur Al. Please bring them back to us. This house is your billet for the rest of the war. We have come to like Australians."

"Thank you Madame. They don't know how fortunate they were to find such kindness and comfort. I'll try to bring them back for a big party when this war is over."

"We would enjoy that Monsieur Al. We would indeed. And pray God that the day is not too far away."

Al withdrew his hand from hers. “We all pray for that.” Turning quickly, he climbed in the truck and motioned to the driver to move on. The men gave three cheers for their hostesses and the women blew them farewell kisses.

“Hey Preacher, you had better watch out. I think Ghislaine has taken a shine to Al.”

“Shut up Darkie.” The tone indicated that Preacher didn’t want to talk and his mood was mirrored by the others. This was the day they’d been looking forward to, and dreading. Tonight they’d be in the line. The truck came to a halt outside the YMCA in Albert.

“Right fellas climb down. You have just got time for a hot brew in the ‘Y’ while I check up on the latest.” Al said.

“Good news and bad news men.” said Al as he approached their table. “The good news is that Jerry is pulling back. The bad news is that the thaw is setting in.”

“Bad news? Surely that’s good news? It’ll be great to see the sun and to feel warm again.”

“Great Preacher for birds, bees and flowers, but not for soldiers. Up to now the ground has been frozen, but the thaw will add to all our other problems. Now we’ll have to contend with mud. Real mud. Mud like you’ve never seen before. Step off a duckboard and you just sink out of sight. I’ve seen a horse swallowed up by it. So, the lesson for today is, once we get off the roads, stay on the boards.”

“Mud, cold, Germans, machine guns, shells, snipers. Bloody lovely place.”

“You forgot a few things Darkie. Now fellas don’t start thinking the war’s over because I don’t believe half of what I hear. If Jerry is pulling back there’ll be a reason, and I don’t think he’s quitting. Anyhow that’s for the Generals to figure out not us poor soldiers. Come on, we’ve a way to go.”

Each man strapped on his equipment and slung his rifle over his shoulder. Al checked each man's gear and then pointed to the north east.

"That's the way men. That's the way to Berlin, but unfortunately there are unfriendly Germans in the way. Form up in single file. Keep about two paces behind the man in front of you. Keep your eyes peeled, especially for trucks and horse-drawn limbers. They tend to skid if they're going at any sort of speed. If you do have to jump to get out of their way, look where you're jumping. Pete King expects me to arrive at HQ with all present and correct. No talking, save your breath and energy. Let's go."

The Corporal wheeled around and set off. The others formed up in single file and followed. There was no conversation. Vehicles moved in both directions. Most were trucks, limbers or wagons, although an occasional staff car wound its way through the congestion. The men were constantly forced from the road to allow vehicles to pass. The drivers moving northward looked worried and ignored the men on foot. The southbound drivers were cheerful and usually called 'Good luck mates,' or 'You'll be sorry,' to the signallers. Their relief at returning from the front was obvious.

On both sides of the road lay the remnants of smashed wagons and the carcasses of horses. Every now and then they saw a small area of land planted with crude crosses, the resting place of men whose luck had run out. And everywhere was the smell; the awful smell of death.

Al Wilson spent some time walking alongside each of his charges. It was a time to assess their feelings and to make sure that each man had focused on the job ahead. He answered questions and pointed out landmarks. This was country over which he had marched, run, and crawled, the previous year, but if the memories of those hideous days haunted him, he gave no indication.

An hour later the group stopped at piles of rubble. Al found a clear space in the ruins. “Welcome to Pozières fellows, or at least what was Pozières. We’ll take a break, and have a bite to eat. Bluey, you and Erik get a fire going and we’ll have a brew. One thing about Pozieres is that there’s plenty of firewood.”

The men scouted around and soon had a fire blazing.

“What was Pozières?”

“A beautiful country town Preacher. This is what war does. A total heap of rubbish and ruin. Once, not so long ago, people lived here. Men, women and children. But last July and August we had one hell of a scrap with Jerry and both sides pounded the village into dust. It was a hard slog and we suffered badly. Just up the road we’ll be passing the Windmill. Not that there’s much to see there, but it has a place in history. We lost over twenty thousand men around here in just seven weeks, but we gave Jerry a hiding.”

Sam pointed to one of the many plots of land covered with crosses. “So that’s why there are so many cemeteries?”

“They’re not really cemeteries. They’re burial grounds. The chaplains try to find a space behind the line to bury the dead, and I guess, when this is all over, they’ll move the bodies to proper cemeteries. Mind you, there are thousands that don’t have a grave or even a name.”

“Shit Al, can’t we talk about something more cheerful?”

“We can Darkie, but death, bodies, graves are now an everyday part of your life. That stench you can smell is death. You’ll never get it out of your nostrils while you’re here, and you’ll never forget it. This is an unreal world you’ve entered. But for you, it’s now the real world, your only world, and will be until we march back down that road. Don’t try to ignore it. It won’t go away.”

Bluey, anxious to change the subject, asked. “Speaking of the road Al, surely it’s dangerous to have all that traffic on the one road? Jerry could cause all sorts of havoc if he got the range of that road. It’s packed with vehicles.”

"Bluey, you're beginning to think like a soldier. But the simple fact is, that there's no other way to the front. In summer, we would stay off the roads and cross the fields, but right now, they're just seas of mud. That's what stopped our drive forward last year. In winter, you can only move along a good, well-built road. Sure, Jerry knows about it, and soon you'll see what happens when he lobs a few shells in amongst the horses. It's not a pretty sight, but there's no alternative. There are thousands of men up ahead and they need food and ammunition. And of course, the artillery need shells, tons and tons of shells. It's a huge job to move all the stuff needed but somehow those blokes and their horses do it. Jerry knows about it, and when he can, he makes life difficult for the transports."

"How far do we have to go to reach wherever it is we're going?" asked Preacher.

"About four miles to the line. It's a pretty well-established front because it's where the weather stopped us last year, and both sides have been well entrenched for some months. We'll pass through the artillery very soon and then on to Brigade headquarters. Right, let's move out." He held up his hand to hold their attention as they stood up. "Now listen real good. If I yell 'down', then get down, and get down fast."

"Why?"

"Sam, do you always have to have a question. We're in range of Jerry's guns. Every now and then he'll lob one over. You can tell by the sound if it's going over or to one side. You can also tell if it's going to land nearby. That's when it's best to get down flat on your face. Better still, dive into a shell hole but get down. You got that?"

Sam nodded. "Yeah, I've got that."

"Good, now cheer up, it's not the end of the world. Come on, stay about three to four yards clear of each other and watch me. Let's go."

The men re-adjusted their gear and set off after the cheerful young man.

"It's all a game to him." muttered Darkie. "I think he actually enjoys all this killing stuff."

"No Darkie, I think not. I think he's putting on a bold front for our benefit." replied Skipper. "Still he's been there and survived, so I guess that's good enough reason to follow his lead."

"Agreed, Skip, but then we don't really have to make a choice do we? I mean, what else can we do?"

Skip grinned. "That about sums it up Darkie. What else can we do?"

The conversation halted as a noise like a rushing freight train reached them. The column halted. The noise came to an abrupt stop and several seconds later the sound of an explosion reached them. Al pointed to the west.

"Long-range gun. Nuisance value mainly, except if he lands nearby. It's the medium guns that cause the trouble, especially if they lay down a barrage. Look over there, you can see our guns. Well dug in. Fritz is probably trying to stir them up but he could easily train onto the road. So, I think we'll leave it here and start off across the fields. There is a pegged route leading to the artillery lines. Come on."

Al veered to the left and set off across the field. The going was wet and the men found it hard going to lift one foot after the other from the clinging mud. "Down." The cry from the corporal startled them all but without hesitating, each threw himself flat on the wet ground. The scream of the shell became much louder and the men felt the blast of air from the explosion. "Up. Keep moving." came the command.

To their right the smoke from the explosion was drifting away from the roadway. Traffic was halted by a large crater.

"Holy smoke Mac! Did you see that?" Bluey spluttered.

"Yes Bluey. Are you thinking what I'm thinking?" Mac answered.

"Probably. I reckon that if we'd stayed on the road we'd have been about where that shell landed."

"Yeah. Do you think Al knew that was going to happen?"

Bluey looked at the retreating back of Al Wilson. "How could he? Maybe experience told him there was a pattern. Anyway, he made the right move at the right time. If he's that clever, he'll do me."

They tramped after their leader. Soon they found themselves passing through the artillery lines and marvelled at the long lines of guns.

"Keep moving soldiers." warned one of the gunners. "Jerry usually gives us a few to keep us on our toes about this time of day and then we repay the compliment. It gets rather noisy and messy."

The men moved on and soon found themselves on a wooden duckboard path. Al stopped and pointed. "Note the wires. We try to keep them as close to the duckboards as possible. These wires run to the artillery from HQ, and to the battalions, where they usually have a spotter. If you have to run them, try and keep on the boards otherwise you could drown in the mud. It's not too bad at the moment because of the freeze, but the thaw has started and until it dries out the mud is a real trap." Any further words were drowned out as the guns commenced firing. Although the shells were high above them, the men instinctively ducked.

Now the scenery changed, dugouts appearing on all sides, with men moving about in large numbers.

"This is the reserve area for the battalions in the trenches," explained Al. "HQ will be somewhere around here and so should Pete King."

"Don't you know where HQ is?"

Al gave Sam a very old-fashioned look. “No I don’t. I know where it was last month but Jerry has this awful habit of rearranging the landscape and things get moved. But don’t you worry, you’re home safe and sound. Here comes Peter King now.”

The burly Sergeant approached the group, stopped and surveyed the men before him. “Bloody hell Wilson, did you crawl to get here? Look at yourselves.”

“We had to duck an eight-inch brick back there. Getting muddy seemed preferable to getting killed.” replied the laconic Corporal.

“Fair enough. Right, follow me.” They followed him to a dugout that was carved into the side of a bank. Sandbags were stacked on the roof and sides. Once inside, the men shed their gear and inspected their new home.

Their quarters were far from spacious, and very remote from luxury. Six crudely-made double bunks, three on each side provided the sleeping accommodation. A table fashioned out of crates took up much of the centre aisle and various boxes served as stools.

“Find a seat and pay attention!” The Sergeant spoke quietly but with authority. “You’re a damn lucky lot. The mob before you spent a lot of time and energy making this dugout comfortable. You can look surprised, but believe me this is comfort. It’s dry and you don’t have to sleep on the ground. Very important. However, I doubt if you’ll be here long enough to fall into the wicked ways of the slothful.”

“We’re moving out?” Al Wilson asked.

“Seems that way. Patrols to the north have found abandoned trenches. Jerry has pulled back in some areas but not all. Anyhow, the word is that the Brigade is going to move to take Bapaume, so there’s hardly any time for training you lot. What I intend to do is this. Starting from now, I’ll take a pair of you out and we’ll run all the lines. Al, you’ll take another pair and do the same. Two of you will man the switchboard at HQ. Al will draw up a roster.

Tomorrow morning, Al and I will repeat the exercise with two more pairs. The odd one left over will be Al's running mate, so I'll leave him to Al. Now remember, what we're doing now is showing you around. Look for landmarks and learn the lie of the land. Jerry is still out there, especially the snipers and the machine gun posts. Get careless and he'll knock you over."

"Now a quick word about our organisation. We have three sections of signallers. You are No.3 Section. Captain Solway commands the three sections with Lieutenant Melroy as his second in command. I am the Sergeant for the three sections and each section has a corporal in charge. The three sections are kept apart as far as possible so that one hit doesn't wipe us out completely. Two sections work the front and one is rested. Now as we go around, Al and I will explain everything in more detail. You will run into men from No.2 Section as you go around and there'll be two of them in HQ for tonight to show you the ropes. As from 8:00am tomorrow, No.2 Section will be withdrawn and you'll take its place. Any questions?"

Before Sam could speak two officers entered the dugout and the men scrambled to their feet. Sergeant King saluted.

"At ease. Please sit down. I'm Captain Solway and this is Lieutenant Melroy. I suppose I should start off by saying welcome, but it seems inappropriate to welcome anyone to this place. However, I'm glad you're here and unlike so many of the new arrivals, I do know a lot about you. Sergeant Phil Reynolds has written and told me some stories about your training. I hope to hear more from you in the weeks ahead. My advice to you is listen to what Sergeant King and Corporal Wilson have to say and learn from them. I have only one rule and that is: 'Never let the infantry down.' No matter how rough it gets for us, they get it rougher, and we know from bitter experience what disasters can befall our troops if communications fail. That is why you're here and that's what you'll do. You'll be seeing plenty of myself and Lieutenant

Melroy during the next few months. It's my intention to keep you as fully informed as possible on what's going on, but sometimes that's difficult because no one knows for sure. Good luck. Oh Wilson, would you please step outside for a moment?" The Captain turned and left the room followed by the Lieutenant and Al Wilson.

Sergeant King looked at his watch. "You two nip over to the cookhouse and get a couple of kettles of brew. It's straight across the square, you'll see the smoke."

Darkie and Erik moved off to carry out his bidding.

"Now, have you been detailed off in pairs?"

"Not officially, Sergeant." Preacher looked around the group. "We do seem to have paired up during training, and unless someone wants to change, perhaps it would be best if we stayed that way."

The Sergeant nodded. "Fine by me. Who drew the short straw?"

"Short straw? I don't follow."

"Well, the odd one out wins Al Wilson as his partner. That's the short straw. Al Wilson does things, goes places, normal signallers avoid. The infantry call him: 'the man the Germans can't kill', but that title doesn't apply to his partners."

"Oh!" Preacher looked at Bluey. "Bluey, you've been the odd one out up till now, but I reckon we should forget the past and draw names from a hat. It seems the fair thing to do."

Bluey shook his head. "Forget it Preacher. After seeing Al Wilson lead us away from that shell today, he'll do me for a partner any time."

"Shell. What shell?"

Preacher explained to the Sergeant what had happened. Sergeant King nodded. "Not surprised. That's about true to form for Al. I don't know what drives him but whatever it is, I wish I could get some of it. He can be very spooky at times. Ah, a brew at last."

All gathered around to get a mug of tea. Al Wilson reappeared and the Sergeant asked, “And what was that all about, or do you and the Captain have secrets these days?”

Al grinned. “You know how I told you about the billet these blokes found and how it didn’t seem quite right. Well, when I went to the Château I ran into Captain Solway and I told him. As two of the girls worked at the Château I reckoned someone would know the background. Captain Solway made some enquiries and found out about the Pruvost family.”

“So?” Everyone was listening intently.

“It’s all pretty simple really. Pruvost senior was a high-ranking officer in the French Army. General staff and all that. He was killed in 1914. His son, Ghislaine’s husband, joined up as an officer when war broke out and he was killed in 1915. It seems some French soldiers were billeted at the farm and played up badly, so the place was put out of bounds to Frenchmen. Next a bunch of Tommies were offered a billet, and they too thought the girls were fair game. More trouble. So, the British put the farm off limits to their troops. Seems there is a notice putting the farm out of bounds to all servicemen, but this mob either didn’t see it, or ignored it. They asked for a billet and were given one.”

“I swear there wasn’t any notice.” protested Preacher.

“Perhaps there was, perhaps someone had taken it down. Anyhow Captain Solway said Madame had not protested to the authorities so it seems there’s no problem. End of story.”

“You mean we can go back?”

“Yes Sam, I suppose we can, but when that will be, who knows.” The Corporal looked at the Sergeant. “Well Sarge, what now?”

“It seems you have a new partner Al. The red-headed bloke.”

Al looked at Bluey. “Well Mr Dowson, what think you of that?”

“No Mr Wilson, what I think doesn’t matter, it’s what you think that counts.”

“Well I hope you’re a quick learner.”

"And I hope you're a quick runner Corporal, because I don't intend to loiter around the paddocks."

"Fair enough. Right, Skip and Mac, you go with the Sarge. Jacko and Sam come with me to Brigade HQ. When I come back, I'll take Preacher and Mick out for a look-see. The rest of you settle in and act as runners to the cookhouse. Evening meal is to be here at 5:00pm, then we'll sort out the rest of the roster. Put your rifles in the corner over there and make sure they're safe."

"Right Al." The Sergeant stood up. "I'll bring these two back by 5:00pm and I'll eat with you tonight. It'll give me a chance to get acquainted with you boys."

"Hang on, I nearly forgot." Al dived into a bag hanging by the door. He held out a pile of blue and white armbands. "Here put these on. From now until you leave the line, you will wear these at all times. It's important that people know you're a signaller."

"Why?"

"Sam, you never fail me. Signallers sometimes have to go where there are restrictions on movement. At other times, you may come upon infantrymen who don't recognise you as one of their battalion and they may assume you're an intruder. That could be fatal. Don't ever let me see you moving about without an arm band. Right Sarge, let's go."

* * *

That evening all the section gathered in the dugout for the evening meal. Those who had been out on their familiarisation tour were relieved, and those yet to go were apprehensive.

"Al."

"Yes Sam?"

"Do you ever get frightened?" It was a question everyone wanted to ask.

"Frightened? Of course you'll be frightened. Only idiots and machines don't get frightened, but you must conquer fear or you'll not be able to do your job. My way of dealing with fear is to recall an old Arab saying: There are only two days in a man's life. One day is the day he is going to die. On that day, no matter how careful he is, no matter where he hides, death will come and claim him. The other day is the day he isn't going to die, and on that day no matter how foolish he is, no matter what risks he takes, death will not claim him. So, each time I get called out on a job I say to myself - well, let's see what day it is."

"And it works?"

"Sam, it works for me. We're all going to die one day, but unless we take our own life, we don't get to pick that day. It's unknown. Today, tomorrow, next year, perhaps in sixty years' time. You don't know when, and you can't control fate. So why worry about it? Just do your job and see what fate has in store for you."

"I'll try."

"Sam, I know you will. All of you will, and I am damned pleased to be your Corporal. Right, let's get some sleep. Early start tomorrow."

* * *

The next morning, Al took Bluey on his familiarisation tour. Just before they came to the top of a slight rise Al stopped. "So far Bluey we've been moving below the skyline so the danger has only been from shells. Once we top that rise, we'll be visible to the other side. The baddies. So, do exactly what I tell you to do, and do it fast. We don't run unless we have to; this wet ground exhausts you too quickly. We just move along. Got it?"

"Lead on. I'm right behind you."

The two moved to the crest and continued following the telephone wire. Suddenly there was a whistling sound just above their heads.

"Sniper!" exclaimed Al. "Don't look up or around, keep moving at the same pace. Be ready to act when I tell you." The next shot clipped the ground a yard in front of the corporal. "Look behind you and then start running as fast as you can."

Bluey glanced behind as instructed and then broke into a sprint. He soon overtook Al and then faltered as the next bullet landed just ahead of him.

"Keep going, get into that crater." yelled Al.

Both men landed at the bottom of the crater at the same time.

"Relax. We're safe." the corporal laughed. "Jeez, you can run. Up to now I've been the ace sprinter of the Brigade but you left me for dead."

"Not a very appropriate choice of words Corporal."

"No, I suppose not."

"What was all that, 'look back' before running stuff. The shot was ahead of us."

"Precisely mate. The first went over our heads. Had we ducked, the sniper would've known that he had gone high. His second was in front of us, so we looked back and started to run. He then decides he has not made enough correction for our forward movement so he lays off further. You nearly buggered it up by running so fast. You nearly caught up with his third shot which should've been well ahead. Anyhow, we're safe now."

"We still have to get out of this crater and he's still out there."

"No, he's given away his position. He'll move out. How do you feel, scared?"

Bluey thought for a moment. "No. I don't think I'm frightened, more like excited. It's exciting isn't it?"

The young Corporal looked straight into his companion's eyes. "Exciting? Yes, I remember my first job at Gallipoli. Yes, it was exciting, and you'll find it continues to be an exciting game until you see your first man killed, and then you know it's not a game, and then you get scared."

"Perhaps I'm scared already but am kidding myself that I'm not."

"Perhaps. Come on, let's have a peep at the scenery and work out how we're going to get out of here." The two men peered across the field towards the German lines. "I reckon he was in that clump of trees over there. What do you think?"

"Probably. There's not much cover around. I wish I had a rifle. I'd stir him up if he's still around."

Al looked at his companion. "You reckon you could hit one of those trees at this range?"

"Easy with a good gun."

"Well you haven't, and we don't carry them. They get in the way and slow you down. Colonel Payne says signallers shouldn't carry rifles. He believes only the infantry know how to shoot."

Bluey continued to stare at the trees. "Jeez Al, there he is!" A figure was running from the trees. "Damn, I could've knocked him off if I had a gun."

"Mate, that's a moving target a long way off. Granted you might have been able to scare him with a bullet around his ears, but to hit him, would have to be one hell of a shot with a lot of luck thrown in."

"Al, if I can find a good rifle, can I carry it? At least let me try. If it hampers my work I'll toss it away, but I feel so bloody naked out here and unable to hit back."

"You're not supposed to be hitting back. Your job is to keep the lines open, but the good book says you're a soldier and the Army has issued you with a gun, so I can't say no. But I believe we carry enough gear now, and another nine pounds won't help. And they are awkward to carry. Still, I can't say no, but believe me if your work as a signaller starts to suffer, I'll soon trade you in for another mate."

"Fair enough. I want to give it a try, but if it's a problem, I'll drop it. Now what?"

"Come on, let's get home. We'll call in on the western battalion and show them on the map where our friend was hiding. They may send out one of their own snipers to try and knock him off."

The two men scrambled out of the crater and started off for the battalion headquarters. As they approached, Al pointed out the various exits and entrances from the complex of trenches.

"Always let them know when you're leaving or coming in. Otherwise you may find an Australian bullet in your guts." He called out and was answered from the wall of sandbags. The two men entered the fortifications to be greeted by a solidly built infantry Sergeant.

"Al Wilson, I might have guessed. I've always said you sigs are mad, and nothing is ever going to change my mind. Who's your mate?"

"This is Bluey Dowson. Bluey, meet Bert Phillips, not a bad bloke considering he's infantry. We go back a long way."

The Sergeant stuck out his hand. "New to the lines are you?" he said as they shook hands.

"Yes Sergeant. Corporal Wilson has been showing me around."

"Showing you around? You sound like a tourist. Do you know anything about this bloke?" he drawled, pointing at the Corporal.

"Not much, but twice he's saved my life, so that's good enough for me."

The Sergeant turned to Al. "Been playing God again Al? You know, one day they'll nail you. You take too many risks."

"No Bert, I take no more risks than I have to in order to do my job."

"Bah! I've heard that before. Anyhow how's things out there, all quiet?"

"Very quiet. No shelling, or very little. No machine guns, just a nasty sniper."

"It's quiet all right. We just heard that the Tommies to our left have found the trenches opposite them abandoned. It's hard to believe, but all the signs are there. Jerry is pulling back without a fight. We're expecting to have a go at him very soon, but this damned mud will make life difficult."

"Maybe the Germans have had enough?"

"Young man, that last statement brands you as a new boy. Jerry is tough, mean and very nasty. He's been sitting over there all winter getting ready for the spring and he hasn't been preparing for surrender. He's up to something, and it's my bet that it'll be something very unpleasant. Now Al, what's this about a sniper? Did you get a fix on his hideaway?"

"Yeah Bert. The boy here saw him. Got a map handy?"

"Collins," roared the Sergeant. "Get your arse out here with a map."

A soldier appeared from a nearby dugout with a rolled map in his hand.

"G'day Jock." said Bluey.

"Well I'll be...Bluey Dowson! So, we meet again." Jock Collins advanced with his hand outstretched.

"Seems like introductions are not required." said the Sergeant.

"I met Bluey during his training but I don't think I know you corporal."

"Al Wilson. So, you met Bluey during training?"

Jock laughed. "Yeah, he caused me great distress. He captured me and made the training staff hopping mad."

"Jock is one of our battalion snipers." explained Bert. "Jock, these two have just been having an adventure with a Jerry sniper. Thought you might stake out the place just in case he comes back to the same spot."

"Fair enough. He's lucky Bluey didn't have a rifle."

"Why's that?" asked Al.

Jock looked from Al to Bluey and back again. "You obviously don't know, but Bluey is a top shot. One of the best in Victoria."

"Ah come off it Jock." Bluey looked uncomfortable.

"How come you're a sig if you're so good with a rifle?" asked the Sergeant.

"It's a long story, but I'm a sig and pleased to be one."

The Sergeant snorted. “You may change your mind after tripping around with Al Wilson for a while. Now where’s that sniper hiding?” He unrolled the map.

“He was holed up there.” said Al, pointing to a spot on the map. “We saw him decamp and run off, but he wouldn’t know that we’d spotted him.”

The infantry Sergeant scratched his chin as he nodded. “Fair enough. Over to you Jock. He might come back.”

“I’ll have a look around Sarge. If he does, I’ll be waiting.”

“Right, we’ll be on our way.” Al paused before moving off. “By the way Bert, dead-eye dick here wants to carry a rifle.”

“He what? Sigs don’t carry rifles Al. The Colonel doesn’t approve. Only real soldiers carry weapons, or so the Colonel says.”

“I know what the Colonel says Bert, but the Army says they can, and they are issued to them. If Bluey wants to play cops and robbers that’s his affair, but it just occurred to me that Jock here might have access to a range of better rifles than the ones we have.”

The Sergeant looked at the sniper. “Well?”

Jock Collins nodded. “Yeah, our rifles are special and I have a spare. Bluey can borrow it for a trial. It’s not a problem.”

“Right, you two sort that out. I’ve got other things to do besides gab to crazy signallers. See you Al, and keep your head down.”

“You too Bert. Come on Bluey. You and your mate can get together later. We’re due back at Brigade.” The four men gave a casual wave of farewell and parted company.

* * *

For the next few days the men of No.3 Section manned the switchboard, ran the wires and delivered messages. They slowly adapted to the fear, noise, smell and discomfort of trench warfare. Each man became infested with lice and the constant irritation caused by the vermin, their ever-wet clothing and lack of sleep caused tempers to fray. The weather became more friendly in the skies but its effect on the ground was devastating. The mud clung to their boots, their clothing and their skins. The miserable life was only made bearable by the rumours that it would soon be all over on the Western Front. Patrols into no-man's land had found deserted trenches and it was evident that a move was afoot.

The expected drive forward was not heralded by the usual heavy bombardment as the battalion moved forward to occupy vacated trenches. By the end of February, the town of Bapaume was under siege. The men were elated. The tide had changed and was now ebbing away from them. It was a phrase often quoted by the politicians and Generals.

"Yeah, it's ebbing all right." said Sergeant King, "But the idiots should know that a tide only recedes so far and then it starts to flow back."

"Yer reckon Sarge?" Darkie was more than happy to believe that the Germans were retreating all the way to Berlin. "They're on the run now and nothing can stop us."

The Sergeant shook his head. "Doesn't make sense. Why sit there all through the winter and then quit? No, Jerry has a plan and we'll soon find out what it is."

By mid-March, Bapaume was in Allied hands and the cautious advance continued. The heavy layer of mud made it difficult for the guns to be moved forward. However, the Brigades pressed ahead.

By the beginning of April, the men could clearly see the imposing defences of the Hindenburg Line and they knew that this was where the ebb of the German tide would cease. From now on they would have to push the enemy back.

It was relatively quiet, a lull before the main event, when Section No.3 suffered its first casualty. Mac and Skipper had been running a line broken by shell fire. They'd mended the line, tested it and reported that they were returning to headquarters.

The men in the trenches saw one figure racing across the ground as fast as he could in the mud. It was an exhausted Mac who literally fell into the trench. "Skip's been hit." he gasped. "A machine gun got us on the way back. I think he's gone. I looked back and there was blood everywhere. He didn't answer me and then the gun started again and I took off."

"Where Mac? Come on, pull yourself together. Think. Where?" Al Wilson's usual happy countenance was now one of grim determination.

Mac pulled himself up and looked over the parapet. "See that tree split down the middle? We'd just passed that when they opened up. Christ Al, we have to do something. We have to try to rescue him."

Al shook his head. "No Mac. That's just what Jerry wants us to do. He's waiting out there."

"But Skip, he might only be wounded. We must help him."

"No Mac. Skip is dead. After they missed you, they would return to Skip and plug a few more rounds in him to make sure. That's the way it is. Sorry fellows, but it had to happen to one of us sooner or later. He was a nice bloke, but it was his day."

There was a silence in the dugout before Sam asked the question. "Al, what happens now? I mean, who recovers the body for burial?"

Al waited a while before answering. He chose his words carefully. "Once the area is reasonably safe, and I stress the word 'reasonably', stretcher bearers move out and pick up the wounded. I say 'reasonably' because at times wearing a Red Cross armband is no protection. They also, if possible, recover bodies and these are laid aside near a first aid post. When time and circumstances permit, a chaplain, with a team of blokes detailed off as the burial party, will bury the dead. However, many bodies are not recovered and many that are recovered are unidentifiable. These are put in a common grave. Skip is dead, don't think otherwise.

If he's in an area of soft mud his body will already be committed to the earth. If not, a stretcher party will collect his remains as I described. Now listen, and listen very carefully. We know that the area where Skip went down is covered by a machine gun. They would have seen Mac and Skip at work, and they know a line runs along there. Now what they're hoping is that the line will be cut again, and we'll have to run it. That may happen. If it does and I'm not here, the two who run the line must remember one thing. Do not get too close together, make life difficult for Jerry. Use the shell-hole to shell-hole method. Change direction often. If you see Skip's body ignore it. Many men have died trying to help a dead mate. Have you all got that?"

"Do we have to run the line in the daylight? It would be safer at night."

"Perhaps, Preacher. Sometimes it's safer, sometimes more dangerous. The single factor is, what do the infantry want? If they need that line, we continue to run it and repair it at any cost, and I mean at any cost. The infantry knows the risks you blokes take on their behalf and they won't ask you to run a line they don't need. But if they need it, we give it to them. Right. I'm off to report in that we're a man short but I don't expect a replacement for a while. Mac, you'll work with Bluey and I'll spend some time running with the others to check on their progress. One last word of advice. If Bluey tries to take on the German Army with that pea shooter of his, knock him senseless. And you Bluey, see if you can compose a letter to Skip's mum and dad. Captain Solway will write the usual formal letter, but they'll be comforted if they hear from one of his mates."

A BLOODY MESS

The attention of the Australians was now turned towards the town of Bullecourt, a fortress in the infamous Hindenburg Line. The engineers had worked relentlessly repairing roads, or building new ones, to get the guns in place and the stores forward. The weather continued to warm and the successes of the past three weeks had raised the hopes of the battle-weary troops. To them the Hindenburg Line was just another obstacle to be overcome. Break the Hindenburg and Germany is finished, was the freely-given advice from the Generals.

It was an excited Jacko who burst into the dugout late one evening. "We're going to get tanks for the big push." he gasped. "I've just heard it over the line."

"Careful Jacko. You could get shot for repeating information that came over the lines from HQ." counselled Preacher.

"Yeah I know Preacher, but I'm safe with you guys. Hell, we hear and see all that secret stuff every day, but this is big. Tanks! Jerry will shit himself when he sees them charging down on the bloody Hindenberg."

“Tanks!” repeated Preacher. “What do you think Al?”

“Think? I don’t get paid to think Preacher. Nor do you. If tanks are the answer to all our problems, then I only ask why didn’t they show up a couple of years ago and spare us all this bloody slaughter. But if Jerry is going to be beaten by tanks, then bring them on. I’ll vote for anything that will end this war.”

Just then the door curtain parted and Lieutenant Melroy entered. The men stood up and Al saluted.

“At ease men. The big push is on, first thing tomorrow. Wilson, I want you to organise one pair to go forward with each battalion. You go with the western battalion and I’ll go with the eastern one. You’ll have to run out lines as you go but the general staff must be kept informed. Two pair are to remain in HQ ready to run the line if communication is lost. By the way, we’ll have tanks in advance so it should be a breeze. All the section are to be in HQ by 3:00am. Men, this is it! The big one, and we’re to be part of it. Grab some sleep for now. I’ll see you in HQ.” Returning the corporal’s salute, the young officer left the dugout.

“See, I told you so. Tanks. Even Lieutenant Melroy says it’ll be a breeze.”

“Perhaps Jacko, but it seems to me we had tanks last year at Pozières and the Germans didn’t run away.”

“That was last year.” said Preacher. “Maybe they’ve improved them.”

“Sure Al. These will be the deluxe model. Bullecourt here we come.” Jacko would not be deterred from his vision of the march to Germany.

“Calm down Jacko. Just remember your job and leave the fighting to the infantry and your precious tanks. Right, now let’s see how we’re going to play this. Bluey, you and Mac go with Lieutenant Melroy, and Darkie, you and Erik come with me. Preacher, you take the rest to HQ and act as switchboard operators and backup to the advance party. I won't ask if there are any questions because I know that Sam will have one."

The men laughed at what was now a common joke.

"Yes Al. Can we ride on these tanks? It should be easier than walking."

"Well I don't think the tank men would want passengers, and I imagine every German gun and rifle will be aimed at the beasts in the hope of stopping them. It wouldn't be too comfortable sitting on the outside. And if tanks drive over your lines they make a bloody awful mess. They tend to pick up the wire and munch it up in big heaps. So, try to stay away from them if you can."

"It's a bit unusual for us to take a wire forward with the assault isn't it Al?" asked Preacher. "In the other advances, we've acted as runners until a forward HQ has been established and then run a wire forward. Why the switch?"

"I suppose the brass think this attack will be different. Personally, I don't like it. Reeling out cable during a frontal attack is not going to be fun. But if we can get the lines operating, at least the battalions will have instant communications with HQ, and it'll save us a lot of running to and fro with messages."

"Bullecourt. This is the Hindenburg Line isn't it?"

"Yes Mac. This is it! Tomorrow we find out just how invincible the Hindenburg is. So, let's not think about it but get some sleep. Wakey wakey call is at 2:30am and be well dressed. It's cold out there tonight."

* * *

Bluey and Mac huddled together in a small depression slightly to the rear of the infantry companies who also lay flat on the snow-covered ground. Between the two signallers lay the reel of telephone wire with a lead running to Lieutenant Melroy, who was positioned further forward with the battalion commander.

"Hell Bluey, I thought those tanks would be here by now. It's getting bloody close to the attack time."

Bluey half raised himself to look back at the Australian lines. "Yeah they should. Funny we can't even hear them. I don't like this at all. If we're still out here when it gets light, Jerry is going to have a picnic."

"Hang on. Something is happening." Mac was monitoring the line. "It's off. HQ just told battalion. It's off, and we have to get back and quick!"

"Wait a minute, let's see what the infantry is doing. We can't act on a conversation you accidentally overheard." Bluey smiled to himself. Signallers never hear things by accident.

Just then Lieutenant Melroy appeared out of the gloom. "It's off chaps. Head back to our lines reeling up as you go, but be smart. We don't want Jerry to know what we had in mind, just in case we have to do a repeat another day."

The men needed no second bidding and started to run the reel back in the direction of their lines. The infantry filed past them cursing the Generals who had 'fouled up again.'

"Hey Sergeant Phillips." Bluey recognised the stocky infantry Sergeant. "What gives?"

"Oh, it's you. Where's your mate Wilson?"

"He's with the other battalion. What's going on?"

"A balls up. We're supposed to go in with tanks, but the bloody Pommy tanks didn't show. What a circus. Only problem is the monkeys are running it, not performing." The Sergeant strode off into the gloom.

"Come on Bluey, let's move. I don't want to be here when it's light. All right for those foot sloggers they don't have to carry this damn reel." Preacher and Jacko appeared ahead of them running a reel of their own.

"We guessed you guys would need some help, so we reeled up from HQ." called Preacher.

"What a wonderful sight. Bless you Preacher." murmured Bluey.

Carrying the two reels the party made rapid progress back to the relative safety of the Australian frontline.

* * *

The signallers were resting in their dugout late that afternoon when Lieutenant Melroy appeared. He brushed aside their questions as to what had gone wrong and who was to blame. “It’s just one of those things that happens from time to time. The tanks had all sorts of problems but they’re here now and so the attack is re-scheduled for tomorrow morning. Same drill as for today except the attack will commence at 4:30am, slightly earlier than planned for today. We’ll retain the same formation. I know that there is a lot of disappointment about this morning, but believe me, the problems have been sorted out and tomorrow night we’ll be in Bullecourt. Take it easy for now and be ready to move out from HQ at 2:30am. Good luck.” The Lieutenant returned a salute and departed.

“A cool customer Al.” observed Bluey.

“Yep. Very cool and very efficient. Stick close to him and you’ll learn a lot. Hell, did you hear those tanks when they finally did arrive? What a noise!”

“Fat chance of surprising the Jerries with them. They’ll hear them long before we move off. They’re a dead give-away.” Darkie was expressing the thoughts of all the troops involved, not just the signallers.

“True Darkie,” explained Sam, “we probably will lose the element of surprise, but if they’re unstoppable, it doesn’t matter if Jerry hears them coming. All that does is give him time to run away.”

“Do you really believe that, Sam?” Al Wilson was not smiling. “You’ve now been in the trenches for what? Six weeks?”

“Seven.” replied the indignant Sam.

“Seven weeks. Seven weeks and you believe that Jerry will turn and run just because he hears a strange noise.”

"But Al, everyone is saying the tanks are the answer. They can't be stopped. They'll simply roll over the wire and the trenches. Don't you believe that?"

"No Sam I don't. And you're only believing what you hear because that's what you want to believe. Jerry has had time to work out how to deal with tanks, and I have no doubt that he also has a few tricks up his sleeve. But enough of this idle chatter. Tomorrow we'll know who is right. If you are, then tomorrow will be a great victory to our side, if I am right, it'll be a day we won't forget. For all our sakes, let's hope you're right."

"Well talking about it now won't alter things." Darkie was never keen to dwell on the unpleasant things in life. "Who's for a few hands of cards?"

"Really Darkie I didn't know you played bridge." Preacher feigned a look of surprise.

"Bridge? Who said anything about that old maid's game. Poker is the game. Now, who's for a few hands?"

"Not me Darkie," said Bluey, "I'm behind with my letter writing."

"And you can count me out." added Preacher.

Darkie looked at the worried Corporal. "What about you Al? You going to sit in?"

"Oh, I'm not sure, Darkie. I don't know how to play and I'd probably spoil it for you blokes."

"Now don't worry about that, Al. You'll soon pick it up. We only bet in pennies so you couldn't do much damage to your purse." Darkie's eyes had lit up at the thought of an innocent victim.

"All right. I'll have a go and see if I can get the hang of it, but not for too long. We all need some shut-eye before tomorrow's stunt."

"No problem there Corporal. This won't take long." replied the suddenly cheerful Darkie.

* * *

At 4:30am on 11 April 1917, the assault on the small town of Bullecourt began. A number of the tanks, in which the high command had placed such faith, failed to reach the starting point on time. Those which did, failed to have the impact their proponents claimed they would. The lines of communication were repeatedly cut by the heavy barrage and the HQ staff had to rely upon reports from visual observers stationed on high ground to the rear of the battlefield. These confused reports indicated the attack had been successful and that Allied troops could be seen in Bullecourt and the village of Riencourt.

It was mid-morning when Bluey appeared out of the dirt and the smoke. He was covered in blood and mud. His face showing anguish and exhaustion. Captain Solway and Preacher ran to meet him.

"Dowson are you all right? You're wounded."

"No Sir, I'm all right, but the battalion is in big trouble. Sir, it's murder over there. The CO sent me back to ask for artillery fire to cover the withdrawal."

"Withdrawal? What are you talking about Dowson? The attack is going splendidly. Come with me. Colonel Payne is here. He'll want to hear what you've got to say. Where's Lieutenant Melroy?"

Bluey shook his head. "Dead Sir. I was standing beside him when something hit him. Some sort of shell I guess. It went through him and left a hole you could put your fist through. It's his blood that's all over me."

"Good God! Come on. You're the first runner to come back from the front and the line has been dead all morning."

Preacher tried to assist the young redhead but he shrugged off the offer. "I'm all right now Preacher. What a mess, at times I didn't think I would get back. Where's Mac?"

"Mac?" Preacher looked at his friend. "We haven't seen Mac. As the Captain said, you're our first contact with the front since you moved out this morning."

They had now reached the entrance to the HQ and here they were met by a group of officers, led by Colonel Payne who'd just arrived from Divisional Headquarters.

"Sapper Dowson Sir." Captain Solway addressed the Colonel. "He has just come from the front and he says things are bad."

"Bad? What do you mean bad? I've just been on the phone to Division and they're very pleased with the way things are going."

"Pleased? For Christ sake Sir, our men are being butchered out there, and the Major I spoke to wants Riencourt shelled. The enemy is massing there and our men need some artillery support to cover their withdrawal." It was a plea rather than a request that Bluey delivered.

"Withdrawal? Nonsense man. I just told you, Divisional HQ is very happy with the attack. Who said anything about withdrawing?" This was not the sort of news Colonel Payne expected, or wanted, to hear.

"The officer in charge of one of the battalions. I don't know his name, but he was in charge. Most of the officers are dead. In fact, most of the battalion is gone, but they need artillery support and in a hurry."

The Colonel was confused. "Why didn't this officer give you a written request soldier? How do I know you're not a deserter making up this cock and bull story to cover yourself?"

Bluey was rapidly losing his temper. "The officer couldn't give me a written order because he had just had his arm blown off. He wasn't in the mood for writing letters. And if I was on the run, I would have by-passed this point and kept going. Colonel, I've just come from hell on earth. You have to help those who are still alive."

"Colonel Payne." said Captain Solway. "I know my men. I know Dowson. If he says the battalions need artillery I believe they do. After all he's been there, we haven't."

"Captain, I appreciate what you're saying and I'll talk to Divisional Headquarters, but they won't like it. No. They won't like it one little bit."

"Can I go Sir?" All eyes turned towards Bluey.

"Go! Where the hell do you think you are going?" demanded the Colonel.

"I told the officer I would deliver his message and return with the answer. I expect you'll have the artillery barrage laid down by the time I get there and I can help with the withdrawal. I also have to find Mac."

"Mac?"

Captain Solway explained. "His partner Sir. Seems like Sapper McKenzie was sent back earlier with a message but didn't get here. Sir, I really do believe that Dowson is telling the truth."

The Colonel stared into Bluey's face. "Tell me boy. After what you've seen out there, knowing what you do, are you really planning on going back to battalion HQ?"

"Yes Sir. Captain Solway has always told us that we mustn't let the infantry down and I'm not going to. I was sent here to deliver a message and then return with the answer. That's what I'm going to do."

The Colonel shook his head. "All right. Off you go. You have convinced me. Tell them a supporting barrage is being organised just as soon as I can persuade Division HQ. Good luck." He turned to enter the building. "Get me Div HQ on the phone," he shouted, "I want to speak to the General, no one else."

Preacher laid his hand on Bluey's shoulder. "You rest Bluey, I'll go."

"No Preacher. You wouldn't know where to go. It's a shambles, and I know the exact spot where they're holed up. But there is one thing you could do."

"Name it."

"Follow me back and check the casualties along the way. Mac has to be out there somewhere. Dead or wounded. Try and find him."

Preacher looked across to the Captain, who nodded. "There's no phones to man here Lacey, so you might as well take O'Brien with you to help with the wounded. Shit what a mess! What a stuff up!"

Preacher raised an eyebrow in surprise at the officer's outburst. "Come on Mick, let's move. Where's Bluey?"

"Out there Preacher. Going like a train. You know he's mad, he'll never get through that lot."

"You're right Mick. He's mad. Angry mad and God help any German he meets. The way he is at the moment he could tear them apart with his bare hands."

* * *

It was just before midday that the remnants of the assault force came walking back across the battlefield. The wreckage of the tanks that made it as far as the front stood out as charred monuments to someone's folly. Sam and Jacko were helping the walking wounded when they saw a familiar figure walking towards them, his arm around a soldier who had a bandage around his eyes. They both hurried forward and relieved the exhausted Bluey of his burden.

"Come on mate." Sam said to the wounded soldier. "Let's get you out of here. Can't you go any faster? Everyone seems to be strolling along as though they were taking a walk along St Kilda pier."

The wounded soldier stopped. "I don't know who you are, but let's get one thing clear. We're retiring from the fight, not running away."

Sam hung his head. "Oh, sorry, I'm always saying the wrong thing."

"Forget it mate. I wasn't being brave or stupid. It's just that I'm too tired to walk any faster. What a day, what a bloody mess. Where's that bloke who picked me up in the line?"

Bluey spoke. "Here soldier. You're in good hands now. They'll get you to a first aid post. I have to check in."

The sightless soldier thrust out his hand and Bluey took it in his.

"Thanks mate. Not much of a speech but I mean it."

Bluey smiled. "It's a bloody good speech. Says it all. Take care and give my love to Aussie when you see it."

"Poor choice of words I think, but I know what you mean."

The two signallers moved on with the wounded man. Bluey walked across to the Headquarters. Captain Solway saw him coming and advanced to meet him.

"Quite a day, eh Dowson. I think the intelligence boys will want to talk to you later on. You did the Signal Corps proud today. Now best you get off to your dugout and get cleaned up."

"Sir, it was hopeless. Right from the start. Completely hopeless. We didn't stand a chance. As for those bloody tanks..."

"Yes Dowson. It was a bad show."

"And Mac? Any news of Sapper McKenzie Sir?"

"Yes, your mates found him. He was concussed by a near miss. Not feeling all that well, but he'll come good with rest. The bad news is that Sapper Pettersen was killed in action with the western battalion. I don't know any details, but Corporal Wilson just phoned in."

"Lieutenant Melroy and Erik. Not a good day. Not a good day for anyone but the Germans."

"Oh, I suspect they've suffered, but their suffering will be tempered by the taste of victory."

Bluey was staring towards the German lines. "Bullecourt. More like Bloodycourt. I'll never forget it."

"None of us shall Dowson. Oh yes, I do have one other piece of information that might lighten your load. No.3 Section is being withdrawn for a rest. Seven weeks is long enough, too long sometimes, for a man to be in the front. Off you go. You did well today."

CHAPTER 13

LIVING IN CLOVER

The eight men stood outside the farm wall, and read the notice nailed to the wooden door.

"It's very clear Al. It says no French or Allied soldiers are permitted to billet at this farm."

"I know what it says Sam, but Madame Pruvost was quite clear with her invitation to us when we left. If she hadn't wanted us to come back, she wouldn't have invited us."

"Oh, for Christ's sake, stop dithering about and knock on the door. If we're not wanted she'll tell us to nick off." Darkie growled.

Preacher stepped past Sam and gave three hearty raps on the door. Footsteps were heard running across the courtyard. The bolts were drawn and the door swung open. Ghislaine stood there bathed in light thrown from the open kitchen door.

"It's you. I knew as soon as I heard the knock. I told mama - it's our Australians. Welcome home." She looked around, "Monsieur Skipper and Monsieur Erik? They are late?"

"No Ghislaine. They're not coming." Al's words were carefully chosen.

She hesitated. "I see. Oh dear, how silly of me. You must be frozen and hungry, and here I am keeping you standing outside. Come." She led the men across the courtyard to the dairy. "The girls and I have been busy getting your quarters ready for you. What do you think?"

Heavy curtains had been hung across the room effectively dividing it into three large cubicles. In the left cubicle, there were ten beds each with a straw filled mattress, a pillow and blankets. The centre cubicle contained the large trough which once had been the milk vat. In the right hand cubicle was a table, chairs, a wood-fired stove and several lounge chairs.

"Please won't someone say something?"

"It would be hard to find the right words Ghislaine." Preacher's eyes had never left the petite French woman. "You said 'Welcome home', and that's how I feel. I'm home. But how did you manage all this?"

"We had a lot of help. Mind you, we didn't always tell people why we were converting the dairy into special accommodation, but we hinted that it was for a good cause, and that was the truth. Now I'll let you settle in. We'll expect you for dinner in thirty minutes. You have bathed?"

"Yes Ghislaine, we're clean. We would've been here much earlier but we had to go through the disinfectant showers in Albert. We got issued with clean clothing, then collected our kitbags from storage." Al explained.

"But I didn't hear a truck."

"We hitched a ride to Lahoussoye and walked from there. Most of us walked. Preacher ran."

"Oh, you must be exhausted. I think a good cognac before dinner is called for. It's so wonderful to have you all back safe and sound." She hesitated, realising what she had just said.

"It's all right Ghislaine. We miss Skip and Erik, but there is nothing to say or do that can bring them back." Al gave her a warm smile.

She ran to the kitchen door calling to the rest of the family "Our men are back. I told you they would be."

* * *

Most of the men slept long into the next day. As if governed by some natural force, Bluey switched from soldier to farmer in one night's sleep. At sunrise, he milked the cows as if it had been his routine for the past two months. He made tea and delivered a mug to each of his companions, but the brew grew cold as the exhausted men slept on. It was past midday when the men started to arrive in the room set aside for eating and recreation. Bluey had prepared a meal and they gratefully accepted the food.

"What's the weather like Bluey?"

"Peaceful Sam. A lovely, sunny, peaceful day. Too good to waste by lying in bed."

"Don't you believe it Bluey. When I get home, I'm going to stay in bed until noon."

"Really Sam. I thought you were going to buy a farm. A farmer has to use every minute of daylight. Lying in bed is not an option."

"Ah yes. What I meant is that I'll lie in bed until I buy a farm, then I'll get up early."

Bluey smiled. "If you want to learn how to milk, you could help me. Good training for when you get home and buy that farm."

Sam thought carefully. "You know Bluey, I don't think I'll have cows on my farm. So, there is no point in my learning to milk."

"And therefore, no point in getting out of bed early?"

"Oh, I hadn't thought of it from that angle."

"Neatly done Sam. I thought Bluey had you trapped there for a moment." Al Wilson had entered the room.

"Where have you been Al? I had breakfast ready about an hour ago but you had disappeared."

"Sorry mate, should've told you. I went into Corbie to check on a few things. We've been given two weeks off. After that, we'll start carrying out the usual duties at HQ, like running messages and manning the switchboard."

Darkie looked up from his meal. "No more running bloody lines."

"No Darkie, unless some clown runs over them with his truck or a stray shell hits them. But you have a duty to do today."

"Duty? You just said that we had two weeks off."

"You know what I am talking about, Darkie. A letter to Erik's parents. That's what you have to do."

"Oh that. Yeah, I'll get around to that in the next day or so. Need time to think about what to say."

"No Darkie, you won't do it in the next day or so, you'll write today." Al Wilson spoke softly. "You were his mate, and you were there when he died. I want to see that letter today."

"Yeah Al, but I'll need some help. What about it Preacher?"

"Sure, I'll help you." Preacher paused. "You know Darkie, you haven't told us how Erik died. I think his friends have a right to know what happened."

Darkie pushed his plate away from him and stared at the table. "It was stupid. It was unnecessary. He should've followed me. I told him to keep moving. But no, he had to stop and help."

"Help?"

"We were on our way back from the enemy lines. It was a mess, a bloody mess. There were no lines, there was nothing we could do. Al said to get out."

"Darkie, you and Erik did well. You did everything you could to get a line open."

"Thanks Al. I never thought we would get out of there alive. Just after we came back through the German wire we came upon an infantry fellow, he was badly wounded. We stopped and gave him a drink, and I said that I would send a stretcher party to get him. He didn't want us to leave him. I said to Erik. Let's go and we set off. We hadn't gone very far when I looked back and there was Eric running back to the wounded bloke. I yelled at him but he took no notice. He reached the bloke and picked him up like he was a little child. There was not much left of them after the shell burst."

"It was his day."

"Damn it Al, I knew you would say that. What if I had stayed and helped, would it have been my day? If Erik had come with me he would still be alive."

Al shook his head. "You don't know that Darkie. Erik could have copped a bullet on the way back with you." He looked around at the anxious faces. "Had Darkie stayed with Erik and the wounded soldier, there is no certainty that the shell would have killed all three. We've all seen it. Three men in a group, a burst of machine gunfire, two cut to ribbons, and one left untouched. Take Bluey's case. Standing alongside Lieutenant Melroy and along comes a shell. End of Melroy, Bluey untouched. Why? Who knows why, or how, or when. The Arab is right, there are only two days. Anyhow that's what I believe."

Before anyone could answer or debate his statement, he added. "That's enough for today. Darkie get started on that letter. Erik was a hero, he died trying to save another's life and his parents need to be told that. Small comfort, but it will be some comfort. That's more than many families will be told about how their sons and husbands died at Bullecourt."

"Al, have you got any idea of how many we lost?"

"It's hard to say Preacher, but down at HQ this morning they reckon about three thousand. A lot of good men for no gain. You should hear Captain Solway. He's still swearing and cursing."

"I heard him. In fact, I was surprised at his language. He seems such a gentleman."

Al laughed. "You reckon gentlemen don't swear? Stick around Preacher. At the right time in the right circumstances, you may even hear a Chaplain let fly. It seems to help to relieve the pent up emotions. But enough of this chatter. You and Darkie get stuck into that letter, the rest of you clear off and get some fresh air."

* * *

Preacher and Darkie had just finished their letter when there was a knock on the door leading to the kitchen. In response to their chorus of "Entrez," Ghislaine appeared.

"Where is everyone?"

"Al has taken them for a stroll around the countryside. Darkie and I have some letters to write." answered Preacher.

"Oh I see. Well, I have some news for you. The family has decided that seeing it's Saturday, we should have a party to welcome you back. It will just be the family and the eight of you. Unless you have made other plans."

"Oh no. We don't have any plans, but you don't have to go to all this trouble just for us. You have already been too kind. Look at these quarters."

"If you have any more of the cognac stuff lady, I'll be delighted to accept." said Darkie.

"Where's your manners Darkie? That is a rather crude way of accepting a kind invitation."

Ghislaine laughed. "No Monsieur Preacher, not crude, honest. Yes Monsieur Darkie, we do have some cognac and the girls are going to get some beer from the Château."

"Beer! Did you hear that Preacher?"

Preacher tried to turn the conversation away from Darkie's obvious fascination with alcohol but Ghislaine seemed amused by his attempts.

"Monsieur Darkie is fond of beer eh?"

"You're bloody right Ghislaine."

"It's all he ever thinks of." snapped Preacher.

Ghislaine raised an eyebrow. "All he ever thinks of?"

"Not so." replied Darkie.

"Enough Darkie. Ghislaine is not interested in your personal likes or dislikes."

"Perhaps another time Monsieur Darkie, but I must go and help the girls prepare for the party. We shall expect you all at seven. Till then." She left the room.

"Darkie I'm warning you."

"Calm down Preacher. Can't you see what she's doing? She fancies you, so she teases you. They say love is blind, and you're a prime example. Don't worry, I won't muck up while we're here. Even a dumb peasant like me knows when he's in clover. And one other thing, I reckon Mac would belt the daylights out of me if Al told him to, and that's something I wouldn't want to happen. Come on, let's walk towards Querrieu and see if we can find the others."

* * *

The evening meal was excellent and it was obvious that the kitchens at the Château had made a significant contribution.

"You really don't fit the image of a bunch of hard-drinking Australians."

"Why's that Nicole?" asked Al.

"Well that's the general impression one gets from reading the newspapers. Big hats, big thirst, big..."

"Nicole." her mother cut her short.

"Now we'll never know." laughed Darkie. "But the big hats part is true."

Al stood up. "Come on you lot, time to hit the hay."

"I beg your pardon Monsieur Al. Time to hit the hay indeed! We said we are going to have a party, and that's what we are going to do."

Al looked bewildered. "I'm sorry Ghislaine, but I assumed that you meant a dinner party."

“No my friends, we are going to have a proper party. Mother, please lead the way.”

The old lady rose from her seat at the head of the table and led the way through a door at the far end of the kitchen. None of the men had seen beyond this door. They were led into a very large room with a chandelier hanging in the centre. The blue and gold carpet felt soft and giving under their feet. The furniture was beautifully carved and ornate, and in one corner stood a grand piano. The whole room proclaimed great wealth of another era.

“You like our drawing room or grand salon?” asked Nicole.

“It’s beautiful Nicole.” breathed Preacher. “But shouldn’t we take our boots off?”

“Why Monsieur Preacher? Your footwear is clean and carpets are for walking on.”

Ghislaine waved her hand towards the piano. “Now gentlemen, we are going to have a concert. The Pruvost family will perform first, followed by our guests. Please find a seat. Yvette, you may start the proceedings.”

After Yvette had played her well-rehearsed number, Marie and Nicole played. When Ghislaine took her seat at the piano, it was obvious all members of the Pruvost family were talented musicians. Next came a medley of songs from the three girls accompanied on the piano by their mother. The men were generous in their applause.

“So now it is your turn gentlemen. Who will begin?”

Darkie lurched to his feet. “I know a couple of good poems Ghislaine. Real ‘dinky di’ Aussie bush ballads.”

“Darkie sit down and behave yourself.” cautioned Al. “I’ve heard that Preacher is an accomplished pianist Ghislaine, so we’ll start with him. Away you go Preacher, don’t let the side down.”

Preacher took his place at the keyboard and gazed at the beauty of the piano. After a pause, he commenced playing. At first there was a hint of the occasional wrong note, but as he warmed to his work the music flowed, and filled the room and the hearts of his listeners. He played on as if in another world. His audience sat enchanted by the sheer brilliance of his playing.

Suddenly he stopped. “I’m sorry Ghislaine, I got carried away. It’s such a magnificent piano. The best I’ve ever touched.”

“Don’t be sorry dear friend. We are the ones who are sorry that you stopped. It was beautiful playing, truly beautiful.”

Preacher blushed. “Thank you Ghislaine. Now we have a special surprise.” Preacher motioned to Mick.

Al frowned and looked at Bluey. “What the hell does that Irishman do?”

“You’ll see.”

Again, the room was filled with music. This time the piano was secondary to Mick’s pure vocal notes. The womenfolk were spellbound. With the final song, they clapped and cheered as if part of a concert audience. Mick looked embarrassed, and Preacher walked across to him and put his arm around his friend.

“Monsieur Mick, that was wonderful, just wonderful. Why haven’t you sung for us before?”

Yvette was bubbling with enthusiasm for the young tenor.

“No one asked me before.” was the simple reply.

“Well you can expect many requests from now on.” said Ghislaine. “Now who is next on this program of surprises?”

“It’s Monsieur Al’s turn.” declared Marie.

“Oh no Marie, I don’t sing very well and I wouldn’t dare play the piano after that masterly display by Preacher.”

“No Monsieur Al, you don’t have to play the piano or sing. You have to play this.” She produced a violin from behind a chair.

They laughed. “I told you she would call your bluff Corporal. She didn’t forget.”

“And you didn’t let her, did you Darkie? Oh well, if I have to, then I have to.” Al unlatched the case and removed the violin and bow. “It’s a very nice instrument Ghislaine. A very fine piece of craftsmanship, and my hands are rough. I'm not sure I should even try to play in case I do some damage."

Ghislaine tilted her head on one side and looked searchingly into Al's face. "You have me guessing Monsieur Al. True, it is a very good violin, but I suspect you are playing a game. If I say go ahead and play, then I am, what do you call it, calling the bluff? If I say don't play, then we will never know if you are teasing us."

"Go on mother." pleaded Marie. "Tell him to play."

"Marie, you are very anxious to hear Monsieur Al play. Now why would that be?"

"Because I have a bet with Monsieur Darkie. A little while ago he reminded me of the conversation we had on that first night, and suggested I produce father's violin. We have a bet."

"A bet?"

"Yes. I bet Monsieur Al could play, and Monsieur Darkie bet he couldn't. So, you must ask him to play."

Ghislaine turned to Al. "I know nothing of this foolishness and I don't approve of my daughter betting, especially as I don't know what the stakes are. So, Monsieur Al, for the sake of my dear Marie, would you please play for us?"

"Certainly Madame. Preacher give me a note or two so I can tune this fiddle."

The two men made a great production out of the tuning of the violin.

"He's bluffing Marie. You can tell by the way he and Preacher are carrying on. You lose."

Darkie was pleased with himself. A kiss is a kiss, and could lead to other things.

"Right Preacher, that should do it." Al turned and bowed to the audience. "If you will take your seats, I will begin." With a flourish Al nestled the violin under his chin and drew the bow across the strings. The noise was awful.

"Told you so." shouted Darkie. "He's a fraud. I win."

And with that Al started to play. The fingers were stiff, and some of the notes off key, but there was no doubt that Al Wilson had once been an accomplished player. He too, seemed to find in music, an escape from the world around him, and the expression on his face, just as with his two companions, showed that he had been transported to another time, another place. When he finally lowered the violin, there was a pause before the applause broke out.

"Thank you Monsieur Al. What a truly wonderful night this has been." Ghislaine was delighted with the way her party had turned out. Everyone was happy, even Darkie, and as all gathered around the piano for a final sing-song, Madame Pruvost senior nodded in approval. "A house without laughter is not a home." she told herself.

* * *

The week passed quickly and quietly. Some days they'd walk to the village of Daours and from there, walk along the banks of the Somme while Bluey pointed out the birds that were preparing their nests. There were blackbirds, warblers, finches, sparrows and many more. He identified the many flowers that were bursting forth into a mass of colour on either side of the river. France had come to life and put on its colourful spring clothing. The men found it difficult to equate this natural beauty with the horrors they knew were going on a mere twenty-five miles away.

They didn't talk about the war, but the subject, though dormant in their speech, was ever active in their minds. One morning as the group sat around the table gossiping, there was a knock on the outer door. Ghislaine crossed the courtyard from the kitchen and then came to the men's quarters.

"Monsieur Al, there are two soldiers at the gate asking for you."

"Thank you Ghislaine. Cheer up. It doesn't have to be bad news."

She smiled. “Yes of course, I worry too much.” and retreated to the kitchen.

Al returned from the gate with Sergeant King and a stranger. “Boys, this is Skip’s replacement. Sapper George Morbey, a Sydney man, but don’t hold that against him.”

As the new man moved around the table shaking hands, Al led the Sergeant across to the stove to get his guest a cup of tea, the universal method of greeting a guest in the Australian Army.

“They seem to be getting older, not younger, these days Pete. How old do you reckon Morbey is?”

“He claims to be thirty-five. Family man. Has four kids, all left school, so he’s probably a bit older than he says. Keen to do well, and Phil Reynolds recommended him. ‘Methodical, but reliable’, Phil wrote.”

“Well that’s good enough for me. What news from the front?”

“Jerry counter-attacked at Lagnicourt but got a bloody nose for his trouble. Our blokes did well. The talk around the bars is another go at Bullecourt early in May.”

“Bloody hell, I hope they plan it better this time. It won’t fuss me if I never see another damn tank in this war.”

Peter King nodded. “As you can imagine, everyone at the Château is blaming everyone else. I get the feeling that our troops are getting a little bit tired of being mucked around by Pommie Generals. Feeling is running pretty high, and if they foul up again, all hell could break loose. How’s your team?”

“Look at them. This house is not a billet, it’s home. Only a couple of them take a drink, they do everything together as a team should, and I think they’ve shown that they’re made of the right stuff when in the trenches.”

“Captain Solway likes them. He expects to get a replacement for Lieutenant Melroy in the next week or two. Come see me next Monday and we’ll see what’s afoot.”

"Thanks Pete, the extra couple of days will be appreciated. By the way, you doing anything Saturday night?"

"Not that I'm aware of. What have you got in mind?"

"Well the lady of the house has organised a small concert for a few of the locals and the section. We all join in and sing for our supper. Why don't you join us? It'll give you a chance to see the lads in a different light. I'll speak to Ghislaine and see if we can squeeze you in at the meal table before the show."

"Sounds good to me. Thanks for the brew. Must be off." The tall Sergeant waved to the men and left.

"Come on Al, what's happening? Whenever you two old stagers get together in a corner whispering we smell trouble."

"Sam you ask too many questions. We were just reminiscing about old times."

"I don't believe you Al." Darkie had got to his feet. "You're part of this team and we should know what you know. It's our right."

Al walked over to the table. "There are two sorts of information Darkie. One is fact, the other rumour. So, let me tell you the facts. Fact. Our unrestricted leave finishes next Monday. Fact. I've invited Pete King to come to the concert on Saturday. Fact. George Morbey is here on Phil Reynolds' recommendation. Fact. Our boys beat off a German counter-attack at Lagnicourt and gave Jerry a bloody nose. The rest is rumour, and I don't pass on rumours. Oh yes, one last fact. The war has not been cancelled due to lack of interest. Don't push me Darkie. I'll always tell you what you need to know. I'll never hide the truth from you, even if it's unpalatable, but I decide what and when information will be passed on. Got that?"

"Sorry Al, we were just anxious in case the Sergeant had come to tell us to hightail it back to Bullecourt."

"I understand Darkie, but he didn't. One day we'll have to go back to the front, but at the moment we have no orders except to enjoy ourselves, so why don't we do just that?"

* * *

As the days became warmer, Bluey's nature walks became very popular. Sometimes one of the girls would accompany them as a guide and to explain to an elderly farmer why the men were crossing his fields.

One day, Ghislaine accompanied the group, and while they rested and ate the food from the picnic hamper, she told them of the history of the area. "At one time, all this land was owned by my husband's ancestors." she said, waving her hand in a sweeping gesture towards the nearby villages.

"You owned all this?" questioned Sam.

"Not me Sam, nor my husband. But last century most of the land you can now see, was owned by his family."

"The town as well?"

"Everything Sam. But times change and so do attitudes, and the big landlords had to change or perish. We still rent out some of the fields around Querrieu, but the house and its surrounds, are really all that is left of the old empire."

"So the family was, still is, titled?"

"Yes and no, Al. There is a title, but my father-in-law never used it, nor did my husband. It seemed so inappropriate once the lands had gone. But as you have seen, we live well, and we still have many of the treasures from the past."

"Indeed you do Ghislaine. The furniture in the drawing room, that magnificent grand piano. Who would have thought it when we first knocked on the door." Preacher seldom took his eyes from her face.

"Ah yes, that was a very lucky day for the Pruvosts. We have had soldiers billeted at the farm before, but they were rough and caused us much concern. I was frightened that they might discover our secret room and vandalise it. That would have been terrible. But fate moves mysteriously, and it was Sam's dreadful accent that told Mama that this group was different. We are in your debt, Sam."

"We all are Ghislaine, if it was Sam's charm that got us the billet. But there is something I want to ask. You have stopped calling us Monsieur, may I ask why?"

"I think Preacher should answer that Bluey." She turned to her admirer.

"Oh it was just a simple remark I made," Preacher stammered. "I mentioned to Ghislaine that using monsieur in front of our names indicated a certain formality in our relationship, and in Australia, it would never be used between friends."

"And the girls and I regard you all as friends."

Darkie spoke. "Ghislaine we have another custom back home. You may have noticed. We tend to call our friends by shortened names or nicknames."

Ghislaine laughed. "Noticed, Darkie? It would be hard not to notice. I don't think I know any of your real names."

"Well there you are. You see Ghislaine, I find your name a bit of a mouthful, and I was wondering if I could call you Gilly for short."

Preacher sighed. "Take no notice of him Ghislaine, it's just another example of his appalling bad manners."

"Oh no Preacher, it's another example of how Darkie speaks his mind." She turned to the New Zealander. "Of course you can call me Gilly. I will tell people that it is my Australian name. What of the girls and Madame Pruvost. Do they get Australian names too?"

"Oh no, I don't have any problems with their names, and I certainly wouldn't call your mother anything other than Madame Pruvost. No, it was just your name that had me stuttering."

"Good, then that's settled. I'm Gilly from now on. Come on, we had better get back to the farm. Bluey has the cows to milk, Mick and the girls have to practise for Saturday's concert, and I have to prepare the evening meal. George, you can walk beside me and tell me all about your family in Australia. I think it's good that this group now has a fatherly figure to watch over them. They take life too carelessly." She realised what she had said. "Oh dear, how stupid of me."

"No Gilly, perfectly true from what you see." Al was quick to stop the discussion proceeding along a difficult path. "You see we lead two lives. Live in two worlds you might say. One we don't talk about, or even think about. The other is here at the farm. Here we have no cares, no worries. For that we are most grateful. But we do care, we care a lot about ourselves, each other, you and your family, and what we're fighting for, but if we appear to be carefree then that is good, it means we're enjoying ourselves."

Ghislaine had stopped and was looking straight into Al's eyes. "I said before that George was a fatherly figure, and so he is, due to his age, but you are the wise one. Thank you. Now George, tell me about your children."

The moment had passed and the group set off for home. Jacko, Sam and Darkie found it necessary to drop in to the local inn at Querrieu to seek refreshments, complaining that the heat had affected them. Al and Bluey walked together at the rear of the group.

Al nodded towards the group ahead. "Look at poor Preacher. She only has to give him a glancing look and he's fired up for a day. It's not a good situation."

"Why? They both like each other."

"Most of us cross from this unreal world to the real world over there," Al gestured towards the north, "by turning some sort of switch in our minds. A quick adjustment. Preacher is likely to start flicking that switch to and fro, and that is dangerous."

"You mean his mind might not be on the job, and he might make a mistake?"

"As usual mate, you catch on fast."

"You playing cards again this evening?"

Al grinned. "I suppose so. Darkie is determined to win his money back, but every night I still have beginner's luck. Strange isn't it?"

It was Bluey's turn to smile. "I've watched you Al. There's no luck in the way you play."

"Ah but you're wrong Bluey. Luck has a part in everything we do. Cards, women, or dodging bullets. The thing to do is make the most of any good luck and minimise any bad luck. It's good advice my friend. Think about it while you heave on those cow's teats. God that must be a boring job."

Bluey didn't answer. He was too engrossed with sorting out in his mind Al's theory on luck.

SIG WITH A GUN

The Saturday night concert was a great success. Ghislaine had asked twelve families from nearby farms and, although it was standing room only, everyone enjoyed themselves. Darkie and Jacko volunteered to escort two of the ladies back to their homes, returning to the farm just before sunrise.

On the Monday, in clean uniforms and shining boots, the group marched to Corbie. There was a spring in their step and they held their heads high. At the Brigade HQ, Al and Sergeant King went inside to talk to Captain Solway. The three returned with a young fair-haired officer.

Captain Solway addressed them. "Well men I think we've been through enough together to dispense with some of the formalities. I hope you've enjoyed your rest. You earned it. Let me introduce Lieutenant Melroy's replacement, Lieutenant James Crowther. He's new to the game, so I'm relying upon you to teach him the ropes, but don't teach him any bad habits. Despite your absence, the war hasn't changed very much. It looks like we're going to have another crack at Bullecourt, but you'll be in reserve and so will miss out on a seat in the front row, something you won't be too disappointed to hear. Jim, I want you to join in with the Section for a couple of days. That way you'll get to know the men and how they work. They're all yours Sergeant."

"Thank you Sir." Sergeant King saluted and turned to the squad. "Right you lot. I know that you've been feeding in a good paddock and are not as fit as you should be, so we'll get into shape by running, reeling and mending lines. You also need to sharpen up your Morse. Three of you will remain here at HQ each night to man the switchboard. Corporal Wilson will work out a roster. There's a room in the back of this building that'll serve as a mess room and sleeping quarters. Lieutenant Crowther, Sir, you will do all activities except the shifts on the switch. Right, dump your gear in the mess room and let's get started."

The next few days were a nightmare. The Sergeant was relentless in his efforts to bring the men up to his standard of fitness and efficiency. Three days later Sergeant King announced that the second battle for Bullecourt had commenced. "Sorry chaps, but you seem to have missed out on the excitement. You're in reserve, but the brass doesn't anticipate you'll be needed. However, we know that sometimes the Generals get it wrong, so keep on your toes. I'll let you know how things are going but I expect you'll know more about it than me seeing you're manning the switchboard."

The men nodded. Each night they had handled the messages flowing backwards and forwards between the commands. At lunch, they discussed the developments. The news wasn't good. Each day the casualty lists grew and from the progress reports, it was apparent that Bullecourt was a hard nut to crack. It didn't come as a surprise when the Division was placed on standby.

"Well sir, it looks as if you're going to see some action."

Lieutenant Crowther shrugged his shoulders. "That's why I'm here Corporal Wilson, and I'm pleased to be going in with a team like No.3 Section. I've learnt a lot in the past days, more than I could learn in the signals school in a long time."

"Oh yes, the school." Al paused as if selecting the right words to use. "Sir, there's something I want to mention but feel I might be out of line."

"Let's have it Corporal. You don't strike me as someone who wastes words on trivial matters."

"Thank you Sir. It's about the relationship between you and the men, you and me..." He paused.

"Go on, I'm listening."

"Well Sir. This training we have been doing has been one in, all in. A sort of get to know the job and each other. For most of us, it's been honing our skills, except of course, George. He's yet to face the music."

"And me. That applies to me."

"Yes sir, it does. But when we get into action, you won't be a worker, you'll be a leader. That's what those pips on your shoulder are for. You'll be telling us what to do and we'll be doing it. Not like here where you have been just one of the team. If you mess up, then we buy the consequences."

Lieutenant Crowther frowned. "And you're worried that I'll mess up?"

Al continued. "Not really, because I now know you can listen. Some officers come out of that school you mentioned with wax in their ears. They can't, or won't listen. My men are good at their job and they can help you. Mind you, in the final analysis, it's you who makes the decision, and it's you who cops the blame if things go wrong. We won't let you down, but if we work as a team, upwards and downwards, the odds become more in our favour."

"Thank you Wilson. I'll let you into a little secret. When I joined the unit, Captain Solway told me he was putting me in the hands of Sergeant King for additional training. I guess my face indicated that I wasn't all that happy. The Captain then gave me some advice. Look, listen and learn from those who have been there. He had a few complimentary things to say about you and Sergeant King. I now know what he meant, and how little I know. So, your words have not fallen on waxed ears. Let the men know that I hope, no, expect them to keep me fully informed, and where they think they have some useful advice, then come forward with it. Fair enough?"

"Couldn't be fairer Sir. Have a nice war."

The Lieutenant laughed. "You sound like the 'maître de' seating me at a table. Thanks corporal, and good luck to us all."

Al Wilson frowned, "Oh yes, luck, that unknown but all important element. Yes sir, let's hope it's all good."

* * *

The call to the front came late the following Monday and No.3 Section left that night for the deployment northwards. The stream of trucks, wagons and ambulances moving south along the roads was evidence of the savage fighting. Al went with the two officers and Sergeant King for a briefing, while the Section cleaned their old dugout. Artillery fire was heavy.

"Bloody hell, Darkie! It looks rough out there." muttered George Morbey, as the morning light filtered through clouds of smoke and dust.

"Yeah, and those poor bloody infantrymen are right in the middle of it."

"Come off it...no one could survive out there."

"Wanna bet cobber? And you had better hope we can, because I reckon in a short while that's where we'll be."

The others joined them to watch the bombardment. After a while the guns ceased and the clouds of smoke drifted away leaving a spectacle of devastation. Men could be seen scrambling towards the rubble that had once been the villages of Bullecourt and Riencourt. The reserve battalions were moving in to relieve exhausted comrades.

Bluey pointed. “I bet we won’t be spectators for long. Here comes Al and Lieutenant Crowther.”

“Right pay attention! Same as before. Lines are out, they’re useless. Too much shelling, so we act as runners. Preacher, take Mick and Sam and join the battalion on the left flank; Bluey take George and Mac to the right flank. Once you find the battalion commander, stick with him. Brigade HQ is forward of here and we’ll go there first. Darkie and Jacko will stay there with me, and will relieve you as you come in with a message. Come on, it’s on in earnest. Bluey, you don’t need that frigging rifle.”

“The last time we were here Al, I could have touched a dozen Germans. This time I’m going to shoot them. It won’t slow me down, but damned if I am going to be chased around there like a rabbit.”

“All right. Come on, move it. Follow me and the Lieutenant. And keep your heads down. Move!”

In single file the men ran across the ruptured wasteland to the Brigade Headquarters, located close to the actual fighting. After a quick briefing from the signallers they were relieving, the two parties set out to find the battalion commanders.

Al stayed close to Lieutenant Crowther. “Well Sir, the men won’t get exhausted from running. I’ve never known Brigade HQ to be so close to the fighting.”

“I don’t think it was planned that way Corporal Wilson. I suspect that in the planning, this particular site was deemed to be somewhat remote from the action. Perhaps the advance hasn’t been as swift as expected.”

Al nodded. “You’re learning fast Sir.”

“Well Corporal, when do we go up and see what’s going on?”

Al shook his head. “Sir, you don’t just wander up there to have a look-see. You go when there is a job to be done.”

“I know, but when will that be?”

"When a battalion wants a job done, they'll tell you. You then decide how to do it. Don't fret Sir. You'll get your chance to see what's going on."

The battle raged on. The hours of hand to hand fighting, became days. The roar of shells, the rattle of machine gunfire, the sound of exploding grenades and the cries of wounded men assailed the ears of all who were there and could hear. And strewn all around the area were men of both sides who could not hear, and wouldn't hear again.

As Al Wilson had predicted there was no respite for No.3 Section. They were alongside the infantry as each assault took place. Through the hail of shells and bullets they ran with their precious messages. Bluey, when not running messages, was on the parapets firing. On several occasions when sent to get a report from a company commander, he found the company heavily engaged in fierce bombing attacks or hand to hand fighting. The red-headed signaller joined in and became known through the Brigade as the 'Sig with a Gun.' Several times Al Wilson reproached him but the only reply he ever got was: 'Am I doing my job Al?'

Corporal Wilson's main concern was Lieutenant Crowther. The officer's enthusiasm, and desire to do well, created problems. He listened to advice, and made quick and decisive decisions, but felt that he should be leading his men from the front. He ran messages like any of the men, but took risks they would've avoided. He seemed to thrive on danger.

"They'll get him Bluey. Sure as hell they'll nail him." commented Al as the officer set off on another mission forward.

"Only if it's his day Al. You know that."

"Touché, my friend. Only if it's his day and... oh shit, come on." The Corporal ran from the lookout point followed by Bluey.

The Lieutenant was badly wounded from shrapnel, but in a state of shock he felt no pain.

"Dowson, get this message to battalion. Go on move!" he gasped. Bluey seized the pouch and started off towards the fighting.

"Right sir, let me give you a hand and we'll get you back to HQ." Al tried to raise the fallen man but both legs were shattered.

"No Corporal, let me rest for a while. Just until I get my breath back. My, that was a near one."

"Yes it was, a damn near one. You know I should've been carrying that message, not you. I keep telling you that running messages is not your job."

"Ah yes, good advice, but I ignored it. But think Wilson, if you'd been carrying it, then you'd be lying here with me comforting you. But then we all have to live by the word of the old Arab don't we?"

"You know about the Arab?"

"Yes. Captain Solway told me that was the law by which you lived and survived, so I decided to adopt it myself. Hell, I'm tired."

Al looked at the shattered limbs. "Sir, you're losing some blood. Let me race back and get some medical gear. I won't be long."

"Don't worry Corporal, I'm ready to go. It doesn't even hurt." With that the young Lieutenant closed his eyes and died.

* * *

Two weeks after the initial assault and ten thousand Australian casualties later, the pile of rubble was declared captured. Only then did No.3 Section find itself reunited as a single unit. For the nine men, it had been ten days of hell. Ten days without a wash, ten days with little sleep, ten days of exhausting work, and always the threat that this might be the 'day'. As the men sat slumped in their dugout George Morbey asked the question, "Is it always as bad as this?" It was a remark that relieved the tension.

"Bad? What do you mean by bad?" Darkie scoffed. "Hell, that wasn't bad. We had them on the back foot from Day One."

"Shut up Darkie." Mac had reached, or even passed, the end of his tether. "No George, it isn't always like that, but thank the Lord we made it. I'll never forget Bloodycourt."

Bluey leant across and patted Mac on the shoulder. "None of us will. You did well mate, especially as Jerry knocked you silly in the first stoush."

Al stood up. "You all did well. Not once did we let the infantry down, and that's the measuring stick. Captain Solway says we have twenty-four off so get cleaned up and get some sleep. You've earned it." He walked outside.

Bluey followed. "What's up Al? Something is getting to you."

"Hell, does it show? That's bad, I thought I had it under control. It's Lieutenant Crowther. I can't help feeling it's my fault he died."

"Come on Al, don't be stupid. I was there. He grabbed that message pouch and took off down the line. Whoosh! Bang! End of story! You had nothing to do with it."

"Yeah that's what happened, but why did an officer race off doing what one of us should've been doing? He knew about the Arab."

"So?"

"Before he died, he said Captain Solway had told him about my philosophy on survival, and he'd decided that was the way to go."

"What do you mean, the way to go?"

"Crowther decided to run risks, thumb his nose at death, because if it wasn't his day, then he wouldn't get hit. Somehow, he got it all mixed up. To him it was a game of hit me if you can."

"Calm down Al. You've us all believing in the Arab. If Crowther had sat in the dugout playing patience, an odd bullet would've whistled in the entrance and nailed him. It was his day, his time, and he went out in a blaze of glory. You must believe that, because if you start to change your attitude it will seep down through the section. It was Crowther's day! Simple as that!"

“Thanks Bluey.”

“You’ll be right, but I’m not sure of one or two of the others. They were pushed to the brink these past couple of days. Is it really over?”

Al looked out across the cratered expanse of countryside still littered with bodies. “Bullecourt? I think so. My guess is that the Germans have had enough for the time being. The Division has taken a fair whack, so I think they’ll pull us out once a new line has been built and fortified. We’ll have to wait and see. Get some sleep cobber. You could do with it.”

Al’s predictions were right. After a few days of helping to establish a new frontline No.3 Section returned to the HQ at Corbie. They were met by Captain Solway accompanied by a very young looking soldier. Gesturing towards the young man the captain said, “This is Pettersen’s replacement, Sapper Simon Young. I understand you have a billet out along the Querrieu road, so I suggest you get cleaned up and move out there. You can use this truck. You’ve earned a rest so check in with HQ in three days time. Off you go.” The men saluted the departing officer.

“For Christ’s sake Al, we can’t turn up at the farm like this. We are lousy, dirty and need new uniforms.”

“You’re right Mac but I’m not knocking back the offer of transport.” Al turned to the young sapper, “What’s your name?”

“Young Sir, I mean Corporal.” They laughed at his embarrassment.

“Right Young, here’s what I want you to do. Take this truck to the QM Store, the driver knows where it is, and ask for Sergeant Harley. Got it?”

“Sergeant Harley.”

“Correct. Tell Ted Harley that Al Wilson wants nine new sets of kit. Everything. Got it?”

“Yes Corporal, but what about sizes?”

"Sizes don't matter. We'll have fresh gear back at the farm. Tomorrow we'll swap the issue stuff for gear that fits. We'll wait here. Now get cracking."

The young sapper saluted in his confusion and climbed on board the truck.

"What the hell was all that about?" asked Preacher.

"Using one's head Preacher. What's the normal routine when you come out of the line? First, we have to hand in our clothes so they can boil and disinfect them to kill the lice. You sometimes wait hours until your clothes are ready to wear again. Then you have to get into a queue to go through the showers, one hour, two hours perhaps, waiting for your turn. Then you have to front up to a doctor. Another hour or two. At the farm, we'll strip off and boil these clothes. Young can do that. Then we hop into the large vat filled with hot water and disinfectant. The whole process can be over in an hour, whereas if we go through the Army routine we won't be finished before dark."

"Small point Al. Disinfectant. We, and our gear, do need a good cleaning."

"There are bottles of it in the barn. Same stuff as the Army uses. Any more objections?"

The thought of getting to the farm and becoming clean once more was too attractive for anyone to suggest an alternative.

But Sam had to have a question. "What about the medical examination Al?"

"Right Sam. We must abide by the rules. Now, hands up anyone who is sick. Come on don't be shy. No one? Good. Medical check-up completed, Doctor Sam. Any more problems?"

Sam shook his head. "One day I'll learn to keep my mouth shut."

"No Sam. Asking questions is a good thing. Clears the brain of worries. Always speak up, better to ask, than die wondering. Ah, here comes young Simon. If he's got what I ordered he's done well." The truck came to a halt and Simon started to climb down. "Stay where you are boy. Did Ted deliver the goods?"

"Yes Corporal. He said to tell you that you and he are now square."

"Fair enough. You ride in the cab. I'm sure you and the driver don't want any of our nasties to jump onto you. Driver, take us out along the Querrieu road. We'll tell you when to stop."

The load of dirty but happy soldiers jumped down from the truck outside the farm wall and at the same time the gate opened and Ghislaine appeared.

"Hold on Gilly. Don't get too close." Al advised.

"Oh? What's wrong?"

"Can't you see, or rather, can't you smell? We came directly from the front so we need to organise a bath routine. All except him." Al pointed at the newcomer to the group. "Ghislaine, meet Simon Young. Simon, this angel is your hostess." The lady and the boy bowed to each other.

"Well, come on. Get into the courtyard and we'll see what has to be done." Ghislaine held her nose between her thumb and forefinger. "You are a bit smelly aren't you?"

"We could go back to Corbie and bathe." Preacher was disturbed that they had imposed on the family in such a manner.

"Corbie? What's wrong with my bathhouse Monsieur Preacher? At least I think you are Preacher. You all look and smell alike."

The men trooped into the courtyard as the three girls and their grandmother appeared from the kitchen. Ghislaine spoke in rapid French and they re-entered the house.

"Right. Hot water is being prepared. Marie and Nicole are getting some old bags from the barn and we can put your clothes in them."

"Thank you Ghislaine. We have replacement clothing so the dirty clothes are of secondary importance. The main job is to get ourselves clean."

"I understand Al. But first things first. Here is Yvette with the immediate essentials."

Yvette appeared carrying a tray with glasses of cognac on it. When each had a glass Ghislaine raised hers in salute. "We welcome back our dirty Australian friends." The men returned the salute and drank.

"Gilly, you are the prettiest Sergeant I have ever seen."

"Really Darkie? From what I have seen of Sergeants, that isn't a great compliment, but it'll do for the present. Here are Marie and Nicole with the bags. Off with your filthy clothes and put them in the bags."

Not a man moved.

"Ghislaine," cried Preacher, "surely you don't intend that we undress in front of yourself and these young ladies?"

Ghislaine raised an eyebrow. "And how else do you think you can get those rags into the bags, my clever friend?"

Still no man made a move. It was Al who spoke. "The truth is Gilly, that we are shy and modest, and so I suggest the ladies withdraw, then we'll undress and put our things in the bags."

Ghislaine burst out laughing. "Oh, you silly men. Did you really think I would allow you to parade naked in front of my daughters. I was teasing. Oh, if only you could have seen your faces. Just like a bunch of little school boys, not the heroes you really are. Good, here is Madame with the necessary articles."

Madame Pruvost emerged from the house carrying a large bundle of towels which she placed on a garden bench.

Ghislaine turned to Simon. "Now Simon, you don't need a bath?"

"No ma'am, I'm clean." The young man was totally bewildered.

"Fine. We ladies will withdraw to protect the modesty of your friends. When the bags are full you can carry them around to the rear of the house. We'll deal with them later. You...," with a wave of her hand towards the group of dirty but embarrassed men, "can wrap towels around your modesty and sit out here until the bath is ready. Simon can help the girls to fill the baths. It's going to take a while to put all nine through the cleansing process. Madame Pruvost will supervise the bathing. Don't look shocked or try to protest, she is not likely to be offended or even interested in your manly bodies. The baths will have disinfectant added and my mother-in-law will put a special lotion through your hair. For my part, I will start preparing dinner." She smiled. "It's good to have the family together again."

After she left, the men quickly stripped off their filthy clothing and Simon, with the bags at arm's length, disappeared around the corner. Yvette had left a bottle of cognac on the tray.

"Is it always as good as this?" George asked, and the men laughed. The removal of the louse ridden dirty clothes was symbolic of their severing of links with the battlefield. As Ghislaine had said, the family was back home.

The bath routine went well, with Simon acting as the water carrier between the kitchen and the big tub. Old Madame Pruvost washed and combed the men's hair with her 'special' lotion, her presence not the embarrassment the men had imagined.

"Just like a matron in a hospital," observed Mac. "She sees us as objects to be helped, not as men."

It was quite late when all the ablutions had been completed and the tired but happy group sat down to a meal. There was little banter at the table as the Pruvost women could see the weariness of the guests. No mention was made of the war. As soon as the meal was completed, the men excused themselves and headed for their sleeping quarters. The long day, the cognac and the heavy meal all contributed to a desire to sleep, sleep and sleep.

As they rolled into bed Jacko called out to Darkie, "You know that little black book that Madame Pruvost kept writing in during our bathtime?"

"Yeah."

"What do you reckon she was writing down?"

"Haven't a clue, Jacko."

"I know," piped up Sam. "I sneaked a look."

"You did? Come on Sam, what was in it?"

"Well you won't believe it Darkie, but she was keeping a score."

"A score? What sort of a score, Sam?" The darkness hid the wide grin on Darkie's face.

"Well, she was awarding a score out of ten on the size of your prick."

"Oh, come on Sam, you're making that up."

"No seriously Darkie. That's what she was doing. Remember, I can read French." Sam was convincing.

"Bloody hell Jacko. Did you hear that?"

"Sure did. Well, go on Sam, who won the competition?"

Sam hesitated. "No, I'm not sure I should divulge that. It could cause jealousy amongst the group." Everyone was listening. "And another thing, Simon wasn't in the competition so he may think it's unfair."

"Stop stalling, Sam. Tell us, and let us get to sleep."

"All right. The winner by a big margin was Preacher."

"Preacher? You sure Sam?"

"Yep Darkie. Preacher won the blue ribbon."

"Hey Preacher," called Jacko, "did you hear that? You're the best hung man in the Section. Congratulations."

"Oh shut up and go to sleep." growled Preacher.

"Yeah give it a rest you fellows. Let's all get some sleep." ordered Al, although he too was laughing quietly.

"Well Preacher," Darkie had to have the last word, "size is one thing, but do you know how to use it?" The room shook with the laughter.

"That's enough Darkie. Shut up and let's get some sleep." Al's voice of command brooked no response.

* * *

With the exception of Bluey and Simon the men slept through the next morning. It was after noon when they started straggling out to the mess room. Nothing was said of the late night conversation which puzzled Bluey.

“You know Al. I would’ve bet that Preacher would’ve come out steaming this morning after what Darkie and Sam cooked up last night.”

“Bluey, he had two options. The expected one was that he’d take offence at the gist of the conversation, an insult to Madame Pruvost, etc. The other, is that he was flattered by the so-called results of the competition. You know, he may even believe that the whole thing was genuine.”

Bluey shook his head. “Poor Preacher. He’s a gem in the field, but once he gets to the farm, he’s hopeless. I hope he and Gilly don’t become too involved. They’re both such nice people, but this must be a temporary thing. I mean, it’s all very well to have a fling, but Preacher isn’t like that. Preacher takes everything so seriously, especially Gilly.”

“Who knows Bluey. My concern is what happens at the front, how Preacher performs back here is his business. They’re two different worlds, and must be kept apart. Preacher has to understand that. Come on, let’s go and check on the new gear. I’m sure Ted Harley will have done us proud.”

The section was not required to report for duty for the next week and soon slipped back into their routine of lazy walks around the countryside and long nights of cards. Al’s beginner’s luck held.

THEY'RE BLOODY MAD

The week away from Army duties passed very quickly for the men of No.3 Section. They had allowed their fitness level to drop slightly but once they returned to duty Sergeant King saw that they soon regained it. But apart from the drill and the route marches, life was not too onerous. The weeks passed slowly. And for once rumours were scarce.

Sergeant King was unable to throw any light on the subject of future activities when asked by Al Wilson. "No one seems to know what they have in mind for the Division, Al. It's almost like a holiday camp up at the Château."

"Well Pete, there must be something in the wind judging by the number of new troops arriving."

"Not really. They're replacements for the losses at Bullecourt. We should be up to strength soon, but no one is talking about a new offensive."

"Come on Pete, we both know different. It's just that they're having trouble finding a new place for the slaughter." Al's sarcastic tongue was not lost on Sergeant King.

"Anywhere along the Hindenburg Line would fit that description Al. But you're right, it's just a matter of where and when, not a question of if. How are the new boys fitting in?"

"Not too badly. Morbey is slow but steady. Young is full of beans but he has yet to see action. I've taken Morbey as my partner and given Young to Dowson. That puts McKenzie and Fleming together. McKenzie won't take any nonsense from Fleming, so all in all, I think we have a good balance. Young could be a problem."

"What sort of a problem?"

"It's sort of difficult to explain. Bluey reckons that Simon is only sixteen and is too young to be sent to the front. But that's not the problem. He's fallen in love with Yvette, the youngest of the girls at the farm. He really has fallen head over heels, and the others tease him unmercifully."

"Bloody hell!" laughed the Sergeant. "Sweet sixteen and all that. Well, keep an eye on him. He won't want to be mooching around the trenches dreaming of Miss Yvette when Jerry is nearby."

"I don't think Bluey will let that happen. It's the opposite that I worry about. I worry about Bluey spending too much time looking after his partner and not concentrating on looking after himself. You can only think of yourself and what you're supposed to be doing out there, you can't be worrying about others."

The Sergeant gave the corporal a long hard stare. "Coming from you Al Wilson, that's total bullshit, and you know it. Your men, their safety, and their welfare, dominates all your thinking. Don't give me that garbage about only thinking of yourself."

"Aw Pete, that's different. I'm a corporal. I'm experienced and I'm lucky. Everyone says so."

"Yes they do my friend, but don't push that luck too far. Good corporals are hard to find."

"Why Sergeant, that's the nicest thing you've ever said to me. I didn't know you cared."

“I don’t. Well, put it this way. I’d miss you if they ever knocked that cocky head off your shoulders. I’d miss you. But not for long.”

“Liar. We go too far back Mr King. Anyhow that sort of talk is not healthy. I’ll keep my head on my shoulders, and you find out what’s cooking. Those blood-thirsty bastards at Corps HQ must have something in mind.”

* * *

The weeks of training in the warm summer sunshine worked wonders for the morale of the battle weary troops. But the Generals did have something in mind, and no one was surprised when the orders came to move out.

“Where are we going Al?” asked the ever inquisitive Sam.

“The Generals have heard about how you are living in the lap of luxury here, so they’re sending you to Belgium.”

Al looked around at the anxious faces. “Come on, cheer up. We’re only going there as a reserve Division. Seems they’re putting all the Aussie Divisions together at last. We leave in four days’ time. You can tell the ladies we’re going to Flanders, but nothing more.”

“That’ll be easy because that’s all we know.” Preacher complained.

“What I mean Preacher is, don’t start dreaming up orders that haven’t been issued. Time for one last concert if Gilly agrees, and then it’s goodbye.”

“You mean we won’t be coming back here?” Simon was disturbed.

“Simon, this is war. Who knows if or when we may return to the Somme. We go where we’re told. No one asks for our preferences. We’re going in four days. That’s all I know, that’s all you need to know.” Al looked around the room. “But like the rest of you, I’ll miss this place and the ladies. They’ve been very kind.”

* * *

Four days later the men took their leave of the five ladies. Even Madame Pruvost senior came to the gate to shake hands with them and to wish them well. The farewells were brief and formal, although the invitation for the men to return to the farm was warm and sincere.

"Where to now Al?" asked Sam, as the farm receded into the distance.

"We board a train at Amiens and go wherever it takes us Sam. We're to be held in reserve so I guess we'll be a fair way back from the line, but I've no doubt you'll be seeing Ypres in the near future."

"Another heap of rubble?"

Al nodded.

"How the hell are these people ever going to rebuild these places after the war?" asked Darkie.

"Same as before Darkie." responded Preacher. "You've seen what a good flood or bushfire can do. Well this isn't much different, except it's taking a lot longer to happen. When it's all over the people will return, just as they've done for centuries, and start all over again."

"Poor bastards." murmured Jacko. "It's not their fault."

"No, it's not. Just like a flood is not anyone's fault, except perhaps God's. It just happens and always has in the history of this planet."

"Well in the case of a flood, God can always turn off the tap, but he doesn't seem to be taking much interest in this bloody mess." observed Mac. "It sorta tests your faith doesn't it? I mean, why would God let men do this to one another? That's assuming, of course, that there is a God."

Al moved quickly to end the conversation. He had heard such discussions before and they usually led to angry and confused debates that disturbed the listeners. "There are many things we don't understand or can't explain. You all could, if you had a mind to, recall losses of young ones, dear ones, long before they had reached old age when death is an expected part of life. Don't try to reason it out. Accept it. Believe it's part of some greater plan, or don't believe it. But you must find something to believe in, and hold fast to that. You don't have to share your belief with anyone, just have it within yourselves. The man who has nothing to believe in, nothing to hold onto, has nothing to fight for, and then the will to survive falters, stumbles, and he collects a bullet. Sounds a bit drastic, but it's the truth. A fact. Lose your will to survive, and you'll lose your life. Right fellas, end of lesson. Sort it out within yourselves. For now, your job is to get down off this truck and move your baggage on to the station. Let's go."

* * *

The men had little idea of where the train was taking them as it wound its way northwards to the Belgian border. At times, they felt they were doubling back, at other times they were left sitting on a siding while freight trains passed them, en route to the Somme battlefields. It was just on dusk when the train reached the northern town of Hazelbrouck and the order was given to disembark.

"Well me hearties, this is going to be a shock to your systems." Sergeant King was waiting outside the station. "No nice warm billet for you tonight, but a good old army tent. I hope you had something to eat, because you have a fair march ahead of you, and I doubt if the cookhouse will be functioning when you get there."

"No real problem Sergeant, the ladies provided us with plenty of bread and cheese, plus a few other goodies," Preacher answered. "There are some left-overs if you're hungry."

Sergeant King glared at the tall soldier. He was about to rebuke him for being cheeky, but changed his mind. "Well, I don't mind left-overs Lacey. Don't mind them at all, seeing I last ate at 0600 this morning." He turned to Al. "You've trained them well Corporal Wilson. Always good to keep on side with the Sergeant."

The men delved into their pockets and produced some sandwiches. "Thank you. Corporal Wilson. Seeing your men have been so kind, you can sleep in tomorrow until 7:00am."

The corporal made a mock bow. "Most kind of you Sir, and where are we heading to for this long night of sweet dreams?"

The Sergeant produced a small map from the top pocket of his uniform. "X marks the spot," he said, placing a finger on the map. "You have a tent reserved and the new member of your section is already there. He's been told to have everything in readiness for your arrival, so you should get a brew before turning in."

"What new member? We came up to strength when Simon joined us."

"I know Al, but seems like there was a spare sapper in the replacement pipeline, and he's been allocated to No.3 Section. You're to get an extra pair of hands."

Al Wilson was not convinced. "Yeah, but everyone is so short of men, it's a bit odd. What's his name?"

"Sapper Colin Bailey. Seems he's an old school friend of the new officer, Lieutenant Crowther's replacement."

"Another officer? We seem to use them up at a fair rate. Anyhow, we haven't the time to stand around talking." Al turned to his men. "Come on, grab your gear and let's go. I don't trust maps marked by Sergeants. This camp could be anywhere in northern France."

"On your way corporal, before I change my mind about letting you sleep in." The Sergeant walked back into the railway office.

* * *

The section had covered close to six miles before arriving at the tent city. A young fair-headed soldier appeared from the shadows of a tent.

"Are you Corporal Wilson with No.3 Section?" he asked in a lilting voice.

"Who wants to know?"

"I'm Sapper Bailey." replied the challenger. "I was told to prepare the tent, and to meet you here so I could show you where it is."

"Well, well, a welcoming committee. And is there by any chance a cup of tea awaiting the weary warriors?"

"Oh yes corporal. Sergeant King said that all sorts of horrible things could happen to me if Corporal Wilson didn't get his hot mug of tea on arrival."

"A wise man, Sergeant King. Right, lead on Bailey. We can do the introductions later."

The group weaved its way through the forest of tents. At their Section tent, they quickly dropped their gear before gathering around the small fire.

"Starting with you Preacher, each man introduce himself." Al directed.

The men volunteered their names.

"There's one name missing."

"What do you mean?" asked Al. "This is No.3 Section, all present and correct."

"Oh, he must've been mistaken." replied Bailey.

"Who's been mistaken? What are you talking about?"

"When I joined the Brigade this morning, Lieutenant Johnson said there was a big man called Pettersen with you, but he's not, so the Lieutenant must have been mistaken.""

"Erik Pettersen was with us but he's..."

"Did you say Johnson?" interrupted Bluey. "What's his first name? What does he look like?"

"Easy Bluey. What's bitten you?" Al was surprised at the urgency in Bluey's voice

"Come on Bailey, tell me!" demanded Bluey.

"His name is Ronald Johnson. We went to the same school in Melbourne. He has a dark complexion with black wavy hair. He's very nice."

"Oh shit Bluey," Darkie moaned. "He's come back to haunt us."

Bluey stared at the flickering flames. "Haunt us? More like hound us."

Al looked from Bluey to Darkie, and then back to Bluey. "From the looks on your faces, this means trouble. So, what's with this Ronald Johnson?"

"It's a bit late in the evening to tell you all about Ron Johnson, Al. Why don't we turn in and we'll tell you about it tomorrow?"

"No Bluey. Tomorrow is too far away. I suppose the rest of you know about this Mr Johnson?" All the men, except Simon and George, nodded.

"Yes Al. Bluey and Darkie and poor old Erik told us what happened in the recruit camp." Preacher said.

"All of you, except Bluey and Darkie, turn in. Now you two, let's hear it. Keep it short, and don't give me anything but facts. What the hell, or who the hell, is Ronald Johnson?"

The three men sat around the fire for the next twenty minutes, while Bluey and Darkie briefed Al on the events that occurred at the training camp, including Bluey shaming Johnson at the firing range, and the altercation between Johnson and Erik. When they'd finished, Al got to his feet. "Time to turn in."

"But Al..." protested Darkie. "What are we going to do?"

"Do? You're going to do your job. Forget about some stupid incident that happened in recruit camp last year. Just do your job. That's all that matters. Now hit the hay. Despite his generosity this evening, Sergeant King may not be in such a good mood in the morning."

* * *

The Section paraded before Captain Solway the next morning and he introduced Lieutenant Johnson. As Johnson walked along the line shaking hands with the men, his contempt of Bluey and Darkie was obvious. Captain Solway briefed the men on the situation around Ypres, and although he couldn't, or wouldn't, give them any specifics, it was obvious that a new Allied drive was in the offing, and that it would include the reserve divisions.

* * *

In early June, the battle for Messines commenced. The Allied plan for the battle went as planned, and the Germans suffered a stunning defeat. The spirits of the men soared as the news filtered back to the rear.

"Perhaps our Generals have learned from the past, Al. Messines seems to have gone according to plan, and the plan was good."

"Yes Preacher it was, and you may be right. They seem now to favour throwing all the weight on a section of the frontline with the aim of making small gains. Apparently, the artillery barrage was superb. Jerry really took a pounding."

"There's one thing I don't understand Al."

"What's that Preacher?"

"People who were there said no one could survive the artillery bombardment, but some must have survived. Look at our casualties."

"True Preacher. Some Germans survived the bombardment. Their reserves were well back but came up quickly, and their artillery took a heavy toll on us, but it wasn't an open field slaughter like Fromelles or Bullecourt. Still that's little comfort to the dead or their next of kin." Al looked around to see that they couldn't be overheard. "Change of subject Preacher. How goes it with Lieutenant Johnson and the Section?"

"We don't see much of him. He informed us that his skills as a planner are much sought after in HQ. Personally, I think he has an aversion to dirt and bad odours."

"That's all right for now, but sooner or later we will go back to the frontline, and this animosity between Johnson and the others could be a real danger."

"I can see that Al, but I don't believe Lieutenant Johnson will get too close to the front. I think he finds war very distasteful."

"Distasteful!" Al rocked with laughter. "Preacher, I have never heard a better description. I must tell Pete King what to do with his distasteful war. Good one."

"Speaking of the Sergeant, I've a feeling he has put himself between Johnson and the Section. A sort of buffer zone. Most perceptive."

"Yes, but that's all part of being a good soldier. Know your enemy, without and within."

"Another useful phrase Al. Mind if I use it on the others at some time?"

"Be my guest. But enough of this philosophising, let's see what our villains are up to."

* * *

Over the weeks the build-up continued. Everyone knew the next blow would be struck in the area to the north and west of Ypres, probably on a scale never before seen.

In mid-September the great assault commenced, with the Australian Divisions committed. The plan for a rolling barrage worked well. The troops, showing faith in the accuracy of their own gunners, walked behind the curtain of shells. Occasionally, a shortfall caused casualties. The sheer weight of the three-day artillery barrage had stunned the enemy and the rolling barrage confused him. Al, Bluey, Mac and Darkie accompanied one battalion whilst the others were on their right with the sister battalion. Everything was going according to plan. After the initial advance the infantry, with the signallers alongside, settled in for a respite before the next advance.

* * *

The battalion officer spoke into the phone, then called out. "Pass the word. Barrage commences in two minutes. The guns will hold their line of fire for three minutes then raise the range by one hundred yards. As soon as the three minutes are up, we are moving out."

No problems were anticipated for this next stage. Right on time the shells descended, but to the consternation of the men in the field, the veil of smoke and dust rose one hundred yards behind them, not ahead of them.

"For Christ's sake, they've got the wrong range. Quick! Get me the artillery on the line."

Darkie didn't need to be told twice. A look of desperation came over his face. "The line is down Sir. It's been cut by our own shells."

"My God! When they raise the range we'll be right underneath it." The men staring at the wall of smoke knew only too well what was about to happen. In two minutes their war would be over.

"Come on Mac," screamed Bluey. "Follow me." He jumped from the shallow foxhole he'd been sheltering in and ran to the wire. He picked up the cable and, running it through the palm of his hand, sprinted towards the inferno. Without hesitation, Mac followed with a phone. As the watchers watched and prayed the two men disappeared into the wall of smoke and dust. Twice the impact from shells knocked them from their feet and their ears rang from the impact of the blasts.

"Got it Mac?" screamed Bluey. Mac couldn't hear above the din, but seeing his companion on his knees hauling the two ends of the broken wire together he realised that the break had been found. Mac tied in the phone and a voice answered, "Artillery here."

Mac failed to hear the sound of a voice but assuming, or hoping, that he'd made connection he screamed into the phone,

"Stop the bloody guns. You're killing our men." As if by an act of God, a silence descended over the battlefield.

"Who are you? Identify yourself."

Mac heard a voice but the ringing in his ears prevented him from understanding the words. "Linesman here. You're hitting our own men. We're putting you through to Battalion."

Bluey took the phone from him. "You're through now. Battalion calling." He replaced the phone. "Come on Mac. Sitting out here is no place for us. Let's get back to the line."

"Bluey, you're mad," whispered Mac. "You're bloody mad. You nearly got us killed."

"We're all about to be killed Mac. What a spot of luck to find that break so easily. And thanks mate for coming with me. I'd forgotten the phone. Come on, let's get back to the line before some Jerry spots us. Here comes Al."

Al took the telephone gear from Mac and helped him towards the trench. As they reached the safety of the trench, the shelling recommenced and Mac cringed against the wall.

Mac pointed at Bluey. "He's mad. No one could go into that hail of shells and survive. And I must be mad to have followed him."

Al shook his head. "No Mac, he's not mad. Neither are you. We all owe our lives to you two. That was fast work Bluey! You were off before I had even thought about what could be done. As a matter of interest, why did you call Mac to follow? Not that I am complaining?"

"Mac can run faster than you Al, and I took off so quickly because I didn't stop to think. Had I given it a thought, I probably wouldn't have gone."

The corporal thought for a moment. "Yeah. Anyway, are you two all right? I could send you back. By the way, the battalion is very pleased with you. Extremely pleased."

"You know Al, what amazes me is the way those guns stopped. Mac yelled out stop shooting and that was it, not another shell. Magic."

Al placed his hand on his friend's shoulder. "No magic Bluey. It was fate, or whatever it is that runs this show. As Mac phoned in to the gunners, they stopped to raise their range. The timing was perfect, thirty seconds later and we would've been mince meat."

An officer dropped into the shelter. "We're on our way corporal. I just wanted to thank these two men for what they did." He looked at Mac and Bluey. "You'll hear more about it later men, but the battalion is forever in your debt. Come on corporal, I need you, your men and that telephone." He stood up, blew his whistle and started forward in the wake of the covering bombardment. The three signallers joined Darkie with the reel and took their places behind the officer. The second assault was back on track.

* * *

Four weeks later a group of officers assembled at the Brigade Headquarters. The meeting was chaired by Colonel Payne, and it was obvious he was uneasy.

"Gentlemen let me try to sum up the discussion so far. The Battalion Commander has put forward the names of two signallers, Dowson and McKenzie, for a bravery award. The artillery HQ wishes to oppose the recommendation on the grounds that it will cause certain reactions at the higher level of command, by people who do not know about the error made during the barrage at Polygon Wood. I tend to agree with the gunners. It was an unfortunate error, an error which can occur in the heat of battle, but not one that one needs to advertise. No one was killed or wounded."

The Battalion Commander raised his hand. "Sir, we do not want to cause the gunners any embarrassment. They do a magnificent job. They have made our job so much easier, but those two signallers deserve some recognition for what was a very brave act."

"Fine John. I hear you, but you do understand that if I send this recommendation forward, giving the details of what happened, someone is going to draw it to the attention of the Corps staff, and that might start an investigation, a witch-hunt." The Colonel had his instructions.

Lieutenant Johnson raised his hand.

"Yes Johnson?"

"If I may Sir. It's a technical point, but I think you could apply it to this case."

"A technical point Johnson. Explain yourself."

"Well Sir, the recommendation states in part, and I quote, 'in the face of heavy shelling these two men...' and so it goes on. Medals are awarded for bravery in the face of the enemy, this was not enemy fire, so this recommendation falls short of the accepted criteria."

The anger on the Battalion Commander's face was plain. "Lieutenant, are you saying that if you happen to stray into a friendly fire zone then it's not dangerous?"

"No sir, I didn't say that. What I said was, medals are struck for bravery in the face of the enemy, and in this instance, this was not the case. I accept that the men were brave, but their action does not meet the criteria laid down by Corps."

The Battalion Commander shook his head. "I hear you, but I don't believe you. Hell's bells, you're one of their officers, and you won't support my submission."

"I can't Sir. From a technical point, I have to oppose it."

The Battalion Commander stared at the Colonel. "Well Sir, is there a technical fault in my recommendation?"

Colonel Payne cleared his throat. "Now that it has been drawn to my attention, I have to take notice of the point made by Lieutenant Johnson. As he said, this was an act of bravery, but not an act of bravery in the face of the enemy, and so I will not be passing it on. However, Lieutenant Johnson, I want you to parade the two men concerned, and in front of their companions express the sincere thanks of the staff, the infantry and the gunners for what they did."

Lieutenant Johnson nodded. "Of course sir."

"Thank you gentlemen." With a wave of his cane, the Colonel led his staff from the room.

"Sorry John." the artillery officer offered his hand across the table to the Battalion Commander. "We go back a long way, and I know how you must feel, but I had to protect my batteries."

"Understood Fred, and I probably would've withdrawn my submission as an indication of our regard for you and your team, except of course Mr Smart-arse here found a technical fault." He glared at Johnson. "I hope, Lieutenant Johnson, we will have the pleasure of your company at the front one day. My men, who owe so much to those two sappers, will be delighted to test out your theory about friendly bullets as opposed to unfriendly bullets. Come on Fred, I'll buy you a beer."

"Damn you Dowson." Johnson addressed the closed door. "One day your luck will run out, and I'll be waiting. Damn you!"

* * *

It was not the Germans who stopped the Allied drive, but the weather. Heavy rain turned the battlefield into a sea of mud. Both sides realised that the Major campaigns for 1917 were over. Another year of bloodshed, tens of thousands of lives lost, a few miles gained or lost. It had been a dreadful year. However, No.3 Section was elated when orders came through that the Division was moving back to the Somme, back to their old stamping ground.

"Christmas at Corbie, what a wonderful thought." mused Preacher. "I can hardly believe our good fortune."

Darkie grinned. "Yeah Preacher, and just look at young Simon. You know Preacher, one day you might become his dad. We could have a double wedding. You and Gilly, and Simon and Yvette. Now that would be a party."

"Oh shut up Darkie." snapped Simon.

"Yes, shut up Darkie." added Preacher. "You're an idiot, always have been."

The men's laughter was cut short by the entrance of Lieutenant Johnson accompanied by Sergeant King. They got to their feet as a mark of respect.

Ronald Johnson looked very pleased with himself. "Having a good time, are we men? That's good. I have just returned from Corbie where I have been organising our accommodation. I understand you have organised yourselves rather well in the Corbie area. Lucky you. Of course, Captain Solway and I will live at the Château. I've been talking to the officers there, and it seems we have a small problem. It appears that most Brigades provide their officers with a batman, but Captain Solway and my predecessors have made do without. Now I think that is an imposition on the others. I put it to Colonel Payne that we have an extra man in No.3 Section, and he has agreed that the captain and I can share the services of a batman whilst we are at the Château."

The men looked around nervously.

"Yes, I can see you're wondering who is the lucky man amongst you, who is to get to live in the luxury of that magnificent Château. Well Dowson, I've selected you."

For once Bluey was dumbfounded, and this allowed Al Wilson to speak before the redhead found his voice. "Sir, as the Corporal-in-charge of Section three, don't I have a say in who I give up from the team to act as your batman?"

"Corporal Wilson, I've been studying your team for the past four months, and have come to certain conclusions, on which I have based my selection."

"You..."

"Quiet Dowson." The voice of Sergeant King carried a warning. "Sir, I must support Corporal Wilson. I feel we need to discuss this matter with Captain Solway."

"Discuss what?" said a quiet voice from the doorway. "I was just passing and thought I would drop in. Well Sergeant, what should be discussed with me?" The Captain gave no indication of just how much of the conversation he had overhead.

Lieutenant Johnson had been surprised by the entry of his superior.

"Sir, I was just explaining to the men how Colonel Payne had approved that you and I could utilise the services of a member of this Section as a joint batman whilst billeted in the Château outside Amiens."

"Yes Ronald, he mentioned it to me. I found it odd that you went direct to the Colonel without consulting me. But I'll take that up with you later. Now what is it Sergeant that you want to discuss with me?"

The Sergeant paused before replying. "Sir, it seems to me that this batman at the Château will sort of be our representative. I mean, the other officers will judge us by the behaviour of our man at the Château."

"Yes Sergeant King, that is a distinct possibility. He will be representing the signallers."

"Right Sir. So, it's important that we get the right man for the job. And bearing in mind he is there to look after you and the Lieutenant."

"I agree Sergeant King. So, who do you have in mind? Who is this man who will ably represent the signallers and tend to my comforts?"

"Well Sir, I don't have anyone in mind, except I am sure of one thing: he must be a volunteer."

"Of course he must Sergeant. That goes without saying. I'm not having some miserable soul pressed into looking after me and

Mr Johnson. A volunteer is required." The shrewd officer ran his eye over the section. "Now men, you have all had a pretty hectic year, and as a Section you have done extremely well. Here's your chance to swap all that mud and filth for the comforts of the Château. All right, hands up those volunteering."

One hand crept into the air.

"Bailey. Good show. I was worried that no one would volunteer. So, there you are Ronald. One of your old school mates. I'll leave it to you to teach him the finer points of being a batman. Anything else you chaps would like to discuss before I push off?"

"Yes Sir." Sam could not resist any invitation to ask a question.

"Well?"

"When's this bloody war going to finish, so we can go home?"

The room filled with laughter.

WHAT'S GOING ON HERE?

The arrival of the men back at the farm was a time of celebration. The neighbours were invited at short notice for an evening of music and fun. The warmth of the greetings given to Preacher and Simon by Ghislaine and Yvette was noted.

Next morning the men held a meeting in their quarters.

Darkie called for attention. "Fellas, we have to give the women something special for Christmas, something they will remember us for after we have gone. You agree Al?"

"I'm sure we all agree Darkie. Something in mind?"

Darkie looked around. "I know you're expecting me to come out with some stupid suggestion, but this time I'm serious. George and I have been talking, and we think we should install running water in the house."

"You mean pipes and taps and all that sort of thing?"

"Yeah Mick, that's exactly what we mean." replied George.

"But we're signallers, not bloody engineers. What do we know about plumbing, and where are we going to get the materials, even if we could do the job?"

"Quieten down Mick." advised Al. "Darkie. Just what do you and George have in mind?"

"We all know the present set-up for getting water into the house. There are two holding tanks in the kitchen, which the women keep topped up with water they draw from the well in the backyard. George and I were carrying in the water yesterday, when George said how much easier it would be if the farm had some sort of a pump, instead of that old bucket and windlass for drawing up the water. I said it was a nice dream, but George reckons it could be done. Right George?"

George nodded. "When I first spoke, it was just a casual comment, but since then I've given it some thought. It's possible, but would depend on getting the necessary material."

"Such as?"

"Well Al, it all depends what we want, a simple system or a complex system, or perhaps something in between."

Al leant back in his seat. "All right George. Let's talk simple for the moment."

"Right. The aim is to get water from the well to the tanks in the kitchen. That means pumping water from the well. Now, you can work a pump by using human power, by using machinery or by using the forces of nature. With a manual pump, the only saving for the women would be the carrying of the water from the well to the kitchen. They would still have to work the pump. At the other end of the scale, we could install an engine. Of course, problems spring to mind. What engine? How do we get one? What about fuel? And remember, it's the ladies who would have to work it."

"And the noise."

"Yes Preacher, the noise, and who fixes it when it breaks down, and all those other messy things?"

Al intervened. "So, we go for a nature-assisted system?"

"Yes Al, that's what I have in mind."

"Nature-assisted?" Mick scratched his head. "Will someone tell me what the hell we are talking about?"

"Use your brain Mick. The wind. We're talking about windmills."

George continued. "Darkie is right. Wind power. What I have in mind is an Aussie-style windmill, pumping water to a tank alongside the house. From the tank, we would lead pipes to the kitchen, this room, the barn, to wherever Gilly wanted water on tap."

"You mean we could fill the tubs here, without carrying the water?"

"Yes Sam. And your modesty would be protected."

Sam grinned. "Yeah, but grandma would miss out on spying on Preacher's manhood."

All laughed except Preacher, who quickly turned the talk back to the topic under discussion. "If we had running water in here George, could we rig up a shower over the tubs? It would make life much easier, especially when we come in from the field."

"It's possible Preacher, but there's one thing that puzzles me. Where is the women's bathroom in this house? Do you know?"

Preacher shook his head. "No George, but I suspect that there isn't one, at least not a bathroom as we know it. Ghislaine said they bathed in here when we were away. I guess this is their bathroom as such. But there is a large tub behind a screen in one corner of the kitchen which could serve as a bath. Makes sense. The kitchen is warm, and the hot water is handy."

"Ah, hot water," mused Sam "What a gift."

George shook his head. "I think we'd be biting off more than we could chew if we started thinking about a hot water system. I suggest we stick to the original idea of getting water from the well into the house."

Al interrupted. "Before we go any further, George. Are we being practical? Are we being realistic to even consider such a scheme?

Say we could get the materials, do you have the expertise, the know-how, to build such an arrangement?"

George looked at the faces around the table. "If we stick to a simple arrangement. Yes, I think I could handle it. Of course, I'd need lots of help from you blokes."

"That you can take for granted George once we have agreed to proceed with the project." Al looked around the table and all the men nodded. "So, what about materials?"

"There is a bunch of Australian engineers attached to the engineering depot just south of here. It's a huge complex. They have everything an army needs, and a lot of stuff it doesn't need, so the materials are there. The windmill is a challenge. We would need help to build one, but favours can be purchased."

"What do you mean by purchased?"

"I suppose Preacher you would call it bribery. I prefer to call it bartering. We want a windmill. So, we find out what the engineers want, and we give it to them in exchange for a windmill."

"Yes, but what do they want?"

George held up his hands. "Preacher, at the moment, I don't know. We have to find out what the price is for a windmill. Once we know that, then we see if we can come up with the goods."

Al once again got the discussion back on track. "Right George, that's hurdle number one. The windmill. What's next?"

"Well Al, we need a tank, pipes, taps, and of course building materials and tools. There's no real problem with those. The Engineers are forever building things, and no one keeps a strict check on the materials. We simply visit projects they are working on and borrow the stuff. A little bit here, a little bit there. And before you speak Preacher. We are not stealing the stuff just redirecting it to a worthwhile cause."

Al stood up. "Right, seems like we all agree. Let's get started. There's a lot to be done."

Bluey raised his hand. "Hang on Al, aren't you going just a little too quickly?"

"Sorry Bluey, I didn't know you had an objection."

"I haven't, I like the idea. But don't you think you should ask Gilly before you start rebuilding her house. She might not want running water."

"I had thought of that. But the first step is to do our homework to see if this scheme can actually be accomplished. Then we ask Gilly. It would be sad if we mooted the idea and she became enthusiastic and then we found out that it was not possible. You agree?"

"Yeah Al, that makes sense. So what now?"

"As I see it, we have three things to sort out. Firstly, the windmill. It just so happens I know a couple of blokes over at that depot."

"As usual," chimed in Sam.

"Well Sam, it's always good to have contacts, friends in high, and sometimes, low places. I'll walk over there with George and we'll see what can be done. I know Darkie and Mick could find us a truck if we turned them loose, but then again, the engineers probably have everything we need. So, we'll try and do a complete trade with them. We'll have a further pow-wow this evening."

* * *

The men gathered around the table that evening to hear Al's report.

"It's looking good. The engineers are on side but only for work they can do on the Base. They won't come over here to work, except to help install the windmill. If we can get a truck, they'll turn their backs while we load the materials. They'll let George use their workshop to bend pipes and thread them, whatever that means, but we only go in and out at times they specify."

"Sounds great Al, and what's the price?"

"Ah yes Darkie, the price..." Al paused. "The price is high, very high," and from his pocket he produced a written list. "Our friendly engineers want to have a very merry Christmas, and to do that, they need a considerable amount of liquid refreshments. Beer, spirits, wine. You name it, they want it. Here, cast your eyes over that Darkie."

Al tossed the sheet of paper across the table. Mick rose from his place and moved around the table, so he could read over Darkie's shoulder.

A low whistle emerged from Darkie's lips. "Shit Al! What are these engineers planning to do? Start up a pub?"

"No. They have been given a week off at Christmas, and are planning to go to the coast for a binge. Right away from the war. They want to celebrate and entertain, if you get my meaning. So, what do you think?"

Darkie continued to run his finger down the list. "Al, there's stuff here I've never heard of. You sure this is for real?"

"Yeah, that's their price. The blokes over there believe that certain liqueurs have a certain effect on a lady's sexual appetite."

Darkie's eyebrows rose. "Any truth in that theory?"

"Not that I know of Darkie. Intoxication is intoxication, and it really does not matter which bottle causes it. Well, what do you think?"

Mick whispered in Darkie's ear.

"Yeah, good point Mick. These here liqueurs Al, would the officers' mess stock them?"

Al frowned. "Yes Darkie, I suppose they would. Why?"

"Oh, just curious. No problem Al, except the time. How long have we got?"

Al shook his head. "You know, I'm already beginning to regret starting off down this path, so my only hope now is that Gilly says she doesn't want plumbing installed. However, if she does, then we have four weeks to do the job and to pay up. What say you?"

"Done. You go and see Gilly. If she says yes, then it's full speed ahead."

Again, Al shook his head. "Come on Preacher, let's go and see Gilly. Maybe the Germans will attack and save our skins, because I can see that this venture is fraught with danger."

* * *

The evening meal was dominated by talk of the new plumbing system. George, supported by Al, tried to restrain the enthusiasm of the girls. The two men pointed out that what was proposed was very basic, and even then, would be dependent upon the unskilled labour of the signallers. The girls wouldn't hear of any criticism of the plan or the men. It was left to Darkie to dampen their spirits.

"Now pay attention girls. No one outside this room must know of our scheme. No one. If a neighbour asks what's going on, you must say the mad Australians are mending the roof because it's leaking. You must not mention the plumbing."

"But why Monsieur Darkie?" asked Marie.

"Because we'll have to borrow most of the material," said Darkie with a long, obvious wink. "You understand? Now someone might miss a few bits and pieces from a store and start looking for them. If they hear that some Australians are installing pipework here at the farm, then they might get suspicious, and we don't want anyone snooping around do we?"

The ladies agreed that secrecy would be the best defence against any possible enquiries.

That night Darkie and Mick briefed the others on their plan. "Just two points to make Al. Firstly, the engineers must take the stock as we collect it. We don't want it stashed here at the farm. Secondly, only Mick and I will collect the goods, so only Mick and I will know where the stuff comes from. In that way, none of you can be implicated should anything go wrong. Oh yes, one other thing, should Mick or myself ask you to do a duty for us, we expect you to do it, as we'll be busy elsewhere. That all right with you?"

Al Wilson threw his hands up in mock despair. "I've heard more than enough already. Phil Reynolds warned me about you lot, and he was right. Yeah Darkie, we're all in this together. But for God's sake, and your own, be careful. The penalty for borrowing grog is death, or something worse."

"Don't worry Al. You just see to the plumbing. Mick and I will look after the other side."

"Yes, I expect you will. All right George, it's full steam ahead. What's the plan?"

"There are ten of us. We will have to provide two switchboard operators each day from next weekend. We leave out Darkie and Mick. So that leaves us with six working hands. Now I want to spend most days in the workshop, and I would like Mac to be my offsider. The four off duty must do the carrying of the goods from the depot to here. A truck would help."

"My department George." said Al. "I have friends in transport. Just let me know a little ahead of time when you want something moved."

"Good. Now Jacko and Bluey. Have either of you ever put up a tankstand, a really good solid tankstand?"

Jacko nodded. "Yeah, I've helped with a few. A stand is not a real problem providing we have the timber."

"I've helped with a few, George." the red head said. "As Jacko said, it's not too difficult providing you have the right materials."

"Fine. You two will be responsible for erecting the stand. I'll sketch what I want, and I'll put the hard word on the engineers tomorrow for timber. You and the rest of the team start digging postholes tomorrow. I'll mark them out before I leave. Al, you bring a truck over to the depot tomorrow afternoon. I'll have the timber ready for loading. It'll be cut to size. The day after tomorrow, we should see a tankstand in place, that is, if you blokes can swing a pick and shovel."

"Don't you worry about the tankstand mate." growled Jacko.

* * *

Over the next three days the men erected four large posts that were to hold the platform in place. These were braced one against the other and the tops carefully levelled. Finally, heavy timbers were laid on the top and bolted to the cross members. It was Sam who asked the question.

"Jacko, that platform is a good twelve feet above the ground. How are you going to get a tank up there?"

Jacko scratched his head. "You know Sam, for once you have asked a very good question. I don't know, and really, I don't care too much. That's someone else's problem. My job was to build a tankstand, and that's what we've done. Ask George when he comes back this evening."

Sam duly put his question to George that night.

"Don't worry Sam, we'll think of something when the time comes. The tank can wait. We have other things to worry about. Come on Mac, get your plans, we've got some measuring to do."

Each evening George and Mac measured, and re-measured, where the pipes would go. During the day, they would cut and bend pipes according to their calculations. Each pipe was given a number and conveyed to the storage area in the barn.

Each day Darkie and Mick would depart the farm to return well after dusk. Each day, a few more bottles were placed in the knapsack which George would carry to the engineering depot. No questions were asked, no explanations were offered. In two weeks, most of the payment had been made but, as forecast by Darkie, the securing of the range of exotic liqueurs was a problem. It was Marie who unwittingly solved Darkie's dilemma. In conversation, she mentioned she had been helping at the Château with the unloading of a truck of Christmas supplies. Her description of the various bottles confirmed Darkie's suspicions. The officers' mess had stocked up on a wide range of 'fancy' drinks.

The following afternoon Al and Bluey were standing in the courtyard when a staff car driven by Captain Solway pulled up. Their hearts sank as they saw Darkie and Mick emerge from the car.

"I knew it was too good to last." breathed Al.

Captain Solway returned the salute of the two men. He waved his swagger stick at the two signallers standing by the car. "Fleming and O'Brien were telling me about this scheme you chaps are working on for Madame Pruvost. Sounds like an excellent way to repay the family for their hospitality. I wish all my teams were as civic-minded as you lot. Care to show me just what it is you are doing?"

Al controlled his fears. "Of course Sir. Darkie, you and Mick organise a brew for us while we show the captain around."

"Right Al. We'll see if Gilly would like to join us."

The captain smiled his approval. "Good idea Fleming. I'd like to meet the lady of the house. Lead on Wilson."

As they toured the courtyard and the barn Al casually asked; "Where did you find Fleming and O'Brien, Sir?"

"Oh, they were up at the Château. Said they had dropped in to see Bailey. I was driving into Corbie so offered them a lift. They told me all about your scheme and persuaded me that I should inspect it. You fellows have certainly put a lot of work into this project."

"Thanks Sir. Now how about that brew?" Al led the way into the messroom where Ghislaine was waiting. She had placed some small cakes and biscuits on the table.

"I'm pleased to meet you, Captain Solway. Of course, I've heard a lot about you from my boys. Only good things, I might add."

Al looked around. "Where are Darkie and Mick?"

"Oh, they said they had some work to attend to, and asked if I would serve the tea. Is something wrong?"

"No." laughed a relieved Al. "Everything is just fine. We would much prefer you to serve us than those two rogues."

"Rogues, Wilson? They seemed a reasonable pair of fellows. In fact, the Snake Section seems to have worked very well."

"Yes, thanks to Phil Reynolds. Have you heard from him lately?"

The captain's face took on a sombre look. "Just a short note. He's not very well, not very well at all. He read in the papers about the deaths of Walters and Pettersen. He wanted to know if their training, or lack of training, was a factor in their deaths. The man should be worrying about his own health, but there he is, worrying about the men he trained and how that training might be improved."

"That's Phil. He'll never change, but I'm sorry to hear he's not well. Please pass on my regards to him when you write."

"I'll do that. Now Madame, tell me about these concerts I hear about, but never get asked to."

Ghislaine smiled. "You will be the first person to receive an invitation to the next concert Captain, but I must warn you, the price of a ticket is you have to perform. Do you sing or play an instrument?"

"If I have to, I'll sing. But one or two lines will be enough for you to cancel that requirement. Now, tell me about yourself and this lovely home."

* * *

Little was said at the meal table about the captain's visit but at the evening round-table conference Al turned on Darkie and Mick. "All right you two, what's all this nonsense about going to visit Bailey? You both detest the man, and why did you insist that Captain Solway come here to see the farm?"

"Al, do you really want to know?" asked Darkie. "I mean, do you really want to know?"

"Normally I'd say no, but with Captain Solway involved, I have to know, so out with it."

"It's quite simple. We needed an odd bottle or two of those strange liqueurs that the engineers ordered, and we found that there were a few cases in the cellar at the Château."

"Oh God, you didn't break in there did you?"

"Break in? Of course not. Mick and I just attached ourselves to a working party that was unloading a truck of supplies, and each time we came out of the cellar we stuffed a couple of bottles in our pockets."

"Bloody hell, you took a risk."

"Not really, they'll never miss the stuff. The cellar is chock-a-block, and there's no accounting."

Al shook his finger at the two sappers. "Now get this straight you two. You're not to go near that cellar ever again. Do I make myself clear?"

"All right Al, all right. Calm down. We've got all we need from there. In fact, we've got all the stuff ordered by the engineers. It was a breeze. This whole area is being swamped with grog in preparation for Christmas."

Bluey spoke. "Tell me Darkie, was it worth the risk? What if the MPs had lumbered you walking away with some bottles of stolen grog?"

"Worth it? Well the prize was, still is, our Christmas gift to Gilly and the family. How can you ask was it worth the risk? And as for walking out with two dozen bottles, we didn't, we were driven out."

"Oh no! You mean you had that stuff stashed in Captain Solway's car?" Al's face had paled slightly.

"Relax Al, he'll never suspect what happened. That's why we had to talk him into coming here. If he'd dropped us off in Corbie, we would've had a real problem."

Again, the corporal shook his finger at the men. "All right, I've had enough for one day but I repeat, keep away from the Château."

"Fine by me." replied Darkie. "Can't stand the place, what with all that brass, and poofters like Bailey swanning around."

"Me too." chimed in Mick. "The place gives me the creeps."

Al shook his head. "You're both mad. But then we're all mad, or going that way. Tomorrow you two are back on the roster. No more foraging parties. Come on, let's hit the sack."

* * *

"It's a strange world Bluey, and it gets stranger every day."

It was Sunday afternoon, and Al and Bluey were walking alongside the river. The two men had formed a close relationship since they had started working as a pair in the field. Their respect and admiration for each other was obvious to all.

"And what is so strange today?"

Al stopped walking and turned to look at his companion. "Something that happened yesterday. Some officer in the engineers' depot came around to the workshop where George and Mac were working. He asked what was going on, and when told, blew his top. He ordered his men to cease any further work on our project. It looked like George and Mac were going to be charged with stealing, and all sorts of other offences."

"Then up drives another officer, a Major Kelty. He hops out of his car and demands to know what is going on. He also is outraged, but then he peers at Mac and says, 'Don't I know you from somewhere?' Mac said he didn't think so, but the Major kept staring at him, and then suddenly he yelled 'AGENOR'. Everyone thought he'd gone mad. He shoved out his hand saying, 'I've always wanted to shake hands with the man who cleaned up that bully on the ship.' He went on to tell the assembled company about some boxing match on the ship. Suddenly, the whole situation had changed. Mac was a hero who deserved all the help the engineers could give him. So, one moment we were in big trouble, then fate intervenes, and now we have unlimited engineering support for the project."

Bluey ran his hand through his red hair. "What a coincidence, Major Kelty turning up. Good old AGENOR."

"Yes, it was. A whole string of unrelated events coming together, at the right time, and in the right place. It must be planned by some higher authority. Everything is planned. Nothing just happens."

"Getting around to the Arab theory are we Al?"

Al paused before speaking. "It's true Bluey. What will happen will happen. What we don't know is when, nor do we know why."

"Perhaps it's best we don't know, but all the same Al, I'd consider it a great favour if you didn't take on the whole German army while I'm with you."

"If you insist my friend, but it's an interesting idea. Come on let's head for home. These days are getting shorter and colder."

* * *

"Two weeks to go. I reckon this'll be the Christmas party to end all parties."

"Steady on Sam. Just because we'll have water on tap for Christmas, hardly makes it rate quite that high on my list." Jacko cast his mind back to some of the festivities he had been involved in. "No Sam, running water doesn't quite equal running beer. Kegs and kegs of the amber fluid, that's what makes a party."

The group was gathered around the well in the courtyard awaiting the arrival of the water tank. They failed to notice the arrival of Lieutenant Johnson and Sapper Bailey.

"So, what do we have going on here may I ask?" The words spoken in the familiar threatening voice brought them to attention.

Al saluted. “We’re awaiting the arrival of a tank Sir.”

“A tank? And what do you intend doing with a tank Corporal?”

“Fill it with water Sir. What else can one do with a tank?”

“Don’t get smart with me Wilson. That’s the trouble with this Section. You’ve had it too easy. You’ve become slack and undisciplined.”

The smile went from Al’s face. “That’s not true Sir. We’ve carried out every duty given to us, and no one has complained, at least not to me, and I’m the one responsible.”

Lieutenant Johnson quickly realised that he’d gone too far with his criticism. “Well corporal, I’m delighted to hear that No.3 Section is at such a high level of efficiency, and no doubt you’ll welcome the opportunity to show me just how good you are.”

“Opportunity sir?”

“A stint in the frontline Corporal Wilson. I’ve volunteered this Section to do a nine-day stint in the line starting on the 22nd. I realise that you’ll be away for Christmas but you’ll be back to spend New Year’s Eve with your friends.”

The gasp from the men’s mouths fuelled the sadistic pleasure of the man. “Now, I must let you get on with your chores, as I think this is your truck approaching...” He paused. “Does Captain Solway know about this work?”

“Yes he does sir, and he thinks it’s a good idea.”

“What about the engineers?”

“Major Kelty is probably in the truck Sir. Perhaps you would like to ask him?” Al was having difficulty in controlling his anger.

“No, I haven’t time to hang around here, I’m very busy. Come on Bailey, we’ll leave this rabble to play with their tank.” Lieutenant Johnson and his fawning attendant returned to the staff car.

“So, help me Al, one day I’m going to kill that slimy creature.” Darkie snarled.

“Enough of that sort of talk. The matter is closed. No doubt Pete King will be along to formally give us our orders. Cheer up, it's not the end of the world. Someone has to be at the front, and it's pretty quiet there at present. We have work to do. Here's our tank."

The truck entered the yard, a large cylindrical tank firmly secured to the tray. A jovial Major Kelty dismounted from the cab.

"Splendid. A real tankstand. Let's get cracking. It's too cold to hang about."

"Your question is about to be answered Sam." Jacko muttered.

The truck was positioned a short distance from the stand and two long planks covered with thick grease were laid from the tray of the truck to the platform on the stand. Long ropes were anchored on the platform and then run under the tank and returned over the tank and back to the platform. The men manned the ropes and the tank was rolled up the planks and on to the platform. The engineers then used a system of ropes and pulleys to turn the tank on to its base. The completion of this stage of the project called for some sort of a celebration and Darkie and Mick quickly provided a brew laced with rum.

"You blokes certainly have got a cosy nest here." observed the Major.

"Yes Sir, but don't get any ideas. Our hostess is very anti-officers. She's a real dragon."

"Really Darkie? I didn't know you thought of me as a dragon." Ghislaine had entered the room unobserved. Darkie blushed and mumbled something about a nice dragon, before he beat a quick exit.

The Officer stood up. "Since no one seems eager to introduce me Madame, I'm Major Kelty."

"I'm very pleased to meet you Major. I am Ghislaine Pruvost, but to Australians, I answer to the name of Gilly. Can I pour you another cup of tea?"

"Thank you Madame. I was just telling these men that this is a very comfortable billet. They are very lucky."

"Yes I heard you Major, and I assure you, I don't breathe fire."

"Never thought you did Madame."

"Oh, please call me Gilly. You sound so formal. Now we have our tank, what happens next?"

The officer nodded towards George. "You had better ask Sapper Morbey, it's his project."

George smiled. It was quite a compliment for an officer, especially an engineer officer, to acknowledge he was in charge of the operation.

"The next thing is to install the piping inside the house, while the engineers complete the windmill. It's all going to be a bit of a tight squeeze in view of our new orders."

"What new orders?" Ghislaine sensed that there was something troubling the men.

"Lieutenant Johnson dropped in to tell us the glad tidings. We're returning to the front on the 22nd for a stint in the line." Al Wilson felt it was his responsibility to break the news. "Looks like our Christmas party will have to wait until New Year's Eve."

"What rotten luck." said the Major. "Still, I hear it's pretty quiet up there at the moment, so that's one blessing in a batch of bad news."

"Yeah, you're right Major. It's best to look for the good things in life, and to push the bad into the background."

"I agree Corporal, but here's what I intend to do, as my way of thanking that boy for restoring discipline to the AGENOR. Things were getting out of hand until that fight. If you haven't completed this job here at the farm by the time you leave, I'll put in a few of my men to finish the job.

"Oh thank you Sir." replied Al. "We'll be close to finishing it, but we would hate to go forward and leave Gilly and the girls without water."

Gilly spoke. "It's very kind of you Major, but we don't want to cause you any trouble. I know some French engineers who were very close friends of my late husband. I'm sure they would help."

The Major sat upright in his chair and looked straight at Ghislaine. "With all due respects Madame, this is an Australian project. If these men can't finish it due to war commitments, then their fellow Australians will see that it is brought to a successful completion. We do not seek help from others."

"Oh Major, please don't misunderstand me. I was only saying that if you were too busy, and I'm sure you are very busy, I could perhaps get some help from my own countrymen."

The Major stood up. "Thank you Madame. Your concern for our workload is admirable, but rest assured, we will see this project through to the end. Now I must go, and I suggest you men stop loafing around the table and get to work. There's plenty to do."

The Major and his men left the room.

"Hell Gilly, you sure touched a nerve when you suggested that you might call in French engineers. The Major was not amused."

"No he wasn't, and I didn't expect him to be. I think we will get all the help we need, plus more, now that we have his commitment to the task."

"Gilly! You deliberately stirred up the Major with that talk about French engineers." Al was amazed. "I bet you don't have friends in the engineers. It was just a story to get the Major stirred up."

"No Al, I never lie. Well perhaps exaggerate a little. I do know some engineer officers in the French army, but they are a long way from here, and I don't think they have the time or inclination to devote their endeavours to a plumbing system at this farm. Still, it doesn't matter. You don't have to worry. Everything will work out fine."

George took charge. "Right, you heard the Major. Work to be done. Come on Mac, let's get back to the depot. Jacko, you and the others tie down the tank, and then start building a slanted roof above the tank. We don't want it to collapse under a pile of snow."

* * *

The plumbing wasn't completed when the men left the house and climbed aboard the truck for the journey to the front. Major Kelty came to see them off, and reassured them that the great plumbing scheme would be operating at the farm on Christmas Day.

"Out to get all the credit and glory for himself, I reckon," snapped Darkie. "I bet he's around on Christmas Day for a free feed."

"Oh shut up Darkie." responded Preacher. "There is no Christmas dinner this year at the farm. The women are waiting for our return. The big party will be on New Year's Eve. We should be grateful to the Major. He's been a tower of strength in pushing the project ahead. It's going to be a far more sophisticated system than we planned, or were capable of constructing. As Al says, look for the positives."

The farm disappeared from sight and the men fell silent, each one remembering the world to which they were returning, the mud, the stench, the lice, the fear.

"I reckon the Somme mud is thicker and nastier than Flanders mud." Jacko waved his hand towards the sides of the road they were travelling along. "A bloody sea of mud."

"Don't knock it. It's that mud that has given us a respite. No army can move across it, not here, nor in Belgium. Something the Generals forgot when it started to rain at Passchendaele. The sad thing is that one day early in the new year it will dry, and the war will start again. Still I reckon we'll have a pretty easy time of it for the next nine days."

"Al, just where are we heading?"

"Somewhere around Bullecourt, Preacher. We're relieving an English Section so we won't be working with Australian battalions this time, but that's no problem. I've worked with the Tommies before. It's all right unless you meet up with a Highland regiment, then there's a problem."

"What's wrong with the Scots?"

"Nothing wrong with them. It's just a language problem. I can't understand them."

Preacher nodded. "I know what you mean, but they say we are hard to understand because of all the slang we use."

"Probably true, but at least the written word is easy to comprehend." Al looked at his watch. "Should be near Pozières soon. I'll get the driver to stop so we can stretch our legs and have a bite to eat when we get there." "Pozières! Seems we stopped there early this year on our way to the front."

"Yeah we did," chimed in Sam. "It's just a heap of rubble."

"True Sam. It's just a heap of rubble, but to me it's a rather special heap of stones, just like Bullecourt is something special to you blokes."

The truck slowed down, pulled to the side of the road and came to a stop. "Right, climb down." ordered Al. "We'll have twenty minutes here and then push on. Don't wander too far and don't try to souvenir any of the junk, it could be unstable, and this is a silly place to die or get wounded."

"You know of a sensible place to die, Al?" questioned Bluey.

"Yes I do Bluey. In an old man's home in Adelaide. That's where I aim to die."

HULLO BRITISHER

The men soon settled into the familiar routine of trench life. The English signallers had made their dugout as safe and comfortable as the conditions would allow. Maps were studied and the lines of communication examined in detail. Red circles on the map highlighted areas where snipers had been active, the only other threat coming from occasional shelling. Within hours of arrival the men began itching from the bites of the hated lice, and the cold seeped into their bodies. Living in the trenches was a miserable existence.

It was just after the night shadows had crept across the cold land that the men in the dugout heard an unusual noise. It was singing and it came from the German trenches. What was more surprising to the men was that the Germans were singing Christmas carols.

"Fancy that," quipped Darkie. "Those murderous bastards are singing our carols."

"And what makes you think they're our carols?" asked Preacher. "They're the songs of Christmas, and Germany is a Christian nation, has been for many centuries."

"They don't act like Christians, do they?" retorted Darkie. "They started this bloody war."

"I doubt, Darkie, that the men over there could be accused of starting the war. My guess is that they're simple soldiers, just like us. Fed up with the war, the cold, the lice, the mud, and wishing they were home." Preacher paused. "I wonder."

"Wonder what, Preacher?" asked Al.

"I have an idea. Maybe it's a silly idea, but let's try it."

"Try what, what are you talking about?"

"Come on Mick I need you."

The Section followed Preacher out of the dugout and into the forward trench.

Preacher turned to his friend. "Right Mick. In your best voice. Let's hear it. Silent Night."

"Here?" Mick frowned at the request.

"Yes Mick. Come on, sing, and put your heart and soul into it."

Mick moved towards the parapet.

"No Mick, I don't want you to be a target. I just want you to sing. Go on."

Mick looked to the others but no advice came. He turned towards the vacant no-man's land and commenced singing. It was a still cold night, and his voice carried across the wasteland. It was an eerie sensation to hear such beautiful words in such an ugly place. When he finished, cheering was heard in the enemy lines and, with this encouragement, Mick started another carol. Again, his wonderful voice, full of warmth and compassion, was greeted by loud applause from the Germans.

"Keep going Mick. All join in. Sing the chorus." urged Preacher.

A small group of English soldiers left their posts to hear this unusual concert. Preacher whispered to Al and the pair left the gathering and walked across to the officers' dugout, a short distance to the rear. When they returned, Preacher was beaming, but Al looked worried. The singing died down as the two men approached. Al looked unhappy.

"I don't like it Preacher."

"Don't like what, Al?" questioned Bluey.

"Preacher has some crazy idea about asking the Germans for a truce over Christmas. We asked the officers but they have been examining the inside of a bottle of scotch and couldn't care less."

"But they did say I could try, didn't they Al?"

"Yes Preacher, they said you could try."

"Fine. Well, here goes." Preacher raised his voice and called out. "Hallo druben. Können Siemich hören?"

"What did you say Preacher? Why didn't you tell us you spoke German?"

"Shut up Sam and listen."

After a brief pause a voice returned the call. "Ja. Wer ist da. Was wollen Sie?"

"He wants to know who I am and what I want." The tall man spoke again in German. "Ich will mit Ihnen auf Englisch reden. Kann jemand da sprechen?"

Before Sam could ask him, Preacher said he was asking if anyone there could speak English. The answer came back. "Ja. Was wollen Sie."

"I want to speak with you, man to man, under a flag of truce. Would you agree to meet with me as a Christmas gesture of goodwill?"

"Meet with them? Preacher, have you gone mad?" whispered Sam.

"You don't have to whisper Sam. They can't hear you. No, I haven't gone mad. It came to me in a blinding flash when I heard them singing carols. They are men. Christian men just like you and me, and it's my bet that they'd like to enjoy Christmas without the fear of someone shooting them."

"So, what do we do now?"

"Wait. No doubt my suggestion has come as a big shock to them, just as it has to you."

"Hullo Britisher. Are you there?" A voice came from the other side.

"I'm here. I'm listening."

The voice from across no-man's land continued. "We agree to meet with you under a flag of truce. Two people from each side. Each man to carry a lantern to indicate his position. You agree?"

"We agree. Two people carrying lanterns. When and where?"

"It is now 6:00pm and we need to pass the word along the line. Both parties leave their trenches at 8:00pm exactly. The ceasefire will last one hour. We will meet you at the pile of concrete which is roughly half-way between the lines. No weapons. Do you agree?"

"We agree. We will depart here at 8:00pm exactly."

"Be warned Britisher. If this is a trick you will pay."

"No tricks. I'll see you shortly after 8:00pm." Preacher turned to his audience. "See, it was simple. They want peace as much as we do. Mick, you'll accompany me."

"Just a minute Preacher, I'm still in charge around here. I'll decide on who goes, and who stays." Al was uneasy at the speed at which events were occurring.

"Of course Al, but your place is back here with the Majority of the Section. I have to go because it was my idea, and I speak German. We may have to resort to their native tongue to clear up any technical problems. Mick should come because it was his singing that charmed them, and besides, we are a pair. And another reason you should stay is because we only have two hours to ensure that every man in our trenches knows what's going on. One loose shot will cause us a lot of problems."

"He's right Al," chimed in Bluey. "It's his hare-brained scheme, and we need to get cracking to make sure the word is passed along the line."

"All right, all right. I get the message. Jeez you're mad, all of you. Right Bluey, take Mac and walk the length of the right hand trench. Don't miss anyone. No shooting between 8:00 and 9:00pm. Jacko, take Sam and do the same along the left. Get going, and check their watches to make sure we're all working on the same time. Off you go. Simon, you back up George, he's on the switchboard. If anyone calls in, tell them it's the Red Cross out there with stretcher bearers. That might keep them quiet for a while, but it's still a hell of a risk. Now move!"

* * *

Preacher and Mick took deep breaths and raised their lanterns above the parapet. As if in answer to a signal, two lanterns appeared above the enemy trenches. The watchers in the trenches saw the lanterns converge, and after a meeting that lasted some ten minutes, the men returned.

Preacher and Mick slid back into the trench. The smile on Preacher's face told it all. "It's going to happen Al. They've agreed."

"Agreed to what Preacher?"

"Peace and goodwill will prevail over this sector of the front for twenty-four hours commencing at 12:00pm tomorrow."

"Shit Preacher! You're a sapper, not a bloody General. You can't negotiate a truce with the enemy. You just can't do it."

"Al, I haven't stopped the war. All we have, is an agreement with the blokes across there to stop shooting for twenty-four hours. In our little neck of the woods, we're going to have a short time during which we can enjoy Christmas." Preacher looked towards the two English Sergeants who had joined the group. "Do you people have any objections?" he asked.

"Just one." replied the Englishman. "Why only twenty-four hours? Why couldn't you swing twenty-four days, even better, twenty-four years?"

Al threw up his hands. "You win Preacher. We're only here to support the infantry, and if they go along with your mad scheme, so be it. What now?"

"I was coming to that. At 12:00pm tomorrow we're going to exchange gifts with the enemy."

"Gifts? Now I know you're mad Preacher. Gifts? Out here? Sure you don't want to dress up as Santa Claus?"

"No Al I don't. At 12:00pm tomorrow, the truce begins and we'll meet with the Germans and exchange some food and drink. That's our priority for now. It sounds like another job for Darkie."

Darkie shook his head. "Not out here Preacher. You got any ideas Al?"

"Yeah, I might be able to come up with something. What about the infantry? Can you fellows help?"

"Yes Corporal, our lads will be delighted to hear the news, and we'll have something here by 1100 tomorrow. We'll also pass the word to the artillery to shoot somewhere else, although I suspect they'll be happy to enjoy their Christmas without manning their guns in this weather. We're with you all the way."

"And what about your officers?"

"Don't worry about them. They'll dress up in their best finery and get drunk, which they would've done anyhow. We'll go and see them, persuade them that it was all their own idea, and thank them for being so caring and considerate to the soldiers. See you at 11:00am tomorrow." The two English Sergeants departed in the direction of the officers' dugout.

Al waved his hands in the general direction of the signallers' dugout. "Get back to your posts. If Jerry is going to cheat, then he might have a go at us tonight. I'm off to the switchboard. Nothing has changed around here until 12:00pm tomorrow. Don't forget that, or you may still miss out on Christmas dinner."

* * *

The men in the signallers' dugout were increasingly concerned as time passed the following morning. Al Wilson would give them no hint of what he had arranged, and all enquiries were met with a curt, 'don't worry.'

It was a little after 10:00am when a truck came rumbling up from the south and Sergeant King alighted.

"Hello Peter, any problems?"

"No Al. You didn't give me much time, but most of the things were organised for pick-up today, so it was just a matter of hurrying things along. Now, what's the score?"

"At 12:00pm, Lacey and O'Brien are to make an exchange of food and drink. The Tommies have agreed to throw in some stuff as a gesture of goodwill. I know it's crazy, but most things that have happened to me since this mob arrived in France can only be described as crazy."

"Yeah I know. Come on you blokes. Don't just stand around gawking. Unload the truck so the driver can get back to Corbie in time for his party."

"Hell Pete, are you staying here?" Al looked surprised. "It's Christmas Eve, and I'll bet the Sergeant's mess has something special planned."

The Sergeant shook his head. "I must be going soft Al. When I heard that you guys had volunteered to spend Christmas in the line I decided I should join you."

"We volunteered?" The corporal looked surprised.

"Yep. That's what Lieutenant Johnson told Captain Solway and myself. Captain Solway suggested to the Lieutenant that it might be a good idea if he came forward and spent Christmas with you, but Mr Johnson wasn't at all keen on that idea, so I said I'd come up here."

"Thanks Pete, it'll be good to have one sane person to talk to. Good God what's that?" Al gestured towards a pile of boxes and bags which had been unloaded from the truck.

Pete King walked over to the pile and selected a blue canvas bag. "Here you are boys, mail from home. I figured this might be the best present I could deliver for Christmas. Seems like half of it is for Dowson. You must be very popular back home, Bluey."

"Don't be fooled Sergeant. They're from the people he owes money to back home." Darkie dodged as Bluey threw a playful punch at him.

"It's not surprising that Bluey collects the most letters Pete, he writes one or two every day, but damned if I know what he finds to write about." Al pointed to the rear. "Ah, here comes the battalion Sergeants with their contribution."

The two English Sergeants joined the group and accepted the offer of a cup of tea.

"Any problems?" asked Al.

"None at all," replied one of the men. "Our officers are delighted with what has been arranged and are going to have a formal luncheon tomorrow." He shook his head. "They're a rum lot."

"Speaking of rum, have you been able to get your hands on any?" asked Preacher.

"Oh yes." The Sergeant opened his bag. "Rum, beer and a heap of tinned goods. Not much, but our Christmas supplies haven't arrived yet. We expect a truck this afternoon. You chaps look as if Santa has already arrived."

"Yes he has, and this is the man in person. Sergeant Peter King." Introductions were made and the group clustered around the piles of goods.

The Englishman let out a low whistle of surprise as the contents of the various bags and boxes were revealed.

"I think I had better explain." said Pete King. "This is not a normal load of Christmas cheer. In fact, it's three separate donations.

In the first place, I had arranged for a Christmas hamper with an occasional bottle of this and that to be prepared for this Section. When Captain Solway heard about your volunteering to spend Christmas in the front, he suggested to Lieutenant Johnson that he might put together a suitable Christmas hamper for you guys."

"Lieutenant Johnson was very diligent in his endeavours, and I didn't see any need to tell him about my little hamper. I'd told the ladies at the farm that I was planning to come up here and so they prepared a few items for me to bring up. There you have it. When Al rang through last night saying you needed some stuff for this exchange, all I had to do was ask people to have their contributions ready a little ahead of time. Oh yes, two other things. You'll each find a small present with your name on. Those are gifts from the farm. The second matter is most intriguing. The young ladies found a cache of grog hidden under straw in the barn. All sorts of exotic drinks, spirits and liqueurs. They sent up a good selection."

Darkie frowned. "Most unusual."

Mick nodded. "Probably left there by one of the earlier groups billeted there. Strange we didn't stumble on them."

"Yes Mick, very strange." Darkie shrugged.

"All right. Let's just pretend Santa's helpers left the stuff there," said Al. "What we need to do now, is make up a couple of bags of stuff to hand over to the Jerry officers. Open all the boxes and let's have a look at what we've got."

After considerable debate the men finally agreed on two kit-bags of food and drink, with the emphasis on drink, which seemed plentiful. Even with the bags filled there remained an ample supply of Christmas fare and cheer for the group.

On the stroke of noon Preacher and Mick clambered over the parapet of the trench and staggering under the weight of their load moved off in the direction of the pile of broken concrete.

As soon as they had shown themselves, three men emerged from the enemy trenches.

"Bloody hell," snarled Darkie, "I knew it was a set-up. They have only one bag. Let's tell Preacher to bring one of ours back."

"Don't be stupid Darkie." snapped Al. "A psychological victory to our side."

"A what?"

"An advantage over their minds, Darkie. When they see what we've sent over, they'll think that it is our normal fare. Soldiers in the field drinking scotch, brandy and liqueurs, whilst they have nothing, or very little in the way of Christmas cheer. In a strange way, this mad scheme of Preacher's may help our war effort in more ways than one. What's going on?"

"They're talking and waving their arms around. Looks like it's going as planned. The Germans have taken the kit-bags and are off back to their trenches. Preacher and Mick are on their way back." Sam, with binoculars, had monitored every movement of the exchange. "Stand by to give them a hand as they come over the top."

Preacher and Mick arrived looking pleased with themselves. Mick was carrying a large bag which clinked as he walked.

"Any problems Preacher?"

"No problems. The officer apologised for not being able to spare more in the way of food, but I told him that the truce was the best gift he could ever give."

"An officer. Did he realise he was dealing with a lowly sapper?"

"No, Sergeant King. Both Mick and I removed all our insignia before going out, but he recognised from our accents that we were Australians. The officer and his batman were friendly. The third man was a very different sort of bloke, a Sergeant, and he wore a green uniform with sniper's badge. He wasn't at all happy with the proceedings."

"Yeah. A real nasty type. What did he say just before we left?"

"Oh that. He forgot, or didn't realise, I spoke German. He said, Wir sollten dich töten, nicht füttern."

"And what does that mean Preacher?"

"We should be killing you, not feeding you."

"So he wasn't too happy about the truce?"

"I should think not. However, the officer turned on him and said, 'Halt den Mund! Ich habe ihm mein Ehrenwort darauf gegeben, und das bedeutet noch etwas.'"

"Translated means?"

"Sorry Sarge. 'Be quiet! I have given my word and that still means something.' The Sergeant didn't take too kindly to being spoken to in that tone, but he shut up."

Mick interrupted. "Jeez Al, you should have seen his eyes. Murder is his game, a real bastard."

Al looked around the group. "Be warned. We'd best be on our toes once this ceasefire is over. That sniper had a good chance to look around and it would appear he's not a friendly soul."

Mick shook his head. "I've seen my share of villains, but that one was pure poison. The hate was seeping out of every pore. I hope I don't meet him again."

"To hell with Jerry, let's enjoy the next twenty-four hours. What's in the bag?"

"Steady Darkie. It's to be shared with the infantry." Preacher opened the bag and began to lay out the contents. "German sausages, bread, wine and beer. Not a bad swap, all things considered."

* * *

Although Christmas Day was cold and bleak, without the fear of an enemy bullet, cheered by the change of diet, and enlivened by alcohol, the men rated it as one of the best.

The war in and around Bullecourt restarted just after noon on 26th December with a sniper's bullet whistling close by Mac as he ran a proving check on a line.

“Business as usual?” asked Al, as the startled Mac dived into the trench.

“Too close for comfort. I reckon Mick’s sniper is back in town for the shooting season.”

“Probably. He had time to survey the land during the handover and it’s obvious he wasn’t there to convey good tidings. Pass the word around, we’ll need to be extra careful until we can terminate his little game.”

“Sure thing Al. There isn’t much work to be done in front of the trenches with such light shelling, but it’s a worry to know he’s out there.”

“Stick to the rules. Head down, keep moving, all the things you’ve learned over the past year. I’ll go and talk to the infantry. They’ll need to watch out as well.” Al turned and walked towards the path that led to the frontline trenches, while Mac headed towards the signallers’ dugout to warn the others.

* * *

The Section was delighted to hear that they’d be relieved at 12:00pm on New Year’s Eve by a Section of British signallers. Just after breakfast, Al called the men together. “We have a small problem. The Brits want two of the Section to stay behind to show them around. It’s not an unreasonable request, and I’ve got them to agree that the two who stay will be released at 8:00pm. Now I’m not going to call for a pair to volunteer or anything noble like that. I’ve decided to run it like a lottery. There are five pieces of paper in this hat. One has a cross on it. Right, one from each pair draw.”

“Go on Simon, draw,” urged Bluey, and smiled when the young man opened a blank sheet of paper. George then drew a blank sheet, followed by Darkie. The remaining four men looked disconsolate.

"It's not the end of the earth fellas. If you leave here by 8:00pm, you can still make the farm by midnight, providing you can hitch a ride"

"Slim chance of that at that time of night. It must be a good thirty miles from here to the farm."

"Yes, I know Mick, but a young fit man like you could march that far in four hours, and if you ran, you could do it in three."

Mick reached and took a slip of paper. "Christ Preacher, I'm sorry, really sorry."

"Don't be Mick. It was meant to be. Al's right, we'll be there for the party, even if we're a little late."

"Preacher, that farm means more to you than any of us. I'll take your place. I'm in no rush to get back."

Preacher put his hand on the shoulder of the young redhead. "Bluey, many thanks, but no thanks. We won the short straw, fair and square. If I was to let you take my place after the ballot and something happened to you, I would never forgive myself. As I said, we'll be there. Don't worry."

"Just make sure you leave something for me to drink." chimed in Mick.

Darkie slapped his friend on the back. "Don't worry, mate. Santa left a few bottles in a second cache, and they won't be touched until you arrive."

"Right, that's settled. Turn to, you blokes. When those Brits arrive, I want this dugout looking as spick and span as Buckingham Palace. Let's show them that Aussies are very house proud."

"Tell me Corporal, even if we do make this place look like Buckingham Palace, how does the King put up with the dreadful smell?" Mick dodged the expected cuff on the ear as he headed for the door.

* * *

It had been a good party to welcome in 1918. The fears, the horrible memories, had been put aside. However, the after-dinner concert was not up to its usual high standard due to the absence of Preacher and Mick. About one o'clock, Ghislaine declared the party over and ushered the men from the kitchen. The girls had offered to help with the cleaning up but Ghislaine had declined. She would often pause and listen, although the men had assured her that Preacher and Mick would have remained in the dugout as the weather had taken a turn for the worse. Heavy snow was falling and a biting wind made travel hazardous.

Suddenly she paused. With a cry, she ran to the door that opened out into the courtyard. She imagined she saw a movement in the yard and called, “Preacher, is that you?”

The tall man appeared from the darkness. Drenched to the skin, frozen to the bone, his face, illuminated by the light streaming from the kitchen, was gaunt and pale.

“Oh my God, what are you doing out there? Come in out of the cold. Where’s Mick? Don’t tell me something has happened to Mick.”

“No Ghislaine, calm yourself. Mick’s all right.” Preacher stumbled into the kitchen and Ghislaine quickly shut the door behind him. “Mick’s all right. He was going to come back with me, but when the weather turned nasty and the British arrived with ample supplies of rum, he decided to wait until the weather improved.”

Ghislaine moved forward to embrace the wet and weary soldier.

“No Ghislaine, don’t touch me. I haven’t been to the bathhouse. I’m still lousy with these damn lice, my clothes are crawling. I’ll go to our quarters and change. All I need is a good rest in a warm bed.”

“You must get out of those wet clothes at once. Get behind that screen and undress.” Preacher hesitated. “You heard me. Get behind that screen and get those wet clothes off. There is a bath there, and thanks to you Australians we now have a hot tap to fill it. Come on, don’t stand there, do as I tell you. You’re not going to go crashing around your quarters waking everyone. I’ll get a bag and you can throw your clothes in it. They can soak in a solution."

"But Ghislaine, they're filthy. They are lousy, and so am I."

"Really Preacher, do you think we farmers haven't had to deal with a few miserable lice before tonight? Get moving!" She gave him a shove in the direction of the screen.

Preacher looked with astonishment at the new bathroom. Before the introduction of running water the family had a large tub behind the screen and this was filled by bringing buckets of warm water from the stove. Now there was a proper bath and two large shining brass taps proclaimed that hot and cold water was available.

"Put your clothes in this and hurry up," ordered the lady of the house, throwing a large bag over the screen.

Preacher soon was settled in the bath, vigorously soaping himself.

"Are you sure Mick is all right?"

"Absolutely sure. The British relief company was late arriving due to the weather, but they carried plenty of rum to protect them from the cold. Mick was in two minds about coming home, but after a couple of rums, he decided to stay put for the night."

"It's nice to hear you call the farm your home."

"Ghislaine, we all think of the farm as our home away from home. What are you doing?"

"Heating up some food for you. I've made some tea. Do you want me to bring it to you?"

"Ghislaine, I'm in the bath, the tea can wait."

She laughed. "I was only teasing you. The others were telling us about your Christmas in the trenches. I'm not sure that mother approves of you fraternising with the enemy, but in the end, I think the others persuaded her there still is a place for goodwill in the world, even if it is rationed. Tell me, how did you manage to get here? It's a dreadful night."

"You'll get no argument from me about that. I have never been so cold. The weather has caused chaos on the roads. I was lucky and managed to get a ride on a truck from Bapaume to Querrieu. If it had not been for that I wouldn't have made it here tonight. It was very difficult to walk through the snow."

"Well you're here now and that's all that matters. How much longer are you going to wallow in that bath?"

"Oh, I'm nearly ready to get out, but, there is a problem."

"Oh, and what is that?"

"I need a towel and some clothes."

"Of course you do." A towel was draped over the top of the screen. "I've been warming it for you. Clothes, now that's a problem. You get yourself dry while I see what I can find."

Preacher waited till he heard the door close before stepping out of the bath to retrieve the towel. He rubbed himself vigorously and then draped the towel around his waist. The door reopened and Ghislaine threw a garment on top of the screen. "Here, try this. It should fit. You're a bit taller than my husband, but not much."

Preacher took the garment. "Ghislaine, this is a nightshirt! A very expensive nightshirt!"

"Of course it is you silly man. It's night time. It's the time of the day people go to bed. Most men, so I'm told, wear nightshirts when they go to bed. Are things different in Australia?"

"Oh no, we wear nightshirts. It's just that I didn't expect you to give me one."

"Oh for heaven's sake, put it on and come and have your meal." Ghislaine sounded exasperated.

Preacher emerged from behind the screen and stood as if on parade and awaiting inspection.

Ghislaine nodded. "It's a good fit. You do look different once you get out of those dull uniforms. What are you staring at?"

"Sorry Ghislaine, I suppose I was staring and that's rude of me."

"What's the matter Preacher? You were looking at me as if you hadn't seen me before. Have I changed?"

"No, it's just the way you are dressed." The women of the house almost invariably wore a tunic type dress that had straps over the shoulders and were cut in a straight line above their breasts. Under this dress they normally wore a blouse, with long sleeves in the winter and short sleeves in the summer. This evening Ghislaine was not wearing a blouse, and the kitchen lights were reflecting off the pale flawless skin of her arms and neck. A gold cross on a gold chain around her neck also caught the light each time she moved.

She looked down. "Oh that. I took off my blouse when I was cleaning up the kitchen. It's hot in here, and I didn't want to get my best blouse dirty. Does it upset you?"

"No, I'm not upset, not at all. You just look so lovely with the light playing on your hair and your skin. You look lovely."

"Really Mr Preacher, I think you are flirting with me." Ghislaine tilted her head to one side. "Are you flirting with me?"

"Of course not." Preacher was floundering. "I just said you looked lovely, and you do. It was a genuine compliment."

"Thank you kind Sir. Now sit down over there and I'll get some food. And what about a glass of wine to toast the new year?"

"That would be nice, yes a glass of wine would be very welcome."

As Preacher was taking his seat, Ghislaine leaned across the table to place his meal in front of him. The front of her bodice fell forward and the wall lights reflected upon her unconstrained breasts. Having set the plate in front of the soldier she moved away, seemingly unaware of the effect her action had had on Preacher.

Preacher started on his meal as if seeking a distraction from the images that were running through his thoughts. No matter how he tried, the vision of the two breasts kept flooding back into his mind. Ghislaine busied herself with the final chores of cleaning up until the soldier had finished his meal. She then returned to the table with a carafe of wine and two glasses. Again, she leaned across the table and once more Preacher's eyes became riveted on the beautiful breasts now fully exposed.

"Really Preacher, I do believe you are peeping."

Preacher's head jerked upright and his eyes met the twinkling brown eyes of the lady. The blood surged to his face. She laughed. "Caught you, didn't I? Tell me dear Preacher," and she leaned forward again, "do you like what you see?"

"I was looking at the cross, the gold cross. That's what caught my eye. It's a lovely cross."

"Really, if you were only looking at the cross then why are you blushing? Be honest Preacher, tell me."

"Oh stop it Ghislaine. I was looking at you. I'm sorry. It was a cheap thing to do."

"Sorry Preacher? What is there to be sorry about? You are a man, I am a woman. Give me your hand." She took his hand and moved it to her breast. "How does that feel?"

"Warm, soft, lovely." Preacher fondled the exposed breast, then half stood and kissed it.

"Ah that's much better, I don't think we need that wine, it is very late."

"Yes of course, it's time to go to bed," mumbled Preacher, totally occupied with showering kisses on the two treasures that were now free of Ghislaine's dress.

"Exactly what I had in mind, my gallant soldier. Come we are wasting time."

Preacher moved back from the table. "Us? You mean go to bed together? Oh really Ghislaine, do you think that is wise?"

"Wise, who is talking about being wise? Look at that thing sticking out of your nightshirt. Do you think he is wise? Come. We have the new year to celebrate, but first give me a kiss."

Preacher moved towards her and gave her a gentle kiss on the cheek.

"That's a kiss?" she asked. "Is that how you kiss in Australia? What a cold lot you must be."

"I'm sorry Ghislaine, I'm not very good at this sort of thing."

She looked down. "Perhaps you are not very good, but it certainly looks as if you are keen to learn. Come, take me in your arms and let me kiss you."

Preacher did and soon the probing tongues and nibbling lips became enmeshed.

"Ah that's more like it. You learn quick my dearest. Come, help me put out the lamps, and then we'll move onto lesson two."

"Lesson two?"

"Yes, lesson two. I am assuming that as you didn't know how to kiss a girl, you are also lacking in experience in the art of making love."

"I have always believed that one should save oneself until the woman you love came along. It's expected of our ladies, why not the same rule for men?"

"A question I will debate with you later, but tell me Preacher what is different about tonight?"

Preacher had just blown out the last lamp and the only light in the room came from the lantern Ghislaine held in her hand. The glow from the light seemed to bathe her in a mystical aura. It took Preacher's breathe away just to look at her. "There is no difference Ghislaine. I love you. I have since the first night I saw you. I will always love you."

"Strong words my gallant soldier. Strong and beautiful, but this is not the time to be standing around talking. Come, and be as quiet as you can. We don't need the family as an audience." Turning she led the way from the kitchen up the stairs to a bedroom. Pointing to the large double bed she motioned Preacher to climb beneath the covers. Ghislaine slipped behind a screen and when she re-appeared she was naked, her hair hanging loosely to her shoulders. She slowly walked to the bedside well aware that Preacher's eyes were watching her every move, studying the detail of her body. She bent over and blew out the lantern then slid into the bed.

"What is this?" she asked.

"It's my nightshirt."

"I know it's your nightshirt but why are you wearing it? You won't get cold, I promise you."

Preacher quickly discarded the garment and returned to embrace his partner. They kissed and gently felt the contours of each other's body.

"That's good, that's nice." breathed Ghislaine.

"Ghislaine?"

"Yes?"

"Oh nothing, forget it."

"Preacher, how can I forget something I never knew. Come, tell me?"

"Oh, it's just something that Sam said a long time ago. It's nothing really."

Ghislaine propped herself up on one arm. "Well my darling, we are not going to progress if you lie there thinking about something that Sam said, and I lie here wondering what Sam did say. Tell me."

"Well..." Preacher paused, "remember the first time we had a bath in the old dairy?"

"Yes. The girls and I were barred from entry. Remember? Mother took charge."

"That's it. Madame Pruvost had a book, and she kept writing things in it. Sam says he saw what she was writing. Sam knows French."

"Yes my dear, I've heard Sam's French. But what is this all about?"

"Well Sam said your mother was giving us all a mark out of ten."

"She what?"

"Well that's what Sam said."

"Really, and what was she marking out of ten?"

"Oh you know."

"No I don't know. What was mother marking you for?"

"Sam says it was a mark out of ten for the size of our manhood."

"Manhood? Oh you mean this?" Ghislaine reached down and grasped the swollen organ.

Preacher shuddered. "Yes that. Sam said I got the highest mark."

"That's interesting. So, what is worrying you?"

"Well is it true?"

"How could I know Preacher. I haven't seen the others, so how could I pass judgement."

"No Ghislaine, what I meant is, was your mother judging us when she wrote in her book?"

Ghislaine's body shook with suppressed laughter. "Preacher, you never cease to amaze me. Did you really think that she would do such a thing. Mother is a stickler for detail, and when we send in our bill for billeting you, she always charges for the number of buckets of hot water used for bathing. I think that's why she is not all that happy with this running water set up."

"Oh, I'm so pleased to hear that. It's been worrying me for months."

"Tell me, when Sam let loose this important piece of information, what did the others say? Were they not jealous of your exalted status?"

"Oh no, they accepted it. The only one who made any comment was Darkie. He said that size didn't matter, it was how you used it that counted. But then, Darkie's always been crude."

"Sounds to me as if Darkie is more of a man of the world than you my darling. So here beginneth lesson two." Ghislaine positioned herself astride the excited soldier. "Easy my darling. There is no hurry. Let me lead you into the real world of love. After tonight, everything will be different."

* * *

The old woman stirred in her sleep, then came awake as an unfamiliar sound reached her ears. She sat up and listened. Satisfied with what she heard she nestled back beneath the bedclothes. As she drifted off to sleep, she smiled. "It's only right that one so young and beautiful should have a man to love."

* * *

The men were seated at the breakfast table when Preacher joined them. They greeted him with the usual questions: where was Mick, what time did he get to the farm, how did he manage in the snow? No one commented on the civilian clothes he was wearing, or that he had appeared from the main house. That he and Ghislaine had finally declared their liaison was accepted as a natural progression of the courtship that had been obvious to all. When the girls joined them to discuss the day's programme it was apparent that they, too, had welcomed Preacher into the family circle.

"It's going to be a great year Al," enthused Preacher. "I've never been so happy."

"Yes Preacher, you look happy and you have my best wishes. But I can't say I share your enthusiasm for 1918. To me, 1st of January 1918 is little different to 1st of January 1916 and 1917. Perhaps I'm getting old, but I'm sick of this war."

A silence fell over the group.

"Perhaps you could find a better war Al?"

"No Sam. We have to finish this one before the Generals can start another. But don't worry, they will. However, let's not sit around brooding. It's a day for celebration, so what are we going to do?"

"Nothing outdoors that's for sure," observed Jacko. "I hope Mick doesn't try to fight his way through this weather."

"Don't worry about Mick. The Brits had enough rum to last out this storm and a few more. Mick's in good company, and Jerry won't be moving for a while."

"No he won't Preacher," said Al in a sombre voice. "Darkie break out the cards, let's see if my luck is still holding."

"If I didn't know you better Corporal, I would almost be tempted to say that you use more than luck when playing cards."

"A profound statement Darkie. Well, who's playing? I know Bluey, you have letters to write. Preacher?"

"No, I think I'll go and talk to Ghislaine and her mother." Preacher rose and headed for the door. There he paused and turned to face the group.

"Thank you. Thank you all," he said in an emotional voice before disappearing into the kitchen.

"What the hell was that all about?" asked Darkie.

"One day you might figure it out, but I doubt it. Now are you girls going to play cards or watch?"

"We're playing," chorused the three girls. "And for real money," added Marie, "I'm sick of playing for matches."

Al smiled. "Welcome to 1918, and the real world."

YOU ARE SCUM, FILTHY SCUM

The cold weather continued well into January and the men of No.3 Section were grateful that they were sleeping in dry beds. The engineers had run a network of pipes behind the kitchen stove and so the men were also able to enjoy a hot shower. During the day Sergeant King kept them busy laying and retrieving lines, manning the switchboard, and practising Morse and Semaphore. One morning the men were surprised to see Lieutenant Johnson awaiting their arrival at Headquarters.

"Trouble coming men," muttered Darkie.

"Couldn't be anything else with that bastard around," replied Jacko.

The squad halted in front of the officer.

"Well men, I've some good news for you. The army is about to introduce a new piece of signalling kit into service, and I have suggested to higher authority that No.3 Section would be the ideal team to test it out under battle conditions."

"May I ask what sort of kit, Sir?"

"Yes of course, corporal. It's a new portable wireless set. Move the squad into the classroom. A sergeant from a British Regiment is waiting to explain all about it."

At one end of the classroom was a trestle table and on it was the new apparatus. Each man looked at it with concern and curiosity.

"Be seated. Sergeant Trounson will be your instructor for the next few days. Your job is to learn how to assemble, disassemble and operate this new equipment. It's going to change your lifestyle on the battlefield. No more wires. You just set up this kit and start sending messages. Right Sergeant Trounson, they're all yours. Today is Tuesday, so I suggest we hold an examination on Friday if that is enough time?"

"Plenty sir, if they're as smart as you claim. Of course, they'll need to be above average with reading and sending Morse code by buzzer."

Johnson looked around at the men and gave a sickly smile. "Don't you fret about that Sergeant. This particular squad is renowned for its skills and initiatives. Right I'll see you all on Friday."

Sergeant Trounson looked surprised. "Well chaps that was a real pat on the back, but we'll soon see how good you are. Gather around and have a look at what we have here on the table."

For the next couple of hours, the Sergeant explained the theory of telegraphy and the capabilities of the wireless set. The facts and figures were impressive. After lunch, the Sergeant instructed the men how to dismantle the equipment and re-assemble it.

"By Friday you have to be able to pull it apart and put it together blindfolded. That's the final test."

"Why?" asked Sam.

"Because lad, I cannot guarantee that every time you have to set up a communication station, there will be light. You may be out in the field in the middle of the night, in a place where torches or lights are not allowed. Don't worry, you soon get the hang of it. The main thing to guard against is connecting the batteries incorrectly. These sets don't like the electricity running amok. Right, three of you come up here."

"Three?" queried Al. "We normally work in pairs."

"Not any more," replied Sergeant Trounson. "Two could carry and operate this kit at a pinch, but what happens if one gets knocked over? No, it has been trialled and tested, and the decision is for a three man team. You can sort yourselves out into teams, but for now any three will do."

* * *

Conversation around the dinner table that evening was subdued.

"Well Al, what do you think?" Preacher's question was the question each man wanted to put to their leader. It would be Al Wilson's decision whether or not the team became a wireless Section and Al chose his words with care.

"It's too early to say Preacher. We've only had the one day to look at the gear and we don't really know how good it is. The big plus is that it eliminates all that work on the lines but I don't think there are enough wireless sets to go around, so the lines will still be the usual way of communicating. Our old jobs will still be there if we want them. What I want you to do is apply yourselves to this course of instruction. Learn all you can and don't worry about teams. Each one of us should be able to slot into any team at any time."

The men nodded. Al Wilson knew what he was doing, they told themselves. The Majority left the table and headed for bed, leaving Al, Preacher and Bluey sipping their last cup of tea.

"This is going to upset your rifle practice," observed Al.

Bluey nodded. "Yes. I don't mind missing one day, or even two, but a whole week is a bit much."

Preacher smiled. “You could always ask that nice Lieutenant Johnson for time off from classes Bluey. I’m sure he would accommodate you.”

“Wouldn’t give him the chance to say no Preacher. In fact, I could never bring myself to ask a favour of that man. He is evil.”

“I agree,” Al frowned. “He’s part of this wireless scheme, but I don’t know why. He wouldn’t volunteer us for the course unless there was something in it for him. Captain Solway is away at the moment leaving Johnson in charge. Normally I’d ask Pete King, but he is up at the front. I don’t like surprises such as Johnson sprang on us this morning.”

Preacher looked at his watch. “Time to turn in, I reckon. We all need our beauty sleep.”

“Yes we do Preacher,” replied Al, “and I hope you’re getting plenty. Sleep I mean.”

Preacher paused by the kitchen door. “Are you trying to tell me something?”

“No Preacher. I only worry about my men when we reach the lines. Back here, I don’t worry about you.”

“Rubbish!” interjected Bluey. “You worry about us twenty-four hours a day no matter where we are. Preacher, we’re all worried about you, even if Al won’t say so.”

Preacher returned to the table and stood looking down at his two companions. “Why should you worry about me? I’d never let you down, surely you know that?”

Bluey looked to Al for help. “I think what Bluey is trying to say Preacher, is that we’re concerned about your future. You’re not someone to enter into a relationship lightly. This affair with Gilly is much more than a brief encounter. Even the girls are talking about you as their replacement father.”

“So, what’s wrong with that?” The tall man was on the defensive. “I intend to marry Ghislaine once this damn war is over.”

"I never thought you would view it otherwise Preacher, but the damn war isn't over, and soon we'll be going back to it. And you know what that means."

"Yes Al, I do, and I worry about what would happen to Ghislaine and the family if I did get hit. We have discussed it, and she knows and accepts the risks, the dangers. She has been through it before you know."

Al nodded. "Yep we know, Preacher. It's just that we care and worry for you and for the family. I hope it all works out."

"Me too." added Bluey. "Preacher, we really are happy for you, but worried. That's what mates are for."

"Thanks Bluey, you too Al. It'll be all right, you'll see. I've never been so happy, and I just know that it'll all work out in the long run. Well, see you in the morning," he paused. "You know it's funny in a strange sort of way. I had to come all this way to take part in a filthy war, to find the two things that I couldn't find back home. Love for a woman, and some real friends. I guess that's a plus for the war." And with those parting words Preacher departed the room.

"A plus for the war?" Al shook his head. "Well that's the first entry in the plus column, although it hardly measures against all the minus signs. Come on, let's hit the sack to dream about wireless sets."

* * *

As soon as the evening meal was over on Thursday the men excused themselves from the chores of clearing the tables and washing the dishes. Once they were seated around the table attention turned to Al Wilson.

"The first thing I want to say is, that I have been most impressed with the speed you blokes have shown in mastering the ins and outs of the wireless set. I know Sergeant Trounson is also most impressed, which makes tomorrow's performance a little more difficult to execute." For once Sam failed to ask a question.

The corporal continued. "I've been asking around and I now know why Lieutenant Johnson volunteered this section. The arrangement is that three teams will be formed from this Section, and each team will be sent to separate battalion headquarters. I'm not part of the scheme, as I'm not part of the vendetta the Lieutenant is waging against you blokes."

"Crap! He can't split us up."

"Yes Darkie, he can. By the time Captain Solway gets back, you will have gone your separate ways. I think he knows the captain and I go back a long way, hence I am spared. But having completed this wireless course, I'm sure the army will find a new job for me." He held up a hand to stop the expected howls of protest. "Before I go on, I would like to hear what you blokes think about the new kit. Bluey?"

"Sorry Al, but I'm not going to pass that test tomorrow. It's too heavy to carry around in the trenches. They might call it portable, but I feel sorry for anyone who has to carry it any distance. And what if Jerry latched onto you? Hell, there's no way you could run and still lug that stuff along."

"Especially if you're also carrying a rifle eh Bluey?"

"Yes, that too."

"Right. Too bulky, too heavy." Al made a note in the book he had in front of him. "Mac, you got any thoughts on the subject?"

"I agree with Bluey, it's too heavy, and I also wonder about its reliability. What happens if the gear gets wet or dirty? Sure, it works a charm in that classroom, but up the front in all that filth and wet? I'm not convinced. It's a solid piece of kit, but there are also some delicate parts."

"Points noted. Any more contributions?"

Jacko put his hand up. "Those batteries are heavy, and to keep the bloody thing going, you'd need a fair number as spares. More bloody weight."

"True." said Al, making another note in the book.

Sam slowly raised his hand. Al nodded in his direction. “I won’t be passing that test tomorrow Al, but not for any of the reasons already mentioned. You see I’ve always had trouble with reading the buzzer. With the lamp, I’m up with the others, but my brain can’t handle the buzzer. There’s no way I can pass tomorrow.”

“Me too,” butted in Darkie. “You can add my name alongside Sam’s. I can’t handle the buzzer, especially receiving. My ears don’t seem connected to my brain.”

Al looked at Simon and George. “You two got any thoughts on the matter?”

It was George who answered. “Al, we didn’t start off with Preacher and the rest, but we’re part of the team now, and we want to stay with the others.”

“Fair enough. So, it’s all in together. As I see it, all of you intend to fail the test. Now how do you plan to do that...”

Preacher spoke. “We’ll think of something Al. Perhaps it’s best if we work it out between ourselves and leave you in the dark. You don’t need to know as you’re excluded from this plan of Johnsons’. Although when it goes wrong, he’ll probably take it out on you anyhow.”

“Possibly Preacher, but that’s my worry. Let’s see how it pans out. Anyone for a game of cards before turning in? Come on, clear the table. Let’s play and forget about Johnson and his infernal signal machine.”

* * *

At breakfast next morning, the men were chattering like school boys. It was clear that they saw the wireless tests as a challenge, a war against an old adversary, a war they were confident of winning.

“You don’t look too happy Al.”

“No I’m not, Bluey. Lieutenant Johnson has gone to a lot of trouble to set this thing up, and when it turns sour he’s going to turn nasty. A man like that is most dangerous when crossed, and we don't have Captain Solway here to umpire the game. Still, the alternative is unacceptable, so we'll just have to wear his revenge. Mind you, what can he do to us? Send us up to the front? That's what we're here for, and I expect we would be going forward in about ten days."

"Cheerful bugger, aren't you?" growled Bluey as he picked up his rifle.

"Bluey, leave Lucy behind today."

Bluey looked at the cherished weapon he held in his hands. "But I always take her with me Al."

"Yes I know Bluey. But I'll make you a promise. There'll be no Germans to shoot today, so leave Lucy here."

Bluey studied Al's face, and as he couldn't detect any sign of levity in the corporal's features, he replaced the weapon in its stowage and joined the others in the courtyard.

* * *

When the Section halted outside the classroom they were warmly greeted by Lieutenant Johnson. Inside the classroom they found a smartly dressed Major from the same regiment as Sergeant Trounson. Lieutenant Johnson introduced Major Ford, and explained that the Major would be conducting the tests. Major Ford then explained the procedure. On the table was a wireless set ready to operate. It would be manned by Sergeant Trounson. Two other sets were sitting on the floor. The object of the test was for teams of three to dismantle these sets, then proceed at speed to sites that had been selected on a hill to the north of the camp.

"Look at it as a competition," said the Major. "Once you arrive at your site, you will assemble the equipment, and call in to Sergeant Trounson. Call signs are on the log book with each set. Once you have established communication with base you will be asked a number of questions. Sergeant Trounson will require each operator to identify themselves as an individual, so he can assess your competence at sending and receiving. Any question? Good. Corporal, detail off your teams."

Al Wilson took out his notebook. "Team A will be Lacey, Fleming and Ralston; Team B will be McKenzie, Jackson and Young. The final team will be Dowson, Morbey and O'Brien."

"Fine, I'm going to time you. The whole thing should take about an hour depending on how fast you can run, and how proficient you are at handling the equipment. Your time starts now."

The two teams descended on the equipment and commenced dismantling it.

"Be careful man," warned the Major, "that's delicate electrical gear," as Darkie dropped a piece of kit onto the floor.

"Sorry sir, I guess I was too eager," replied Darkie.

The men seemed to have all sorts of difficulties dismantling the equipment, and at times, it was hard to work out which piece of kit belonged to which wireless set. Eventually both teams scrambled out the door and set off at a trot towards the selected outposts. Al and the members of the third team retreated to the rear of the classroom.

"Not very good Johnson," said the Major looking at his watch. "In fact, very poor. They didn't seem to have a clue."

"Nerves sir. This is very important to them. They're as keen as mustard." Johnson might have sounded confident, but he had a worried look.

Time passed, and the wireless set in the classroom remained silent.

"For God's sake, what are they doing? Call them."

Sergeant Trounson tapped the buzzer key. There was no reply.

"Johnson, the whole exercise should take about an hour, and it's almost that now and not a word."

"Don't worry Sir, they'll check in at any minute now."

As if in answer to his prayers the wireless sprang to life. Sergeant Trounson acknowledged the call and asked the sender to identify himself. The dots and dashes came in slowly. The men in the classroom stared at the machine.

"I don't believe it!" exclaimed Major Ford. "That's about the speed I expect from a raw recruit who has never used Morse code before. Who is sending?"

"It's difficult to say Sir. It's a jumble of letters, but I think it's Sapper Ralston."

"Well tell him to get off the line and let someone else have a go."

"Yes Sir." Time and time again the Sergeant sent the message to Sam to change operators, but all he received was: "Please repeat."

"Give him a jamming signal." ordered the Major, and the Sergeant pressed his key for a continuous signal. "That should get him off the air."

The Sergeant released the key and the room fell silent. They all stared at the wireless.

"Call Team B."

In answer to the Sergeant's call came the Team B call sign, but again it was painfully slow.

"Identify yourself." instructed Sergeant Trounson.

Back came the long drawn out reply from Jackson.

"Get him off the line, Trounson. Tell them to change operators."

Again, the man at the other end seemed to have difficulty in reading the instruction, and when Simon finally did come on the line, he was almost as slow as Jacko.

"Damn you Johnson, these men are hopeless. They are morons. There's no way I would let them loose in the field with a wireless set. They're incompetent. Don't you teach them anything in Australia? Get them back here Trounson."

The sergeant had great difficulty in passing the recall message and the Major's anger and frustration continued to grow.

"Damn it Johnson. We have been here for two hours, and virtually not one message has been passed."

"I'm sorry Sir. Really, I am sorry, but could you please test the last three? I do need to find a wireless team." pleaded the Lieutenant.

Major Ford swung around to look at the three sappers. "You," he said, pointing his finger at Bluey. "Get on that key and show me what you can do."

Bluey took the Sergeant's place at the set and tapped out a message at high speed. Sergeant Trounson smiled but said nothing. Major Ford nodded. "Right, you can handle Morse, so you're to be the operator. Just as soon as the other imbeciles get back, you three take one set and move to the outpost." He swung around to Lieutenant Johnson. "I'm telling you now Lieutenant, I've wasted nearly a whole morning, and if anything goes wrong with this lot, I'm off, and your commanding officer will be hearing from me."

Johnson's embarrassment was saved by the door crashing open and the two exhausted teams filed in. Despite their apparent weariness, Al thought he detected the odd twinkle in their eyes.

"You men are a disgrace to the signallers," roared the irate Major. "You are useless, and I thank the heavens that you are in the Australian Army and not the British Army."

The men sheepishly deposited the equipment on the floor.

"It's too heavy Sir." Sam was exhausted, but defiant.

"And so is your stupid brain soldier. I've never heard such poor Morse. Never. Right, you three. Take one set and off you go, and be quick about it."

Bluey, Mick and George grabbed the gear and hurried away. The remainder settled down to wait. Ten minutes later, the door opened and George entered.

"Sorry Sir, we forgot to take the batteries. We got the two sets mixed up."

The Major catapulted out of his chair and confronted Lieutenant Johnson. "Did you hear that Lieutenant? They forgot to take batteries! Did anyone tell them that the wireless operates on batteries? Did anyone tell them anything about operating a wireless? Did anyone ever teach them Morse code? They are useless, utterly useless. I'm off, but you'll hear more of this." Without looking left or right the Major strode to the door held open by George, and disappeared outside. The men turned to face a very shaken Lieutenant Johnson.

"Get those other idiots back here, Wilson. Get them back here at once. My God I'll make you pay for this. I'm going to see the Colonel right now. When he finds out you have disgraced the Australian Army, I hate to think what he will do, but whatever he does it won't be enough. You are going to pay for this, and you Corporal Wilson, are in this right up to your neck. Your precious Captain Solway won't be able to save you this time." He glared around the room. "You are scum, filthy scum, and scum should live in filthy surroundings, and I know where to find such a place for you." He stormed from the room slamming the door behind him.

"Your Lieutenant seems to be out of sorts today."

"Yes Sergeant he does, and I worry about a man whose judgement is clouded by such anger." Al was not smiling.

"George, tell the others to come back, and be quick about it. The rest of you reassemble that wireless set and tidy up this room."

Order was quickly restored to the room and the equipment. Sergeant Trounson watched with interest. "Neat and fast. Just what I would have expected from you blokes. Why? Why the stuff up? I was puzzled until that red-headed fellow got on the key, then I realised that it was a put up job."

"Don't worry about it Sergeant," replied Al. "You did a good job. We had our reasons for not passing the test, but you don't need to know about them."

"Well I'm off. Please reassemble the other set when it arrives and then return the key to the guardhouse. And good luck. I've got a feeling you'll be needing it." The Sergeant looked out from the doorway. "Here come your mates now. They look like signallers, but we know different don't we?" He laughed and walked away.

* * *

That night, the men took up their positions around the table laughing as they relived the events of the morning. "Tell me Al, why did you make me leave Lucy behind?"

"I had a feeling that today something might go wrong, and if you'd heard what Johnson called us, that temper of yours might have flared up a bit too high."

"You don't think I'd waste a bullet on that bastard?"

"Yes I do Bluey. He's mean and vindictive. I worry that one day he'll push you just that bit too far, and of course, when you retaliate, he'll have won. A man who carries that much hatred inside him is a man to be watched. Remember that. Now what was that message you tapped out that Trounson read? It was too fast for me."

Bluey laughed. "I was hoping no one would be able to read it, but of course Trounson is a professional. I sent: 'Now is the time to stumble and fall, better to walk the wire, than hear a wireless call'."

"Pretty weak," mused Al, "but I guess it sums it up. That's what we'll be doing, mending wires for the rest of the war."

The sound of a vehicle interrupted their talking.

"Corporal Wilson?" said a voice from the darkness. "Orders from HQ. Please sign for them." A soldier appeared carrying an open book, on which lay an envelope. Al took the envelope and signed.

"Thank you, Corporal," said the messenger before disappearing back into the darkness.

"Well, what have we got here?" asked Al as he held up the envelope. "Johnson's revenge. We can guess what it says. The question is when?"

Al opened the envelope and read the message. "The time is 7:00am tomorrow. Sorry boys, but we are going back to war. Preacher, best you break the news to the ladies. The rest of you start putting your gear together. I'll inspect each man before breakfast tomorrow. Preacher, ask Gilly if we can eat at 0615. That's it, men. We won the battle, but lost the war."

LIKE STALKING DEER

The departure next morning was a very quiet affair. The women said little as they bustled around making breakfast. From the piles of sandwiches that had been prepared it was obvious that the girls had been working in the kitchen since the early hours. Ghislaine's red eyes belied her cheery conversation and demeanour. The over-riding emotion of the men was anger. It was a dangerous sign and was recognised as such by Al.

Farewells were brief. Yvette took Bluey aside and whispered something to which the young redhead nodded. With a lot of waving and cries of, "Take care, be careful, come back soon", the truck, with No.3 Signal Section on board, set off.

Al gave the men time to settle down before calling for their attention. "There're a few things I want to say, and I want you to listen hard. The plain truth of the matter is this. If we hadn't crossed Lieutenant Johnson then we might have had a few more days at the farm. All Johnson did, was bring forward our departure date. We're not in France to have a good time, we're here to fight a war. The farm is a very pleasant diversion from reality, but that's all it is. So, I don't want you becoming occupied with silly thoughts about getting revenge on Johnson. Put that behind you. If you don't concentrate on the job ahead you will make mistakes, and mistakes can cost lives. Tomorrow you'll be sniper bait. There are people who think we're a lucky section, but luck is a very fickle lady, and she can play strange tricks. I like to think we make our own luck by the way we carry out our tasks, and that's the way I want it to stay. Put Lieutenant Johnson out of your minds. When the war is over, you can tar and feather him. In fact, I might even give you a hand, but right now he's nothing. So, start thinking about where we're heading, and what we have to do. Think of nothing else." The young corporal paused and waited for Sam's question.

"Where are we heading Al?"

"Belgium. We're to join up with our old Division at Messines. You'll see some familiar faces, although there've been a lot of changes. Right, now check your gear. Let's not make it too easy for the enemy."

The mood slowly changed, and the men began to relax. Their admiration and respect for their corporal was overwhelming. Each man held a firm conviction that Al Wilson would bring them safely through the ordeals that lay ahead. Al Wilson wasn't so sure.

* * *

The cold days were detested, yet welcomed, by the men in the trenches on both sides of the battlefield. In the sector where the Australian battalions faced Prussian regiments, both sides took advantage of the lull in the fighting to reinforce their positions. The front was on a series of low hills separated by an expanse of flat land that had once been home to several farming families. It was almost impossible to imagine what that wasteland had been like before the fury of war. No farmhouses, no fences, no trees remained. Roads coming from nowhere, going nowhere, started and stopped at shell crater edges. This was ‘no-man’s land’, but in reality, it was ‘nothing land’. Nothing moved on that desolate landscape.

While the Generals on both sides pondered their next moves, the men in the trenches made the most of the respite from hostilities. The war had diminished in intensity but not abandoned them completely. Shells from both sides occasionally whistled overhead as the gunners polished up spotting procedures, or trained newcomers to the battery. Small detachments of soldiers manned the shooting platforms to observe the enemy’s movements. Common sense, and the desire to survive, dictated that the men not expose themselves to the sharp eye of a sniper. The range between the frontline trenches was close to the maximum for a rifle. But you could never be sure, and the chance of a ‘lucky’ shot finding its target made men move with caution.

The lookouts on the platforms were doubled at night and strict silence was imposed along the lines. Both sides sent out night patrols into the wasteland to gather information and to test the enemy’s defences. Occasionally, opposing patrols would meet and a fierce skirmish would take place, but survival was the key factor in these mini-battles and both sides would try to quickly disengage from the action.

With the lull in fighting the Australian battalions improved their living conditions. In the reserve area, to the rear of the frontline, they burrowed like moles into the sides of slopes to make their dugouts roomier and safer. Timber, normally sought as fuel for fires, was now also sought to make furniture. Tables, chairs and crude beds were constructed. Men no longer slept on the lice-ridden ground and, feeling safe and secure in their earthen cocoons, they slept soundly and dreamt of a world at peace.

Small parties were allowed each day to march to billets in the villages behind the lines, and for twenty-four hours the men would try to forget the world they’d just left. The YMCA and

Salvation Army had established rooms equipped with the essentials for letter writing. Hot showers, and facilities for washing clothes, were in great demand as the battle against the hated lice was waged and won, if only for a short time. Hot wholesome meals, sometimes washed down with wine or rum, were much appreciated. Despite the best endeavours of their superiors, a quantity of rum managed to find its way back to the frontline, where it became valuable for drinking, bribery or barter.

This brief interlude was designed to give the men time to relax, to enjoy home comforts, to forget the war. But the war had become their total existence, and they seldom spoke of home. When they had first arrived in France, surviving and going home was all they thought about. In the beginning, there were endless rumours about an early end to the fighting, and men would seize on any mention, any suggestion, that peace was possible, imminent. Clutching at straws, they added their own interpretations to the whispers, embellished the half-truths, until they convinced themselves, and anyone who would listen, that the war would soon be over and they would be going home.

But the never-ending attacks and counter-attacks had erased any hopes of an early return. To the men the end of the war was death or, if you were lucky, a wound serious enough to warrant a ticket back to an English hospital. And so, they waited, knowing that one morning they would climb out of their trenches and race across that barren wasteland, and then their war would probably end.

* * *

Across the shattered landscape, facing the Australian trenches, the men of the Prussian regiments also rested and regrouped. They and the Australians were old foes, and although each side hated and despised the other, they also had a deep respect for the courage and fighting qualities of their enemy.

Sitting in a concrete pillbox which they had recently commandeered as their observation post sat two German soldiers. Their green uniforms identified them as belonging to a Bavarian regiment and their equipment identified them as snipers. Gunther and Herwin were cousins and had grown up in the Bavarian mountains, where they had acquired skills as hunters and marksmen. These skills had attracted the attention of the German High Command and so they found themselves drafted into a special sniper unit commanded by Herwin's brother Rolt. Rolt had requested that the unit be allowed to operate as an independent sniper section and, as his family was related to Crown Prince Rupprecht of Bavaria, Commander of the German Armies on the Western Front, the request was approved.

The group had over two years earned a reputation for skill and bravery, and commanders vied for the use of their talents. However, it was normally left to Rolt to select the sphere of operations, and it was he who had chosen the Australian sector for their next operation. Herwin's eyes glistened with excitement as he explained to his cousin his plan of operation.

"It is so simple, Gunther. You see that pile of rubble?" he said, pointing to a heap of broken concrete that lay forlornly in the barren wasteland.

"Yes, but you can't build a hideout there. One shot, and they would be onto you. You would never get back."

"Wrong, cousin. I went out last night with a patrol. It's a perfect hide. There's a small concrete block that can be pushed aside to give a peep hole. It gives a limited arc for firing, but as soon as I have fired, I push the block back into place, and slide down into my secret tunnel."

"Secret tunnel?"

"There is an old ditch, a channel, that leads from near the front of our trenches, across no-man's land. It passes by the heap of concrete. I've talked to the engineers and the infantry, and they have agreed to cover the ditch with planks and to cover them with dirt. I will then have an access route to the hide."

"Why would the infantry and engineers go to all this trouble for you?"

"Because nothing is happening at the moment, and I happened to mention how pleased Prince Rupprecht would be when he heard about their co-operation."

Gunther nodded. "So, when is all this going to happen?"

"Tonight they start, and I expect it will take three or four days. I want you to check that the earth cover they put over the planks blends in with the surrounds. I don't want a line of new dirt pointing like an arrow to my hide."

"It will be damn cold and wet Herwin, and a long crawl out there."

"Not really. What I'll do is walk out there during the night, and settle down during the day to observe what is going on. Once I've got a feel for the comings and goings of the enemy, I'll start causing them problems."

"Can I have a go?"

"Perhaps Gunther. First, we must see how good our Prussian friends are at roofing in that channel. I wish Rolt was here. He'd like this idea."

"Where is your big brother?"

"Silly question. The bright lights and good company at headquarters demand a lot of his time these days."

"Half his luck," muttered Gunther. "Being an officer has its advantages doesn't it?"

"Yes, but then we get some benefits from having Rolt as our Commander. The other men don't drink our class of wine with their meals."

"No, nor do they get to eat as well. Speaking of which, how about a little something to hold off the pangs of hunger?"

Herwin sighed. His cousin's appetite was well known. "Help yourself Gunther, it's only an hour or so since we had lunch." He shook his head. "I don't think you will ever make it to the hide. You'll never get that gut of yours through the tunnel."

* * *

No.3 Signal Section had been in the trenches for just over a week and the men had quickly dropped into the routine. The smells, the lice, the cold, the fear, all were there, and the state of the ground meant that great care had to be exercised when traversing the country. This made it easier for the enemy to predict the route the men would travel. To deviate from the duckboards could spell disaster if help was not close by. And another threat had been added to the already long list of perils. Gas was now an ever present menace, and both sides experimented with this insidious weapon. Men listened to the sound of exploding shells and learnt to recognise the difference between the high explosive, the anti-personnel and the gas shell. The Germans developed a strategy of mixing up bombardments with high explosive and sneezing gas, which made the men take off their gas masks. Then would come the phosgene or mustard gas shells, with dreadful consequences.

* * *

Bluey entered the dugout to find Al Wilson sitting at the mess table staring at a map. He made himself a cup of tea and sat down alongside the corporal.

"Problem?"

"Not really, Bluey. I was just looking at this map and realised that I know this area better than home. I've lived in Adelaide all my life, but I can't remember any of the streets as clearly as I can visualise these roads and tree lines."

"Probably you walked around Adelaide without someone shooting at you Al. All you had to do was go from A to B, without a care."

"Guess you're right. Not like you in the bush."

"True. But in the bush a tree, or rock, can act as a signpost, so you have to notice such things and remember what they look like. As Dad always said, 'See what you are looking at'."

"Good advice."

"You know Al, we don't know much about you. We know you come from Adelaide, we know you were at Gallipoli, so you have been in the army for the past three years, but what did you do in civilian life?"

"Not much. Dad was a grocer and owned a corner store. A comfortable existence, but Dad worked long hours. I went to the local state school. Two things became evident about the time I went to high school. I was good at the academic side of things, I never had any problems passing exams, but more importantly, I was a natural at sports. I played cricket, tennis and football for the school. Towards the end of high school, I was encouraged to go to university in return for playing cricket and football for the local clubs. It was all too easy. In my first year at university I was selected for the state cricket squad, and during the winter played football in the state league. I loved sport. I loved the challenge, the competition. Then along came the war. Some of my mentors suggested they could pull strings and have me classified as an 'essential' worker. What a farce! No, to me the war was another challenge, a bigger game."

"After what you've been through, what you've seen, any regrets?"

"A few, but I see each day as a challenge, and I seem to thrive on it. My blood races, the palms sweat, and the fear returns. But I still look forward to it."

"Here we are in the middle of hell on earth, everyone hoping and praying for the war to end, and you say you look forward to the challenge. What the hell are you talking about?"

"Survival. That's what it's all about Bluey. Staying alive, beating the odds, it applies to all of us, although you probably regard survival as something desired, not a challenge."

Before Bluey could answer, a shell whistled overhead. More followed. They looked at each other.

"Bastards," snarled Bluey. "Gas?"

"I reckon. It's becoming pretty common. That gas is one of the worst things I've seen in this war. God men can be cruel."

"You call the Germans men? More like animals in my book." ventured Bluey.

"Are they, mate? Remember Christmas?" Al looked at his watch. "Who's running the lines?"

"Preacher and Mick. They should be back by now, they are..." The rest of the sentence went unspoken as rifle fire broke out and raised voices could be heard. Both men ran from the dugout, Bluey pausing to grab his rifle. As they ran along the communication trench they could hear men calling, "Keep moving Preacher. Catch up Mick. Keep moving."

Al and Bluey reached the forward trench and took up positions on the parapet. Mick and Preacher had about one hundred yards to cover in sight of the enemy and both men were now sprinting towards the safety of their own trenches. The enemy infantry had opened fire in the hope that a stray bullet would find a mark, and the Australian infantry were returning fire to add to the problems of the enemy riflemen.

Preacher dived into the exit trench as Mick let out a dreadful scream and fell to the ground, thirty yards short of the safety.

"Christ, he's been hit." breathed Al.

"Yes, and a gut shot too," added Bluey as Mick writhed on the ground, hands pressed to a gaping wound.

"Help me, for Christ's sake, help me." Mick's screams were like a knife being driven into the ears of the onlookers.

Preacher having reached the safety of the trench joined his companions on the parapet. His face went ashen as he took in the scene before him. “Do something Al. You have to do something.”

“Do what Preacher? What can anyone do? To go out there to help Mick is inviting a bullet. He’s hit bad Preacher.”

Mick’s screams continued. “Bluey, please Bluey, shoot me.” he cried. “Bluey, for God’s sake, you wouldn’t let one of your precious animals suffer like this. Bluey.”

All eyes turned towards the young redhead, who stood cradling his rifle.

“Bluey, end it, please Bluey.”

Bluey slowly raised his rifle and looked along the sights.

“For God’s sake Bluey,” whispered Al. “Do you know what you’re doing?”

“No, I don’t know Al. You’re my superior. Tell me what to do.”

“Bluey I can’t order you to shoot him, you know that. It’s your decision, but I’ll back you.”

Any further discussion was interrupted by a battalion officer shouting, “That man. Return to the trench immediately.”

Unnoticed, Preacher had dropped down from the parapet and, seizing a rifle which was lying in the mud, had re-entered the exit trench. He was now standing at the entrance to the trench, holding the rifle high over his head. On the muzzle, he had tied a white handkerchief. A total silence fell upon the watchers.

“Preacher, it’s no good.” shouted Al. “Those bastards won’t recognise a flag of truce. Come back. Think of Gilly.”

These last words caused Preacher to turn, as if he had changed his mind, but then he nodded towards his friends, and started to walk slowly towards his fallen comrade.

“Al, they’re not shooting.”

“No Bluey, not yet.”

The onlookers watched in disbelief as the tall soldier walked slowly towards Mick.

"Preacher, I knew you wouldn't leave me. Oh Christ, Preacher it hurts."

"I know Mick, I know. But everything is going to be all right. You'll be in the first aid post before you know it." Preacher knelt down beside Mick ensuring that the rifle, with its pathetic white flag, remained vertical. Preacher undid the buckles on Mick's gear and eased the equipment from his shoulders. He then put his arm around the fallen man. "Please Mick, try and stand. I know it'll hurt but you must try."

Mick nodded, and with Preacher lifting he managed to get to his feet.

"Fine, just fine Mick. It's going to be all right. Now one step at a time. Slowly now."

Mick managed three or four paces before he slumped to the ground pulling Preacher with him. The rifle fell from his grasp. The mesmerised onlookers gasped as they heard the shot which shattered Preacher's head. A second shot hit Mick in the chest. It was all over.

"The bastards. Those lousy bastards."

"Yes Bluey, those lousy bastards. What did you expect?"

"For God's sake Al, Preacher was out there under a white flag of truce."

"Another rule, another so-called law of war. You can't fight a war with rules Bluey, it's not how it's done. There is only the one rule. You must know that by now."

Bluey nodded. "Why did they wait? Those two shots were clean kills. Why didn't they finish off Mick with a second shot once he hit the ground? Why wait?"

"A good question but I doubt if we'll ever know the answer. Come on, there are other things to be done. The stretcher bearers will recover the bodies tonight."

"What things?" The young redhead was staring at the bodies of his friends.

"Letters. Letters to Preacher's parents, to Mick's mother and to Gilly."

"Oh God. Gilly. Who's going to tell her?"

"Well we can't, that's for sure. I'll write to her and tell her what happened, but first I'll get a message to the padre in Corbie, he can break the news. You can get started on letters to the parents. I'll help later on." Al looked across towards the fallen men. "I told you. Lady Luck is very fickle."

"And what about the Arab?"

"This was their day to die." The corporal looked into his friend's eyes. "Tell me Bluey, were you going to shoot Mick, if Preacher hadn't gone out there?"

Bluey looked down at the rifle he held. "I don't know Al, I don't know. But I was thinking about it, and that makes me sick in the stomach."

"Well don't think about it, because you didn't do it. Come on, let's get started. George?"

"Yes Al."

"Take Simon and report to battalion headquarters. You're a pair now."

"Looks like we've graduated."

"Yeah, but remember, keep your head down. Someone out there can shoot straight."

Bluey's head snapped around. "What did you say Al?"

"I said someone out there can really shoot. You said it yourself. Two clean shots."

Bluey looked across towards the enemy lines. "Yeah, someone over there can really shoot."

* * *

The atmosphere in the German battalion was electric. The regiment commander, Major Edel Manfried, was quivering with rage. The object of his unbridled anger stood before him, looking very relaxed.

“Sergeant,” the Major hissed, “you are a disgrace to your uniform, a disgrace to your country.”

“Not so Major. You have it all wrong. I was doing my duty as a German soldier. I was...” He paused as an officer entered the room.

The newly-arrived captain wore a green uniform, which identified him as from a Bavarian regiment, and the insignia on his arm announced that he was a sniper.

“Well Herwin, what seems to be the trouble?” asked the tall handsome captain, totally ignoring the Prussian Major.

“A misunderstanding Rolt.” replied his brother. “I was occupying my shooting site when two enemy soldiers came into my line of sight. I managed to wound one, and he fell. After a short while the other soldier returned to help the wounded man escape. I then shot both of them.”

“Is that so, Major?”

“Yes Captain Von Monsor, that is what happened, but the Sergeant forgot to mention that he shot the men while under a flag of truce.”

“Is that so Herwin?”

“No Rolt. The man who returned to assist the wounded man had a white flag attached to the muzzle of a rifle. I respected the flag of truce, until he put it down. I then considered that the truce was ended.”

The captain looked at the Major. “Did the enemy lower his flag of truce Major?”

“They stumbled and the man dropped the rifle. An accident.”

The Captain’s eyebrows raised. “An accident? How can you be sure it was an accident? Perhaps they had some sort of plan to deceive you. Who knows? The question is, did Sergeant Von Monsor shoot a man who was holding a flag of truce? By your admission, you have confirmed that he did not. I think that ends the matter.”

"Oh no it doesn't Captain. I intend to make representation to higher authority. This is a disgrace, a slur on the honour of my regiment."

"Really Major. Do you know who I am?"

"Everyone knows about Captain Von Monsor and his riflemen."

"Yes Major. They do. Even the enemy knows about us. I feel I should inform you I am related to Crown Prince Rupprecht, he's a close relation, and so your representation to higher authority will come to nothing. That I can promise you. Sergeant Von Monsor was doing his duty as a good German soldier. Now I have heard enough of this nonsense. Come Herwin, I want to talk to you about this new site you have developed. It sounds interesting."

Ignoring the infantry Major, both men left the room and crossed to the small concrete structure which served as their quarters.

"Thank you brother. That Major was beginning to get on my nerves."

"I could see that Herwin. Just as well I happened along when I did. He could have made things difficult for you. Tell me brother, did you really shoot those men while they were under a white flag?"

"No, the man put down the flag, so I shot him. Shot them both as a matter of fact. They were Australians. I have been watching their operations for a couple of days, and today I decided to do something about it. It's a strange thing Rolt. Those two, were the men who talked the regiment into that stupid truce at Christmas. I didn't recognise them, until the tall one came walking out with his idiotic white flag. There was something familiar about him, something about the way he walked. I said back at Bullecourt that we should be killing them, not feeding them, so in the end I got my way. Two dead Australians."

"Good for you brother. A dead Australian is a good Australian. Now I want to have a look at this hide you have built. How safe is it?"

"Very safe. I could crawl from here along the tunnel, but it's very muddy and damp. What I do, is go out just before sun-up and hide in the far end of the tunnel. From time to time I move out of my hiding hole, and crawl up to the blocks of concrete. One of them can be rotated slightly, and that gives me a peephole. My field of vision is limited, but if the enemy comes into view, he is a sitting duck. It's simple and effective as I have demonstrated."

"But after today won't they be on to you?"

"My bet is that all eyes were on the wounded man and his good samaritan. As soon as I had the second shot off, I closed the peep-hole. Even if I hadn't, I doubt if anyone could pick out that small gap in a heap of rubble. We sent over one of our aircraft yesterday, and he couldn't spot the trench. It's a great hide, and those Australians are going to suffer a lot more before I pull out of it."

"It sounds good. I'll come out with you tonight and check it out. It's your idea, so it's your operation, but be careful Herwin. I doubt if I could face mother if anything happened to you."

"Relax brother, nothing is going to happen to me. This is just like stalking deer in the mountains. Totally safe, with the odds in my favour."

* * *

Next morning Bluey was standing on the parapet, gazing across the wasteland towards the spot where Preacher and Mick had fallen. He didn't notice that he had been joined by another soldier until the man spoke.

"A bad business Bluey." the man said.

"Jock Collins. What a surprise! How are you?" They shook hands. "Hell's bells, I never expected to see you again. They tell me a sniper's life is limited out here."

"No more than a linesman's. The way you blokes expose yourselves to Jerry makes my hair stand on end. I saw what happened yesterday. That little bloke, wasn't he with you the day you jumped me on that training exercise?"

"Yeah. You were real careless that day, but you obviously learnt your lesson, or you wouldn't be here today."

"I've learnt a lot in the past year Bluey, and whoever shot your mates yesterday can shoot real good."

Bluey frowned. "That's what I told Al Wilson. But seriously Jock, he couldn't have got those two shots off so quickly from their trenches. No one is that good, or that lucky."

"I agree. Too far for two clean hits."

"So, he had to be closer, and the only cover is that heap of rocks."

The sniper shook his head. "He wasn't there mate. I've learnt a lot in the past year, and while you were all looking at your mates, I had my eyes on that pile of stones. To get off those shots he would've had to pop up above the stones, or at least show some part of him, or his rifle. He didn't. I swear, nothing moved over there."

Bluey continued to stare at the pile of stones. "You and I agree those shots, coming so close together, and being so accurate, could not have come from the trenches."

"Yep, that's a fact."

"Right Jock. We agree. We know that both men took hits on the left side, so the shots came from the right."

"And the pile of rubble is on the right."

"Correct, Jock. So, the shots must have come from the rocks. It's in the right position and it's the right distance. That's where our man was."

Again, the sniper shook his head. "I swear Bluey, I was watching those rocks. It's my job. Nothing moved."

"He was there Jock." Bluey continued to stare at the rocks. "He could be there now. Somehow, he can fire between the rocks, and doesn't have to show himself above the skyline."

"That sounds a logical explanation Bluey. But I've studied those rocks. There aren't any gaps."

Bluey continued to stare at the rubble. "No Jock, not from here. But let's move to a position where we can line up the spot where Mick fell."

"It's a long shot, but worth a try. I wouldn't mind a shot at that bastard."

"You can Jock, if I miss him. He's mine. I owe it to Mick and Preacher. Come on."

The two men picked up their rifles and climbed down from the parapet. They moved along the trench to the position nominated by Bluey. Jock was about to scramble onto a shooting platform when Bluey placed a restraining hand on his shoulder.

"Easy. We must not startle him. If he thinks we've spotted him, he'll be off. Wait here." Bluey disappeared along the trench and returned with two observation periscopes. "Better we stick these up in the air rather than our heads. That Jerry can shoot."

Both men settled down with the periscopes held against the trench wall.

"Only put it up far enough to see the stones, no farther." warned Bluey.

"Don't tell me how to do my job. I've spent half the war looking through one of these gadgets," snapped Jock.

"Sorry mate, I forgot." Both men cautiously raised their viewing devices. For ten minutes they studied the rocks without success.

"What now?" asked the sniper.

"He's there Jock, I know it. We just have to be patient. He's stalking us and we're stalking him. We have to get him to make a move."

"How?"

"Think Jock, as if it were you out there. You are blind, until you open your peephole, so what else can you rely on?"

Jock frowned. "What else is there?"

"Your ears. You hear something. You don't know what it is, so what do you do?"

Jock grinned. "You have a look."

"You're a quick learner."

"Hell Bluey, if we start shooting to make a noise, he'll keep that trapdoor shut, and you can't very well yell out, 'Hey Jerry, open up'."

"No you can't. Besides the only man we had who could speak German was Preacher, and he's gone. No, we have to make him curious."

"Curious?"

The young redhead frowned. "Yesterday I was talking to Al in the dugout when we heard shouting. The men were calling out to Preacher and Mick to hurry. They were encouraging them to run faster."

"I know, they usually do when they see you linesmen out in front."

"That's the key. He heard the shouting, opened up his peep-hole, and Mick and Preacher came into his line of sight. He missed Preacher the first time, because he was about thirty yards ahead of Mick."

Jock peered at the sapper. "You're guessing."

"Yeah I am. Stay here and watch that pile of concrete." The young sapper set off at a trot in the direction of the communi-cations trench.

* * *

Bluey was back thirty minutes later. "Jock, it's all fixed. Twenty minutes from now, the boys will start cheering. You see any-thing?"

"Bluey, you were right. Get your periscope and have a look." Carefully both men raised the upper mirror to the top of the trench.

"No change as far as I can see," said Bluey after carefully examining the nondescript pile of rubble.

"He's there. He opened his peephole about ten minutes ago. See that large slab that has a weird design blasted onto its surface? It's at ground level, slightly to the left of centre."

Bluey moved his viewing device. "Got it."

"Good. Now, his peephole is directly above the right hand side of that slab. It's about two foot, maybe twenty inches, above it. You can't see anything at the moment. It's a very snug fit, but ten minutes ago that's where a gap appeared."

Bluey stared at the spot Jock had indicated. When he was finally satisfied, he lowered the periscope, took his watch from his pocket, and set it on a ledge beside him. "We're only going to get one chance Jock. The boys will start cheering in exactly twelve minutes. We will watch the rock in turns for the next eleven minutes. We're directly in his line of vision, so if we pop up too soon, he'll spot us. What we must hope for is that he has the gap shut when the cheering starts. With luck, we'll have laid our sights on it. There won't be any time for polite manners about who shoots first. Once you have that hole in your sights, start shooting."

Jock nodded. "How far do you reckon he is Bluey?"

"My guess is 300 yards, give or take a couple. I'm not really guessing. I had a look at the map at battalion headquarters and they measured it off for me."

"Christ, you think of everything. Three hundred it is."

"Have a peep will you, while I double check Lucy."

"Lucy?"

"My rifle. Darkie named it. He said I went to bed with it every night as a substitute for the real Lucy."

"Oh. Have you told the real Lucy?"

"Not yet. I'm not sure if she would take it as a compliment or an insult. What can you see?"

Jock applied his eye to the periscope. "So far so good. His door is closed."

"Let's hope it stays that way for a while yet."

Bluey checked his rifle and when satisfied took over the role of watcher, while Jock went through the same procedure, except the sniper had a telescopic sight to adjust and clean.

Jock looked up. "I'm ready. Still got his head down?"

Bluey nodded. "Yeah. We have a minute and a half to go. Climb up and get set. If that gap appears shoot. Don't wait. Let me know when you're set and have your sights on the spot."

The sniper climbed onto the shooting platform and wedged his rifle in a gap between two sandbags.

"I'm on Bluey. Up you come," he called.

Bluey mounted the platform and looked at his watch. "Thirty seconds to go," he declared, pocketing the watch and settling himself in the firing position.

"Bloody hell, I hope Jerry over in the trenches can't see us." muttered Jock.

"Probably can, but it's too long a shot, and anyhow they don't know what we're up to."

"You hope my friend. Stand by. That's our cheer squad."

A chorus of shouts reached their ears as the men to their right commenced to urge on the phantom linesmen.

"Come on you dumb bastard." whispered Bluey. "Are you deaf as well as dumb?" As if in answer, a stone moved and a small black hole appeared. Both rifles spat fire, the men quickly reloading and firing again.

At the first shot the cheering subsided, but then there came another sound. A scream. The sound of a man in great pain.

Jock and Bluey jumped down from their platform and embraced.

"You bloody beaut Bluey. You were right about everything, and we did it."

"Yes Jock, we did it. May the bastard rot in hell."

* * *

Captain Rolt Von Monsor strode into the concrete dugout. In one corner, on a make-shift bed, lay his brother, face covered with blood and his uniform soaking wet and coated with mud. The captain brushed aside the men who were bathing the Sergeant's face.

"Herwin, for God's sake what happened? Are you all right?"

"Do I look all right brother?"

"Hell, I thought you were dead. At least that's the message I got. Let's have a look." He knelt down and took a cloth from one of the orderlies, and with tender care sponged the blood away from the wound. "My God, you're lucky Herwin."

"Lucky? I'm dying, and you say I'm lucky."

"Dying? I don't think so. The bullet has merely caressed your cheek. Mind you, it's made an awful mess where it kissed you, and I suspect your good looks have gone forever, but you'll live. A centimetre to the right and it would have been a very different story."

"Oh God it hurts Rolt."

"I'm sure it does. Where's Gunther?"

"He's probably cleaning up. He crawled down the tunnel and helped me back here. It was wet and foul but he did a good job."

"Good. Perhaps I will promote him to corporal as a reward for saving my brother. What happened?"

"I don't know. Somehow those Australians discovered my hide. How I don't know. I heard a noise and opened the peephole. That's all I remember, except for the pain. There was blood everywhere."

Rolt stood up and looked down. "You badly underestimated your enemy. A serious mistake but you'll survive. Make sure you learn from your error. Next time you mightn't be so lucky. I'll get you off to hospital and from there you can take some leave. A wound of honour. That should impress the ladies." He took his brother's hand. "Remember Herwin, not all our enemies are fools. Give my regards to all at home and don't linger too long in the beer halls of Munich. I need you here."

"Don't worry Rolt, I'll be back soon. I have a very personal debt to settle."

GET DOWN YOU IDIOTS

The cold miserable wintry conditions of January slowly abated and the hours of daylight increased. The soldiers waited while the Generals planned the courses of action they could take when dry ground would allow the slaughter to recommence.

No.3 Signal Section took its turn in the frontline but work was mainly routine. There was however, one problem, a problem created by Lieutenant Johnson.

"It's not necessary Al. To run a line in front of the trenches is operationally stupid, and from a safety point of view, it's madness. We're asking for trouble."

"I know Bluey. I've pointed out the facts to Johnson but he has a bee in his bonnet about keeping the men on their toes, realistic training, etc. We'll just have to put up with it and exercise every care."

"Damn him. You know it was he who sent us up here in the first place and as a result we lost Preacher and Mick. He's to blame."

"Enough of that talk Bluey. I told you on the way up here, this is where the war is. This is where we're expected to be, not lounging around at the farm. If Preacher and Mick hadn't been killed that day, then they might have copped it the next, or the day after that. It happens." He looked at his friend. "Something upsetting you mate?"

"Yeah. Had two letters today, one from home and one from Lucy. I know my Mother is ill, I can read between the lines, but all Dad says is, she's as well as can be expected. What the hell does that mean? As well as can be expected?"

"It's just a saying Bluey. You probably write home and say things over here are as well as can be expected, and back home they wonder what you expect. And how is the lovely Lucy?"

"Well that's another problem. I've been trying to find her twin brothers ever since we arrived in this area, but their battalion always seems to be in reserve when we're in the line and vice versa. Now I find out from Lucy, that Len was killed at Passchendaele and John badly wounded."

"How bad?"

"She doesn't know. He got hit and was gassed."

"Doesn't sound good. When we get out of the line, ask the padre to enquire for you. They have a very good old boy net."

"Good thinking Al." He looked at his precious watch. "Time for me to run that damn line. I'll take Simon with me."

Al looked up sharply. "That's another thing Bluey. How come you seem to partner Simon so often these days?"

Bluey paused at the doorway. "I promised Yvette I'd look after him. I'm slowly getting him to talk a bit about his life back home. I think he lied about his age so he could enlist and leave home. He's a good kid, but he's had a rotten life."

"I thought it was something like that. You had no right to make that promise to Yvette. It puts an extra load on your shoulders and that's not fair. Out here, each man has to pull his weight. We all have to be equal links in the chain."

"Like Bailey?"

"No, Bailey is not part of the team, never will be."

"You know Al, there are times your lectures sound a bit hollow."

Al frowned. "Hollow? What do you mean?"

"You lecture me about my concern for Simon, but I notice you keep a very close eye on George. I've seen you run a line on your own when George was available to go with you."

"Oh that. Well, that's different. George is older and has a wife and children back home. He needs to survive for their sake, so I sometimes let him stay back. Why expose him to an unnecessary risk if the job doesn't need two people?"

"No argument Al." Bluey smiled. "But remember the links in your chain."

"Point taken. You look after Simon and I'll keep an eye on George. Now get cracking. Lieutenant Johnson will get upset if that line isn't run."

"Lieutenant Johnson. Bah! I wish he'd come with me," snapped Bluey. "I might manage to lose him out there." He looked at his Corporal but got no response. Bluey pushed the doorway curtain aside. "Come on Simon, there's work to be done."

* * *

In their concrete shelter opposite the Australian lines, the Bavarian snipers watched the enemy's activities with interest, but little more, the distance between the frontlines being too far for effective fire from their rifles. Besides being bored by their inactivity, Gunther and Herwin were appalled at the attitude of the Prussians. They could not understand the hatred the men had for the war. But then, the Bavarians did not join in the suicidal charges across the killing fields. Such actions soon cooled one's enthusiasm for war.

The area of operations was welcomed by Herwin, whose good looks had been ruined by the Australian bullet that had gouged an ugly scar across his right cheek. Herwin had a score to settle with Australians and had pleaded with Rolt for a chance to wreak revenge.

Rolt was absent on one of his reviews of the situation along the frontline so Gunther and Herwin settled into a pattern of watching and recording the enemy's activities. There was little movement to be observed except for the occasions when two Australian linesmen would move along a telephone line laid in advance of their trenches. The linesmen were experienced and moved quickly and cautiously along the line. The German snipers had little hope of securing a hit at such a range, but as they were the only targets of opportunity presented, the two snipers would fire, more in hope than in expectation of a hit. It was a game, and they were amused when the Australians dived for cover in a shell hole, a sure indication that a shot had gone close.

Finally, Rolt arrived back from his travels and Gunther and Herwin made their report.

"There is something strange going on Rolt. The enemy is running a line in front of his trenches from a point directly opposite this observation point, to an entry point about three kilometres to the west. Why run such a line when it could easily be routed behind the trenches. Why expose their men to our fire? Why take the risk?"

"Gunther is right." added Herwin. "There must be something special about that line. They maintain the line most conscientiously. It seems they run it as a matter of routine."

"Why do you say that?"

"Well, they run the line two or three times a day, and with the limited amount of shelling I don't believe the line is being broken by shells that often. Yesterday morning at first light, two men ran the line and I didn't hear a single shell all night. It couldn't have been broken. Anyhow, I got off a couple of shots at them just to ensure they had their minds on the job, but they are old hands and they don't dawdle. If I could get a bit closer I'd knock them off, but at this range and with a moving target, it's hopeless."

"That's the problem." added Gunther. "We're too far away. To get closer we would have to move well outside our wire and those Australian sharpshooters would have a field day once we gave our position away by firing."

Rolt gazed across the shell scarred land. "Let me go over what you have just said. The first point is that the Australians are running a line from over there," pointing as he spoke, "to another terminal about three kilometres to the west. Each day they run the line with a two-man section, sometimes two, sometimes three times a day. We don't know why, but we suspect they are doing it as a routine and not because the line needs repairing."

"But why?" Asked Gunther.

"Now cousin, don't try to fathom out the whys and wherefores, but stick to what we know. The line is there and the linesmen religiously maintain it. We must therefore assume that the line is important to the Australians, and that makes it important to us."

"All right Rolt, the line is there and it's important." Herman shrugged. "What can we do about it? I have passed on the information to our gunners but they seem loath to bombard a single telephone line."

"You can't blame them for that brother. Dozens of shells to break a telephone line which our friends across the way would soon fix. No, we must do something. Something that will make the Australians reel up their line and take it elsewhere. Now what would make them do that?"

"Obvious." Herwin smiled. "Shoot a couple of those linesmen."

"I agree brother, and that is what we are going to do."

"Easy to say Rolt, but how? We need to get closer and that sounds like a suicide mission to me."

"No Gunther, we are not in the business of getting ourselves killed. Our business is killing the enemy. We know where the line is, we know the Australians run the line at first light and just before dusk...”

“...and sometimes during the day, usually around 11:00am.” interrupted Herwin.

“Yes, but we can’t plan on the day sortie, it’s not a regular part of the program, whereas the morning and evening runs are. So, our plan must revolve around one of those two runs.”

“Rolt, whatever you have in mind must mean one of us setting up an ambush out there. Once you have fired and given away your position, all hell will break loose.”

“Right Herwin. Whoever does the job must get in, kill, and get out before the enemy knows what has happened. The loss of two linesmen should be enough to convince the Australians that the line should be re-routed behind their lines. If we force them to stop using that line, then we have achieved a victory. A small victory, but a victory nonetheless.”

“And if they continue to run the line?”

Rolt frowned. “That would confirm that the line is very important. Why? I cannot guess. But if they are prepared to continue risking lives to keep it open, then it must be of considerable value to them. And if it’s important to the enemy, then it’s important to us. The more I think about that line the more important it becomes. It’s almost as if they are flaunting themselves in front of us, teasing us, daring us to do something. Well, we will do something, and it will be something they won’t like.”

“And just how are we going to do this something?” asked Gunther.

Rolt continued to gaze at the enemy lines. “I don’t know, but for every problem there has to be a solution, and I intend to find a solution for this particular problem. From now on I want you to log everything that happens along that damn line. Times are important, try to identify the men. Do they always operate as the same pair? Do they vary their methods? Write down everything you can about them."

"And where will you be while we are doing all this watching and writing?"

"I'm going to headquarters to talk to the intelligence people. We must have detailed maps of the farm lands. After all, we owned them last winter. Oh, and one last thing. Don't take pot shots at them from now on. Let them think we have lost interest in them. They may relax and get careless. I'll be back in two days."

* * *

Directly opposite the German observation post another meeting was taking place in an unfriendly atmosphere. Bluey and Simon had run the line this morning, and Bluey was upset.

"This whole bloody thing is stupid. Just what are we supposed to be doing out there besides giving the Jerry snipers some target practice?"

Lieutenant Johnson, seated at the table, was not amused. "Dowson, watch your language and remember who you're talking to. There are good reasons to maintain K5 line and the Section will continue to do so until I order otherwise."

Sergeant King could see that Bluey's anger and frustration had reached boiling point and that meant trouble. He interceded before Bluey could speak.

"Sir, these men are the best in the Brigade and they've been running lines for a long time. I'm sure if they were acquainted with the reasons for keeping K5 open they would accept the risks they're taking."

"Sergeant King, I'm surprised to find you taking sides with these men. It should be quite sufficient for them to know that it is my order to keep K5 open and I expect my orders to be obeyed. But since you have decided to enter into this discussion I will elaborate on why K5 is important to this company. It's training Dowson. Training. The war seems to have got bogged down and men are becoming stale and undisciplined. K5 is an operational training aid and I intend to keep it that way."

"Training! Are you saying that after all this time in the field we need training? You're out of your mind! Simon and I had to dodge a couple of shots out there this morning. I don't know who was on the other end of the rifle but he knew his stuff, and I don't care to be his bunny."

"Dowson, I'll ignore your insubordinate remark for now, but again I warn you to watch your language. As to your encounter this morning, that sniper or rifleman was merely reminding you how dangerous the war is and no doubt you reacted in the appropriate manner. Excellent training for Young."

Before Bluey could answer, Captain Solway entered the dugout. "Something the matter Ronald?"

"No Sir. Just a small matter concerning my training methods which Dowson had not appreciated. But now I've explained it to him, I'm sure he understands and accepts why K5 must be kept open."

"Ah yes K5. I've been worried about that myself. We wouldn't want any casualties from a training exercise. God knows we suffer enough from the real thing."

"There is no danger Sir. In fact, Sergeant King and I will run the line this evening to prove my point."

"All right Ronald. But please, no heroics." And with that advice the captain departed.

"Dismiss these men Sergeant. I'll see you at the exit point at 5:00pm. Warn the infantry that we will be out there in case we need covering fire."

The two sappers saluted and left the room. "Well Bluey, what do we do now?"

"Nothing, we'll head back to our dugout to get a few hours sleep before the circus at 5:00pm."

They walked along in silence. Bluey was troubled. The arguments put forward by Lieutenant Johnson rang true. Discipline had slipped. Earlier, when danger threatened, the men responded like automatons, orders were never questioned, the men never argued amongst themselves. All that had changed. The men lolled about the trenches with an air of indifference. Men put themselves and their companions at risk by sleeping when on guard, and there was constant bickering. Perhaps Johnson was right. It was fear that kept you on your toes, kept you in a high state of readiness. Bluey was not sure he accepted the logic of the Lieutenant's argument and later that afternoon he discussed it with Al Wilson.

"Bluey, there isn't much danger in running that line if you keep moving and use the shelter of the craters. I bet you and Simon were running in a fairly straight line along the wire, close together and not diving into the occasional shell hole."

"You're right Al, we were taking it easy until that sniper let fly."

"See, you have just confirmed the Lieutenant's rationale."

"Perhaps. Come on, let's watch the bastard and Peter King run the line. It'll be a joy to watch him wet his pants when that sniper opens up, and with a bit of luck he might even score a hit."

"Bit short on charity aren't we?"

"Al, I don't like this set up, and I don't like Johnson. I have a bad feeling about this stunt."

The two men arrived at the observation platform shortly after the officer and the Sergeant had set out along the line. The pair moved quickly and frequently changed their direction of advance. No shots were fired.

Bluey was disappointed. "Bloody Germans. You can't trust them. Today they could've done us a great favour and they didn't even try. We'll be hearing about this run for weeks to come. Damn him!"

"Relax Bluey. It's only a training run. You're letting your imagination run away."

"Perhaps you're right, but I still don't like it."

* * *

Rolt strode into the observation post three days later with an air of confidence. He had a plan and the excitement of what lay ahead made the adrenalin surge. To Rolt, this minor operation had escalated into a Major conflict. He and his team were going to inflict a decisive defeat on the hated Australians. His eyes sparkled.

"It really is very simple. I have convinced HQ the telephone wire is essential to the enemy's defences, and they want it stopped."

"Hang on Rolt. You don't know what that line is for, so how could you persuade the Colonels that it is important?"

"Gunther, I may have been a little generous with the truth, but at the mention of a significant blow to the enemy's communications, they were all ears. I think the signals to Corps HQ are already being drafted. Corps wants some good news to send back home, and we're going to give it to them."

"Slow down brother. Remember who you are talking to. We don't get carried away with all this talk of significant blows to the enemy. Perhaps you could be a little more specific as to how this great victory is to be obtained."

"Get me a cup of coffee Gunther, while I set up this ground map of the area. I also have some excellent photographs taken from an observation balloon, just what I wanted."

Rolt became meticulous and precise in his briefing.

"Let me recap the situation. The Australians are running that line from here to here." He pointed to two crosses on the map.

His brother nodded. "Yes Rolt, we know all about the situation, probably better than you, as we have been here with our eyes glued to the binoculars for days. Nothing has changed."

Rolt continued. “The problem is to find a suitable position out there in the farmland for a man to hide close to the telephone wire. A spot where he can get off two quick killing shots. Our man needs to be able to reach his firing position and withdraw from it without being observed by the enemy. This can be done either by using the cover of darkness, or by using natural cover provided by the terrain. Perhaps a combination of both. Once our man is in position, the next move must come from the enemy, and we would like to control that move.”

There was total silence in the post. All Rolt had done so far was state the obvious, but both Herwin and Gunther knew their leader had also found a solution to each of the problems.

Rolt continued. “Let me work backwards from my last statement regarding movement by the enemy. We are dealing with a telephone wire. If the line is cut, the enemy will send out a repair party. So, we have the mechanism for controlling his action. Our man needs to cut the wire and then position himself in a spot where he can easily and quickly eliminate the linesmen. There is an ideal point about half way along the wire that would serve our purpose well. At this point, the wire runs about seventy metres south of an old sunken road. See here on the map. If you look closely at the same point on this photograph, you will see the remains of an old stone fence. It will make an excellent hide for the sniper. So how do we get there and back undetected?”

“I can see that one might sneak up there in the dark Rolt, but once you have given away your position by shooting, the chances of coming back are slight. The Australians can shoot. Ask Herwin.”

“Right Gunther. The Major problem is getting to the hide and returning, but it can be done. We can’t move about no-man’s land in daylight so we must move to the hide at night.”

“And risk running into one of those damned patrols the Australians send out.”

Rolt shook his head. “No Herwin. I have learned from intelligence that all patrolling is carried out between 10:00pm and 2:00am, perhaps a little later. If we leave here at 3:00am the risk of encountering a patrol is almost nil.”

“So much for getting out there Rolt, but coming back? Surely you don’t intend that our man remains out there in the hide all day waiting for darkness to make his retreat?”

“No Gunther, that wouldn’t work. I am banking on a kill early in the morning. Two quick shots. Our man then crawls along the sunken road in this north easterly direction. The sunken road and the remnants of the stone fence give him a shield about sixty centimetres high from the enemy’s eyes.”

Herwin interrupted. “That isn’t much cover for a man who will have a whole army looking for him.”

“No, it’s not, but think. The two linesmen arrive at the break, and stop to mend the line. Usually they would find the ends in or around a shell crater, but this time the break will be on flat ground. I’m betting they will mend it then and there, and not seek the shelter of a crater. Our man lets them mend the wire and then shoots them.”

“Why wait for them to mend the line?”

“Because, at the first sound of a shot, the reaction of those in the trenches will be to test the line. The line will be working. Confusion. Should someone see the men fall, he then has to alert the lookouts along the front. It is most unlikely that the observer will have pin-pointed the position the shots came from. All attention will be focused on the fallen men and this will give our man time to crawl along the road. And the longer he has to move undetected, the further he will distance himself from the scene of the action.”

“Hell Rolt, it might work.”

“It will work. If the fools mend the line on open ground, their officers and comrades will suspect that they were careless and were killed by shots from our lines. As they won't know how it happened, they will look for an easy explanation, and decide that the men had been careless and unlucky."

"And they will re-route the line."

"If they do Herwin, then victory is ours. But who can predict what these people will do. This whole business of the telephone line is strange. What they do after the event is something I'm not even going to think about at this time. Now, what have you two observed over the past few days?"

"Well, you are going to find this hard to believe, but we think that this running the line is a drill of some sort."

The remark startled the officer. "What! A drill in front of the enemy, within rifle range? No one's that stupid."

"Well, we have had trouble convincing ourselves, but everything points to it being a set pattern exercise. The first party runs the line at first light. Then a new pair comes on duty. They run the line between 11:00am and 12:00. Another pair runs the line about 5:30pm. Same drill. Our guess is, that each pair runs the line while the relief pair is having a meal. Note, that the running of the wire is always east to west. They don't return via the wire. It's all too regular. It has to be a drill."

Rolt had trouble in believing what he was hearing. "They must be mad. Anything else?"

"Yes," said Herwin consulting his notebook. "There are four pairs and they seem to work as set pairs. On two occasions, an NCO ran the line with one of the regulars, as if he was checking up on their technique. It's most odd."

"What do we know about the linesmen?"

"They are fit, move quickly, and know their job. They move their shifts about so you don't know which particular pair is going to do which duty."

"Well it doesn't matter which pair we eliminate."

"One last point Rolt. One of them carries a rifle. You would think that it would hamper him in his work, but he is as quick as the others. I wonder if he can use it."

"Don't worry about that Herwin. If he's on tomorrow morning, he'll never get the chance."

"Tomorrow morning!"

"Yes, tomorrow morning. It should be fun."

* * *

It had been a beautiful starlit night, and to those watching the darkness surrender to the first rays of sunlight, it seemed difficult to believe that this was a world of evil. A world of death, a world of darkness, and yet before their eyes shafts of light combined with the shadows to create images of beauty. The patrols had returned safely and the guns on both sides had remained silent throughout the night.

Darkie looked out and called to his companion. "Wake up Princess, it's time to go."

Mac yawned and stretched. It had been a wonderful dream and he was loath to leave it. "Give battalion HQ a call and tell them we are on the way. A brew would be most welcome on arrival. Milk and two sugars for me."

When Darkie reached the phone, he gave the handle a vigorous turn. He waited for the acknowledging ring but the instrument failed to respond. "Come on fellas, wake up." he muttered as he gave the handle a further turn.

"Mac, they don't answer," he called to his partner.

"Probably sound asleep. Ring them again and this time put a bit of elbow grease into it," snapped Mac. It had been a wonderful dream and he was still upset with its sudden ending.

Darkie assaulted the telephone handle with gusto but still the return ring did not come.

"Line must be broken Mac."

"I could work that out for myself, but how? There's been no firing. More likely they've knocked out the plug at the other end and no one's noticed it. Come on, let's go over there and point out the error of their ways."

"Shouldn't we tell Al before we go?"

Mac was not in a good mood. "Tell him what? Please Al, the telephone at battalion doesn't work. Come off it Darkie, you're a big boy now, and you have me to hold your hand. Grab your gear and let's go."

A quick word to the infantry lookouts and the men moved cautiously through the access trench under the barbed wire. Darkie picked up the telephone wire and moved forward letting the wire run through the palm of his hand. They moved forward at a brisk pace, content there was no danger in the half light. The enemy lines were almost lost in the low light and drifting mists.

After a while, Darkie felt the wire slip from his hand. He stopped to retrieve it and then looked ahead for the other end. Sure enough, there it was lying on the ground a few feet away. "There's something strange about this Mac. This wire has been cut, not by a shell but by someone with pliers or a knife."

"Probably a Jerry patrol out here last night."

"Yeah, that would be it. Come on, let's fix it and be on our way. I need that brew."

Both men crouched over the line as Darkie quickly tied the ends together, a simple task and soon completed.

"Ring through and check Mac, and then let's get to hell out of here."

Mac turned the handle and the response was immediate. "We're on our way in so don't get trigger happy. Two white teas with sugar please."

Neither had noticed the dark figure that had risen to the kneeling position some sixty yards away. Two shots in rapid succession. For Darkie Fleming and Robert McKenzie, the war was over.

Back in his dugout Bluey raised his head. Two shots and they sounded close by. Two shots and then silence. Hardly the outbreak of hostilities he thought, and nestled down for an extra few minutes of blissful sleep.

* * *

Gunther and Herwin also heard the shots but the morning mist had obscured their view of the ambush. They waited for a volley of shots from the Australian trenches but none came.

"He's pulled it off, he's done it."

"Calm down Gunther. It's not over until Rolt makes it back."

"It is over Herwin. Look to the right of that broken tree. You can occasionally see movement as he crawls along. He was supposed to stay out all day under cover, but I guess he's changed his mind."

The two men waited by the concealed access trench as Rolt carefully inched his way towards the entrance. Herwin had thoughtfully brought a flask of cognac with him and this, Rolt happily accepted. The Bavarians revelled in the acclamation of the Prussians. It was the victory they had promised.

"No problems Rolt?"

"None. I can't believe how easy it was. I cut the line between two craters and waited. Right on schedule, the two linesmen appeared. They didn't seem to have a care in the world. They found the break and squatted on the ground to mend it. I could hear every word they said. They even rang through to order tea to be waiting for them when they reached the end of the line. When they had finished they stood up, and presented me with two perfect targets. I got in two head shots and then crawled away along the sunken road. Nothing happened. I really believe I could have walked away from the area in perfect safety. As there was no immediate reaction from the enemy and the mist gave me good cover, I decided to crawl back here. Has there been any reaction yet?"

"Yes. About twelve minutes after you had fired two linesmen ran to the spot. It was a bit hard to see everything. Stretcher bearers appeared about ten minutes later and took the bodies. I'll bet there's hell to pay over there."

"You are probably right Gunther. Now we have to wait and see how they react. It should be interesting."

* * *

Lieutenant Johnson sat at the table with Sergeant King standing beside him. Al Wilson and Bluey stood facing the officer across the table.

"I warned you. It was a stupid senseless idea and now we have lost two good men. And for what?"

"Shut up Dowson." snapped Sergeant King. "I agreed to you coming to this meeting on the clear understanding that I would do the talking. So shut up."

Bluey opened his mouth then closed it.

"Thank you Sergeant King. Before anyone says anything that he may come to regret, let me put a few facts before you. Facts, not wild emotive statements. K5 is a valuable training exercise. It was, and still is, designed to keep the men on their toes. To run that line, requires strict adherence to the principles we teach, and to heed the lessons learnt under combat conditions. Sappers Fleming and McKenzie ignored the rules. Firstly, they did not ring Battalion Headquarters to tell them that they were about to run the wire."

"Perhaps they couldn't Sir." interjected Al Wilson. "Where we found them, there was a join in the wire. Perhaps they had stopped to repair it."

"Point taken Wilson. Let us assume there was a break. Why didn't they inform the stand-by pair there was a problem? Then back-up would have been readily available. You say you found them lying in the open. Can we then assume that they carried out the repair in full sight of the enemy? Another breach of basic procedures."

The two sappers' initial anger receded as they came to accept that Mac and Darkie had failed to observe the basic rules of their trade.

"We know that the line was working just before the men were killed. They rang in to advise they were coming in, and when they didn't arrive, Battalion rang through to ask where they were. You took the call Dowson."

"Yes Sir. I asked the infantry on the shooting platforms if Darkie and Mac had gone out. They also told me about the two shots."

"You then called Corporal Wilson, and together you ran the line and found the bodies?"

"Yes Sir."

"And did you see anything out there that might give us a clue as to what happened Dowson?"

"No Sir. It's hard to believe that someone could loose off two shots at that range and get two perfect head kills. Jerry must have some new kind of rifle and sighting gear."

"So now you are an expert on weaponry, Dowson?" Lieutenant Johnson knew he had won this particular battle.

Bluey, confused and concerned by the outcome of the discussion, would not be drawn into any further debate.

It was Sergeant King who brought the conversation back to the matter of Line K5. "It seems sir, that Sappers Fleming and McKenzie disregarded the rules and as a result of their carelessness, lost their lives to enemy fire. The question now to be resolved is the future of K5."

Lieutenant Johnson chose his words carefully. "The future of K5? Because those two men acted in a foolhardy manner is no reason to abandon a valuable training aid. You may wish to tighten up some of the procedures for departing the lines and for back-up parties Sergeant King, but otherwise it's business as usual. Dismiss the men, and everyone get back to work."

Al and Bluey walked slowly back to their dugout. The loss of their companions weighed heavily on their minds.

"Well he certainly turned that one back on us. Damned if I know what Darkie and Mac thought they were doing out there, but whatever it was, it wasn't very clever."

Bluey stopped and gazed at the enemy lines. "I don't believe it Al. No one could shoot so accurately at that range. Two shots, two head kills. It's impossible."

"Are you suggesting someone from our side did it?"

"No, but whoever did it was closer than their trenches."

"Doubt it. No one from our side saw anyone or anything move out there, and the platforms were manned."

"I know. Remember I was talking to Battalion on the phone not long after the shots, but you couldn't really see anything due to the low light and mist."

"Well you heard the man. It's business as usual, but we will all stick to the rules from now on. What's the time?"

Bluey pulled out his precious watch. "Time for a brew. Let's go and tell the others the glad tidings."

* * *

Next morning as the sun rose and the mists cleared, Herwin gazed through his binoculars. "Rolt, come here. I don't believe it."

His brother moved swiftly to the observation slit rubbing the sleep from his eyes.

"What's up?" asked Rolt.

"Look across there."

The two men watched as two Australian linesmen ran across their line of vision. They moved as a well drilled team, using the shell holes as shelter. Both would disappear from view then one would appear, sprinting forward to another shell hole, once he had gained its safety the second man would sprint from his shelter to join him. The procedure would then be repeated.

"Like a couple of rabbits looking for their burrow." remarked Rolt.

"I like hunting rabbits. It was an Australian rabbit that scratched my cheek. Can I have a go?"

"Well, the aim of our exercise was to force the enemy to give up using that line, and it looks as if we haven't succeeded. We'll have to repeat the dose."

"Tomorrow morning." Herwin's eagerness was obvious.

"No Herwin. You saw them, on their toes, moving quickly and expecting trouble. Let them have a couple of days playing at soldiers then they will relax and let their guard down. And we must review our plan."

"Why? It worked for you. Why change?"

"To keep on top of the situation, we must control it. I'm sure they have checks and balances to cope with a line that is mysteriously cut, so we need a different approach."

"What do you have in mind?"

"Let them run the line without any problems for the next three days. We need two complacent linesmen running the wire without a thought of something being amiss. Then, at the ambush point, we need something to catch their attention. Something that will make them stop and look. As soon as they do that, bang, bang. Two dead rabbits."

"And just how do you propose to bring them to a stop Rolt? Perhaps you could bring out one of your girlfriends to pose out there. That would certainly make them stop. In fact, you would stop the whole army."

"No Herwin, nothing quite that startling. We need something that will just catch their attention for a moment. Something they wouldn't be expecting to see, and I have an idea."

"What?"

"You'll have to wait and see. I need to see a couple of friends to help in the making of my secret weapon. You'll know in three days' time."

"I suppose that means you are off to the flesh-pots around HQ while we continue to watch and wait?"

"Correct. We don't know yet if these Australians are serious about keeping that line open so we must continue to monitor their actions."

Herwin gazed at the Australian lines. "They are crazy if they do, but then that line's been a puzzle ever since we arrived."

"I agree. Keep those stupid Australians under surveillance. This really has developed into a great game."

* * *

"Al, wake up."

"What's wrong Sam?"

"Time to run the line. Jacko and I are ready to go. You and George are the back-up team."

"Damn the bloody line. Give George a kick and we'll be right out there. Don't go until we're there."

"Don't worry, we're in no hurry. George, stir yourself."

A grunt greeted this last remark but George, like every man in the dugout, had awakened when Sam had first called. It was three days since Darkie and Mac had died and there had been no further incidents on K5.

As Al and George pulled on their clothes, Bluey sat up. "Want me to come along Al?"

"No mate. All we're doing is manning this end of the line and watching Sam and Ken. Trust me, I can handle it."

Bluey smiled. His faith in Al Wilson was unshakeable. "Pity he's not a General," he would tell the others. "we would soon sort out Jerry."

Bluey rolled over and resumed his interrupted sleep as Al and George departed the dugout.

The air outside was clear and cool with the sun's rays just starting to remove the night's blanket of darkness from the battlefield. Sam and Jacko were standing by the entrance to the exit trench.

"Take care Sam."

"Don't worry about us Al. It's a clear morning and the infantry have been alerted. It's like performing before an audience so we'll give them a top class show. Watch my feet move, my body sway."

"Right, off you go, but remember, you also have an audience on the other side, so make those feet move quickly and that body sway fast. Don't dawdle."

The two sappers left the trench and Sam picked up the line. They set off at a brisk pace moving from crater to crater.

"No problems Al."

"No George. Jerry seems to have lost interest in us."

The men were well along the line when Al leapt to his feet. Sam had stopped in one crater and had motioned to Jacko to join him. Together they stood up to look at something.

"Get down you idiots. Get moving." screamed Al, but at that distance they wouldn't have heard his shout. In fact, they wouldn't have heard him even if they had been much closer. As the sound of the shots reached the trenches, both men fell. Rifle fire broke out along the lines.

"What's up?" Bluey appeared from nowhere.

"Sam and Ken are down and it doesn't look good. How the hell did you get here so quick?"

"I was outside having a piss and heard you shout. Heard the shots too. What are the infantry shooting at?"

"Damned if I know. Come on let's go and see what the damage is, but I don't like it. They haven't moved. George, tell Battalion we're moving out. Come on Bluey. This is bloody awful."

"Wait a moment Al, I'm not dressed to run around in front of a lot of Jerries and I haven't got Lucy."

Bluey was back in minutes and together he and Al exited the trench. Sergeant King and Lieutenant Johnson arrived as the two started down the line. George briefed the two new arrivals.

“Sergeant, call those two men back. There is nothing they can do and we must assess the situation before doing anything rash.”

“Wilson, Dowson, return to the line.” shouted Sergeant King. There was no reaction from the two sappers. They continued to move quickly from crater to crater.

“I don’t think they can hear you Sergeant.” suggested George.

“You mean they don’t want to hear me.” replied the Sergeant.

“Sergeant, I want those two men up before me on a charge when they get back.” Snapped Lieutenant Johnson.

“Sir, with all due respect, they’re doing what every man in this unit would do. They’re going to the aid of their mates.”

“All right Sergeant King. Perhaps Wilson and Dowson can bring back some evidence that will help to explain how this unfortunate incident came about.”

George, who had not taken his eyes off the two figures, exclaimed, “They’ve reached the spot. That’s where Sam and Jacko stopped to look at something.”

“What did you say?”

“They stopped to look at something. Al yelled at them to get down, but it was too late.”

“So Sergeant, we have another stupid break of procedures and two more fools have paid the price. What are Wilson and Dowson doing?”

George, who had the binoculars, gave the running commentary. “Bluey is in a shell hole with his rifle ready. Al is crawling forward. He’s got something and is now crawling back towards Bluey.”

“What did he pick up?”

“I can’t tell from here, Sir.”

Just then the phone rang and Sergeant King lifted the receiver. He listened intently “Understood. Take care.”

“And what was that all about Sergeant?”

“Wilson phoning in Sir. Ralston and Jackson are dead. He wants a stretcher party to pick them up. He and Dowson have collected their gear and will complete running the line.”

“But what did he pick up? What was it?”

“Didn’t say Sir. No doubt we’ll find out when they get back.”

“Why the hell didn’t you ask them while you had them on the phone?”

“Wilson did the talking, Sir. From the tone of his voice, I reckoned it better to let him talk and for me to listen. He sounded upset and I guess he has every right to be so.”

“I see. Right, I’m off to breakfast and to brief Captain Solway on this unfortunate affair. I’ve no doubt he’ll want to see Wilson and Dowson just as soon as they return.”

Johnson returned the Sergeant’s salute and walked away.

“Shit Sarge, I wouldn’t want to be in his shoes when Bluey gets back.”

“Enough of that talk. Get on the phone to Battalion and ask if a couple of stretchers can be sent down under a white flag to recover the bodies. Bloody officers. Bloody hell, what a bloody mess.”

* * *

Herwin had retreated from the ambush position as planned and although tempted to crawl back to the lines in daylight, common sense, and the whistle of bullets passing overhead, told him that many eager eyes had the wasteland under close scrutiny. Some four hundred yards along the sunken road, Herwin found the shallow grave dug by one of the night patrols as planned. In it he found a couple of water bottles and a ground sheet. Knowing that he was safe under the eyes of his own infantry, he rolled himself in the ground sheet, pulled the makeshift cover over the top of the grave and rested.

READ THE INSCRIPTION

The four survivors of No.3 Section and Sergeant King waited in the command post for the arrival of the officers. The morning had been spent writing their individual accounts of the incident and they now awaited the Command's findings on the matter. Sergeant King called them to attention as Colonel Payne entered, followed by Captain Solway and Lieutenant Johnson. The Colonel took a seat and opened the file he had placed on the table.

"Stand the men at ease Sergeant. I have just come from a session with the Brigadier and he is not very happy. No, not very happy at all."

The Colonel looked from man to man as if expecting some sort of response to his remarks but none came. "I have studied your reports and discussed the matter with your officers and it seems your section contains, or did contain, a lot of slow learners. Lieutenant Johnson has explained to me what an excellent training scheme K5 is, and I agree with him. It was a scheme designed to keep you on your toes but it seems you men, or at least your late companions, paid little heed to the procedures laid down for operating in a hostile environment. A sad and unnecessary waste of men. We cannot afford any more such casualties, and although I personally consider K5 should continue, the Brigadier has directed it be shut down. I'm sure you will all be relieved to hear that."

The Colonel waited for some response to confirm that the decision was welcomed.

After a pause Bluey spoke. "Sir, do I have your permission to speak?"

His companions exchanged glances. Dowson's temper was legendary and he didn't usually ask for permission to speak.

"Go ahead soldier. What's on your mind?"

"Well Sir, I don't think closing down K5 is a very good idea."

All eyes were now riveted on Bluey's face. The Colonel looked at the two junior officers in the hope that one of them would be able to shed some light on this unexpected turn of events.

"You don't eh? It seemed from the discussions I've had with your officers, that you men were strongly opposed to the operation of K5. Now I find you opposing the decision to shut it down."

"Yes Sir. If you had ordered K5 to be shut down a week ago, we would have been very happy. But things have changed."

"How do you mean, changed?"

"The situation with K5, and the fact that you want to hand Jerry a victory."

"Be careful of your words soldier. I don't hand anything over to Jerry. You tell me that to shut K5 down is a victory for Jerry. I don't see it that way. Tell me, why should K5 remain open?"

"In the beginning K5 was, as Lieutenant Johnson said, a training scheme. To us it was a pain in the arse, but we do as we are told. A week ago, that all changed with the deaths of Darkie and Mac. Today we lost two more good men. For what? I believe Jerry saw K5 as a challenge, an affront. There we were, running that line in broad daylight in full view of his trenches. We were getting under his skin and he had to do something about it."

"You could be right Dowson. And he did do something about it, didn't he?"

"Yes Sir, he did. He sent out one of his best men to put a stop to K5. If we close it down, then he has beaten us. One man against the Australian Army, and it's the Australian Army that retreats."

Bluey could see that he had struck a sensitive nerve. The Colonel's face was darkening. The word retreat was not in his vocabulary.

"You said one man. One man has shot these four linesmen?"

"That's rubbish Dowson." interjected Captain Solway. "There were dozens of men watching Ralston and Jackson this morning and saw them fall. Someone would have seen your phantom marksman. There was no one out there."

"Well soldier, how do you answer that?"

"Sir, it's true that many people saw Sam and Ken fall. But they then looked across to the German trenches to see if they could spot where the shots had come from. They even started shooting, for all the good that could do. No, the sniper was close to the killing spot, he was concealed in a hide of some sort."

"A hide? Good God man, this is not some sort of an animal hunt."

"I think it is Sir. In this case we are the prey, but the same rules of hunting apply. I believe I could go out there under the cover of darkness and manufacture a hide and no one in the trenches would be able to spot me. When Sam and Jacko fell, people were looking at them or across to the Jerry trenches. No one was scanning the middle ground."

Colonel Payne glared at Bluey. "You say one man. Why not two? And how can you be sure of this 'hide' theory?"

"Firstly, the range Sir. I've discussed it with our battalion snipers. From the German trenches, a body hit would be a fluke shot.

Two head shots would be impossible. Then there is the sound of the shots, both times very clearly heard in our trenches. Almost at the same time as the men fell. Those shots were fired from somewhere near here, not from the Jerry trenches."

"But only one man?"

"Yes Sir. The shots were consistent with one man using a bolt action rifle. Whoever he is, he is good, very good. If there were two men they would fire together, the shots would sound almost as one. So it's one man, and I would guess he's holed up somewhere between one hundred to two hundred yards from the killing place, perhaps even closer. This bloke hasn't missed with a shot. All four have been head shots."

"Well gentlemen, you have heard Dowson's theory. Anyone want to dispute what he has said?"

"A question Sir." Captain Solway was confused. "All four men were stationary when hit. What if they had been moving, running the line as they should have?"

"Well Sir, I reckon Jerry would have only got one man. The other would have stayed low in a shell hole and waited for help. That's why he went to the trouble of distracting Sam and Jacko. They should have known better and been more careful, but they weren't."

"All right lad. You have convinced me that is how the enemy is operating, but he won't get another chance, because the Brig has directed K5 be closed down."

"But you mustn't close it down."

The Colonel snorted. "Are you telling me what I must or must not do Sapper?"

"Sorry Sir. We ran K5 right under the German noses, and I bet hundreds of German infantry have watched us run that line. We dared them to do something about it and they did. Now the man they used is good, an expert. I bet he has already got a chest full of iron crosses with more to come. Look at what he has done.

Crept right up to our trenches and executed four of our men right under our noses. Now if we abandon K5 then his victory is total. One German has defeated an entire Australian brigade. One German against two thousand Aussie soldiers. You can't let him get away with it."

The anger showed in the Colonel's face. "Don't be stupid Dowson. We'll fix him. We'll shell the hell out of the area. Nothing will survive."

"Won't work Sir. You have to know he's out there before you start shelling, and you also need to know where he is. But he won't care if K5 is closed. That's the prize. If we keep K5 open, we win, close it down and he wins. And one other thing. Our battalions know that K5 is a challenge to Jerry, and I bet the German battalions see it the same way. You can't walk away from it, not now Sir."

"I'm not going to walk away from it son, but the Brig will need a lot of convincing to keep that line open. This is war, not a bloody game."

"Sir, perhaps if you showed him that wreath, he might change his mind."

The Colonel picked up the wreath that lay on the table. "So, this is what the two boys this morning stopped to look at."

"Yes Sir," replied Lieutenant Johnson. "A stupid ruse and they fell for it."

"Well I suppose it did come as a bit of a shock to see someone had laid a wreath in memory of two of their comrades out there in no-man's land."

"No Sir. It wasn't for Darkie and Mac." All eyes turned to Bluey. "Read the inscription."

The Colonel turned the wreath around to study the printing on the ribbon. He read aloud: "In memory of two stupid Australian soldiers, and it has the date."

"You still don't get it do you Sir? Look at the date. It's today's date. That wreath was laid in memory of Sam and Jacko. They were looking at a wreath commemorating their own death."

"The bastard. What a cheek! Well he's not going to get away with this. We'll bloody well show him. I'll see the Brig immediately, but once he hears what I've got to say and sees this, I'm sure he'll agree to keep K5 open." The Colonel rose and picked up the wreath. "I'm sure K5 will remain open so I hope you chaps have a good plan to put paid to this sniper bastard. Johnson, you can accompany me back to HQ. K5 is your idea so the Brig should hear all about it from you."

Returning the Captain's salute the Colonel and Lieutenant Johnson left the room.

"Relax men," muttered Captain Solway. "take a seat. Morbey, see if you can rustle up a brew. I think we all need one."

The men found seats around the table and made small talk until six mugs of tea arrived.

"Well Dowson you certainly surprised me this time, and judging from the looks on the faces of your mates, you surprised them too."

"I surprised myself Sir. I had this idea of how Jerry was operating, but I didn't want to speak out because I wanted K5 to be closed. But it hit me while the Colonel was speaking. We owe it to the others to get square with the bastard."

"You are not getting any argument with that Dowson, but Colonel Payne put his finger on it. How do we get square?"

"Sir let's go over every detail we can collectively think of concerning the two incidents. We must establish what we know about him and then use that to knock him out."

"All right Dowson. You kick off. The rest of you chip in if you think he's missed something."

"Right Sir. I'm sure I'm right about the one man-ambush. Twice he has struck in the one place, but my bet is he will change the site now. He's no fool, and he would assume that we would concentrate our efforts in that area."

"Bloody marvellous. You mean that we can now expect him to hit us at any point along the line?"

"No Al. There are some points that he just couldn't get close enough, so we know roughly where he will be waiting."

"Where?" asked Simon.

"Look at this map. My guess is he will be somewhere between these two points."

"Hell Bluey, that's about five hundred yards. Can't you do better than that?"

"Perhaps Simon, but I will need to go out with a night patrol to examine the lie of the land. But don't despair, we are now in control of the situation. Up to now he's been running the show."

Captain Solway pushed the hair back from his forehead. "All right Dowson. We roughly know where. The next question is when?"

"Must be at first light Sir. He needs the cover of darkness to get out there and settle himself in. Mind you he could wait in hiding all day, but that would increase his risks."

Al interrupted. "Bluey. If you're right, how come no one has seen him returning to his trenches."

"Because no one has been looking for him. We've all been looking at the killing site or at the trenches."

"Can't we set up an ambush for him? I mean leave a few of the infantry out there to knock him off."

"Perhaps Sir, but we have the question of when. Put men out there night after night and they'll soon get fed up. Anyhow they would say it's our problem so we should sort it out, and I agree. They'll give us any support we ask for, but this bastard is ours to nail."

The Captain shook his head. "Dowson, you are a bunch of signalmen not gunfighters. I can't see how you can handle this on your own."

"As I said before Sir, we must control the situation. Remember, if we catch him out there the tables are turned. He has been in control up to now. Deprive him of that control and he may do something stupid."

The screen door at the entrance to the dugout parted and Lieutenant Johnson entered. He frowned as he saw the men seated around the table with mugs of tea.

"Well Ronald, what did the Brigadier say?"

"K5 is an excellent training aid and is to remain open."

"Wonder where he got that idea from," said Bluey.

Captain Solway spoke before the Lieutenant could reply. "Ronald, just what did he say about eliminating our sniper friend?"

"Well Sir, he rather left that to me, and I gave him my assurance that we would take care of the matter."

"Splendid Ronald. Now tell us how you intend to do that."

Johnson realised his error. "Well, it was merely a phrase I used. What I meant was the Section would handle the matter. Dowson had plenty to say to the Colonel. What's he got to say now?"

Knowing that he had an ally in Captain Solway, Bluey took his time before answering.

"The section can handle it but it'll take a combined effort. We can't ask for replacements as that would be a bit tough on the new boys. This is not the time to be teaching some novice how to stay alive."

Lieutenant Johnson replied. "I can assure you Dowson, there'll be no replacements in the short term. The Brigadier was quite clear on that point."

"Right, so we have four teams."

"Wrong Dowson, you have two teams, or are you planning to do single-man runs."

"No Sir. As I see it, we have Captain Solway and Sergeant King, you and Bailey, Al and George and myself and Simon. Four teams."

Johnson looked to the Captain for help.

"Dowson is right, four teams is the absolute minimum. Looks like you and I are going to get our hands dirty Ronald."

"But Bailey hasn't been in the field. He's not trained. I can't work with him."

"Ronald when I agreed to Bailey being your batman, I also said he was to pull his weight with No.3 Section. I am aware Bailey has spent most of his time at the Mess looking after you and your gear. If Bailey's not up to scratch in the field then it's your fault."

Johnson was shaken by the unexpected turn of events. "But this is dangerous, really dangerous. Only the most experienced men should run that line."

"K5 was your idea Ron, so you can't have any quibble about running the line. Recognising our shortages in manpower I'll certainly team up with the Sergeant and we'll do our share. That leaves you with Bailey. Now Dowson what's the plan?"

"There is no plan Sir. We run the line as usual morning, lunch-time and evening. No change to our pattern. I will go out with a patrol tonight to examine the area where I believe he's been hiding. My guess is that he'll be surprised to see us still in action. He'll then plan his next move. If the past is anything to go by, it will be three, perhaps four days, before he makes his move. So today and tomorrow should be safe but we must act the part. Total adherence to the rules for running a wire under action conditions."

"Anyone disagree with that?" There was no reaction.

Sergeant King looked at his tea mug and his question seemed to be directed to that utensil. "And when day three comes, what then?"

Again, all eyes turned to the redhead.

Bluey raised his hands above his shoulders. “I really don’t know, but we have time to think about it. We must all keep our wits about us. My father used to say; ‘See what you are looking at, know what you are hearing’. We are looking for something different. Doesn’t matter how small, how insignificant, note it and report it. If a man is added to the scenery out there then there is something new to be seen. A rock moved, a mound where there wasn’t one before. Use your eyes, look for the unusual.”

“All right men, that’s about all for now. Wilson, draw up a roster for the line. Whenever a team is out there, a back-up team is to be manning the phone and watching them.”

The men stood up as the Captain walked to the door. “Come on Ronald. You had better break the news to Bailey and give him some exercising, or you’ll have to carry him along the line.”

Lieutenant Johnson followed, his face a mixture of fear and hate. He paused as if about to say something, then strode from the room.

“Bluey, you had better watch your step. Captain Solway backed your play today, but Johnson doesn’t like you and he has the ear of the Colonel. If he gets a chance, he’ll fix you, one way or another.”

“I know Al, but for the moment, that Jerry is my worry, not that oily bastard Johnson. How are we going to play it?”

“As you believe that the next few runs will be incident-free, George and Simon can run together. George, you lead. We must have flexibility within the section.”

“Don’t roster me with Johnson Al. One of us mightn’t come back.”

The corporal smiled. “I’m not sure which one I would want to come back Bluey. Johnson got us into this bind but it’s you who kept us in it. But don’t worry, I’ll keep you apart. At least for now.”

“Gee, I’d like to see Bailey’s face when he hears that he’s coming up to the line.” chuckled Simon.

* * *

Gunther shifted his body from side to side to ease the pain caused by stones sticking into him. Rolt had selected a site, some two hundred meters to the west of the previous ambushes. It meant that Gunther would have the extra distance to crawl to the daytime retreat, but Rolt had insisted the enemy would be concentrating his attention on the previous sites and so a move was necessary. The hide was only fifty metres from the line. His targets would be sitting ducks.

There had been a flurry of activity in the German trenches over the past three days. Generals and Colonels had visited the sharpshooters' lair to receive briefings on the operation that had caught the imagination of the troops. Three men versus the Australian Army. It was on everyone's lips. One General had arrived with Iron Crosses for Rolt and Herwin, and there had been speeches and champagne to mark the occasion. "Now it's my turn. Tonight, there'll be more speeches, more champagne and a medal for me." He'd already written a long letter to his mother telling her all about the three-man war against the Australians and his part in it. He tapped his pocket to reassure himself that the letter was still there.

A dull glow of light in the east heralded the approach of a new day. Soon the German guns would start their sporadic barrage of the Australian trenches with a number of rounds falling short in the area where the telephone line lay. The object of the barrage was twofold. Firstly, it would be blamed for the break in the line which Gunther had made some minutes earlier, and secondly, the smoke shells included amongst the high explosives would shield the ambush area from watchers in the Australian trenches. Rolt knew that the enemy would be looking for trouble and had intended to carry out the action himself, but Gunther had reminded his cousin of his promise to let him make the third ambush if one was necessary.

"Gunther, this one is going to be different. They will be using their standard method of hopping from crater to crater so you may only be able to score one hit. One must assume that in the event of a man going down, they will have a contingency plan. One is enough."

"Don't worry Rolt. I'll get one for you, but if the other sticks his head up, I'll take it off too."

"Right. Now the artillery will keep up the bombardment until we see you safely back in the retreat. Keep low and don't hurry. They can't see you. The eyes of the German Army are on you. Off you go, and good luck."

Gunther smiled to himself. He liked that part. The eyes of the German Army are on you. Well, I'll give them a show they won't forget. Just then the first of the German shells whistled overhead and exploded close to the Australian trenches.

"Beautiful," whispered Gunther to himself. "Smack on target. Now my little Australian rabbits, where are you?"

* * *

The Australian trenches came alive at the sound of the first shell. Infantry manned the shooting platforms and stared across the wasteland towards the enemy trenches now visible as the darkness faded.

"What the hell is Fritz up to?" asked the Battalion Commander. "He hasn't left his trenches so it's not an assault, although I'd like him to try. We'd cut him to ribbons if he tried to cross that stretch of land."

"Funny sort of a barrage isn't it?" rejoined Captain Solway, who had been manning the signal post. "What do you make of it Sergeant King?"

"Most odd Sir. Most unusual." They both looked at each other. 'Look for the unusual', those had been the very words of Sapper Dowson.

"Are you thinking what I am thinking King?"

"Probably Sir, but here come Dowson and Wilson so we'll soon know."

The two sappers were still pulling on their clothes and equipment as they arrived in the observation post. "What the hell is going on?" Al asked.

"Jerry has decided that it's a good morning for gunnery practice, but he's not all that good, as a lot of the shot is falling short."

"Falling short Sir? You mean in and around K5?"

"Yes Dowson and he's mixing it up with smoke."

"Anyone tried the line Sir?"

"Not yet. Sergeant, give them a call."

All waited while Sergeant King turned the handle and listened. After several attempts he replaced the handset. "No answer. Looks like he has managed to hit the line. It's out."

Bluey gazed at the area now shrouded in smoke. "Al, I think our friend has arrived. Notice where the shells are landing. I think that's where he is today."

"You can't be sure though can you Dowson?"

"No Sir, but everything is happening as we discussed. We are supposed to assume the shelling has cut the line and therefore we go out and repair it. The shelling is his diversion for today."

Captain Solway felt very uneasy with the situation. "I don't like it. I don't like it at all. Perhaps I should call Colonel Payne and explain, then our gunners can blast the area."

"I disagree, Sir. That might give us a minor victory, but no doubt they could replace their man and we would have to repeat the performance another day. We have to nail him at his own game. Jock Collins and a couple of his sniper mates are up there on the lookouts hoping to pick him off but I don't think they'll have much luck with that smoke. Jerry is being very clever and very persistent. He is putting a lot of effort into this stunt."

"So, what now?"

"Sir, Al and I have agreed that this run is ours. We have been around the longest and Al can smell trouble a mile off. We will work about thirty yards apart and both will carry phones. We will try to stay connected by using a working cable. We will use about forty yards of working cable so we have some latitude for movement. We will avoid using the same craters as we progress. That way, only one of us will be moving at any one time, and Jerry won't know which way we're going to jump. Snagging the working cable could be a problem but we've been experimenting, and it can work."

The Captain turned to Al. "Do you go along with this scheme Wilson? It sounds bloody dangerous, especially for the man in front."

"Bluey has his rifle and there's no better shot in the Brigade. We have a pretty good idea where he is, so let's hope Bluey can get a shot at him."

"Damned if I like it, but I don't know what else we can do. What about some infantry to follow and provide cover?"

"Sir, if we need infantry to cover us every time we go out to mend a line, we'll become the laughing stock of the Army. Excuse me, but there's a couple of calls I want to make, and then we'll be off."

Bluey plugged a line and spoke to someone at the other end. He then made a second call.

"Jock Collins and his boys are on the shooting platforms but they can't see very much. Who knows, the wind might get up and blow all that crap away and then they'll be in business. The second call I made was to the gunners. They are about to answer Jerry's fire but they will drop their bricks about four hundred yards over K5."

Captain Solway looked at Bluey as if he had gone mad. "You mean to tell me that a sapper calls up the artillery and orders a barrage just like that?"

"No Sir. They contacted us a couple of days ago. The Colonel had issued an instruction that the K5 operation was to be given maximum support so they phoned in to see if they could help. I think Major Andrews still feels he owes the section from that incident last year."

"Incredible! The whole bloody Army is throwing all its resources into keeping a line open. What if we fail? Just think of the damage it would do to morale."

"Not to mention our hides Sir."

"Sorry Wilson. You're right. It's you and Dowson who are sticking your necks out."

At that moment, a shell from the Australian battery whistled overhead and landed in the wasteland.

"Whacko," said Bluey. "Spot on."

"But it's well over K5. You said four hundred yards didn't you? Why so far away from where you think Fritz is hiding?"

"It's all part of the plan. Our shells will move across a line four hundred yards beyond K5. When they have traversed that line, they'll lower the range fifty yards and traverse again. I'm hoping this will do two things. Firstly, it will hide proceedings from the Jerry lines as I have no doubt they're all out there watching this pantomime. Secondly, it will give our friend out there something new to think about. No one can feel comfortable if a creeping barrage starts coming his way. We must get control of the situation. With our new method of running the line, together with the shelling, we now have created a new set of circumstances. Jerry has to change his plan, and in changing it, he may make a mistake. Now we'll see just how clever the murdering bastard is. Ready Al?"

"Ready as I'll ever be."

"Let's go. Oh Sir, one last thing. Would you act as spotter for the guns and make sure they don't come down too quickly in range? It would be a bloody shame if we got clobbered by our own guns."

"All right Dowson, I'll see to that. Good luck to you both" Captain Solway walked to the phone as the two men crawled into the exit tunnel and started along the line. "Madness. Bloody madness." he said to himself as he plugged into the artillery line.

* * *

The first Australian shell whined over Gunther's position and landed some three hundred yards behind him and to his right. He turned to look at the rising dust and smoke. A second shell landed, quickly followed by a third and a fourth. It seemed as if the gunner was bombarding an east-west line in the middle of no-man's land. 'Why?' The smoke and dust had now formed a screen obscuring his own trenches from his view. Gunther considered his position. This was not part of the plan but obviously the enemy had some reason for this new turn of events. "Of course." he reasoned. "They think the linesmen were shot from our trenches so they're putting up a protective screen while they run the line. It couldn't be better. They'll think they're safe and relax. Come on rabbits. Where are you?"

As if on cue, two figures appeared out of the gloom to Gunther's left. He frowned. These men were not operating as they normally did. One would appear from a hole and quickly disappear into another. Then the second would make his move and sprint for a different hole. At no time did they come together in the same crater. "Damn you rabbits, I won't be able to get you together but it doesn't matter. I'll wait till the leader stops at the wire break and nail him. Then the second man will pop his head up to see what happened and bang. Two dead rabbits, one Iron Cross. Simple."

* * *

The two Australians were making slow progress along the line. When one reached a crater, he would shout "Go", and the other would then scramble from his refuge and head for his next hiding hole, making sure he didn't get too close to where his companion was. They were zigzagging their way along the line and the short bursts of sprinting with full gear was very tiring. Fear helped. It lent wings to their boots. Bluey's eyes constantly searched the landscape while Al concentrated on keeping in touch with the line.

Suddenly Al shouted, "Break" and at that very instant Bluey screamed, "Down."

Al hurled himself sideways into a crater as the bullet whistled past his head. It was close, very close.

"Are you all right Al?" shouted Bluey.

"Yes but that was close, too bloody close for my liking."

"Don't worry Australian, the next one will be much closer."

"Who the hell said that?" asked the shaken corporal.

"I think we have company, Al."

"Yes you do you stupid Australian rabbits. But don't worry, we won't be together for long."

"The phone Al! The phone!" called Bluey.

"What phone you stupid Australian? You didn't take the line with you. You are trapped, you can't call for help. Soon I will put you out of your misery."

Connecting their phones to the working cable Bluey and Al talked quietly. "Al, I have a rough idea where he is. I saw the stones and the end of his rifle move just as you called 'break.' Keep him talking while I try to get a line on him. And keep your ear to the phone."

"Hey Fritz. Where did you learn to speak English?"

"My cousins and I attended Cambridge for a couple of years and I learnt a lot from the idiotic English."

"Well you didn't learn how to shoot. You missed me."

"My mistake. I went for a head shot and you moved too quickly. I expected you to stop at the break. Don't worry, I'll not miss next time."

Bluey had removed his beloved watch from its case and opened the lid. "Well Dad, you said the mirror on the inside of the lid was useful for observing people without them knowing they were being watched. Let's hope you were right." Pressed against the side of the crater, he raised the watch so the mirror was just above the rim. "It works! Bloody hell it works!" Bluey grabbed the phone. "Al keep goading him about his piss poor shooting and see if you can get him to let off a shot. I want to see him in a firing position."

"Hey Fritz, you the guy who killed our mates on this line?" yelled Al.

"No, Rolt and Herwin did those jobs. Neat eh?"

"Yeah, but you missed. You must be second class."

"That's not true. I'm as good as either of them. I made the national rifle team just before the war. You'll soon find out how good I am but you won't be alive to tell anyone."

"Oh yeah? I think you are a born loser Fritz. You couldn't knock your granny off a piss pot."

"Try me you loud-mouthed Australian. Just try me and then you'll see who is second rate."

"Right Fritz I'll try you. If I am going to die I don't need this tin hat any more. Let's see if you can hit it." With that Al hurled his tin hat like a discus from the crater. A shot rang out. The twang of a bullet hitting metal was clearly heard.

"Now do you think I'm a second-class shot Mr. Rabbit?" Gunther was pleased with his effort.

"Shit Bluey, he's no mug with a gun." whispered Al.

"No Al, but he raised himself up to get that shot away. Here's what you have to do. Make up a package or parcel of some sort. Use your tunic and boots."

"You're mad. I need my boots for running."

"No mate, we're not running anywhere. This is it. One way or the other. While you're making up the bundle keep him talking, we have to make him mad."

"Why?"

"Because when people get mad they sometimes do things without thinking, and I want him to raise himself up a couple of inches more when he fires at the bundle."

"And if he doesn't fire at the bundle?"

"Well mate he'll then be firing at you because I want you to come out of that hole an instant after you have tossed the bundle out in the opposite direction. I want him mad and I want him to let off a shot at the bundle. He then has to work the bolt and my guess is he'll still be in the raised position while he does that. That'll be my time."

"And if you miss?"

"Two things. Either you or I will be dead. Perhaps both. Quickly, keep talking."

"Hey Fritz, did you shoot the Preacher?"

"Who is the Preacher?"

"One of our guys who went out to help a mate back in January. He had a white flag but some bastard shot him."

"Oh yes I remember. It was my cousin. Herwin said he didn't have a white flag at the time he fired."

"That's rubbish, he did. It was a bastard of a thing to do. The sort of thing a coward does. But then we got him in his little hide-away, didn't we?"

"Herwin is no coward you stupid Australian. You didn't kill Herwin. You only wounded him. He's pretty mad at you Australians."

"You know Fritz, when we get to Germany I'm going to fuck your mother."

"What did you say?"

"When we have won the war and we march into Germany I'm going to find your mother and I'm going to fuck her."

"No you're not Mr. Rabbit. You're wrong on two points. You are not going to win the war, and you are about to die."

"You're the one who's wrong Fritz. I suppose she is one of those great fat ladies with hair on her face. Well she might be ugly, but I'm still going to poke her, and then I'll start on your ugly sisters."

"Damn you Aussie. You don't talk about my family that way. You are going to die a slow death. A horrible death. No head shot for you." Gunther was angry and slightly confused. How did he allow the situation to develop this way. He had to act, and act quickly.

"Al," whispered Bluey into the phone, "are you ready?"

"Yes, but I'm not sure I like it."

"Listen the shells are getting closer. There's one now. When the next explodes it will be fairly close to him. He'll feel the blast. Heave the bundle out one way and you go the other. Good luck."

Bluey said a silent prayer as the next shell whistled overhead.

"Here Fritz. Cop this." shouted Al as he threw the bundle out of the crater and launched himself in the opposite direction.

Gunther had reached boiling point and automatically raised himself and fired at the package. His eyes saw Al making a break and he quickly worked the bolt. At the same time he caught a glimpse of movement to his left and realised the danger. The bullet from Bluey's gun removed the upper part of his head. For Gunther, the war was over.

"Al? You still with me?"

"Yes mate. Thanks."

"Any time fellow. Get your boots and then fix the line."

Bluey ran and knelt alongside Gunther. "So, the bastard who shot Preacher is still alive is he?" Bluey removed the papers from Gunther's pockets and ripped off the metal badges from his tunic. He then picked up the sniper's rifle.

"Come on Bluey. We're to return to start point. The line is through. Our gunners are about to close down so let's get to hell out of here."

As they entered the dugout both were surprised to see Colonel Payne seated at the table. “Well boys, tell me about it.”

“He got careless Sir, and Bluey got him.”

“Excellent. Excellent. And what do you have there?”

“Some papers he had in his pocket. Also, his uniform badges and his gun.”

“A Mauser sporting gun. What a beauty! I’ll take this back to HQ and give it to the Brigadier. It’s magnificent! He will be very pleased with the way things have turned out. Well done Solway! Well done Johnson!” He walked to the door. “Oh yes, one last thing. The Brigade is pulling out tomorrow so you can forget about K5. I think it’s done its job. Sound idea of yours Ronald. A very good ploy. Given Jerry a bloody nose haven’t we? Yes, a damn good job.” He left the room followed by Lieutenant Johnson.

“I think the Colonel forgot to say ‘well done’ to you two. You did very well. Sorry I can’t buy you a beer, but one day I’ll shout the bar. For now, you’ll have to settle for a cup of tea.”

“Thanks Sir. We accept. There is just one last thing about K5.”

“One last thing? What’s that, Wilson?”

“The Colonel said to forget about K5 but we have to run it one more time. So far Bluey has been spot on with his assessment of the situation. The prize is the line. Open, we win. Shut down, they win. So, this evening Bluey and I will run K5 for the last time to show Jerry that it’s still up and working.”

“Al’s right Sir. We have to do it, or all this has been for nothing.”

“No, you two are not going to run that line.”

“What? Why not?” the two sappers chorused.

“Because we three are going to do it. I’ll lead and you two can follow. Do try to keep up because I won’t be dawdling. It’s the least I can do for those four men I lost. On your way, I’ll see you at the exit trench at 4:30pm.”

“We’ll be there.” The men rose, saluted and left.

“He’s all right, that Captain Solway.”

"Yeah Al, he's all right. Pity there's not more like him. I must say you surprised me with all that talk about raping Jerry's mother and sisters."

"Surprised myself Bluey. I guess I was very angry, as well as being bloody scared. It was a close call. I've never been so frightened in all my life. Sorry about that German gun. It really was a beauty and now it's the Brigadier's toy. By rights, it should be yours."

"Well, he won't get too much pleasure from it until someone finds him some ammo." Bluey pointed to his bulging pockets. "Silly old bastard was so excited about getting his hands on the gun he forgot to ask about ammo. Sometimes I wonder if those senior officers have any idea about weapons. Let's grab some tucker. I'm famished."

* * *

The senior German officers were upset and their anger was not hidden from the two Bavarian snipers. The Staff had been roused early in the morning from their comfortable quarters and brought to the observation post to witness 'a significant German victory'. All they had seen was clouds of dust and smoke although the sound of shots was heard. When the dust and smoke finally cleared, the body of the German marksman was clearly visible.

"In future Lieutenant, I would be happy to receive written reports rather than spend my valuable time watching some idiotic side-show. Come gentlemen we have a war to run." With that, the General and his staff strode from the post leaving a disappointed Rolt and Herwin to themselves.

"What went wrong Rolt?"

"I don't know Herwin. Somehow, I think we underestimated our foe, or else Gunther didn't follow his orders. The fact that the enemy put up that screen makes me think we sent Gunther into an ambush, and it's my fault. Those Australian troops have been in the field a long time. They aren't novices."

"Well what do we do now? I don't think High Command will give us any further support for this venture."

"No Herwin. We will move on and find new fields in which to exercise our talents." He looked across towards the enemy. "You know I have the strange but strong feeling that there is a special personal enemy over there. It's as though I've been pitting my wits and skills against one man and he has won."

"Well, won this round Rolt. Remember, on numbers we are ahead. Four of their men against one of ours. If you look at it from that angle, we won."

"No Herwin. The prize is the telephone wire. If they keep it open then they have won. But you're right, It's only one round. Perhaps we'll come up against that group again and next time I'll be more careful. Enough of this morbid talk. I'll go look along the lines to see if we can find greener pastures. You stay here and see what happens. Oh, by the way, you had better write to Gunther's family. He died a hero."

Before Herwin could answer Rolt left.

Herwin gazed across the wasteland. "Rolt is right. You Australians are going to pay for the death of Gunther and for my disfigurement." Herwin fingered the ugly scar on his cheek. "Yes, I feel it too. This is now a personal war and in the end, we'll get even. Damn you Gunther, why did you have to die? It was to have been our most glorious hour. Damn you Australians, but your turn will come."

ABSOLUTE BLOODY CHAOS

Al, Bluey, Simon and George sat disconsolately around a table in the mess hall. The day after the incident with the German sniper, the Brigade had withdrawn to a reserve area, but Al and his companions could find no reason to celebrate. They realised that with their reduced numbers, the Section was no longer an operational unit and there was a real threat it would be disbanded. If that happened, the four of them would be posted to other units to make up for losses suffered elsewhere.

"What do you think Al?" asked Bluey.

"Think about what?"

"Us, Al. What happens now?"

"That's the sort of question I would have expected from Sam," answered the Corporal and immediately regretted he had spoken.

Simon spoke. "What's going to happen to No.3 Section, Al?"

Al Wilson looked at the youngster. "I don't know Simon. Peter King sent a message to meet him here in the mess hall. I guess he'll have the answers." Al nodded in the direction of the mess hall entrance where the tall Sergeant was hanging up his coat and slouch hat. "George, rustle up a brew. We won't get any answers out of Peter King until he has a cup of tea in his hand."

They stood as the Sergeant approached.

"Morning men. What's the chance of a brew?"

"On its way Pete. Pull up a chair."

The Sergeant sat down at the table. "Bloody cold out there, but the ground is beginning to dry."

"You mean the Generals are getting restless?" Al suggested.

Sergeant King nodded. "That too. It's been a long winter for them tucked away in their nice warm billets. It's not good for Generals to be idle. They have too much time to dream. I guess it's the same on the other side. Generals are pretty much the same whoever they are."

"It will be no surprise when the big push comes. It's merely a matter of who starts the ball rolling. Us or them."

The Sergeant accepted a mug of tea from George. "Thanks." He looked back at Al. "My guess Al, and it's only a guess, is that it won't be us. We have spent the winter preparing our defences. I think the brass are expecting Jerry to attack and are pinning their faith in our ability to hold him. Unless an attack is overwhelmingly successful, it's the attacker who suffers the worst. My guess is that our Generals are hoping Jerry will attack so that we can inflict heavy losses on him. Then, with the support of the Americans, we will counter-attack and knock him out once and for all."

Simon chipped in. "Americans? I haven't seen any. Where are they?"

"Oh they're here Sapper Young. They're coming over in great numbers and Germany must know it. The Yanks are the key to the whole thing. They're fresh and have the numbers, but we must hold out until they're ready for the frontline."

"One more battle to fight, eh Pete?"

The Sergeant looked at the weary Corporal. "Just one Al? I think not. Even if we hold Jerry, he's not going to lie down and give up. No, I think we'll have to march into Germany to end all this, but I don't expect you'll be involved, at least not for a while."

The last sentence caught the interest of his four listeners.

"What do you mean? We won't be involved?"

"Relax. I wasn't being personal about this group. I was referring to the Australian Divisions. For some reason, after the thaw sets in, the mud in Belgium stays wetter than that of the Somme. You have seen the mud at Messines. No one could advance through that, as we found out at Passchendaele. Yet here it is, the first week of March, and the ground in the Somme is much firmer. So, nature dictates where the assault will take place and the arrival of the Americans dictates that it will probably happen sooner rather than later."

"Have you told the Generals all this?"

"No Al. There's an old saying: 'You can always tell a General but you can't tell him much'."

They laughed. Everything Peter King said made sense. Common and military sense, but they also believed that such an assessment might not be appreciated or understood by their superiors. So many seemingly senseless decisions had been inflicted upon them that their faith in the higher command had been badly shaken.

Al felt it was about time that the question was asked. "Pete, that's sorted out the war, but what about No.3 Section?"

"Ah yes, No.3 Section. Captain Solway has given a lot of thought to this group. The simple solution would be to allocate you four to other sections, but the Captain isn't keen to do that. It seems he has a certain admiration for the way you work together, and he feels it would be wrong to break up such a team. So, he has decided that you are to become the Brigade reserve pool of signallers."

"Reserve pool?" Al frowned. "You mean we are to sit back here on our backsides for the rest of the war?"

The Sergeant laughed. "I can't imagine you sitting still on your bum while there's a battle going on Al Wilson. I've known you too long. No, the Captain wants you held in reserve for special stunts. For instance, should HQ lose comms with a battalion, you blokes will be sent out to find the battalion HQ and restore communications. One small point: you will need to be proficient with all, and I mean all, communication equipment. So you had better start brushing up on your Morse using lamps, flags and buzzer. And get to know all about those wireless sets that were such a problem a while ago. There will be occasions when a wireless set is more useful than a landline. In short, you four will become our communication experts and, when things go wrong, you'll be expected to fix them. Got it?"

"Yep Pete. We've got it." Al had a huge smile on his face. "We stay together and we do our own thing. That's fine by us."

"Steady on Corporal. I didn't say you could do your own thing. I said you fix things when they go wrong. That doesn't give you a free hand."

Al was still grinning. "You don't fool me Peter King. If things go wrong we fix it, right? We work out how to do it, and then we do it. To me, that means we do things our way."

The Sergeant considered this bold statement for a moment. He then rose from his place at the table. "I guess you're right. We give you the problem, you solve it. But knowing you lot, I can only offer one small piece of advice, keep your heads down. This war is about to explode."

"Thanks Pete. We appreciate all that you've done for us. I know your intervention kept us together as a team."

Again, the tall man considered the words of the Corporal. "Men, I know how desperate you are to stay as a team and this solution meets that wish. But please don't think that what we have set up is a soft compromise. I'm not sure how it will work, but what I do know, is that where the fighting is the heaviest is where things go wrong, especially with communications. So, what we've done is selected you to go where the odds on survival are lessened. For that I don't deserve any thanks. However, good luck. I'll see you around from time to time." He turned and left the room, picking up his coat and hat at the door.

No one spoke for a while. Then George looked up from his mug of tea and asked. "Al, he meant that didn't he? We are going to be right in the middle of the bad stuff. That's the price we have to pay for staying together."

"Yes, that's what he said, and that's what he meant. If you don't like it, there is still time to ask for a transfer. That goes for all of you."

Bluey shook his head. "So, what's new? We've been there and survived. Why should it be different now? We know our job. That's all we'll be doing, our job. Hell, we could be in any part of the front and cop a shell or bullet. It's business as usual as far as I can see."

"I'm with you Bluey." said Simon.

"You mean Yvette told you to stick with me, don't you?"

Simon blushed and said nothing.

"So George?" asked Al.

"I'm staying Al. You lot have looked after me ever since I reached France. No matter what they throw at us, we'll handle it."

"Good, that's settled. Now you heard the man, let's get some sort of routine organised for refresher training. Every day. Flags, lamps and buzzer. Eat, sleep and dream of Morse code. I'll hop over to the store and place an order for our own wireless set. We'll practise by tuning into other stations and develop our own techniques. We haven't much time if Pete King is right. Jerry could move very shortly."

"Yes Al, but not here. Pete said he would hit the line in France."

"Yes George he did say that, but you don't expect the Australian Divisions to be sitting in reserve in Belgium while the main action is on the Somme do you? Which reminds me, we need our own transport. I'll see if I can get my hands on a truck. Can you blokes drive?"

"Not me," replied Bluey. "Wouldn't have a clue."

"Nor me." chimed in Simon.

George put his hand up. "I can. Used to drive for the firm back home."

"Right, George and I will do the driving, you two can be navigators. It'll be good to be able to move quickly to trouble areas."

"Or in the opposite direction." interjected Bluey.

Al raised an eyebrow in mock alarm.

"Joking Al, just joking. You know there's one name that never seems to rate a mention these days."

"Bailey. Yes Bluey, you're right. Seems like he's made himself indispensable to the officers' mess. Anyhow we can do without him. He would be a liability if he joined with us now. Come on, there's work to be done. Bluey, you and Simon find a hut or room somewhere which we can use as our classroom and store. George and I'll go hunting for a truck and a wireless set."

* * *

The men's already high opinion of Sergeant King as a strategist was further elevated when two weeks later rumours started to circulate that the great German offensive had begun in France. At first there was a strange feeling of elation that the battle had begun. The men in the field believed this would be the last great encounter. They were confident that the Allies could hold and then turn the tide, and that would be the end of Germany, the end of the war. The anticipation that the end of the war could be near kindled a strange excitement. Men were anxious, even eager, to join in the final act. However, their excitement began to turn to concern as news of the German advance reached them. Names of towns they had fought for and captured the previous year, fell again into enemy hands. It was unbelievable. All those men sacrificed for nothing. It would now have to be done all over again.

As the situation rapidly deteriorated the Australian Divisions in Belgium were deployed to France to help halt the onslaught.

* * *

The three sappers were loading their newly-acquired truck when Al came running down the road. “Here’s trouble.” observed George. “I’ve never seen him run like that before. It must be something big.”

“You’re right George. The last time I saw Al run like that, a sniper was urging him along.” Replied Bluey.

The exhausted Corporal reached the truck and leant against its side to regain his breath.

“Are we loaded?” he gasped.

“All but your personal gear. We going somewhere?”

“Yes mate, the Somme, and in a hurry. George, here’s a map. You’ll be driver for the first leg. Study the map with Simon. We head for Amiens but will try to stay off the main roads as much as possible. They’ll be choked with traffic.” He thrust the map into George’s hand. “Come on Bluey, give me a hand to pack my gear.”

In minutes, the Corporal and Bluey returned with Al’s gear. George had already started the engine and Simon was alongside him in the cabin, the map spread across his knees.

“Happy George?”

“Yeah, we’ve picked out a route but God only knows what the roads will be like.”

“Only one way to find out. Let’s get moving. Don’t try to break any speed records. The object is to arrive as soon as possible, with the emphasis on arriving.”

Al climbed over the tailboard as the vehicle lurched forward. He settled down in the back alongside his comrade. “Holy smoke Bluey, what a shambles at HQ. People running everywhere.”

"I gather the news is bad?"

Al shook his head. "Yes mate. Very bad. No one seems to know exactly what the situation is, but it's not good. Jerry is heading for Amiens, and at the moment, it's difficult to see how we can stop him."

Bluey looked up in alarm. "Amiens. That means Corbie will go. Christ, I hope Ghislaine has moved the family from the farm."

"I hope so, but let's not get too worried just yet. Much of what I heard was rumour, just rumour. Oh, I nearly forgot. I offered to give your favourite Lieutenant and his batman a ride to Amiens but he said he wasn't packed and wouldn't be ready to move until tomorrow. I have the distinct impression that Lieutenant Johnson doesn't care to get too close to the nasty side of the war."

Bluey grinned. "Just as well he didn't accept the offer. There's not enough room in this truck for him and me. One of us would have to run along behind and I bet it wouldn't be the fancy Lieutenant."

Al laughed. "Oh, that would be a sight. You running from Ypres to Amiens. You know, it's probably never been done before. You might have created some sort of record."

Bluey stopped smiling. "Maybe it hasn't been done before, but by the look of those infantry, it's going to be done in the next day or so."

On both sides of the truck marched the infantry. For miles, they could see the moving lines of men. No banter this time, no cheery wave. These were men who knew they had a long way to go and had no idea of what awaited them when they reached their destination.

Bluey stared at the never-ending line of khaki dressed men. "Bloody hell Al, they won't make them march all that way surely? They won't make it, and if they did, they won't be in any shape to fight."

Al shook his head. "No, I reckon they're heading for the railway." He consulted a map he had taken from his tunic. "Yeah, I reckon they're going there." He pointed to the map. "Now, if we can beat them there, which I'm sure we can, we can grab some food from their kitchens and also some fuel."

"We have a few cans under the canvas."

"Yes, but I want to keep those for emergencies." He opened the small sliding door that linked the cabin with the back of the truck. "How's it going George?" he asked.

"Right as rain, and so far, Simon hasn't got us lost."

"Well keep it that way. Bluey and I will relieve you in an hour. Be careful. I wouldn't want you to run over any of these infantrymen. They don't look very happy."

"Right you are Al, I'll try to miss them but there are so many of them. The whole Division must be on the march."

"All Divisions are on the march. Thousands of men all heading in the one direction. Let's hope they get there in time." He shut the sliding door and looked at Bluey. "Oh no, not here. How can you?"

The redhead was trying to write a letter, despite the lurching ride. "Best I do it now Al. Once we reach the Somme there may not be too much spare time."

"By the way, did you get any news of Lucy's brother? The one that was wounded?"

"The padre got some information, but it wasn't good. He's bad, very bad."

"Sorry mate."

"It happens." The sapper had stopped writing.

Al Wilson was staring at the long lines of marching men. "It happens. Now isn't that the very truth of the matter? It happens. When, where, how, we don't know, but we do know that it happens."

"Not to us Al. We're going to beat the Hun and then we're going home."

"Yes Bluey, we are. It won't happen to us." They were brave words spoken by Corporal Wilson but neither men really believed them.

* * *

As they approached Amiens, refugees were streaming away from the battle zone. People trudged alongside horse-drawn carts carrying all their worldly possessions. In some cases, the carts were hauled by humans. No young men to help, so the women hauled or pushed the wagons, old women, tired women, even small children. The men felt a strong urge to stop and help, but there was no time to stop and there were so many needing help.

Al sought information at Amiens while the others scouted for fuel. Petrol was now more precious than food, as petrol could get you safely away from the danger zone if you had a vehicle. After much bargaining, threatening and stealth, the three sappers were able to acquire a number of petrol cans which they poured into the truck's tank.

"Perhaps we'll see the family." volunteered Simon.

"Perhaps, but I doubt it." replied Bluey. "Gilly is smart enough to realise that the roads to and from Amiens would be choked. If they did move I feel certain she would skirt the city."

"Can we go to Corbie and find out?" asked the anxious young man.

"Ask Al, not me."

The Corporal appeared, pushing his way through the crowd.

"Chaos! Absolute bloody chaos! No one knows what's going on. We'll have to go forward and see for ourselves." The Corporal looked angry. "Everyone is busy packing up and getting ready to move out. It's as though they've given up the fight already. Come on, climb aboard."

"Where are we going Al?"

"Damned if I know Simon. Oh, I know what's on your mind, and as Corbie is in the general direction of the front, we might as well go via there, but only for a quick check."

"Great Al. Thanks."

"Thanks for what Simon? I have no orders, no ideas, so Corbie is as good a place as any to start whatever it is we're going to do. Drive on George. What's our fuel situation Bluey?"

The two campaigners settled in the back and discussed their options.

"Perhaps we should try the Château Al. Someone might still be there."

"Yes Bluey, someone might. Then again that someone might speak German."

"Then we'll know where the enemy is. Isn't that what we're supposed to find out?"

"True my friend, but if Jerry is there and we drive up in our truck, I doubt if we'll be allowed to pass the word around."

Bluey nodded. "I wasn't actually suggesting we drive up to the front door."

Al leant over and slapped his friend on the knee. "I know Bluey. It was a joke. Hell, we're making slow progress."

"Yes, it seems like half the people in France are using this road. What a mess!"

The two fell silent as the truck slowly forced its way through the mass of people moving in the opposite direction. The countryside was familiar, and they remembered the long walks along this very road with the others of No.3 Section. Finally, with much shouting by Simon, the refugees allowed the vehicle to pull off the road alongside the farm wall. Simon sprang down from his seat and rang the bell. A voice they all knew said something in French, to which Simon called out, "We're back Gilly. It's us."

The gate swung open and the Frenchwoman ran into the arms of the men, hugging and kissing them in turn. The tears ran down her face, uncontrolled, but no one cared. Alerted by her welcoming cries, the three young ladies of the house came running. Suddenly Nicole pulled away from hugging Bluey, looked at the truck parked outside the gate and cried out. "You've come to save us. Oh thank goodness. We are safe."

Bluey looked at Al who took a step back from the group.

"Well Nicole, that rather depends on how you interpret the word 'save'. If you mean we have come to help you flee, then the answer is no. We are heading in the opposite direction, as are all the Australian Divisions, to try and stop the Germans. So yes, in a way we have come to save you."

"Can you stop them?" asked Yvette, clinging tightly to Simon's arm.

"Of course they can." snapped her mother.

Al looked into the tear-stained face.

"Oh Gilly, what faith you have. I hope it's not misplaced. Things don't look too rosy at the moment."

Ghislaine returned the Corporal's look and her chin rose slightly. "You will stop them. Now come and have something to eat. How long are you staying?"

"An hour perhaps. No longer."

As the men entered the kitchen, they each approached Madame Pruvost senior and bowed slightly. The old lady remained seated and acknowledged each man with a nod of her head. Turning to her daughter in law, she said something in her native tongue.

Ghislaine nodded and smiled. "Mother and I have been having a slight disagreement on what we should do in the present situation. I was in favour of moving the family to the south but mother refused to budge. I couldn't leave her so that meant I stayed. Then the girls rebelled and refused to go unless mother and I went. So, we have had a crisis in the family, but now mother tells me she was right."

"Pardon Gilly? How was she right?" asked Al.

"She just said, 'I told you so. They have come back and they will stop the Hun'."

"Oh dear." said Al. "Another believer in the invincibility of Australian troops. It's not like that Gilly. Things are not going well."

"No they're not," chimed in Marie. "It's a real mess at the Château."

"The Château," exclaimed Al. "You've been at the Château? When?"

"This morning. Nicole and I only arrived home a few minutes before you did. The British officers are still there but they are ready to move out at short notice. Everything is packed up ready to go."

"Except the food, which the girls took pity on and helped some of it to escape." laughed Yvette.

Ghislaine clapped her hands. "Oh, I wasn't thinking. Girls, get moving. Prepare a meal for the men and hurry. I want to talk."

The three girls hurried to the stove and benches. Simon followed offering his services as assistant to Yvette. George excused himself saying he wanted to check the windmill and the plumbing. The old lady returned to her knitting.

"Gilly, I'm so sorry about Preacher. We all are."

Ghislaine reached across the table and took Al's hand. "Can you talk about it? I know how close you all were to one another. Can you bring yourself to tell me what happened?" The tears started to flow.

"Yes I can tell you. It helps to talk about such matters instead of having them drowning all other thoughts."

Holding her hand Al recounted the events. Ghislaine listened. When he had finished she said, "Thank you Al." and left the room.

Bluey stared at the table for a while and then raised his eyes to look at the young leader. "Well done mate. I couldn't have told her without breaking down myself."

"Thanks Bluey. Tell me, as my second in command, what are your recommendations for our next move?"

"Second in command? Big title for a small outfit. Well, we know the Château is still in our hands and I guess that's where our Divisional staff will head. So, I suggest we stick with Plan A and go there."

"Agreed. There must be someone there who has some idea of where the frontline is, although I suspect there isn't an established frontline at the moment."

"I haven't heard any guns Al. Plenty of planes but no gunfire, so I don't think they're too close. Come on, let's eat and get moving."

GOOD NEWS BAD NEWS

George drove the truck up the sweeping roadway that led to the front door of the Château. "The girls were right. Looks like everyone is packed and ready to move out." Cars and trucks were parked under the trees in the expansive Château gardens, their drivers awaiting orders.

"George, take the truck to the old car pool and scrounge whatever petrol you can lay your hands on. Simon, head for the kitchen and help yourself to some of the food the girls mentioned, especially tinned goods. Be back here in thirty minutes. Bluey, come with me."

The two soldiers entered the old house and found a door that bore the sign 'Operations Room'. Al pushed open the door and the two men entered. A group of four officers was gathered around a table studying a map.

"Who the hell are you? Who said you could come in here?"

"We're Australian signallers Sir. We came on ahead of the Divisional staff. We had orders to report here and get ourselves familiar with the situation."

The Lieutenant Colonel frowned. "What Division?"

"Well Sir, all the Australian Divisions are headed this way but we managed to beat them here. Seeing we're here, can we be of any use to you?"

"Use to us?" the Colonel snorted. "How many are you?"

"Four Sir."

"Four? Four? I need four thousand right now." The Colonel looked and sounded like a desperate man. A young captain wearing tartan trousers had been studying the two newcomers. "Excuse me Sir, maybe these men can help," he said in a broad Scots accent.

"You heard him Captain. Four men."

"Yes Sir, but signallers. That's the point. Tell me Corporal do you have any equipment with you or are you travelling light?"

"We have our own truck and our own wireless set. We're self-sufficient." Al was making an impression on the group.

"Splendid. What about it Sir?" the Scotsman turned to his superior.

"What about what Robert?" replied the Colonel.

"We need to find out where our regiments are and where the enemy is. It's ages since we had any really reliable information. These men could take their vehicle and go and make contact and relay the information back."

The Colonel frowned. "Well you heard Captain MacDonald. Could you do that?" he growled.

"Yes Sir. That's what we're trained for. That's what we're here for. Do you have a wireless set here?"

"Of course we do, but no one has called for over twenty-four hours. I suppose it still works." The Colonel raised an eyebrow in the direction of a smartly-dressed Lieutenant.

"It does Sir." replied the signal officer. "We've been receiving messages from Army HQ constantly."

"Questions you mean Patrick, not messages. Questions, and we haven't had many answers lately." The Colonel paused. "You're not under my command Corporal so I can't really order you to go out there and see what's happening, but we would appreciate it if you could help."

"Always thought we were on the same side Colonel." replied Al. "We will try. Seems to me that time is the essence of the matter. Could I suggest your signals officer takes Sapper Dowson to your signals centre so that they can agree on frequencies and call signs, and perhaps a very simple form of coding, while your staff points out the areas you think we should explore."

The Colonel nodded. "Off you go Patrick. Come here Corporal and have a look at this map."

* * *

An hour later, the truck carrying the four Australian signallers, departed the Château and turned north. With the small door connecting the cabin to the rear of the vehicle open, Al briefed the others.

"Firstly, note this and note it well. I carry a letter from the Colonel to identify us to Allied personnel. If anything happens to me, someone must take custody of the letter. It must not fall into enemy hands. If you can't burn it then eat it. Understood?"

The three men nodded.

"The plan is simple. We head north until we find friendly troops. We find out from them what is going on. Bluey and the signals officer have devised a simple reporting form for all units. It's a matter of who you are, where you are, what your strength is, where is the enemy, what is his strength and any comments. We will then code this information and send it back. No one knows very much at the moment about where our troops are, or the Jerry."

"You got a form for Jerry to fill out Bluey?" asked George.

"Shut up George, this is not the time for jokes." snapped Al.

"Sorry."

Al continued. "Our usefulness will cease if we're knocked off or captured, so we'll keep the truck and the equipment out of harm's way if that's possible. Once we get a feel for a situation, we'll establish the truck as a base and then go forward to gather information. I'm hoping the infantry will be able to provide us with all the relevant information for relaying to the Château. Once we make contact with the infantry tonight, we'll edge our way eastward and see if we can establish a rough idea of where the frontline is or rather, how far Jerry has advanced. You got a problem Bluey?"

"Yes Al. Planes. Jerry seems to have control of the skies and if he sees us, then we're in for a pasting."

"Yeah, the planes are a real worry. So, when we stop, we'll move the wireless set and all its gear into some sort of shelter. The wireless is the key to the whole thing. If the truck gets hit, then we'll try to find another or a substitute."

"Substitute?" asked Simon.

"Yes Simon. Out here we're not going to find many petrol dumps, so sooner or later we'll have to abandon the truck and then move by foot or some other means of transport."

"You mean horses?" asked Bluey.

"Horses, donkeys, I don't care, but we must be mobile."

"Right Al, I'll keep my eyes open. Horses are my cup of tea."

"Yes. I remember Preacher talking about you and your horses. Mind you, I think the farmers most probably have taken the horses with them."

George turned in the driving seat. "We've plenty of petrol Al. It should last a day or two depending on how far we've got to travel."

"Yes George, I can see we've plenty of petrol on board. I just hope I'm not sitting on these cans when Jerry drops a bomb alongside."

"Hell, I hadn't thought of that."

"Well don't think about it now and concentrate on your driving." Al looked at his map. "At this speed, I reckon we should make contact with some of our infantry at dusk. That's in an hour or so. Keep your eyes open."

The stream of refugees had dwindled to a trickle as the truck moved northwards. Occasionally they encountered a military vehicle speeding in the opposite direction. From the occupants Al was able to gather limited information on where the Allied forces were located.

Just after dusk flashing lights warned George to slow down and to pull over to the side of the road. Shadowy forms appeared from out of the darkness.

"Hold it right there. Who are you?"

"Australian signallers on a recce." answered Al.

"You got any rations?" was the unexpected reply.

"Yeah." replied Al. "Who are you? Identify yourselves."

A Sergeant pushed his way through the group. "Australians! What are you doing here? You're going in the wrong direction."

"Are we?" replied Al. "Simon, dish out some grub to these blokes. They look like they could use it."

"You're not wrong there, Aussie."

"Right Sergeant, take me to your officer."

The British Sergeant looked at the Corporal. "Why? Do you want to identify the body?"

"Like that is it? Sorry. Come over here and let me explain what we're trying to do. Simon, get some food. Sergeant, tell me what you know about the situation so I can get it back to HQ."

The weary Sergeant sat down beside the Australian Corporal and began his story, a story of heartbreak and hell. The defending troops were no match for the overwhelming assault troops and had suffered dreadful casualties. Al wrote down the salient facts and then composed a brief summary.

"Here Bluey, earn your keep. Get onto the buzzer and pass this message back to HQ. Now Sergeant, what do you know about the regiments to your east?"

"There's a Scottish regiment immediately to our right. We've had some contact with them but they've copped a hiding too. We all settled in along this ridge mainly because we were too buggered to fall back any further. I think the laddies are the same. The left flank just doesn't exist but luckily for us Jerry kept coming straight ahead, otherwise he could've bypassed us and cut us off. Tell me, do you think they can get reinforcements here by dawn, because Jerry is sure to come at us then?"

"Not a chance Sergeant. The question is can your men still march, move, or crawl to the rear, because that's what you'll have to do. This place is untenable."

"How far back?"

Al scratched his head. "I don't know, but hopefully we'll hear soon. What I suggest is that you start pulling what's left of the regiment back to this point and then set them off along this road to the rear. You sure all your officers are dead?"

The Sergeant shook his head. "Who knows. Maybe there are some still alive out there, maybe not."

Al stood up. "Give me two of your fittest men, men who can still run if they have to. I'll take one and scout to the left. Bluey can take the other and move across the right. We'll try to contact as many of your men as we can and we'll direct them back to here."

"I'll come with you." replied the Sergeant.

Al shook his head. "No, you stay here and take charge of the men as they come in. We need your two men to ensure that the blokes out there don't shoot us as spies or agents, someone to vouch for us."

"I understand. I'll have a look at my team and pick a couple of lads to accompany you."

"Hey Al." Bluey emerged from the darkness. "Got through and here's the reply." he said, thrusting a piece of paper into the Corporal's hand.

Al shone his torch on the message pad. "Good news and bad news Sergeant. The good news is that our battalions are now arriving in the rear assembly area; the bad news is that HQ has decided on where the new lines will be established."

"Why is that bad news?"

"Well Sergeant, you and your men are going to have to hoof it about fifteen kilometres back from here." Al spread out his map. "Look, head for this village and dig in there as best you can. We'll tell HQ that's where you are so our troops don't mistake you for Germans." He wrote a brief message on the pad.

"Here Bluey, give this to George to send. You and I are going to scout around to see if we can find some more of the Sergeant's regiment."

When Bluey returned two young English soldiers were standing beside Al.

"Bluey, this is Henry and this is William. Doesn't like to be called Bill. You take William and head to the east. Be bloody careful. If you meet any of this regiment tell them to hightail it back to here and the Sergeant will then get them moving in the right direction. If you make contact with the Scottish boys, keep going along their line and try to find someone with some sort of authority. Tell them to pull back to this point." He stabbed the map with a dirty finger. "Go as far along the line as you can. Take this message from HQ as your authority. It's now 9:30pm. At 12:00am, I'll move our truck eastward along this road here and we'll wait here." Again, the dirty finger stabbed the map. "You make sure you're there by 4:30am, because I want to start back towards our lines before it's light. Got it?"

The Sergeant snorted. "How the hell do you expect that man to race around in the dark in country he's never seen and then meet up with you at some point on a map. A map which he hasn't got?"

"Can't afford two maps Sergeant. Off you go Bluey. Remember, William is not as fit as you so take it easy. Send him back to here with the troops from his own regiment and make sure he knows the way."

"No problem Al. Come on William. No, leave your rifle, it's just a weight to carry and we'll be moving fast. Anyhow I've got Lucy. We'll be right." The two men moved off into the darkness.

"Lucy? Who the hell is Lucy?" The Sergeant asked.

"Tell you later Sergeant. Come on Henry, let's move." answered Al.

The hastily-arranged plan worked and soon small groups of men were making their way to the rendezvous, where Simon had a cup of tea and some rations ready. As soon as they were fed and organised, the Sergeant sent them off towards the rear.

Around midnight, Al and Henry arrived at the truck, and shortly afterwards William arrived with the last of the men who had been dug in on the right flank.

"So far so good, eh Sergeant?"

"Better than good Corporal. We can easily make the village before first light. We owe you a lot."

Al smiled. "You're not home safe and sound yet Sergeant. Jerry won't be far behind." He shone the torch on a sheaf of messages that George had handed to him. "Well, HQ is really burning the midnight oil. An advance party will already be in place at the village by the time you get there. If only Jerry will oblige and continue to push straight ahead we might be able to give him a bloody nose. But if he goes around the flank it will be a different matter. Right, we're off. Got to find Bluey and his highland chums."

The Sergeant held out his hand. "Goodbye. Thanks and good luck. I hope next time I meet you, we'll be in a pub and the shout is on me."

"I'll keep you to that Sergeant. Good luck. Drive on George but take it easy. These roads are the very devil and we don't want to break down out here."

The truck moved slowly off into the dark watched by the small group of British soldiers.

"Good luck to them." muttered the Sergeant and, turning to the young soldier standing by his side said, "William, what was all that nonsense about Lucy?"

* * *

The truck carrying Al and the two sappers arrived at the rendezvous just in time to meet the first of the survivors of the Highland Regiment, sent there by Bluey. The infantry were close to exhaustion, but after a cup of tea and some food, their spirits and shoulders lifted and they set off for safety.

An officer appeared out of the gloom. His head was bandaged and his arm was in a sling.

"You must be Corporal Wilson." he said, ignoring Al's salute. "I was told to report to you."

Al studied the man's face to see if he was being funny or was in a state of shock. "I beg your pardon Major, but officers don't report to corporals. However, I am Corporal Wilson and pleased to meet you."

The officer sat down and accepted the offered cup of tea.

"I'm well aware of the Army's protocol Corporal, but the young man who stuck a rifle into my belly, gave me very explicit instructions. I was to make my way here and report to a Corporal Wilson. So here I am. There didn't seem to be any point in arguing. He was very insistent."

"I'm sorry Sir. Sapper Dowson tends to get carried away at times."

"Oh no Corporal, I'm not complaining. At first, I thought he was a Jerry. He just appeared from nowhere. No noise, nothing. I was convinced my war, if not my life, was over until I heard this Australian voice say: 'you in charge here?' I admitted to being an officer but I didn't think I was in charge at that moment. I was then given a comprehensive brief of the situation and told to move out and report to you. Then he vanished. It was all so sudden, but he convinced me. I just did as I was told."

"That's Bluey all right. Where is he now?" asked a bemused Al.

"Said he had to get the rest moving and with that disappeared. Here comes A Company now, or rather what's left of them. They were on the right flank so they may know where your man is."

A group of tired, dirty soldiers walked into the light of the campfire. A young officer snapped to attention and saluted the Major.

"Good to see you again Angus." said the senior officer as he returned the salute. "Come and take the weight off your legs. You look as though you could do with a rest."

"Thank you Sir. You're right about that. We're all very tired." He sat down and accepted a mug of tea.

The Major looked at the men lining up for food. He frowned. "Where's the rest of your company? Surely this isn't the..." his voice faded without completing the question.

"Aye Sir. This is A Company in its entirety. We got a good hammering yesterday and the day before. And today didn't look too rosy until that Australian emerged from nowhere."

"Gave you a fright did he Angus?" laughed the Major.

"Fright! He was just there! Came out of nowhere. Asked me if I was in charge and then told me to collect my men and move out quick smart. I could see he wasn't the sort to waste time or words so I gathered up the men and moved. Who is he?"

"An Australian sapper. Belongs to this communications outfit." The Major gestured towards Al Wilson.

"Pardon me Lieutenant, if your company is the last of the regiment to be pulled back, where is Sapper Dowson? Why isn't he with you?"

"He told us to go on ahead and he'd just pop down and have a look at what Jerry's up to. Then he was gone. What the hell is he, a phantom?"

Al chuckled. "No, not a ghost, he's a bushman."

"Bushman!" exclaimed the Lieutenant. "I've heard of them. There was one I recall named Kelly. They hanged him."

"No a bushman, not a bushranger. But enough of this idle chatter." Al turned to the Major. "I suggest you move along Sir. You've got a fair hike ahead of you. I'll inform HQ you are coming in so you don't cop a bullet from some trigger-happy outpost."

"Thanks Corporal. Thanks for the food. Thanks for everything. The regiment owes you a great debt of gratitude."

"Part of the job, Sir."

"And what of you and your men Corporal? As of now, this part of the country is no-man's land. Not a very healthy spot once Jerry starts forward, which I assume he'll do shortly."

"We don't plan on staying around any longer than we have to Major. Just as soon as our bushranger returns, we'll be off after you, so we'll probably see you later today."

"I hope so Corporal Wilson." The officer held out his hand which the Corporal took. "Again, many thanks." Turning to the seated men he called out, "Fall in, single file. We're not retreating men, we're redeploying. Sergeant, move the column out."

The three Australians watched as the remnants of the proud Scottish Regiment stepped out as one man for the long march ahead.

"Not bad for a bunch who haven't had a decent rest or meal in three days." observed George.

"No George, not bad at all. Now where's that idiot Bluey? Popped down to see what Jerry's doing! He's gone off his rocker!"

"You said to meet here at 4:30am, so he probably thought he had time to fill in." ventured Simon.

"Time to fill in be damned. We need to get moving. If he's not here at 4:30, too bad for him. We're off. Put that fire out and make sure everything is loaded ready to move." Al looked at his watch. "Twenty minutes I'll give him. Not a second more. If he wants to play cowboys and indians, then he can play them on his own."

"Strewth Al! You wouldn't leave Bluey out here on his own would you?" George was stunned by his leader's threat.

Al looked at the two sappers. "Let's get this straight. We've a job to do and so far, it's going well. If we hang around here waiting for Deadwood Dick Dowson to do his stuff, then we all might become statistics of war. That wouldn't help us or our side. At 4:30 we go, and that's a promise."

The minutes ticked by as the three men stood by the truck peering into the dark.

"One minute to go." muttered Al. "Damn him."

"Damn who Al?" Bluey had walked up behind the trio.

"Oh for Christ's sake Bluey, don't do that." shouted Al.

"Hush Al, keep your voice down. There's a Jerry patrol about five hundred yards away to our left. I suggest we get to hell out of here and fast. They probably heard that shout of yours."

Al motioned towards the truck. "You drive George, Simon forward lookout, Bluey and I in the back." George started the vehicle and it moved off along the narrow lane. Al moved to the communication slat and spoke. "Slow it down George. We can't afford a broken axle or buggered wheels right now. Safe and sure is the name of the game." Satisfied that the driver had comprehended the message, Al returned to the tail-board when Bluey sat cradling his rifle. "That wasn't very smart." he said.

"What wasn't very smart?"

"Leaving our departure to the very last minute and leading a Jerry patrol in our direction."

"You don't mean that do you Corporal? Firstly, we had an agreed time for rendezvous. I stuck to it. Secondly, the Jerry patrol had come through from the east sector and were ahead of me or at least between me and you blokes. I had to go around them. You know, I could hear you blokes a mile away. You were asking for trouble."

Al gazed out into the dark. "Sorry mate. You're right, we were slack. Even had a camp-fire going to lead them in. I guess we thought Jerry would be tucked up in bed getting some rest before the next attack."

"Well most of them are, but they have forward scouting patrols out. By now they'll know that those hills are deserted, so I expect they'll move forward at first light." He paused as he took out his precious watch. "It'll be getting light in about two hours and I guess we can expect his planes to be overhead at about that time. How far have we got to go?"

"About fifteen miles. If we average about eight miles an hour without breaking down we should be all right. The last of the Scots left just before 4:00 and were stepping off at a brisk pace when they left us. If God is good to us, we should all be behind our new line by first light."

Bluey shook his head. "Doubt it Al. Those laddies might have started off at a steady pace, but I doubt if they can keep it up. They're buggered, totally buggered. One of their guards was so sound asleep I had to slap his face to wake him up. If Jerry had pressed on, he would have slaughtered them. So, I can't see them marching fifteen miles in two hours."

"But they're well on the way and should be clear of Jerry ground troops by first light."

"Yeah mate, they're probably clear now except for attacks by aircraft."

"Aircraft? Well if we expect Jerry aircraft to be over us at first light, why not tell HQ and perhaps some of our boys can be there to meet them. Come on mate, let's see if we can work this bloody wireless set while still moving."

"It's not going to be easy to send Morse with all this bumping around, but why not? Let's give it a try."

The two men set about the task with more enthusiasm than confidence. After many repeats, they got a message through. Bluey looked at his watch.

"Nearly 5:30 Al, and I reckon we've only made five or six miles in the past hour. We might need that air protection ourselves."

"Reckon you're right Bluey, but George can't go any faster on this cart track." As he spoke the truck came to a halt. "Now what's the problem?" The two men in the back of the truck hopped out and walked to the cabin. The reason for the stop was evident. They had caught up with survivors of A Company sitting by the roadside. The Major and the Lieutenant stood up and crossed the road to the truck.

"Good to see you again Corporal Wilson."

"You too Sir, but I was hoping you'd be a bit closer to our line by now."

"Me too, but my chaps are very tired. We'll get there but in our own good time. I hope Jerry's not too close behind you."

"Doubt it Sir. He'll move off at first light into your old positions so we have a good start on him. The problem I see will be aircraft. It will be light a little after 6:00 and his scout planes will be out. Then we can expect trouble. Can we help you in any way?"

"Well yes, we have five chaps who are wounded. They can walk but they're getting very weak and are slowing the column down. I won't leave them. If you could give them a ride it would help."

Al thought for a moment. "Better than that Sir. Put your wounded in the back of the truck plus another ten of your men. That's about all there is room for. We'll walk and then every ten minutes you can change over the ten fit men and give another ten a rest."

The Major's eyes lit up. "Och, what a grand idea. Angus, you heard the man. Quick get the men aboard before they change their minds. Come Corporal walk with me, I want to hear about this outfit of yours." He looked around. "Where's that bushranger of yours?" You didn't leave him behind did you?"

"It's all right Al." Simon explained, "Bluey said something about a group of old women having a roadside chatter and forgetting about Jerry. He's gone back down the road to make sure we aren't being followed."

Al nodded. "Right as usual. Let's go." The truck with its escort set off once again in the direction of safety. Slowly the darkness eased in its intensity and visibility improved. There was no talk, no chatter amongst the troops. Every ten minutes the truck would stop, and a quick change over of the resting soldiers would take place, and then it was forward again.

"Not long now before it's fully light." remarked the Major.

"No Sir, not long. But we still have a good three miles to go before we reach the village."

"Perhaps the truck can speed up a bit now the driver can see better." suggested the officer.

Al looked back at the following vehicle. "Perhaps, but this rough old cart-road is not made for speeding vehicles and I don't think your men can raise a gallop."

"No, definitely not. Three miles to go doesn't sound very far normally, but this morning it sounds more like thirty."

"Yeah. Save your breath Major, and keep your ears open. We will probably hear him before we see him."

The Major nodded. Ten minutes passed and another stop was made to change over the passengers. The houses of the village ahead were visible.

"So close and yet so far." said Simon.

"Yeah," agreed Al, "but we'll make it." He paused, hand in the air. "What was that?"

"Shots Corporal." replied the young Scot Lieutenant. "Two or three, maybe more. Came from back there."

"Bluey's in trouble, Al."

Al stared to the rear. "Someone's in trouble Simon. Not necessarily Bluey."

"You want me to send a couple of men back there to give him a hand?" asked the Major.

"No Sir. He can look after himself. We must press on."

"Aircraft Sir," shouted a soldier pointing to the east.

"He's seen us." cried another as the plane banked and turned their way.

"Take cover everyone. Clear the truck. Hurry." shouted Al. The aircraft was already commencing a shallow dive towards them.

"Spread out men. Hug the bank. Keep your heads down."

The men didn't need a second warning as the oncoming aircraft started to fire its machine gun. Bullets whistled overhead striking the opposite road bank and the truck.

"Shit Al, the petrol cans."

"Can't be helped George."

There was a dull roar, then a louder noise and finally a deafening explosion as the spare cans of petrol exploded. The men closest to the truck were showered with burning liquid which their companions quickly doused. A few of the burns were serious, but most were superficial.

"Well, we all walk from here."

"Yes Al, but not everyone." George said quietly.

"What?"

"Some of the wounded just jumped or fell out of the truck and crawled under it." George pointed towards the burning wreckage.

"Damn! What a way to go and so near to home!" Al looked across towards the Major.

"Not your fault son. No one's fault. Has that plane gone?"

Everyone sat up and looked around the sky. There was no noise to be heard, nothing to be seen.

"Right, let's go. No doubt he'll be sending his comrades out to visit us just as soon as he can get home. He wasn't very clever, was he?"

"I don't follow you Corporal. He got the truck, which is probably what he was after."

"Yes Sir, he did. But if he had positioned himself ahead or behind us and flown along the road, we would have been sitting ducks as well as the truck. Let's go."

The column reformed with the able men assisting those who were wounded. The speed of advance was much slower.

"You'd reckon our guys in the village would've seen the attack and send out some trucks to collect us."

"Why George? Jerry will soon be back with some of his mates and trucks make easy targets. And remember they don't know how exhausted this mob is. We'll get there."

"Look Al." said Simon pointing to the rear. "It's Bluey."

"Yes, and he's moving rather fast. Shit that's all we need, some ground troops in pursuit."

The Major spoke quietly. "Don't you worry about that Corporal. We may be tired but we can still fight, and if the Hun wants a stoush, then we'll give him one."

"Well we'll soon know Sir. Here comes your bushranger."

Bluey trotted up to the leading group. Ignoring the officer, he fired his question at Al. "What the hell did you do to the truck?"

"A Jerry plane caught up with us. No time to hide it. What's your news?"

"Nothing really. I saw the smoke and flames and guessed you were in trouble so I came galloping to the rescue. It seems I can't leave you blokes alone without you getting yourselves into hot water."

"Sorry about that mate, but what were those shots we heard?"

Bluey snorted. “A Jerry patrol. Four of them were following your tracks. Mind you, all they had to do was follow the noise of the truck. I don’t think they intended to attack you, just wanted to see who you were and where you were going. They misjudged your speed and were getting a bit too close so I persuaded them to return to their unit. Well one got away. I really need more rifle practice Al. I’m very rusty.”

“Aircraft!” came the cry and the men threw themselves against the bank of the roadway.

“Oh Christ,” shouted George. “There’s a dozen of them up there.”

“Come on men,” called the Major. “We’re home. Those are our chaps. Move on. Not far to go now.” He was right. The column was close to the outskirts of the village and as battle was joined overhead the men walked into the Allied lines.

The Scots Captain who had farewelled the Section from the Château, was waiting. He and the Major exchanged salutes and then embraced each other warmly. It was obvious they were old friends.

“Thought I’d lost you this time Hamish.”

“You nearly did Robert, you nearly did, but thanks to these bushrangers we made it.”

The Captain turned to Al. “Thank you Corporal. Your plan worked even better than we had hoped. A great show. Right Hamish, I’ve a convoy of trucks ready to move you to the rear. The Australian divisions are taking over this sector. It’s all hands to the pump. British, Canadians, New Zealanders, French and Australians. We’re going to stop the Hun right here.”

“I hope to God you do Robert. By the way, these signallers have lost their truck and they also have some very recent intelligence on the enemy. Can you fix them up with a ride?”

"Already arranged. They're to report back to the Château. I'll take them with me. You and Angus can use the staff car. Your men will go in trucks to Amiens."

"Fine Robert. I'll just go and say a few words to them and then see you back at the Château. A wee dram or two is called for I think."

"Aye Hamish, I'll have a bottle ready. You ready Corporal?"

"Ready and keen to be off Sir. This area is going to be very busy in a short while and, much as I would like to be here to see Jerry cop a hiding, I can think of better things to do."

* * *

The men in the back of the truck were very tired but the swaying and lurching of the vehicle made it difficult to rest. There was, however, an even greater distraction to sleep than the motion of the truck. It was the military scene they were passing through. The roads were lined with infantry moving north. They strode forward with a look of determination etched into their features. This was the battle they had waited for, anticipated, hoped for. This would be the end of the German advance and the beginning of its rout. To many of the men it was a reward for all the privations and suffering they had endured. No one spoke or thought of defeat.

As the miles passed, the procession going north seemed to further increase in numbers. Occasionally the truck would pull off the road to let a convoy of artillery pass. On a few occasions tanks rumbled by It was a thrilling, inspiring sight. A huge army on the move.

The many delays encountered on the road meant it was late afternoon when Captain MacDonald and the four sappers arrived at the Château. As they alighted from the back of the truck, Bluey swore.

"What's up mate?" queried Al.

"That's what's up," replied Bluey pointing to the immaculately dressed officer crossing the lawn and heading in their direction.

"Bloody hell! Johnson! Just what we need." sighed George.

"You men. Stay where you are. I want a few words with you." The words rang out clearly and the tone indicated that Lieutenant Johnson was not in a friendly mood. Captain MacDonald stood by the truck watching.

Al called the section to attention and saluted. The salute was not returned.

"Wilson, I want answers and I want them quick. Is this the truck you borrowed from the transport depot?"

"No Sir."

"And where is your truck?"

"What's left of it is smouldering out in no-man's land. A Jerry plane caught up with us." Al's usual laconic voice had a cutting edge to it.

"You mean you lost the vehicle? What about the communication equipment? I hope you saved that."

"No Sir we didn't. We lost the lot. It couldn't be helped."

"Couldn't be helped! Corporal this is a very serious matter. There will have to be a court of inquiry into this. You were told to wait here for the arrival of the Divisional staff and when we got here you had gone off on some wild goose chase. And now, when you have finally decided to return, I find you have lost your vehicle and all your gear. Now get yourselves cleaned up and report back here in one hour. By then I should have drawn up the charges against you."

"But Sir..."

"No but's Corporal, do as I say." the Lieutenant was screaming with rage.

"Sorry to butt in Lieutenant, but there is an explanation, and these men can't go away to clean up just yet. They have an appointment to keep." The Scotsman's voice was soft but the anger was there.

"Appointment? What the hell are you talking about and who the hell are you?" It was then the Lieutenant noticed the badges of rank of the other man. "I'm sorry Sir. No offence meant. I didn't realise you were involved."

"Obviously Lieutenant. I am involved and my orders are to take these men to see the Brigadier immediately on their return from the front. Then I feel sure Intelligence will wish to talk to them. And then, I suspect they will need a bath, a good feed and some sleep. That will give you plenty of time to write up the charge sheet won't it?"

Lieutenant Johnson was lost for words. His mouth moved but no words came forth.

"Come on men, can't keep the Brig waiting. By the way Lieutenant, what is your name?"

"Johnson Sir. Lieutenant Ronald Johnson, Australian Signals."

"Thank you Lieutenant Johnson. I'll remember you." With that, the Captain turned and led the four soldiers into the stately building.

* * *

After a brief meeting with the Brigadier-General the men went to the operations room where they recounted their story.

"Tanks?" questioned one officer. "Any sign of tanks?"

"No Sir. No tanks, at least not in this sector." said Bluey pointing to the wall map.

"We've had rumours that Jerry has got tanks there. Are sure young man?"

Bluey looked to Al for support.

"Tell them Bluey."

"Well Sir, I'd some time to fill in last night, or more correctly early this morning, so I went down to their lines and had a snoop around. There were no tanks there, at least not in this particular sector."

"You had time to fill in, so you went snooping around?" The officer wasn't convinced.

"It's true Sir," volunteered Al. "He did have some spare time."

"Gentlemen," the Colonel spoke, "I think we have extracted as much information as we can expect from these four men. I am convinced there are no tanks there. You did well chaps, very well indeed. Have you got quarters allocated?"

"Yes Sir. They're near Corbie, so we would appreciate a ride if that's possible. And could someone tell our commanding officer Captain Solway what has been going on, or we might be in trouble."

"Of course Corporal Wilson. Patrick, see to that. In fact, ask Captain Solway to drop by, I would like a word with him in person."

* * *

It was an early call from Ghislaine that roused the exhausted men next morning. From under the bedclothes, Al called out, "What's the matter?"

"Sergeant King dropped in last night after you had gone to bed. He said to tell you that the Captain wants to see you at the Château at eight o'clock."

"Holy smoke," answered the now wide awake Corporal. "What time is it?"

"Six o'clock. You don't have transport so you will have to walk to the Château. The water's boiling and breakfast will be ready by six thirty. Is that all right?"

"Marvellous Gilly. Many thanks. Come on you blokes, stir yourselves."

As the men sat around eating their breakfast, the talk was mainly on what the future held.

"Johnson was really mad yesterday." observed Simon. "He'll do anything to break us up."

"Johnson is mad, we all know that," replied Bluey. "Anyhow it's up to Captain Solway to decide what to do with us, and I reckon we did all right yesterday."

"Yesterday. Was it only yesterday? It seems like a month ago."

Al stood up. "Check your gear and your uniforms. I want to put on a good show for the Captain. We'll walk the first couple of miles then march into the Château as a squad." He looked at his watch. "Be outside in ten minutes, ready to move."

Ghislaine and the girls farewelled the group at the courtyard gate.

"Will you be back tonight?" asked Yvette.

"Impossible to say young lady." answered Al. "We haven't any idea what they've in mind for us, but we'll soon know."

"We'll get a message to you somehow." enjoined Simon. "If they keep us at the Château, we might see you girls over there."

Al looked at Ghislaine. "Any chance that you might reconsider moving south?"

She shook her head. "You heard mother. You will stop the Boche."

* * *

Sergeant King was waiting for them as they marched up to the Château. Al halted the squad and turned to his old friend.

"What news from the front, Pete?"

"Seems like Jerry ran into a hornet's nest. Heavy fighting late yesterday afternoon and into the night. If the telegrams are to be believed, he's taken heavy losses."

"All in accordance with your plan eh Sergeant?"

"We do seem to have stopped him this time. But he'll try again. Anyhow what the hell have you lot been up to? Johnson is frothing at the mouth. Says you disobeyed orders, lost a truck full of special gear and a whole heap of other misdemeanours."

Al started to tell his story when the Sergeant held up his hand. “Save it Al. You’ll have to tell it all to the Captain so there’s no sense in doing it twice. Come on. Have the men fall out and follow me.”

Inside, the men were ushered into a spacious room. The walls were covered by maps showing unit strengths and positions. Captain Solway was studying a map with Lieutenant Johnson when they entered.

“Ah, the missing Section!” he exclaimed as the men came to attention. “At ease.” The Captain took a seat at a table.

“Now Wilson, take me through the events step by step. Start with your departure from Belgium.”

“Shouldn’t we start with the orders I gave to the Corporal before he left?” interjected Lieutenant Johnson.

“All right Ronald. What were your orders?”

“I clearly instructed Corporal Wilson to take these three men and the truck with its valuable equipment from Divisional Headquarters to here and await further instructions.”

“Well Corporal Wilson? Were those the instructions you were given?”

“Not quite Sir. As I recall, Lieutenant Johnson said we were to locate Divisional Headquarters and then we would be given further instructions.”

“A subtle difference eh Ronald?” queried the Captain.

“The same thing really Sir. I can’t recall the exact words I used.”

The Captain persisted. “But you didn’t issue any written orders?”

“No Sir. It was all done in a great hurry as you know.”

Captain Solway nodded. “Ah yes. Things were a bit hectic. So, there may have been a slight misunderstanding. However, let’s hear what happened.”

Al recounted the story of the trip to the Château. Bluey noted he didn’t mention the stopover at the farm. Al told of the meeting with the British staff officers and the subsequent foray to the north. He made light of problems in contacting the British troops in the dark and failed to mention Bluey's visit to the German lines. He did however, extol the value of having a mobile wireless set and expressed the opinion that it was the innovative idea to employ the Section as a mobile reporting unit that led to the success of the venture. Bluey noted the half smile on Sergeant King's face and realised that both he and the Sergeant had arrived at the same conclusion. Al Wilson was well aware that it was Captain Solway who had first mooted the idea of a mobile wireless unit. Al was also hoping that if the Captain could be convinced of the success of his idea then No.3 Section might be allowed to continue in that role. When he had finished the Captain looked up in surprise. "Is that all Wilson?"

"Yes Sir. I'm sorry we lost the truck and its equipment, but the aircraft was on to us before we could protect it."

"Last night in the mess I had a drink with a certain Major from the Scottish Regiment. He had a lot more to say about the initial contact he had with your Section, and he certainly had a lot more to say about the return to our lines."

Al shrugged his shoulders. "Oh well Sir. You know how it is. Infantrymen do talk a lot."

"Oh really Corporal Wilson? However, it seems to me that things went rather well for all concerned. I presume that, as our Divisional Headquarters were not here on your arrival, you went looking for them in accordance with Lieutenant Johnson's orders."

"No they didn't, Sir." interjected the Lieutenant.

"Oh yes they did Ronald. You told them to locate Divisional Headquarters. We weren't here so they went to find us. Right Wilson?"

Bluey could have sworn that the Captain winked at Al.

"Yes Sir, that's what we did. I knew you would be where the action was, so I went in that direction."

"Naturally."

"Sir, I protest." Lieutenant Johnson was furious. "They went off on some hare-brain scheme devised by the British staff."

The Captain raised his hand. "Ronald, before you say too much, let me tell you, that I also had another discussion last night. The British Divisional Commander and our Brigadier met and I was present. The British were very lavish in their praise of the part these men played in locating the exact position of the enemy and our Brig was very pleased because it gave him the information he needed to establish the new frontline. So far, things seem to have gone very well, so I would suggest you don't start calling this stunt a hare-brain scheme. Do I make myself clear?"

Johnson nodded.

Captain Solway continued. "Good. I'm glad we have cleared up that misunderstanding. Now for the future. It would seem from the results obtained in this particular incident, there is a role for a mobile signal section and so we shall continue to operate No.3 Section in that role. Equipment and transport are at a premium at present, so you'll need some help to re-equip yourselves. Ronald, I want you to take charge of this problem. You have the blessing of the general staff to fit out the section with the necessary equipment. So, with that backing, you shouldn't have any problems getting a new truck, wireless sets, etc. If you do encounter any opposition you can't handle, let me know. I expect No.3 Section to be fully operational by midday."

"Midday! But Sir that's only a couple of hours away," gasped the Lieutenant.

The Captain looked at his watch. "Goodness me Ronald you're right! Thank you for drawing the time to my attention. Well there's no time to lose. Off you go with your shopping list. I'll inspect the Section immediately after lunch." He rose from the table and the men came to attention. The Captain stopped in front of Al Wilson. "You push your luck Corporal. One day you'll push it too far. I wouldn't like that to happen."

"I wouldn't like it to happen Sir. I'll remember your sound advice. Thank you Sir."

The Captain smiled. "Keep your head down Corporal."

"As always Sir. As always."

"Good. Thank you men. You did well." They saluted as the officer left the room. All eyes now turned to the Lieutenant.

"Sergeant, get these men out of this room at the double. The sight of them makes me sick."

"Yes Sir. Right you men, you heard the officer. Clear off. Muster outside this building at 12:00pm."

Once clear of the building they regrouped.

"Will he do it Al?" asked Simon.

"Do what?"

"Get us a new truck and all that equipment by noon?"

Al laughed. "Yes Simon he will. You see, he'll be telling Pete King now, to get off his arse and get the gear as directed by the Captain. It sounded like a tall order, but I know the Captain and Peter King. My bet is that this decision was taken sometime last night, and Sergeant King has been using his exceptional talents to arrange for the truck and the gear to be ready. When it turns up on time the Lieutenant will take all the credit."

Bluey shook his head. "Thank God you, the Captain, and Sergeant King think alike Al. I could have sworn that the Captain winked at you at one moment."

Al looked astonished. "Whatever gave you that idea Bluey? Whoever heard of an officer winking at a Corporal? What a crazy idea!"

Bluey studied his friend's face carefully looking for a sign that Al was joking, but the Corporal kept a stern face. "Perhaps I was mistaken Al but it sure looked like a wink. What now?"

"The canteen of course. Lead on Simon. If there is food to be found, you'll find it."

* * *

A truck loaded with communications gear was parked outside the Château by 12:00 noon. The men came to attention as the Captain and the Lieutenant approached.

"You have done well Ronald. I had my doubts as to whether or not you could muster all this gear in the short time I allowed, but here it is. Well done indeed."

The Lieutenant gave the Sergeant a quick glance. "It really was quite simple Sir. A bit of push here, a bit of shove there. These stores people need a bit of hurry up from time to time."

"Right Wilson, get this stuff sorted out and in working order. Things have stabilised at the front but Jerry is bound to try again somewhere along the line. You'll operate under the direct command of Brigade Headquarters, but I expect you to use your own initiative should the situation demand. Just make sure Sergeant King knows where you are and what you're doing. Any questions?"

"No Sir." replied the Corporal.

The Captain turned to leave and then turned back. "My advice of this morning is still relevant. Keep your heads down. From all accounts, you lot have used up all your nine lives plus some."

Al nodded in agreement. "Yes Sir. We've been rather lucky. We know it, but we'll be careful Sir, very careful."

The Captain smiled. "You don't know how to be careful Corporal Wilson, but I hope your luck holds out." He returned Al's salute and departed with the Lieutenant at his side.

WHAT'S HE DOING OUT THERE?

The general feeling amongst the higher command of the Allied armies in April 1918 was that the war had reached a point of final crisis. If the German attacks could be held, then the great German war machine would grind to a halt and finally crumble. The German High Command would realise that the influx of large numbers of fresh American troops into the opposing forces would signal the end of Germany's aspirations. The German Army attack on the Somme was halted, and then began the Allied counteroffensive. Everyday, the rumours circulated that the Germans were about to surrender. Every day the battles continued.

Summer passed, autumn crept across the land and soon the icy winds that warned of the approach of winter blew across the battlefields. Peace had not come although the Allies had pushed the hated foe back to the Hindenburg Line, and in some places beyond. Soon the armies would have to stop and prepare for another winter wait.

The men of No.3 Signal Section had followed the Australian Divisions through such places as Villers-Bretonneux, Hamel,

Morlancourt, Péronne and Mont Saint-Quentin. Names that were in time, to become part of Australian Army folklore.

On a cold November afternoon Al and Bluey were huddled around a fire.

Bluey was upset. "What the hell is Johnson up to now?"

"I don't know mate. I never try to rationalise anything that man does." "You'd go mad if you tried," answered his companion.

"Well I don't like it. He arrives this morning with that toad Bailey in tow and announces he is taking over personally, and that Bailey will be part of the team. Why?"

"Bluey, calm down. I don't know why and I wouldn't try to guess. All I know is that Bert Phillips' battalion is pulling off some sort of a stunt this evening and we are going forward with them to act as spotters."

"Spotters? What sort of spotters? Artillery? Aircraft?"

"I don't know Bluey. All Johnson said was that we're going forward with a line and he will act as a spotter."

"All of us?" Bluey's anger had not abated. "You mean the six of us are going forward as one body?"

"No Bluey. Five of us. One has to stay behind at battalion HQ to man the telephone."

"No doubt that'll be Bailey's job," muttered the redhead.

Al nodded. "I thought the same as you, but Johnson said to leave one of us behind. So, Bailey is coming forward with us."

"Damn it Al. He's hardly been in the trenches. He'll get in the way."

"Perhaps, but I wouldn't leave him on the other end of the line with our fate in his hands. No mate, we're better off keeping him in our sights."

"I hope to God he gets into Jerry's sights."

"Bluey, I know how fond you are of him but let's put that aside for now. Do you want to man the phone?"

Bluey shook his head. "No. Can Simon do it?"

Al nodded. “I knew you were going to say that. Why all this attention to Simon? He can look after himself. He’s a good soldier.”

Bluey turned to his friend. “I know that Al. I guess I’m being too protective, but I can’t help feeling sorry for him. He ran away from home, or rather his stepfather kicked him out, and he joined up when he was only fifteen. He’s never had a family life. Well, not since his dad died. I’ve promised he can come home with me after the war. Mum and Dad will welcome him and we’ll find him a job.”

“That’s if he wants to go home.”

Bluey stirred the fire. “Ah yes, Yvette. That’s another matter. They’re very much in love and I promised Yvette I would look after him.”

“So you try to keep him out of harm’s way?”

“Try. That’s the right word Al. I have tried, but you know as well as me, that Simon has pulled his weight in every stunt we’ve been in. He hasn’t been living a very sheltered life has he?”

“He’s been as much a part of the team as you or me.”

“Or George. George has done his share.” Bluey added.

“True. We’re a team in every sense of the word, except for tonight.”

Bluey frowned. “It’s very odd. Still, it’s only a battalion stunt, it shouldn’t be too bad. In fact, it can’t be bad at all if Johnson is coming along.”

“Yep, I guess you’re right. But keep your wits about you. I don’t like having so many people in the one place at the same time. Especially as two of them are inexperienced.”

* * *

The attack, launched by the battalion just after sunset, had been preceded by a short artillery barrage. And after some fierce hand to hand fighting the infantry, using Mills bombs and bayonets forced the enemy back to his reserve trenches. The enlarged Signal Section established a post in the ruins of an old German pill-box to the western side of the captured trench from where they could look along its length. Four of the men crouched amongst broken slabs of concrete while Al Wilson perched on the rim of the ruin and gave a running commentary on the action. Lieutenant Johnson manned the telephone and relayed the corporal's messages to headquarters. Occasionally he asked to be connected to divisional headquarters and on these occasions, he passed a colourful description of the attack, stressing at times the grave danger of the situation.

A lull came over the area as the Australians braced themselves for an expected counter-attack. They didn't have long to wait before the enemy artillery began to shell the area. Amid the thunder of exploding shells, Al suddenly cried out and toppled backwards.

Bluey and George scrambled to him.

"Dowson." screamed the sheltering officer. "Get up there in Wilson's place. I must know what's going on."

"Then send Bailey up there. My mate's been hit and needs help."

Johnson gasped at the insubordination but motioned to the frightened Bailey to take up the look-out post.

"How bad is it Al?"

"Not good Bluey. There's something sticking into my head. I can't see."

Bluey looked with dread. Al was right. A piece of shrapnel was protruding just above his right eye.

"Pull it out mate." whispered the wounded man.

"No chance Al, I haven't a clue how far in it has gone. You'll have to go back to the first aid post."

"Never make it mate. I can't see and it hurts like hell."

"Don't be stupid Al. I can't touch it. George here will lead you back, it's your only hope."

"What sort of a hope do you reckon I've got? Jerry shells raining down and me blind. I won't be running very fast, and what about poor old George?"

"Don't you worry about me Al Wilson," responded George. "I'll get you back, and anyhow, I never did like running."

"George?"

"Shut up Al," snapped Bluey. "You're wasting time. Come on George, let's get him to his feet." They carefully got the wounded man upright. Bluey looked at the older man. "You sure you want to go George? I could take him and you stay here?"

George shook his head. "You've got more trouble cooped up in this hole than there is out there. Don't fuss. I'll get him home safe and sound. Tell Simon we're coming back and need some help. You ready Al?"

"Ready George, or as ready as I'll ever be. And you Bluey, keep your bloody head down and that temper of yours under control."

"Oh shut up and get moving," was the curt response. Bluey watched as the two men slowly disappeared into the gathering dark. He turned and crossed to the telephone. "Tell battalion HQ we're sending back a wounded man with escort," he snapped.

"You seem to have forgotten who's in charge here Sapper Dowson. I'm not here to send your messages and who gave Wilson permission to leave his post?"

"He's wounded, badly wounded, and it's probable that he and George won't make it back. Send the bloody message or else get off that telephone and let me do it. Then you can get up there and act as a spotter, which I believe is your job anyhow."

The Lieutenant looked at the angry face and then at the rim of the ruins. "All right Dowson, I'll tell HQ. You relieve Bailey as spotter. His reports so far have been incoherent."

"I'm not surprised seeing it's dark out there. But if it means getting away from you, I'm happy to relieve the fag."

With that parting shot, Bluey climbed over the rubble to where Bailey was crouched. "Piss off stupid," he snarled. "Your mate down there wants your company."

Bailey quickly scrambled down to relative safety at the base of the rubble.

After a while, Bluey heard a noise behind him and Lieutenant Johnson appeared out of the darkness. He had the telephone set in his hand.

"Anything happening Dowson?"

"Nothing I can see or hear. They've stopped bombarding but they don't seem to have launched a counter-attack. It's very quiet."

"Good. Let's hope it stays that way. I've been recalled to HQ. I'm taking Bailey with me and I'll send out someone to keep watch with you. Here's the phone."

Bluey took the instrument and set it down. "Don't send Young out here. Get a battalion sapper to come out."

"If that's what you want." replied the officer as he slid out of view.

Bluey pondered on these words. They were too obliging. They seemed to hold a hidden threat, but he couldn't think of what the threat might be. He checked his rifle and then turned to stare out into the dark. See what you're looking at, know what you hear. He smiled. Good advice Dad, very good advice.

* * *

He awoke as dawn broke and instantly shuddered with alarm and disgust. Alarmed that he might have missed something that would've been important to his mates in the infantry; disgusted that he had allowed himself to fall asleep while on duty. He looked to see if his companion had noticed his lapse, but there was no one there. Confusion now crept into his mind. What had happened. Why was he here alone in no-man's land? It didn't make sense. He raised himself up and looked along the enemy trench. Vacant except for the German dead. No Australian infantry, no Australian bodies. He was very much on his own in a most inhospitable environment. He looked back towards the Australian lines but could see no sign of movement. Why? None of it made sense.

He then remembered the telephone and mentally castigated himself for not thinking of it sooner. He spun the handle and held the handset to his ear. The line was dead. He tried again with the same result. Slowly he replaced the handset and looked back to the friendly trenches. "Come on Simon, you know I'm here, answer me." he whispered to no one. "Think man, think fast and clearly," he told himself. "You're missing something obvious. You must be here for a reason, so think."

In his mind, he went over the events of the previous night. The attack, Al Wilson's wounding, the withdrawal of Lieutenant Johnson and the wimp Bailey. Bluey shook his head. "Come on, wake up man," he told himself. "This is serious. What did that bastard Johnson say: I'll send out someone to keep watch with you, and I said don't send Simon." That was all. But no one had come and so Bluey had maintained the watch on his own, right through the night. He had heard noises coming from the direction of the captured trench but these he took to be the evacuation of the wounded and the men preparing for the inevitable counter-attack next day. Suddenly he realised the noises were in fact the infantry withdrawing. Why the hell hadn't Simon called him, and where the hell was Simon now?

* * *

At that very moment Simon and George were making their way back to the headquarters communication centre from their dugout after a quick wash and a hearty breakfast.

"Strange that Bluey didn't come back to the dugout last night." remarked Simon.

"I expect he went to the field hospital to check on Al. You know how close those two are." replied his companion.

"Possibly, but why would he stay there all night?"

"Who knows? Perhaps Al didn't make it, although the doctor I saw wasn't all that concerned."

"Not concerned? I saw him when you came in George. He had a piece of metal sticking out of his skull and you reckon that's not bad?"

"Easy Simon. I was as worried as you, but the doctor said on first glance it didn't look as if it had penetrated the bone. They were going to open it up and see. That's when I left to come back to you, only to find you had left HQ and returned to the dugout."

"Yep. Lieutenant Johnson said there was no need for me to hang around as the stunt was over and all our chaps were pulling back. He said Bluey was following them and bringing in the wire. I tried to call him but no answer, so I guessed he had disconnected the phone."

"Well, he might have stayed in HQ. We'll soon know. By the way, what day is it?" asked George.

"Monday."

"No Simon. What's the date? I seem to completely lose track of time these days."

"11th of November." replied Simon. "But who cares? One day is the same as any other out here. To me there are only two things to consider, day time and night time. They come around in a very regular fashion."

"Can't argue with that. There's Pete King and that infantry Sergeant outside HQ. Looks like they want to talk to us." The two sappers crossed to where the two Sergeants were standing.

"Where in the hell have you two been?" demanded the Signals Sergeant.

"Back in the dugout Sarge." replied Simon. "Lieutenant Johnson said to stand down after the recall was ordered last night."

"And where is Dowson?"

"We don't know. We think he might have gone back to the field hospital to check on Al Wilson."

Both Sergeants frowned. "Al Wilson. Did he cop a hit?"

"Yes Sarge." replied George. "A piece of shell caught him in the head. I took him to the rear but the doctors thought he would be all right."

"Did you see Dowson come in Sapper Young?" Peter King was angry and worried.

"No Sarge. Lieutenant Johnson said he was following him and reeling up the wire. I called Bluey but got no response. Then Johnson said to push off, so I did."

The two Sergeants looked at each other. Bert Phillips spoke. "Are you sure that's what the Lieutenant said?"

"Yes Sarge. He said Bluey was following him and Bailey. What's wrong? Something's wrong!"

"You're dead right there Young. Something is very wrong. Come up here and have a look."

Simon stepped up to the periscope. "What am I supposed to be looking for?" he asked.

"Your mate Dowson." replied Sergeant King.

"Bluey? Out there?" Simon pressed his eye to the glass. "Oh shit. It's Bluey. What the Christ is he doing out there?"

"A very good question. We were hoping you could tell us."

Simon stepped back and George peered through the glass. "It's Bluey all right." he said, then his face lit up. "He's got the telephone alongside him. Call him up Sarge and ask him."

"We're not altogether stupid Morbey. We've tried but the line is dead. A shell must have cut it last night. But that's not the problem. He's out there and it's now daylight. I doubt if he could make it back without Jerry knocking him off. It's too far and too open."

"Let me call him up by light Sarge." Simon volunteered.

"No Young, not at the moment. If we start flashing a light in his direction, Jerry will tumble to the fact that someone's out there. I doubt if they know he's there and that might work in our favour. Ah, here comes Captain Solway and your favourite Lieutenant. Perhaps we'll now get some answers."

The men saluted the officers and Sergeant King quickly told the Captain of the situation. Captain Solway applied his eye to the periscope to make his own assessment of the situation. "Damned odd Ronald. Why would he stay out there?" he asked.

"I really can't say Sir. When we got the recall message I told him to follow us, reeling in the line as he came. I even volunteered Bailey to assist him but he said he preferred to do it on his own."

"That's strange."

"What's strange Sergeant King?" asked the Captain.

"Well it takes two men to reel up a wire. Why would Dowson decline the assistance of Bailey?"

Lieutenant Johnson smiled. "Bailey and Dowson are not on very friendly terms Sergeant, and Dowson is fiercely independent."

The Sergeant was puzzled. "True Sir, but he's a professional, and he would know how difficult reeling up would be on his own."

"Maybe he had decided to stay for some strange reason of his own. He was very upset when Wilson was wounded." Lieutenant Johnson was not convincing.

"Are you suggesting Ronald that Dowson is suffering from some sort of shock?" Captain Solway asked.

"Well Sir, he was very upset. Perhaps in his mind he has decided to wreak his revenge on the enemy for what happened to Wilson. He was very disturbed."

The Captain looked at Sergeant King. "You believe that Sergeant?"

The Sergeant thought for a moment. "Hard to believe, but it's possible I suppose. Why else would he stay out there on his own? The question is, what are we going to do about him? I don't think

Jerry knows he is camped on their doorstep, but if or when they do find out, he'll be in big trouble."

Captain Solway nodded. "I think he's in big trouble now. Where's Wilson and Bailey?"

"Wilson's in the field hospital but we don't know how bad he is. Bailey has returned to the Château. He found the events of last night very stressful Sir." The Lieutenant appeared nervous as he awaited the Captain's reply.

"Stressful Ronald? Your man Bailey has hardly seen the war up till now. But I'm not concerned with him. It's Dowson I'm worried about. Anyone got any ideas?"

"May I speak Sir?"

"Yes Young, I'm ready to listen to anyone."

"Sir, what about we get the artillery to put some smoke between us and Jerry. Land it right up close to that trench. That will give Bluey the cover he needs. Just before the shells start landing, I'll call him by light and tell him to start running with the arrival of the first shell."

The infantry Sergeant shook his head. "Won't work Sir."

"And why not Sergeant Phillips?"

"All firing has been put on hold. The message we got last night when we were recalled, said to hold our position and not engage in any hostile action. That applies to everyone. The artillery have stood down. I spoke to them on the phone to see what the hell was going on. The usual rumours of course, but there is obviously something in the wind."

Captain Solway nodded. "I saw the signal, Sergeant. You're right. There's to be no hostile action until further notice. Perhaps the Germans have been given the same orders. If they have, Dowson is safe. But I don't think we can bet on that. No, for the moment let's hope Dowson keeps his head down and Jerry doesn't find out he's there. I wonder why he's there. It's all a bit of a puzzle."

* * *

Huddled amid broken pieces of concrete, Bluey watched the enemy trench and his own lines. There was no movement in either. His mind wandered back over the past weeks, months, years. He remembered the first time Al Wilson told them about the two days in your life. All the original squad had been there, and now they were all gone, even the indestructible Al Wilson. Now it was his turn. Stranded in no-man's land, he had no illusions as to which day it was. He was not frightened but very angry.

"Come on Fritz." He eased his rifle into the space between two blocks of concrete. He could see clearly along the line of the enemy trench. "Come on Fritz, let's get it over and done with" he snarled.

* * *

In the enemy reserve trench, joined to the front trench by a communication passage, the tired and dispirited German troops waited for the next assault. They had been taken by surprise by the Australian attack the previous evening and had suffered heavy casualties in the fighting. They had had enough of the war, and survival was their only goal. Their commanding officer, Major Edel Manfried of the Prussian Regiment had fought against Australians in many places at different times, and knew their ferocity. He felt this time there would be no escape, no prisoners taken. He looked up as two men in green uniforms pushed their way along the trench.

"Good morning Major," said the tall dark Captain. "Had another setback have we?"

"As you can see Captain Von Monsor, we have been savaged by an Australian raiding party. But if you would like to stay, no doubt you will be able to help when they make their assault on this trench." The sarcasm in the Major's voice did not escape the attention of the Bavarian officer.

"You say they're waiting out there to attack Major? Why are they waiting?"

"I don't know, and frankly I don't care. But when they come we'll give as good as we get."

"Brave words Major, but you and your men don't look like you could resist a bunch of one-armed cripples. This place is a disgrace and so are your men. Come on Herwin, let's see if these phantom Australians are really there." Captain Von Monsor had little respect for the exhausted Prussian infantrymen. He checked his rifle and moved forward along the communication passage.

His companion followed a few steps behind him. As they neared the junction of the frontline trench and the communication passage, Rolt held up his hand and put his finger to his lips. The two men listened intently but could hear nothing. Rolt shook his head. "The birds have flown Herwin. Come."

They advanced silently. At the junction Rolt gestured to Herwin to stay back and with a light jump he leapt forward into the trench. His eyes darted from side to side, the rifle following his movement. Then he looked up and to the right. He threw his rifle to his shoulder, but before he could squeeze the trigger another shot rang out. The German officer lurched backwards. Herwin sprang forward and seized Rolt by the arm and dragged him into the passage. "Major!" shouted Herwin. "Stretcher bearers at the rush." He knelt beside Rolt. He did not need to unbutton the tunic to know the wound was serious.

"He's good Herwin." The Captain was gasping for breath. "A snap shot and he got me. Fast and accurate. Too fast for me."

"Be quiet Rolt. The stretcher bearers are coming. We'll soon have you in hospital. I'll see to the Aussie sniper."

"Be careful my friend. He's good, and you know..." Rolt paused to gasp for breath. "You know Herwin, I seemed to recognise him. He was outlined against the sky. But then how could I?" He started to choke.

"Be quiet Rolt. Save your strength. The stretcher bearers are here." The men gently lifted the Captain onto the stretcher and followed Herwin back to the reserve trench. “Major, get onto the telephone. We need a field ambulance to meet us at the other side of the wood. Tell them it’s a priority.”

The Prussian officer looked at the man on the stretcher. “I don’t think so Sergeant.” he said.

“Don’t think what, you fool?” snarled Herwin.

The Major ignored the insult. He had seen death in all its forms over the past three years. “Your Captain is dead. There is no priority for an ambulance.”

“Dead? Oh my God no, not Rolt.” The distraught man knelt beside the stretcher and took his brother’s hand. At the touch, he knew that the Major had spoken the truth. “I don’t give a damn about your priorities Major. Get that ambulance and have Captain Von Monsor conveyed to the hospital. Do it or else I’ll see your name reaches the highest levels of this army.”

“It’s of little consequence to me Sergeant, but you can have your ambulance.” He motioned to one of his men to pass the message.

“It’s not my ambulance Major, it’s for Rolt. I’m staying here and, with your help, we are going to exterminate the bastard that killed him.”

* * *

The observers in the Australian lines saw Bluey rise up and fire. The sound of the shot brought men running from the command post.

“Have they found him?” questioned Captain Solway.

“Sort of Sir,” replied Simon.

“What do you mean, sort of?”

“Well Sir, someone must have stuck his head out in the trench and Bluey took a shot at him. I don’t know if he hit anyone, but now they sure know he’s there.”

“Damn him. Why didn’t he lie low?”

"Who knows why Dowson does anything these days?" answered Lieutenant Johnson. "They'll bomb or blast him out of there for sure and we can't do a thing about it."

"What the hell's going on?"

The voice startled the group who were all looking towards Bluey's hideaway. They turned and Sergeant King exclaimed. "Al Wilson. What are you doing here? God man, look at yourself. You should be in bed, in a hospital."

Al Wilson did look a sight. His uniform was caked in blood and dirt. He wore no helmet and had a bandage around his head.

"Sorry Pete, but I couldn't stay back there. There are all sorts of rumours rushing around, and if this is going to be the end then I want to be here with my friends, not in some stuffy hospital."

"Bluey's in trouble Al," blurted out Simon.

"Trouble? What sort of trouble? What's going on?"

"Come into the headquarters Wilson and I'll try to explain." said the Captain. "You two," pointing at George and Simon, "keep your eyes open and let me know if anything happens."

Al accompanied the two officers and Sergeant King into the communication dugout where the Captain explained the situation to an incredulous Al Wilson.

"It can't be true Sir. Bluey wouldn't stay out there for fun or revenge, or however you want to describe it. Peter, you don't believe that do you?"

"I don't know what to believe Al. I've given up trying to figure it out. The only thing that matters is that he is over there and now Jerry knows he's there. It's not looking good."

"Christ what an understatement! My mate is out there on his own in Jerryland, and we're leaving him there. I can't believe it."

"Corporal Wilson. We've been together a long time." The Captain's voice was low in tone but hard in delivery. "This is not a good situation. We don't know how or why Dowson came to be out there, but I can tell you one thing, I'm not risking other lives to save his. To throw your own philosophy back in your face, let's see what day it is in the life of Sapper Dowson."

"It stinks Captain Solway. It stinks and it's all my fault."

The Captain tilted his head to one side. "Your fault? How do you work that out?"

"Because, Sir, I got in the way of a piece of flying metal. If I hadn't left the stunt none of this would have happened."

Captain Solway shook his head. "A poor excuse Corporal, but we won't hold it against you. It's a waiting game now, but the odds are not looking good for Dowson."

Al stood up. "Mind if I go and look Sir? Maybe I can figure something out."

"You wouldn't try to pull one of your crazy stunts would you Wilson? I meant it when I said I won't risk other lives to save Dowson. To lose him is bad enough. To lose any more would be tragic."

Al held out his hands in a gesture of hopelessness. "What can I do? But I want to keep my eye on him. I reckon Bluey will make a move on his own."

"Off you go then. Sergeant King, you had better go too, just to keep an eye on things. And Al, I'm sorry, really sorry. He was..." the Captain checked himself, "he's a good man."

* * *

Twenty minutes later the quiet atmosphere of the front was shattered by a fusillade of shots. The two officers ran from the dugout.

"What the hell's going on?" demanded the Captain.

"It's Wilson Sir." replied Sergeant King. "He arranged with the battalion to give him covering fire and there he goes. He's gone to join Dowson."

"Covering fire? Get me the battalion commander. The orders were explicit, no hostile action of any kind. The brass are going to go raving mad when they hear this. And what does Wilson think he's going to do now he's out there with his mate?"

"I don't know Sir. He spoke with Sergeant Phillips and then when my back was turned, he took off with the infantry giving him covering fire."

A bewildered infantry officer appeared running along the trench with Sergeant Phillips close behind. "Will someone tell me what's going on?" he demanded.

"You tell me Lieutenant. It was your men who opened fire," countered Captain Solway.

"Not true Sir." interjected Sergeant Phillips. "My men were testing their weapons. They didn't aim at the enemy trenches. In no way could their actions be regarded as hostile."

"Really Sergeant Phillips? And can you also explain how Corporal Wilson seemed to know that your men were about to test their weapons?"

"Sir, I wouldn't know what Corporal Wilson knew or what he planned to do. Al Wilson is his own man, always has been."

The Captain sighed. "Yes Sergeant Phillips. You're right. He is his own man. But tell me, do you have a schedule to test your weapons again this morning?"

"No Sir."

The Captain's eyebrows raised. "Is that so. Then how does Corporal Wilson intend to return?"

"As I said Sir, Al Wilson is his own man. I have no idea what his next move will be, but we're not involved."

The Captain nodded. "Thank you Sergeant." He turned to the Lieutenant. "Why would your men risk all sorts of consequences as a result of breaking the orders, just for the sake of one Corporal?"

The Lieutenant shook his head. "I think Sergeant Phillips had better answer that one Sir."

"We didn't do it for Al Wilson Sir. Well, he asked the favour, but we did it for Bluey Dowson. He saved the battalion at Messines from our own artillery. We owed him one and Al reminded us of that." The infantry Sergeant saw no reason to offer an apology for the actions of his men.

"I see Sergeant. Thank you for being so frank with me. Any soldier would know that rifles have to be tested from time to time. It was a routine test of course. Thank you Lieutenant. I would like to say that your men have been a great help but I can't. Now I have two men out there instead of one. I can't see what we gained from that little exercise."

* * *

The volley of shots startled Bluey, who had been concentrating on the enemy trench. He looked across the uninviting land and was surprised to see someone running at full speed.

"Bloody hell, it's Al!" he exclaimed. "Run Al, run like hell." Instantly he remembered the danger and threw Lucy to his shoulder but no enemy appeared. As far as he could tell, the shots from the Australian trenches drew no response from the Germans.

An exhausted Al Wilson threw himself into the scooped out hollow at the base of the concrete pile. He lay there puffing and panting.

"Getting a little out of condition are we?"

Al looked up. "You're a stupid bastard Bluey Dowson. What the hell are you doing out here? Can't you ever do as you're told?"

Bluey frowned. "Look mate, I'm over the moon to see your somewhat disfigured face. I was convinced you had cashed your chips in last night, but if you came all the way out here just to abuse me, then I suggest you turn round and hightail it back to the lines."

"Hang on until I get my breath. Any sign of Jerry?"

"No, and that's very odd." replied Bluey. "I hit one a while back, but so far there's been no reaction. And they didn't try to pick you off as you ambled over."

"Ambled? I'll give you ambled. Hang on, I'm coming up." Slowly Al scaled the slabs of concrete until he was sitting just below where Bluey kept his watch.

Bluey stretched down his hand. "Welcome my friend. I think the sight of you running across that paddock was one of the greatest sights I've ever seen. I really did think you were a goner last night."

Al firmly grasped the offered hand. "Can't remember much about it myself, but George says you took charge. Thanks pal. Now what the hell is going on? Why are you out here?"

Bluey kept his eyes on the enemy position as he related to Al the events of the previous night.

"You sure Bluey? Absolutely sure? Johnson told you to wait for someone to come out to join you?"

"That's what the man said. 'I'll send someone out.' I remember I made the point of asking him not to send Simon."

Al looked back towards the battalion lines. "No wonder the Captain is tearing his hair out. Someone is bending the truth back there."

"What does Bailey say?"

Al shook his head. "No one has seen hide or hair of Master Bailey since last night. Hell, I nearly forgot."

"Forgot what?"

"My reason for coming out here." Al reached into his tunic pocket and produced a wad of envelopes. "I stopped off at the mail office after I left the hospital and picked up your mail. They get cranky if Sapper Dowson doesn't collect his mail. Its sheer volume tends to block the system."

"You beaut. Thanks mate." Bluey took the battered envelopes and stuffed them into a pocket.

"Aren't you going to read them?" Al asked.

"Hardly the time or the place is it? Any minute Jerry is going to come roaring out of that trench and the only thing that might stop him or at least slow him down is Lucy."

Al stood up and looked into the trench. "Here give me that rifle. Even I could hit something at that range. You climb down and read your mail. We're not going anywhere, at least not for a while."

Bluey smiled. "What a way to end the war. Just the two of us against the German Army. Odds certainly favour us don't they?"

"You're gone in the head Bluey Dowson. Sit down and read your mail while I hold the Hun at bay."

Minutes passed with the silence disturbed only by the rustle of paper as Bluey read his mail. Suddenly he gave a strange cry. Al looked down at his friend who was staring into space. Tears were gathering in his eyes.

"What's wrong mate?" he whispered.

"It's from Dad. Mother passed away last month." Bluey spoke in a stifled whisper.

"Jeez Bluey. That's tough. I'm really sorry mate. To think I came out here to bring you that sort of news."

"Don't blame yourself mate for bringing bad news. I'm really very grateful to you. Poor old Dad. He'll be lost without Mum. Lucy has been over there helping out. That's good."

"From what you've told me about home, I think he'll have lots of support from friends." Al looked back to the Australian trenches. "Speaking of support from friends, we could do with some right now."

"Are we going to get any?"

Al shook his head. "There's something very odd going on. Bert Phillips' battalion was told to pull back and not to commit any further hostile act. What sort of a war is that?"

Bluey shook his head. "I don't try to work things out nowadays Al. I just do as I'm told, and try to stay alive. Here, give me the rifle. The way you shoot, I reckon I'm in as much danger as the enemy. And where the hell is the enemy? What's he up to?"

* * *

In the dugout of the German reserve trench the atmosphere was tense. "They are fools, damn fools, the lot of them." ranted Sergeant Herwin Von Monsor.

"I doubt it Sergeant." replied Major Manfried. "Higher Command probably has a better idea of what is going on than we do. Our orders are very clear. Stay where we are, make no advances, take no hostile action. It appears to me that peace is at hand. Thank God!"

"Damn you Major. Is that all you can think of? Peace? What about victory? Do you ever think of that?"

"Victory? You're a fool Sergeant. An honourable peace is all we can hope for. The only other alternative is a crushing defeat. We have lost the war Sergeant. Each day we get weaker and the enemy gets stronger. Our hopes of winning were finished with the arrival of the Americans. Even a fool like you should have been able to work that out."

The Sergeant looked around the room. No friendly faces here. "Damn you all. You saw what happened this morning. Rolt shot down in cold blood. All I want is for a few volunteers to back me up and I'll settle the account."

"You won't get your volunteers from my Regiment Sergeant, and after all those phone calls I don't think you're going to get help from anyone else. Why don't you just settle down and wait like the rest of us?"

The Sergeant glared at the Major and returned to a slit in the sandbags through which he could see the hated enemy lines. Quietly to himself he whispered, "Don't fret Rolt. I will avenge your death, those bastards will pay. That's a promise."

AN UNSAVOURY AFFAIR

It was mid-morning when Colonel Payne arrived at the battalion headquarters. He looked smug and self-satisfied. Captain Solway and the battalion commander went forward to meet him.

The Colonel was in a good mood. "Good morning gentlemen. What a lovely day it is."

The two officers looked at each other.

"Yes Sir, it is. Very quiet, but we do have a problem."

"Problem Solway? What sort of a problem?"

"Well Sir, one of my men got stranded out in no-man's land last night and now he's been joined by Corporal Wilson. The enemy knows they're there, as Dowson took a shot at something or someone."

"He what?" exploded the Colonel. "The orders were very, very clear. No hostile action of any sort."

"Ah, yes Sir. The orders were very clear but it appears Dowson wasn't told. For some reason, he remained at his post last night after being told to return."

"Has he gone mad? Stayed out there after being told to return? Who was in charge of this fiasco?" demanded the irate Colonel.

"Lieutenant Johnson Sir. But he insists that Dowson was given an order to reel up and return."

Colonel Payne was unimpressed. "Why didn't you phone him and re-issue the order?"

"Couldn't Sir. The line was dead. However, he'll know about the no hostile action now as Wilson is out there with him."

"Show me Solway. Where are these two idiots?"

Captain Solway led the Colonel to the viewing platform and pointed to the two figures huddled amongst the ruins.

"I see," growled the Colonel. "Well leave them there."

"Just like that Sir? Leave them there? I was hoping for your permission to give them some covering fire so they could at least try to make a break for it. We could alert them by signalling lamp."

"No lamp. No covering fire." The Colonel looked at his watch and smiled. "I'll save your men Solway. I'll save them. You'll see. Oh, there you are Johnson. Headquarters tells me that you did well last night. Good show."

Lieutenant Johnson, Simon and George had retreated from the lookout when the officers had approached.

"Just doing my duty Sir," responded the Lieutenant. "What's happening?"

"Be patient Lieutenant. Be patient." The Colonel once again consulted his watch. "I'm expecting a very important message from divisional headquarters any moment now. A very important message."

The men surrounding the Colonel looked at each other. There was something in his attitude that was different. He had a secret that he was bursting to tell them but had to wait for the all clear from higher command. If anyone suspected what that secret was, no one was game enough to speak up. Too many times in the past their hopes had been raised, only to be dashed in renewed fighting. But each hoped that perhaps this time things would be different.

Captain Solway motioned to Simon. “Sapper Young, report to the signals centre and act as messenger for the Colonel.”

“Yes Sir,” replied Simon taking off at the run.

Again, the Colonel looked at his watch. “What time do you make it Solway?” he asked.

The Captain removed a fob watch from his pocket. “A minute or so before 11:00 Sir.”

“I agree. That message should be here by now.”

As if on cue Simon emerged from the signals dugout running. “Your message Sir,” he said thrusting the piece of paper into the Colonel’s hand.

The Colonel unfolded the paper and read the message. Solemnly he folded the paper and put it in his pocket. “Well gentlemen, I regret to have to inform you that as from this moment, you’re unemployed. The war is over.”

A spontaneous cheer erupted from those in hearing range. The news passed quickly along the line and the cheering grew.

“Please Sir. Can I tell Al and Bluey?” asked Simon.

Captain Solway looked at the Colonel. “Why not,” said the senior officer. “I said that I would save them. Anyhow it’s time they came back don’t you think?”

Captain Solway grinned. “Yes Sir. Off you go Young.”

Simon forgot to salute as he left the parapet and started to run towards the two men, waving his arms in the air.

* * *

Al and Bluey were alerted by the cheering that rang out from the battalion positions.

“What the hell is going on? What have they got to cheer about?” asked Bluey.

“Could only be one thing mate and we’ll soon know. Here comes Simon. It must be all over. Look at him.”

They watched as the young man ran towards them shouting and waving his arms. A shot rang out. Simon recoiled from the blow of a bullet and crumpled to the ground.

"No," cried Bluey, "not Simon. Not now." He scrambled down from his perch and ran towards the fallen soldier closely followed by Al. On reaching the fallen soldier Bluey dropped to his knees and cradled the young man in his arms. A quick glance at Simon's chest told him that the young man's life was quickly ebbing away.

"Bluey," gasped the boy. "It's over. The war's over. We're going home, just as we planned."

"That's great Simon. That's wonderful. Now you take it easy. You've been hit. We'll get you to a hospital."

"Sure Bluey. I need to get better. Yvette's waiting. Bluey..." The rest of the words were lost for all time as Simon gave a dreadful shudder and died.

Gently, Bluey laid his friend on the ground. "Look after him Al."

Al looked at Bluey. "What's there to do?"

"Just one thing mate, and I have to do it." said Bluey rising to his feet and picking up his rifle.

"No Bluey. No. You heard him. It's all over. Finished."

"Not quite Al." With that Bluey turned and ran towards the German trench.

"No Bluey. Don't do it. Don't go in there. They'll kill you." Al screamed but in vain. Bluey leapt into the German trench and was lost to his view.

* * *

As the shot that felled Simon rang out, the cheering in the Australian trenches stopped.

"Stand to," cried Bert Phillips. The men grabbed their rifles and checked their safety catches.

"No. Don't fire," shouted Colonel Payne. "No man must fire. The war's over. Don't give them the excuse to start it again. Put your weapons away."

Everyone turned to look at Colonel Payne. His face was red with rage and his body shook. "Do as I say Sergeant. Tell the men to put their weapons away. One shot could re-ignite the powder keg."

"As you so rightly say Sir. One shot. And those bastards fired it, not us."

"No Sergeant, don't return the fire. There's obviously been a mistake. We'll sort it out peacefully."

"We might be able to do that Sir, but I don't think Sapper Dowson has a peaceful solution in mind at the moment." The Sergeant pointed to where Simon had fallen.

Everyone turned to watch as Bluey, rifle at the ready, went charging towards the enemy trench.

"Oh dear God, that madman again." breathed the Colonel. "Solway, do something."

The Captain watched Bluey disappear into the enemy trench. "It's out of our hands Sir. It's Dowson's war now, and nothing can stop him."

* * *

The Germans had seen and heard Bluey approaching. As he emerged from the communication passageway into the reserve trench three German soldiers fell on him wrenching his rifle from his grasp and crashing him to the floor. Bluey struggled and swore but it was of little use. Other soldiers moved in to hold his arms and legs. Finally, exhausted from his struggles, he fell silent. He heard a voice, a strange voice, speaking in English.

"Pay attention Australian soldier. Any further resistance on your part is useless and will only annoy me further. Nod your head if you're hearing me and understanding me."

Bluey thought for a moment, then nodded his head.

"Good. Now if I order my men to release you, do you agree not to create any further disturbance?" Bluey did not move.

"Think about it Australian soldier. You're unarmed in a trench full of German soldiers. Your enemies. You can't hurt us, but we could hurt you if we wanted to. For my part, I would like to talk sensibly to you. There are matters I wish to explain."

After a short pause Bluey nodded. The Major motioned to the soldiers who were holding him down. They released their grip and one helped him to his feet. He found himself face to face with a Prussian officer.

"I am Major Edel Manfried of the Prussian Regiment." said the officer quietly. "Who are you?"

"Sapper Dowson, Australian Army."

The Major looked puzzled. "A member of the Signal Corps, and yet you come charging in here like an infantryman?"

"I had a score to settle with you bastards. The war is over, but you still killed my friend."

"Not quite true. Your friend was shot by Sergeant Von Monsor." He indicated Herwin who was watching the scene with interest and loathing.

"You miserable bastard." Bluey spat the words out. He then noticed the different uniform and its badges. "A bloody sniper! Just like the one I knocked over back in Belgium."

Herwin stiffened. "You shot someone wearing a uniform similar to this?" he asked.

Bluey nodded and then looked at the ragged scar that ran along the side of Herwin's face. "Oh my God, it's you."

"What are you talking about soldier?" asked the Major.

"Another friend of mine was shot in cold blood in Belgium. He was carrying a white flag. I set a trap for the man who killed him and I thought I had got him. But the bloke who tried to ambush us one day while running a line said I had only wounded the bastard. It was you, wasn't it?"

Major Manfried spoke. “We know all about the unfortunate incident concerning the soldier with the white flag. I want you to know that my regiment had nothing to do with what happened.”

“How could you do this to me?” snarled Herwin, running his finger along the scar. “And how could you shoot Gunther? You’re a miserable signalman, a messenger boy. You wouldn’t know how to use a rifle.”

“Wrong, you piece of shit. I can use a rifle and better than your mate this morning. Tell me, did I get him fair and square in the guts?”

Herwin stared at the young redhead. “You shot Rolt? You?” his voice broke and in a swift movement he swung his rifle towards Bluey. The men in the trench reeled from the percussion of a shot. Bluey stood still, his mouth open as Herwin slumped against the wall of the trench. His eyes projected hatred and he tried to speak but no words came. Slowly he subsided to the floor. The Major stood and watched Herwin’s last gasp before returning his pistol to it’s holster.

“You see Australian, there are still some people of honour in the German Army.”

“Yeah Major. I see that. And I’m very pleased that one of them was here today. I thank you.”

The Major frowned. “Your friends will have heard the shot and they may well assume that we have executed you. That could cause problems.”

Bluey scratched his ear. “You could be right. You had better let me go back and explain. Better still, you come with me, and we’ll both explain.”

“Ah. You want to take me in as your prisoner?”

“No Major. Let’s just walk over there together and sort things out. But I do need my rifle.”

The Major looked at Bluey then at the body on the ground. “Yes, we must not let this unfortunate incident turn into something much greater." He spoke in German and the man holding Bluey's rifle removed the magazine and handed the weapon to the young sapper.

"Don't trust me Major?"

"Just being careful. If someone over there wants to restart this war, I don't want you around with a loaded rifle. We have seen how good you are with that weapon. Come. Let's try to placate your friends. I suggest you go first."

* * *

At the sound of the shot the Australian infantry again manned the sand-bags.

"A nasty business Colonel. First Sapper Young and now Sapper Dowson. I don't think I like peace." Captain Solway was a very angry man.

"It's all your bloody fault Solway for leaving Dowson out there in the first place."

The Captain looked at Lieutenant Johnson. "At least Corporal Wilson will have some answers. I'm sure Dowson will have told him why he didn't come in."

The Lieutenant frowned. "He probably cooked up some cock and bull story Sir, just to cover his actions. Why is Wilson waiting out there with Young?"

"I suspect, like us, he is waiting to see what happens next," replied the Captain.

"Sir." Sergeant King was pointing towards the enemy trenches. "It's Dowson. They didn't shoot him."

The Colonel levelled his binoculars. "You're right Sergeant. It is our man and he's got a prisoner. A Jerry officer. Tell the men to relax. It's all over."

The men nearby let out a yell which was taken up by others further down the line. Al Wilson walked across to join his friend and together the three men walked towards the Colonel and his group.

Bluey, looking pale and drawn, came to attention in front of Colonel Payne and saluted. "Sir, this is Major Manfried, Commanding Officer of the German Regiment facing this line." The Major saluted the Colonel.

"Good God Dowson, are you mad? Your prisoner is armed. Seize him."

Bluey held up his hand. "Sir, he's not my prisoner. The Major expressed a wish to meet with you to discuss how the ceasefire should be implemented. As for his pistol, I'm sure he'll hand it over to you if it worries you."

"Of course Colonel Payne. It was thoughtless of me to carry it." The Major unbuttoned the flap on the holster and carefully withdrew the weapon. He held it out butt first to the startled Colonel.

"Thank you." said the Colonel, accepting the proffered sidearm. "You speak English."

"Yes Colonel. Do you speak German?"

"No I don't Major, never had any need to learn it. Before we go any further, there are a few things you need to explain. Your men shot one of mine after the deadline. I take a very serious view of the matter."

"It's finished Sir?" interjected Bluey.

The Colonel looked at the sapper. "Oh, finished is it Sapper Dowson!"

"Yes Sir. One of the German soldiers was very upset by an earlier incident and in his anger, shot Sapper Young. I hasten to add that he was not a member of Major Manfried's regiment and the man disobeyed orders."

"Really Dowson? And you consider the matter closed just because the man was angry and disobeyed orders?"

"No Sir. The man responsible was found guilty of the crime and executed. I saw the sentence carried out."

"Is this true Major?" asked the Australian officer.

The German officer nodded. “Regrettably it is Colonel. I hope the action taken against the culprit is sufficient to enable our discussions to proceed.”

The Colonel paused. “Right Major. It was a most unfortunate incident but you seem to have taken the necessary action. We'll consider the matter closed. It just so happens that I have an excellent bottle of Scotch with me and I suggest we adjourn to the battalion HQ to discuss how we're going to implement orders I have been given.”

Led by the battalion commander, the Colonel, the German officer, and Captain Solway walked to the battalion command centre.

Al Wilson tugged at Bluey's sleeve. “Come with me mate. There's something I want you to look at. George, get a couple of stretcher bearers and bring in Simon.”

The two signalmen walked back towards the enemy lines.

“What are you looking for Al?” asked Bluey.

“Well my friend, the first thing I wanted to do was get you away from Johnson. I know how angry and upset you are. The second thing is, I wanted you to see the wire. Here it is.”

In silence, the two men walked along the telephone wire that had connected the signal centre to the observation post. They stopped, both looking down at the clean break in the wire.

“It was cut Al. That's a clean cut. The bastard.”

“Steady Bluey. Perhaps the enemy did it.”

“No Jerry came out of those trenches last night. Johnson cut it, and Bailey must have seen him do it. Why?”

Al looked at his friend and spoke softly. “Why? You ask why? Because he hates you. You have frustrated him at every turn. You and the others. The harder he tries to impress, the worse you make him look. Still, It's all over now. It's finished. Right Bluey?”

Bluey was staring at the small group of men standing on the observation platform. “Yeah Al. It’s finished.” but his words were without conviction.

“Right, let’s go back. And keep a lid on your emotions.”

“I’ll try Al, but I want to see Bailey. He’s got a few questions to answer.”

“Forget it pal. He’s no better than Johnson.” The two men were walking towards the lines. “Let it go mate, we’re going home. Soon you’ll see Lucy and your Dad. Don’t do anything silly.”

The redhead didn’t answer.

“Dowson.” snapped the Lieutenant. “You have caused a great deal of trouble and anguish by disobeying orders and staying out there last night. As a result of your stupid actions, Young has lost his life.”

“Sir,” interrupted Al, “I don’t think this is the time or the place to discuss the matters of last night.”

“Shut up Wilson. This man has a lot to answer for. Well Dowson. We’re waiting.”

All eyes were on Bluey but it was Al who saw the slight movement of the rifle as Bluey eased it forward in his hand and his thumb eased off the safety catch.

“You left me there to die, you bastard. You said you would send out another signalman. You or your poofter mate Bailey cut the wire. You left me out there and as a result Simon died.”

“Steady Bluey. He’s not worth it.”

“You’re right Al, he’s not worth it. He is a worthless cur and doesn’t deserve to live.”

Bluey’s action was swift but Al was quicker. He knocked the barrel upwards and the bullet passed over the head of the panic-stricken officer.

“You’re dead Dowson. You’re dead. Attempted murder in front of witnesses,” gasped the shaking Lieutenant.

The Colonel and his guests came hurrying from the dugout.

"Now what's up? Who fired that shot?" demanded the Colonel.

"An accident Sir." Sergeant Phillips was quick to speak before Johnson could gather his wits. "Looks like Jerry removed the magazine from Dowson's rifle but left one shot in the spout. Dowson didn't realise this and accidentally discharged the weapon."

"Damn it man." The Colonel turned on Captain Solway. "I've told you time and time again, soldiers carry weapons, not signalmen. This could have been a most unfortunate incident. Dowson, give that rifle to Sergeant Phillips before someone gets hurt."

Bluey held out the offending weapon which Bert Phillips accepted.

"Right. Now Major, you'd better get back to your regiment in case they think we've shot you. God what a business that would be. Ha Ha."

The German officer didn't appear to understand what was so funny, but shook hands with the Australian officers and set off for his own lines.

"Good heavens Ronald, you look very shaken. Still I've got the remedy for that. You can ride back to Divisional Headquarters with me and we'll have a Scotch or two on the way."

"Thank you uncle."

The assembled group stared at the Lieutenant.

"Oh dear Ronald, you've let the cat out of the bag. Still it doesn't matter now." The Colonel was very relaxed. "Yes gentlemen, Ronald is my sister's boy. I said I'd make a man of him and it looks like I've done a pretty good job. Right Solway, I'll see you at the Château tonight. It should be quite a party. What a day. What a wonderful day. Come on Ronald, let's go." Those remaining behind saluted the senior officer who had his arm around the shoulders of his nephew. "Carry on men. You did well. All of you," were his departing words.

* * *

No one spoke for a while as they watched the car lurch off along the uneven road.

Captain Solway looked at Bluey. "You let me down Dowson."

"I beg your pardon Sir?"

"I said you let me down. For months, I have been arguing with Colonel Payne that you're as good a rifleman as any of his infantry and now you accidentally let off a round which seems to have given Ronald Johnson a terrible fright."

"Yes Sir, I'm sorry. It was very careless of me."

The Captain looked from man to man. "You're all a bunch of liars, but I don't think I want to know any more. Sergeant King, you come with me to Divisional Headquarters to arrange some sort of communication plan for the new arrangements. Wilson, you and your Section can stand down until further notice. I know where to find you if I need you." Without waiting to acknowledge their salutes he turned and strode off, followed by Sergeant King.

Bluey turned to Bert Phillips. "Thanks Sergeant."

"Don't thank me digger. If you'd hit the bastard it would've been a different story. Thank Al Wilson. He saved you. And here, keep your bloody rifle. Your Captain was right. You're as good with a gun as any infantryman. Take care Al, we finally made it." The Sergeant thrust out his hand which Al clasped tightly.

"Bye Bert. See you back home."

"Yeah. Back home. Boy that sounds good, doesn't it?"

* * *

It was early in the evening when Bluey reached the farm and found Al and Ghislaine seated in the kitchen. After embracing Ghislaine he sat down opposite his friend.

"What have you been up to Bluey?"

"Oh, there were things I had to attend to. We buried Simon in a plot near Peronne, then I hitched a ride to Corbie, got deloused and collected some clean clothes. Then I went to the Salvation Army hall to write a few letters. Where's George?"

"He reckoned it was a bit too quiet around here so he took off for Corbie to celebrate. Are you all right? It's been one hell of a day."

Ghislaine placed a bowl of soup in front of Bluey and sat next to him. "Al told me about your mother Bluey. I'm so very sorry."

Bluey patted her hand. "Thanks Gilly. Where are the girls? Does Yvette know about Simon?"

"Yes Bluey. Al broke the news to us early this afternoon. There was much crying from all three. Yvette was devastated. But she's young and she'll get over it."

"Where are they now? It's not a good time for young ladies to be out and about. There are a lot of very drunk soldiers out there."

Ghislaine nodded. "I know Bluey. I didn't want them to go out, but an officer from the Château arrived by car with a request that the girls assist with serving drinks and food this evening. Apparently, there is a party planned for the officers' mess. The officer promised they would be returned here by car, so I agreed. At first Yvette said she wouldn't go, but then she changed her mind."

"Well, as long as they're being escorted home I guess it's all right Gilly. Mind you that party could go on all night." Bluey paused. "There's someone coming across the yard now."

Ghislaine rose to go to the door, but before she could reach it, the door swung open and Yvette stepped into the room. With a cry of anguish, she ran across the kitchen and threw herself into Bluey's arms. The three adults waited for her sobbing to subside and as she dried her eyes on the handkerchief offered by Bluey, her mother asked, "Where are the other girls Yvette?"

"They are still at the Château. I couldn't stand it anymore. Everyone is having such a good time. It's not fair, is it Bluey?"

"No Yvette, it's not. I'm so sorry, I tried to keep my promise." He shook his head. "I'm sorry."

Yvette gave him a hug. "I know Bluey. Al has told me all about what happened and how good you were to Simon. It wasn't your fault."

"Yvette," said her mother sharply, "if your sisters are still at the Château, how did you get home?"

"I ran Mother. I ran all the way. Don't fuss, it was perfectly safe. All the soldiers are in the towns drinking. I came along the back roads. I didn't see anyone."

"That's not the point young lady. I gave specific instructions that you girls were to be escorted home."

"Oh Mother, don't go on. I told Marie and Nicole that I was leaving. I couldn't ask any of the officers to drive me here. Anyhow they are all too drunk."

"Perhaps Bluey and I should go over there and see the girls safely home." suggested Al.

Ghislaine shook her head. "No, they'll keep together and will be all right. The only one I was worried about was this young lady. And now she's back safe and sound."

"Of course I am Mother. You worry too much. Now I think I'll go to bed and leave you old folk to talk."

Yvette rose and walked around the table to kiss the two soldiers and her mother. As she reached the door she turned and said, "Bluey, it was Lieutenant Johnson's fault that Simon died, wasn't it?"

Bluey studied the tear-stained face before replying. "Perhaps Yvette. Things were a bit confused this morning."

"But it was the Lieutenant's fault you were left out there."

"It seems that way Yvette."

She paused. "It was his fault, and that led to Simon's death. But my Simon will now rest in peace." She left the room, gently closing the door behind her.

They all stared at the door.

"She's very upset," Ghislaine said. "Now, I know you two don't usually drink anything stronger than your precious tea, but perhaps on such an occasion you might join me in a glass of wine?"

"All right by me." said Al. "What about you Bluey?"

"Why not. What about your mother Gilly? Would she like to join us?"

"Mother wants to be on her own. I think she is disappointed that Germany still exists. She wanted the Allies to march into Berlin and burn the city to the ground. Anything less she regards as failure on the part of our leaders."

Ghislaine had just set the glasses on the table when a knock was heard on the front door. She opened it to find Captain Solway and Sergeant King standing outside. "Oh good, more welcome guests. We need cheering up. A glass of wine gentlemen?"

"Thank you Ghislaine," replied the Captain. "I'm sorry to intrude, but we have a problem which I need to discuss with Wilson and Dowson."

"A problem Captain? I thought all our problems disappeared this morning."

"No Al, they didn't. I wish they had." The weary officer sat down at the head of the table and accepted the glass of wine Ghislaine offered.

"Perhaps I should withdraw from this gathering?" Ghislaine had remained standing.

"No Madame, it's your house and you may be able to help." replied Captain Solway. He turned to look squarely at Bluey. "When did you get here Dowson?" he asked.

"You mean here at the farm?"

"Yes."

"Well Sir, I guess it was about forty minutes ago."

"I can vouch for that, Sir. So can Gilly."

The woman nodded her head in support of Al's statement.

"Fine. Now Dowson, tell me what you have been doing, and where you have been, since I left you at the front this morning?"

"What's this all about Captain?"

"Never mind Dowson. Just answer the question. I'll explain later."

Bluey thought for a moment. "Well, after you left, I packed up Simon's gear and then went to see the padre who was at Divisional Headquarters. He agreed to bury Simon. A grave-digging party was working at a small plot outside Peronne, so we took Simon there and buried him. The chaplain offered me a lift back to Corbie, which I accepted. I returned Simon's gear to the store. I then drew a set of clean clothes and went to the bathhouse."

"Did you see anyone there that you know?"

"No, not at the bathhouse. The padre can vouch for me up till the time we reached Corbie and the clerk in the store would confirm that I returned Simon's gear."

"After your bath, where did you go?"

"I went to the Salvation Army hall and wrote some letters."

"Oh yes, I heard about your mother. I'm sorry."

"Thank you Sir, but what's this all about?"

"All in good time, all in good time. Captain Solway continued his questioning. "Now, how long did you stay in the Salvo's hall?"

"About two hours I would think. There was a padre there who took my letters. He said he was returning to England tomorrow and offered to post them for me. We had a bit of a chat. His name was Robert Hall. He could vouch for me being there."

"So you haven't been near the Château?"

"The Château? No, why should I go there?"

The Captain looked at Sergeant King who had been taking notes. "Well Peter, what do you think?"

The Sergeant shook his head. "I believe him Sir. There's no way he could have gone to the Château and still done all these other things."

"I agree. So that puts you in the clear Dowson. Now Al, what about you?"

"Me? What about me? Sir, what the hell is all this about?"

The Captain held up his hand. "Soon Al. Now what were your movements this afternoon?"

"George and I caught a ride to Corbie, arrived there about 2:30pm, and then walked here. I guess we arrived here about 3:00. We had a shower and changed. Then Gilly fed us. George left for Corbie about 4:30. Ghislaine can vouch for us, except when we were in the shower." The joke drew no smiles.

Captain Solway again looked at his Sergeant. "Well Peter?"

"I think Sir you had better tell them. They may be able to shed some light on the matter if they know what has happened."

"I agree. Right. Earlier this evening there was an accident at the Château. A serious accident. Lieutenant Johnson fell from an upstairs window, broke his neck and died."

The captain watched to see the reaction to the news.

After a while Al spoke. "I'm not going to waste words by saying how sorry I am to hear the news, because frankly, I'm not. However, I'm confused as to all the secrecy and all the questions. You said it was an accident."

"I understand Al, but we had to do it this way. Colonel Payne, Johnson's uncle, is not convinced it was an accident. He is extremely upset and made some rather wild accusations after the body was discovered. I gather Johnson had told him all sorts of things about No.3 Section during their drive back to the Château this morning."

"Including the fact that I threatened him I suppose."

"Yes Dowson. There was talk that you'd threatened him. Colonel Payne wanted to send the military police to question you, but I prevailed upon the Brigadier to let me do a preliminary investigation. I felt sure you had nothing to do with Johnson's death, but I needed to confirm my beliefs."

"We understand Sir, and thank you for looking after our interests." Bluey frowned as he spoke. "What about that creep Bailey? He still has a few questions to answer."

"Ah yes, Bailey. Now there's another puzzle. You see, Bailey is also dead."

"What?" chorused the two signalmen. "How? When?"

"Good questions, and if we knew the answers they would probably explain everything. Bailey was found in the stables of the Château just after Johnson fell from the window. He had been shot in the head. There was a service revolver beside him."

"Suicide?"

"One possibility, Al. Could have been suicide, could have been murder. Thank you Madame." Ghislaine had decided that the glasses on the table needed refilling.

Sergeant King took up the narrative. "There are a number of possibilities in this affair. Let me run through them, and please make comments as I go. The first. Sapper Bailey pushes Lieutenant Johnson out of the window and then goes to the stable and commits suicide."

The Captain interrupted. "The question that springs to mind is, why would Bailey want to kill Johnson?"

Al looked at Bluey. "You care to comment Bluey?"

"No, you know the story, and you're better with words than me."

"Right. Well Sir, it's a long story but I'll keep it as brief as I can." Al described the confrontations between Johnson and No.3 Section culminating in the incident at the observation post the previous evening. "I believe the version as given to me by Bluey is correct. But the only person who could confirm that is, or was, Bailey."

"But it works both ways Al. If Johnson and Bailey stuck together, then it would be the word of two against one and, Johnson being an officer, people would tend to believe his version."

"Correct Sir. But there is another factor. They were lovers."

"Lovers!" Captain Solway almost fell off his chair. "Peter did you hear that?"

"Yes Sir." Sergeant King was staring straight ahead, not daring to look at his superior officer. "It's a problem I have been wrestling with for quite a while. I knew it, everyone in the Sergeant's mess knew it, the troops knew it."

"Then why in thunder wasn't I told?" demanded the Captain.

"That was my problem." replied the Sergeant. "Should I tell you, or was it better if you didn't know. Let's face it Sir. If I'd come to you and said that Johnson and Bailey had an unnatural relationship, what would you have done?"

Captain Solway shook his head. "I don't know Peter. Was there any proof, or was this just speculation?"

"Oh it was real enough. But if you mean were they ever caught in bed together, I can't say."

"Gilly, I think the Captain needs another drink."

"Ah yes, thank you. You're right Al, I do need something. So, let's see what we have now. Two men engaged in an unsavoury affair, and that relationship further complicated by their involvement in the incident last night. So, they could have met in Johnson's room, had a quarrel, ending with Bailey pushing, throwing Johnson out of the window. Then, realising what he'd done, he stole a pistol, went to the stable and shot himself. Is that what you're saying?"

Al spoke. "It's one possibility. Another is that Johnson arranged to meet Bailey in the stable to get their stories straight about last night. Suppose Bailey refused to go along with Johnson. So, Johnson shot Bailey to prevent him speaking out. Then Johnson went back to his room, realised the enormity of what he had done, and jumped from the window."

The room was quiet as the two possibilities were considered.

Sergeant King spoke. "There is a third possibility."

"What's that Peter?"

"The two possibilities you have put forward are based on the assumption the two deaths were linked. I mean physically linked. Assume Bailey did commit suicide, shot himself without having any contact or discussion with Johnson today. Perhaps he felt jilted, or had a guilty conscience, who knows. Then what happened to Johnson? Did he too have a guilty conscience and commit suicide, or was he so drunk he accidentally fell. Or did someone help him?" added the Sergeant.

"I'm sorry Peter, you've lost me."

"What I'm saying Sir, is that there may have been a third person involved. Someone who pushed Johnson out of the window. He had plenty of enemies."

"True Pete. He was not a popular man. But the man who had the most reason to settle a score with Johnson is here, and we know Dowson didn't go near the Château."

"So, what do we have. Let's take Bailey first. Bailey either suicided, and there are a number of reasons why he might take that course of action, or he was murdered. If it was murder, then Lieutenant Johnson had a strong motive. We don't have any other suspects that we're aware of."

"Go on Peter. You're behaving like a real Sherlock Holmes."

"Thank you, Sir. So now we come to Lieutenant Johnson. There are three possibilities. He fell accidentally, he deliberately jumped, or was pushed. If he was pushed, then Bailey has to be the prime suspect, the other suspects have alibis." The Sergeant returned his notebook to his pocket. "The question is, which story is the truth of

the matter?"

Captain drained his glass before replying. "Something we don't have to worry about Peter. My concern was to make sure Dowson wasn't involved and he wasn't. The rest is up to the military police, although I suspect it'll be recorded as a suicide for Bailey and an accidental fall for Johnson. That should keep people happy. I think when I tell the Brigadier what I now know, he'll quieten Payne down. And talking of keeping people happy, we had better get back to the Château and head off the bloodhounds." He stood up. "Thank you Madame Pruvost for your kind hospitality."

"Thank you, Captain, and thank you to all your men for what you have done for my country. We'll never forget the Australians. Will we see you again before you leave for home?"

"I take that Madame as an invitation to return and I'm sure I'll be able to find time to join you for one of your splendid concerts before we pull out."

Ghislaine smiled. "We would like that, and of course Sergeant, you are also invited."

"Thank you Madame. I'll look forward to it. Keep your eye on these two rascals. I've never seen them touch a drop of grog before tonight. They might be a problem."

Amid laughter Ghislaine accompanied the officer and the Sergeant from the room. Al and Bluey sat staring at the table.

"It's a strange world Al. Two hours ago, I would have cheered if someone had told me that Johnson and Bailey were dead. I would have said, 'serves them right'. But now I just feel empty. It's all been such a horrible, useless waste. What did happen to them?"

Al looked up. "I think we should consider the matter closed, finished. You heard the Captain. It's a problem for the military police, not us. Well, look who's here."

Ghislaine returned to the room with Marie and Nicole. The girls gave each soldier a kiss and a hug.

"Did you hear the news about the officer who fell from his room at the Château? It was awful."

"Yes Marie. We heard. And why did you let Yvette come home alone? You know what my instructions were. Stay together."

"Oh she wasn't enjoying herself Mother. Every now and then she would burst into tears and then she said she was leaving and off she went. Is anything wrong? She is here isn't she?"

"Yes, she's here. In bed asleep, and that's where you two are off to. Say goodnight."

The girls gave their mother and the soldiers a goodnight kiss. At the door Marie turned and addressed Bluey. "Can I ask a question Monsieur Bluey?"

"Of course Marie. What is it?"

"Will you milk the cow tomorrow morning?"

Bluey nodded. "You can sleep in Marie. It'll be a pleasure."

The door closed behind the girls and Ghislaine started to collect the empty glasses.

"I guess we'll turn in now." said Al. "Bluey hasn't slept for the past forty hours so I doubt if that cow will get an early milking."

"Al? Bluey?" She didn't turn to face them. "Is it over? I mean, is that the end?"

"Yes Gilly, that is the end. The end of the war, the end of everything."

She turned. "Really? You're not just saying that?"

"No Gilly, it's over. Now you go off to bed. You look very tired."

She gave them both a light kiss. "Thank you both." and quickly left the room.

"Al, is it all over?"

"Yes mate. I know what you're thinking, but I reckon it's finished. The damned war, and the Johnson affair. It's time we went home and started a new life."

"Home. A new life. That sounds great to me, but it's not going to be easy. I mean after what we've been through. How do you tell the folks back home about what happened over here. I mean, how could they ever know what it was like?"

"They won't Bluey. They'll never understand, and we'll never forget. It's something both parties will have to adjust to. But don't worry, Lucy will be there waiting and she'll help."

"We were lucky Al. I mean we're here, we survived."

"Lucky? That's one way to describe it. Me, I still believe in the Arab. Our bad day didn't come. God I'm tired. What's the time?"

Methodically Bluey extracted his watch from his pocket. He stared at the precious timepiece. "You're right Al. It's time to go home."

THE MILITARY POLICE

Bluey awoke to a strange noise. He sat up in bed, tilted his head. He smiled. It was children laughing, a sound he hadn't heard for a long time. He looked around and was surprised to see Al still sleeping. Normally Al was shaved and dressed long before any of the Signal Section stirred. Bluey thought about this and the answer came to him, it was Tuesday, 12th November 1918. This time yesterday there was the senseless fighting and killing of World War 1, today the world was at peace.

Another noise came, a gentle lowing of a cow waiting to be milked and fed. Bluey rose and pulled on his clothes. Ever since the Section had been billeted at the farm, it was Bluey's task to milk the two cows. It was a chore he enjoyed as it reminded him of home. Gilly, the lady of the house, had left the milk bucket at the kitchen door. Bluey picked it up and went to the outer barn where two hungry cows greeted him. He'd just commenced the milking when Al Wilson appeared. "Morning Al. I don't think I've ever had an audience before, but you're very welcome to observe and if so inclined, take over?"

"No way Bluey! I wouldn't have the first idea on how to extract milk from those poor animals. Even if I tried, I'm sure the beast would object."

"Probably not Al. Remember you're doing them a favour by relieving them of a heavy udder. Anyhow you could make yourself useful by putting the billy on and brewing up a cuppa?"

"Already underway Bluey, however listening to George snoring I don't think he wants to be woken for a brew right now."

Bluey smiled. "I wonder where he went last night?" Al paused for a moment. "Well, he told me he was going to the canteen in Corbie for an ale or two. I don't blame him. It was a day to celebrate but I didn't feel in the festive mood, not after what happened to Simon. What a way to finish the war after all we'd been through."

Bluey stopped milking and looked at his companion. "It wasn't fair, was it? Either Johnson or Bailey or perhaps both have something to answer for. That wire had been cut and I reckon that one of them was responsible." Bluey returned to his milking. The Corporal nodded. "You'll get no argument from me on that score but it's all water under the bridge now." Al turned to leave the barn. Again, Bluey stopped milking. "So that's the end of it?" asked Bluey.

"Yep," replied Al, "that's the end of it, but it'd be nice to know what happened at the Château yesterday. However, I guess we'll never know." Al departed and left Bluey to finish his chore.

* * *

A short time later Bluey entered the room that'd been adapted as a living space for the soldiers. At the table, Al was pouring two steaming mugs of tea. Bluey left the milk bucket next to the door which led to the kitchen and crossed to the table. "Always a luxury to start the day with a hot cuppa," he said as he slumped into a chair.

"No argument from me," replied Al. "I still marvel at our good fortune at finding this billet. What a pity Sam isn't here to take the credit. He always maintained that it's his command of French which persuaded Gilly to take us in."

Bluey smiled. "Sam, and all those questions. I don't know how Jacko put up with it. He never stopped asking questions."

"Just think about it Bluey. Jacko wasn't one for making conversation but with Sam as his mate all he had to do to be sociable was to answer Sam's never-ending questions. He never had to think of something to say. That suited Jacko and we all should be grateful that he kept Sam occupied for most of the day."

There was a knock on the door and the lady of the house appeared.

"Good morning gentlemen. I thought I heard voices."

"Morning Gilly", the men said in unison.

"Thank you, Monsieur Bluey for the milk, I knew I could depend upon you. I hope you gentlemen will join the girls and myself for breakfast. I am having a little trouble getting them started today but they should be ready by now."

"It will be a pleasure Gilly, but don't expect George to join us. He seems to have had a long night and needs his beauty sleep. We think he may have overdone his celebrating."

"Perhaps Monsieur Al, but you soldiers have every reason to celebrate. It's just so sad that the others are not here with you. You were always such a happy group. We were so lucky that you were billeted with us."

Al laughed. "That's odd Gilly. We were just discussing how lucky we were to find this farm and the lovely people who live here."

Gilly smiled, "We were all very fortunate. Now how about some breakfast?" The two men followed her into the kitchen. There they found Gilly's three daughters seated around the table. After exchanging the usual greeting with the family, Al and Bluey took their places.

"Madame Pruvost not joining us today Gilly?" Al asked.

"No Monsieur Al, my mother-in-law has decided that now the war is over she can relax and be pampered. Now girls, what about some breakfast?"

Suddenly the bell above the outer door rang. Gilly left the room to see who could be calling at such an early hour. "Don't tell me they have managed to restart the war?" quipped Bluey. "Not funny mate," his companion replied.

The door opened and Gilly led a Sergeant and two other soldiers into the room. The red caps they wore made it easy to recognise them as Military Police. Al rose to his feet. "Well, look who's here. Looking for a free breakfast Charlie?"

The Sergeant looked at Al. "Al Wilson! It's been quite a while since our paths last crossed. So, this is where you've been hiding. Looks like a very nice set up but then you always did have style."

Al made a mock bow. "Thank you, Charlie. Now let me introduce you to our hostess. Gilly, this tower of virtue is Sergeant Charlie Morris, guardian of the law and all that is good. Charlie, this is Madame Ghislaine Pruvost and her family. They have been wonderful friends to our Section for the past two years."

The Sergeant made a bow in the direction of Gilly. "You have my deepest sympathy Madame if you have had to billet this unruly mob for so long. Such service must surely be above and beyond the call of duty."

Gilly looked bewildered. "Unruly? My men have been perfect guests and I won't hear you say otherwise."

"Relax Gilly," Al was smiling broadly. "Charlie and I go back a long way and his poor efforts to make a joke are well known. However, I am curious as to the reason for this surprise social call."

"Sorry Al, it's not a social call, I'm here on business."

"Really Charlie, I can't think of any possible business the Military Police might have with this happy household."

"My understanding is that Sapper Morbey is a member of your Section?"

"Correct Charlie but he is indisposed at the moment."

"Indisposed or not, I wish to talk with Sapper Morbey now." The tone of the Sergeant's voice suggested his reason for wanting to speak with George was serious.

Al realised that the Sergeant was in no mood for small talk. "Well Sergeant Morris, that might be a bit difficult now as George is indisposed and not available. Perhaps you and your men would like to join us for a cup of tea and some toast. I'm sure our hostess will oblige."

The Sergeant glared at the Corporal as if trying to decide if Al was serious or joking. "I'm not here to play games Al. I want to talk to Morbey, and I want to talk to him now. Where is he?"

"Well Sergeant, George has had a tiresome war and is now catching up on some well-earned rest. Can't you leave it with me, and I'll get him to your office later this morning? I promise he'll be there."

"Al Wilson you're testing my patience. We came here to apprehend Morbey and that is what we'll do." He turned to the two MPs with him. "Go search the barn. I suspect that's where you'll find him."

"Steady on Charlie. This is a private residence, and you have no right to send your men rampaging through it. As it seems very important for you to talk with George, I'll ask Sapper Dowson to fetch him." Bluey stood up and moved towards the door.

"Not so fast Sapper Dowson. My men will accompany you. We don't want Sapper Morbey doing a runner."

Al shook his head. "Doing a runner? Charlie what's this all about? George hasn't committed any crime and he's certainly in no condition to run."

"Al, I don't like this any more than you do. I'm just doing my job. So, get Morbey and we'll be on our way."

Bluey and the two policemen left the kitchen. "Right Charlie, a cuppa while we wait?"

The Sergeant smiled for the first time. "Thank you. A cup of tea would be most welcome. Al, I know you always do the right thing for your men, but my orders are to apprehend Sapper Morbey and hold him for an investigation into two serious offences. I respect the rights of the owner of this farm but the apprehension of Morbey is of paramount importance. If he is sheltering here, it is important that I remove him before he does any more harm."

Al shook his head. "What the hell are you talking about? What two serious offences?" Al stopped speaking as George appeared in the doorway firmly held by the two MPs.

Sergeant Morris switched his attention to George. "Soldier what is your name and serial number?"

George answered and then asked, "Al, what the hell is going on?" Al shook his head. "George, it is obvious there's been some sort of stuff up somewhere along the line. Don't worry, we'll soon get it sorted."

Sergeant Morris shook his head, "I hope you're right Corporal Wilson, but I doubt it. There are a lot of unanswered questions."

"Such as? How can anyone answer questions when we don't know what George is accused of doing. You haven't told him what he's being accused of."

Sergeant Morris ignored Al. "Sapper Morbey, you are charged with that on Monday 11th of November 1918 you did murder Lieutenant Johnson and Sapper Bailey of the Australian Army."

"Murder!" shouted Bluey. "Murder! You're mad. George never went near the Château yesterday. How could he be responsible for the death of those two rats. He was never near the place." The famous Bluey temper had risen to new heights.

"Steady Bluey." Al recognised the signs and gave a silent word of thanks that Bluey no longer had his faithful rifle at hand.

"George, tell the Sergeant you didn't go near the Château yesterday and we can soon sort this out."

"Sorry Al but I did go to the Château yesterday. Plenty of people would've seen me but I didn't have anything to do with what happened to Johnson and Bailey. I swear I didn't."

Sergeant Morris held up his hand as if directing traffic. "That's enough talk. We're taking Sapper Morbey to headquarters. I suggest all of you refrain from any further remarks until he has a lawyer. You could be doing him more harm than good. Thank you Madame for the offer of tea. Now we'll be off." With that, the police escort wheeled George around and they left.

The two soldiers and the Pruvost family sat still, eyes riveted on the door, as if they expected the Sergeant to re-appear and announce it was all a practical joke.

"Bloody hell Al," Bluey asked, "what do we do now?"

Al shook his head. "Well, if it's all right with Gilly, I suggest we have breakfast. This could turn out to be a long day."

TIME, OPPORTUNITY AND MOTIVE

It was a quiet breakfast after George and the MPs departed. So many questions but no answers. Several times Bluey began to speak but was stopped by Al. "Bluey, we all want answers, but we'll have to wait until we can talk to Captain Solway or Sergeant King. Hopefully they'll be better informed than we are."

"I understand that Al, but the whole thing is so stupid. George wouldn't hurt anyone, even scum like Johnson and Bailey. It's a horrible mistake."

Al nodded, "I agree, but why did he go to the Château? He admitted he went, but why?"

"I don't like that Sergeant Morris. He's a nasty bit of work if you ask me."

"No, you're wrong Bluey. Charlie Morris is a fair man. I've known him for quite a while. He's just doing his job and a fairly thankless one it is. No one has a good word for the Red Caps. Let's get on the road and see if we can't sort out this mess. Thank you, Gilly. A lovely meal."

"You are easy to please Monsieur Al. Will you join us for dinner tonight?"

"Delighted to accept Gilly." He stood and headed to the door followed by Bluey. Gilly continued, "And you will bring Monsieur George home with you?"

Al turned to look at his hostess. "Gilly, we'll try." And with that, he and Bluey departed.

* * *

Al and Bluey walked to Corbie. There was little conversation as each was deep in thought. They made their way to the Australian HQ. To their surprise, Sergeant Peter King was standing outside Captain Solway's office. "Well, Al Wilson, you certainly took your time getting here! The Captain and I had a wager on just how long it would be after the visit of Sergeant Morris."

"I didn't expect the Captain or you would be out of bed this early," replied Al. "Don't you know the war is over?"

Sergeant King shook his head. "The war might be over but there is little peace at the Château. Come on, the Captain is waiting. "The Sergeant led them into Captain Solway's office.

A sombre-looking Captain Solway was seated behind a desk. A wave of his hand indicated the three men should take seats opposite him. "I should say good morning, but I don't think there is much good about it. Now, fill me in on what you know about this affair."

Al paused as if he were gathering his thoughts. "I think you probably know more about the situation than Bluey or myself, Sir. We had no idea that George had gone to the Château yesterday afternoon. When he left the farm, he said he was going to Corbie to have a pint or two. I assumed that's what he did. What puzzles me is, if someone had seen him at the Château yesterday, why did they wait until today to come forward?"

"Good question. It seems the Mess Manager saw Morbey and Bailey arguing in the main passageway yesterday afternoon. He intervened and Bailey ran off. He reprimanded Morbey and escorted him off the premises. He thought that was the end of it. Then, this morning at breakfast, he heard Colonel Payne talking about the deaths of Lieutenant Johnson and Sapper Bailey. The Mess Manager told Colonel Payne he'd seen Sappers Morbey and Bailey arguing and that was all it needed for the Colonel to rush to the Brigadier demanding Morbey be arrested."

"Two men arguing hardly warrants arresting one for murder! Surely what the Brigadier needed to do was order an investigation. He'd need something more concrete than an argument before ordering the arrest of George."

Captain Solway nodded. "I agree, and I made representation to the Brigadier along those lines, but he said the lawyers would sort it out in due course. If you ask me, the Brigadier just wanted Colonel Payne off his back."

Bluey was angry. "We don't need lawyers. If the Military Police are competent then they'll investigate, get to the truth and drop the charges."

"I have no doubt the MPs are competent Sapper Dowson, but I think they'll be operating under severe pressure from higher authority in this instance. And what is the truth?" Captain Solway had just finished speaking when his phone rang. He answered and listened. He told the caller ten minutes would be fine and replaced the receiver.

"Well gentlemen, things are moving. That was Lieutenant Whyborn. He's a lawyer attached to HQ and has been appointed as Morbey's defence lawyer. He'll be here in ten minutes, so save your questions until then."

"Do you know him Sir?" asked Sergeant King.

"No, I don't," replied the Captain, "but soon we all will. And while we're waiting, I have another matter to discuss. It concerns us all. The question of going home. The decision has been taken to repatriate our troops based on first-out, first-home. Simply put, it means your sailing date for home will be judged on when you arrived here, or in many cases Egypt. So, Peter and Al, as you were in the first convoy in 1914, you will be at or near the top of the list."

"Don't forgot yourself Sir. We all came over in the same ship. Dear God, it seems so long ago."

"You're right Corporal. A long time ago, and a lot of water has flowed under the bridge since we sailed from Albany."

"And a lot of blood," chimed in Bluey. "I wonder what the chiefs have in mind to keep me occupied until my number comes up?"

"Don't worry Dowson. They'll find some way to keep you busy. They always do. There is one other matter. Sometime soon, you'll receive your embarkation instructions. The documents will tell you the name of the transport and time and place of departure. However, you must register at the Australian Embarkation Assembly Point in Salisbury the day before your departure. From there you'll be transported to your ship. I cannot stress this enough - if you don't check with AEAP in Salisbury the previous day, you'll be removed from the passenger list and you'll go to the end of the queue. That could add another year to your time spent overseas. Do you both understand the importance of what I've said?"

The men nodded and Sergeant King spoke. "A man would be a complete idiot if he missed the boat home."

"Spot on Peter. Now I think we have the man we're all anxious to meet."

A tall, thin, spectacled officer walked into the room. Captain Solway rose and extended his hand to the newcomer. "Welcome Lieutenant Whybrow. Meet my team." After introductions, the lawyer sat alongside the Captain. "I think it is probably best if you bring us up to date Lieutenant Whybrow. By the way, what's your given name? We try to keep things fairly low key in this group."

"William but most people call me Bill, and I'm happy if you do the same."

"Right Bill. Let's get on with it. Are they going to release George Morbey?"

The Lieutenant took some papers from his brief case and laid them on the table. "Before I begin, I think there are some matters you should be aware of. Firstly, I am not a barrister. Before joining the Army, I was a solicitor in a small Victorian town. My court room experience consists of an occasional defence of a local who had had too much to drink and had caused a nuisance. I feel totally unqualified to conduct the defence of a man accused of murder."

Bluey's anger erupted. "Just a minute, we're talking about George Morbey. His only crime, if you can call it that, is that he was seen at the Château yesterday. There must've been dozens of people there. Are they going to be arrested?"

"I'm sorry but it's not that simple. Sapper Morbey was seen at the Château arguing with Sapper Bailey. He has admitted that. Another source has told me Sapper Bailey was threatened by members of the Section. Is that true?"

Bluey shook his head, "I guess that source is his uncle, Colonel Payne. He would say that. But I'm the one who threatened Johnson, not George."

Lieutenant Whybrow looked to the Captain for advice. Captain Solway nodded. "Calm down Dowson. Wild accusations or confessions aren't going to help. Just what is the state of play Bill?"

"The news is all bad. Higher authority wants a speedy resolution, and a trial date has been set. Sapper Morbey will be tried before a court martial on Thursday 22st of this month. I have lodged a protest that this does not give sufficient time to prepare a defence, but I suspect my protest will fall on deaf ears."

There was complete silence around the table as each man considered the implications. It was Lieutenant Whybrow who broke the silence. "I suspect some people have already made up their minds about this. Certainly, some I talked to this morning are convinced of Sapper Morbey's guilt. Time, opportunity, and motive. They're all there. And Sapper Morbey is not being very helpful. When I asked if there was anyone, he could call to support him, he said no. Although he maintains his innocence, he seems resigned to being found guilty. Unless we can find some sort of defence, I fear things will go badly. Now we know Bailey was alive when Morbey was escorted out of the Château. We need to find someone who saw him after he left the Château."

The men stayed silent. Sergeant King broke the silence. "Well Sir, perhaps we can find someone who was at the canteen and saw Morbey there, or even better still, had a drink with him."

"A long shot," said Al. "George is a quiet man, and I don't think he would join the celebrations that were going on. He would take his beer into a corner and drink alone. But it's something we must explore. We might get lucky."

"Right. That's a job for you and Dowson. Is there anything else we can do?"

The Lawyer spoke. "Sir, can you or one of your men talk to Morbey, and get him to co-operate with me? At the moment he is reluctant to say anything except he went to the Château, and he didn't kill Bailey or Johnson."

"Well Al, that's a job for you and Dowson. You two are his mates and must know him better than anyone else."

"Right Sir. Is there any problem with us having access to George?"

The Lieutenant frowned. "I'll have to take that up with the legal department. It may be the prosecution will subpoena you for evidence of an alleged vendetta against Lieutenant Johnson. If that is the case, then it wouldn't be appropriate for witnesses to meet with the accused. It may be more acceptable if Captain

Solway and Sergeant King talked to Morbey. I'll make enquiries and let you know."

"Thank you, Bill. Wilson and Dowson, see if you can find anyone who saw Morbey at the canteen. Peter, you go and see Sergeant Morris and see if you can talk with Morbey. I'm going to see the Brigadier to try and get this whole matter back on track. I'm certainly not happy the way it's shaping up." With a wave of his hand, the Captain dismissed the men.

* * *

It was late afternoon before Al and Bluey arrived back at the farm. Both were weary from an unproductive day of visiting as many Army groups as possible, in the hope someone might've seen George at the canteen. But not even the bartenders could recall seeing him.

"It's almost as though he didn't go to the canteen," said Bluey.

"No mate, don't think like that. If George says he went to the canteen for a few beers, then that's where he went. Most of those guys we spoke to wouldn't have noticed if Santa Claus was there. We have a real problem. Let's hope the Captain and Peter King have a more successful day but right now I'm all for one of Gilly's great meals and then a good night's sleep."

"I'm not sure I'll sleep - too much to think about."

"Well, you can do your thinking while you extract milk from your two friends. Or had you forgotten them?"

"Hell, I'd better get cracking and get that done before we report to Gilly. Maybe one of the cows will have some advice on how we can help George."

* * *

It was a sombre meeting next morning in Captain Solway's office. The Captain was the last to arrive and he didn't look happy. "I've just come from meeting the Brigadier and his senior staff officers. I'm very disappointed in their attitude towards the plight of Morbey. They believe he is guilty and that the court verdict will be the same.

Colonel Payne has been pushing the line that the deaths of Johnson and Bailey was a result of a vendetta by the Section. There'll be no delay in the trial date and as far as most are concerned, it is a mere formality. I'm so angry and disgusted with their attitude. The Brigadier keeps saying that justice will be done but he doesn't say what sort of justice. I can only hope that you folk have something more positive to contribute. Bill, let's hear from you."

Lieutenant Whybrow shook his head. "I've spoken to all the witnesses the prosecution intends to call, except Colonel Payne. They're simply going to place Morbey in the corridor of the Château on the afternoon of the 11th. This really is all the prosecution intends to do. Motive and opportunity are all they're looking for, and in Morbey's case, they believe they can establish solid grounds for both."

Bluey interrupted, "Sir, can't you call me as a witness? I will expose Johnson as the scum he was. I know the whole story going back to initial training."

Lieutenant Whybrow spoke, "That's exactly what the prosecution would like. Confirmation of bad blood between the Section and Johnson. You'd be helping them convince the court of a vendetta. No Dowson, you may well be right about Johnson being a bad apple, but we don't want your differences aired in court."

"So, Bill, you're not optimistic about Morbey's acquittal?"

"No. I've been hearing similar opinions being expressed by junior officers like you heard from the senior staff this morning. I don't like our position one little bit. Unless we can come up with some sort of miracle, I fear the worst."

"Let's hear from you Peter. Any miracle?"

Sergeant King shook his head. "I did speak with Morbey but with much the same result as Lieutenant Whybrow. He admits he went to the Château to speak with Bailey. He admits he briefly saw Bailey in the corridor, and they exchanged words. He says he then left the Château and went to the canteen. He didn't meet anyone there he knew. It's the same story he told Lieutenant Whybrow. He believes if he tells the court his story, they'll believe him because it's the truth."

"Al, what have you and Dowson been able to unearth?"

"We haven't found one person who can recall seeing George at the canteen. Mind you, most of them wouldn't have noticed if a kangaroo hopped into the bar. It was serious drinking time. And I don't have any suggestions as to the next step."

"We need George to give us something we can pursue, but unless he changes his attitude, we're at a standstill. Do you agree Bill?"

"Yes Captain. As I said yesterday, I don't have the expertise nor the experience to adequately handle this situation."

"Bill, no one is criticising your efforts. You were handed a poisoned chalice. I wonder how many senior lawyers ducked the case before they dumped it on you?"

"Thank you for those remarks Sir, but it still doesn't help Morbey."

"No, it doesn't, but then we don't seem able to find anything to help Morbey. Perhaps something will turn up. Let's hope so. Al, you look like you have something on your mind."

Al Wilson looked embarrassed. "I was hoping to first discuss this matter with Bluey, but I guess now is as good a time as ever to get it out into the open. This morning while Bluey was milking the cows we had a visitor at the farm – a messenger with a letter for me. A special letter. Next Wednesday I am to embark on a ship sailing for home. I must report to the AEAP in Salisbury no later than Tuesday. I'm sorry Bluey. I wanted you to be the first to hear this news, but I'll be leaving here on Friday morning."

AMEN

The statement about Al's departure stunned his audience. Captain Solway was the first to recover. "That's great news Wilson. I didn't expect the Army to get its act together so quickly."

"Yeah, just think Al, you'll probably be home for Christmas, or at least in Australian waters." Sergeant King gave Al a pat on the shoulder.

Bluey was visibly upset, "You can't go Al. You can't go, not at this time. What about George? You can't leave him. You just can't. After all we've been through, you just can't leave him."

"Now calm down Dowson," advised Captain Solway. "Corporal Wilson has earned his ride home, in fact more than earned it. And before you get too carried away about Sapper Morbey, just ask yourself what can Al Wilson do - nothing. That's what we've been discussing this morning."

"But you don't understand Sir. We're a team, always have been, and we stick together, always have. We just can't walk away from George. We have to help him!"

Captain Solway nodded, "You're right Dowson. We must do everything we can for Sapper Morbey, but what to do – that's the question. But it seems there's nothing we can do. You're suggesting that Al Wilson gives up his chance to go home just so he can sit here twiddling his thumbs. It seems you're not being fair to Al Wilson."

Al spoke quietly, "Bluey, I've been struggling with this decision all morning. If there was any way I could help George, I'd stay. But there isn't. Everyone here agrees, that unless George gives us something to chase, it's pointless our being here. That may sound heartless but it's the truth."

"Al, I've never questioned your judgement in the past and heavens knows there've been many times when I've been thankful it was you making the decisions. But after all we've been through, this is a dreadful way to finish up."

"Amen to that my friend!"

"Right!" Captain Solway sought to conclude the session. "Although things aren't looking bright, we must keep hoping and trying to find a way to help Morbey. Bill, if the prosecution isn't going to subpoena Al Wilson, do you think the powers that be might allow him to say goodbye to Morbey?"

Bluey started to interject but the Captain held up his hand. "No Dowson, I don't think it's a good idea for you to talk to Morbey. To put it plainly, I believe you're too emotionally involved and you may well lose that famous temper of yours and take it out on the MPs who are just doing their job. I think we can make out a case for Al to say goodbye. It's a long shot but Morbey might tell Al something that will help us."

Lieutenant Whybrow took his time before answering. "Captain Bob Sampson is the prosecutor. Bob is a reasonable bloke and we get on well. I will approach him with the request that Wilson be allowed to say farewell and I think Bob will probably agree, but please don't do anything to annoy him."

"Do you hear that Dowson?" asked Captain Solway. "Let's not upset anyone. We need all the goodwill and help we can find."

"I understand Sir. I don't know what I'd say to George if I did go to see him. What can you say to a bloke who is on death row?"

"Enough of that. Despite everything, we must stay positive. Okay Bill, go see your friend and let Al Wilson know the result." Captain Solway turned to Al. "If you do get to see Morbey, let him know we're all working to help him. He must not lose faith in the system. We meet here again tomorrow, hopefully to hear some good news. Off you go!"

* * *

Al and Bluey walked out of the building and stopped in the Town Square. "Right mate, I'm going to hang around here and wait for the word from Lieutenant Whybrow. Hopefully I'll get a chance to see George to say goodbye. Where are you going?"

"I know it's of no use, but I'm going to continue speaking with anyone who might've been in the canteen last Monday.There's nothing else for me to do. I'll see you back at the farm this evening. I hope you have good luck with George."

With a wave of his hand, Al turned and re-entered the HQ building.

* * *

When Al returned to the farm that evening, he found it was milking time. "A never-ending job, this milking," he observed as he took a seat on a bale of hay.

"You're right Al. These ladies don't know what a holiday is but come on, what's your news? Did you see George?"

"Yeah, I did. We had about an hour talking, mainly about his family and life before he become a soldier. We touched on the present situation, and he said something which I think is important. He was talking about the events at the Château and he said, "when we left". I jumped on the word 'we' but he quickly said it was a slip of the tongue and he meant 'I'. That was the end of any discussion about Monday so I switched to general chatter about his family. He is currently writing a letter to his wife and he wants me to carry it to Australia and post it there. He believes that if he sent it through normal channels the censors would butcher the contents."

"That could be right but surely censorship has stopped. But then I guess George has little faith in the Army after what he's going through." Bluey stood and removed the milk pail. "Come on Al, let's get cleaned up for dinner. For me it's been another frustrating day. No one saw George at the canteen."

Al followed Bluey into the room. "Bluey, put on your thinking cap and try to imagine who could have accompanied George from the Château. I don't believe it was a slip of the tongue, but who is George friendly with, beside us? I've never seen him talking to anyone outside the Section."

"I agree. He and Simon were pretty thick and that's why he took Simon's death so hard. I'm sure he didn't have friends outside of the Section but I'll give it more thought, but we'd better get a move on or else Gilly will be upset we're late."

"I think you'll find it's Madame Pruvost Senior who likes things to run by the clock. She doesn't say much but she's in charge."

"Mmmm, I'll be more attentive to the old lady. We don't want to upset she who has the power."

* * *

The signallers plus Lieutenant Whybrow gathered in Captain Solway's office the following morning. Captain Solway asked, "Well Al, I hear you were allowed to visit Morbey yesterday. Anything to report?"

"Yes sir. George was reluctant to discuss the situation and most of the time was spent reminiscing about our adventures and talking about family back home. The only hint I was able to glean about his visit to the Château was when he said, 'when we left'. I jumped on this, but he quickly said he meant 'when I left'."

Sergeant King spoke. "So, there's another person involved. Who could it be? You two must know the mates of Morbey."

"Problem Peter. Firstly, you're assuming there was a second person involved which George denies. And secondly, all of George's mates are present in this room. He really is a shy, reserved type."

"So, not much to go on." Captain Solway lifted his hands in despair. "Is there anything else?"

Al spoke, "Yes sir. George is wearing prison clothing - no belt, no boot laces and so on. He wants to be tried in an Australian Army uniform. Sergeant Morris is willing to hand it over to us so we can get it washed and cleaned. Sir, does he need permission to be tried in uniform?"

"Sounds reasonable to me." Captain Solway turned to Lieutenant Whybrow. "Who do we approach to get approval for Morbey to appear in uniform?"

"I'll talk to Captain Sampson. I'm sure it can be arranged. Sapper Dowson, perhaps this is a task for you. Get Morbey's belongings from Sergeant Morris and have it ready for Morbey by next Thursday. It won't do our cause any harm to have a smart-looking soldier in the dock instead of someone looking like a felon."

"Good thinking Bill. So, it seems the only thing left for today is to say goodbye to Al. It's been a long and at times dangerous journey and I thank you for your contribution, Al. Perhaps when we all get back to Australia, we can arrange a get-together. Time and place to be advised."

"Thank you, Sir. It has been a privilege to serve under your command. I'll stay in touch and we'll get together in the future. I'm not very good at saying goodbye so let's leave it at that."

Sergeant King held out his hand, "I'll look forward to the reunion Al. Have a safe and happy homecoming."

"Thanks Peter. It was quite an adventure, wasn't it?"

The Sergeant nodded, "One way of describing it. Don't worry about Dowson, I'll keep an eye on him."

"Thank you Peter. At times, it's a full-time job. Come on Bluey, there are loose ends to tie up."

The two men left the room. Captain Solway shook his head. "You know life will be different without Wilson. From those first days at Gallipoli he was always there. I've never known anyone like him. His guardian angel must've worked overtime when you think of some of the scrapes he was in."

"Amen to that," replied Sergeant King. "I think his guardian angel was very keen to get him away from France and so arranged his early departure. I wish my guardian angel would get me on a fast boat to Australia."

"All in good time Peter. Let's get on with our work."

* * *

The dinner at the farm was quiet. Although everyone was happy that Al was going home, the thought they may never see him again was a cause for sadness. After emotional farewells, Al and Bluey retired to their sleeping quarters. "I've arranged a truck to pick me up at 5:30am to take me to Amiens railway station. I'll try not to wake you so we should say goodbye now."

'Rubbish. I'll be awake. What are your plans when you reach London?"

"I have several friends there and I want to take one last tour of the city. It's a fascinating place. I never tire of it."

"Well, enjoy it. You've certainly earned a holiday. And don't worry about me. I'll manage even without the help of the man they couldn't kill."

"Don't ever believe that nonsense Bluey. I just happened to be very lucky, and so were you. Together we made a good team, but we both knew it had to end sometime. Maybe we'll get together back home and start up some sort of business. And I don't mean a dairy farm!"

"Now that's a thought. Goodnight Al. I'll see you in the morning."

CHAPTER 29

THE BUSHRANGER

True to his word, Bluey was up early making a cup of tea for his departing friend. Neither had much to say. A long, strong handshake said it all as Al left to board his truck. Bluey stood in the doorway watching it depart. He heard a sound behind him and turned – a tearful Gilly stood in the room. "Has he really gone, Monsieur Bluey?"

"Yes Gilly. He really has gone, and I don't know what I'll do without him. He taught me so much and he got me through this war. How do you ever repay a friend like that?"

"We will all miss him. And you Monsieur Bluey, what will you do now?"

"I don't know Gilly. I guess the Army will have me stay for a while, at least until the trial is over, but after that I have no idea. I didn't come over until 1915 so I'll have to wait until it's my turn to go home. Sergeant King says the Army is forming squads to dig graves and relocate the fallen into formal cemeteries but they can't start until there's been agreement with the French about where the cemeteries will be. It could take some time and it's not a job I look forward to."

"The girls and I will be happy for you to be here for as long as you can."

"Thanks Gilly, I appreciate that. This farm holds a lot of happy memories for me although the past few days haven't been all that happy. But now I must get off to see if there's any change in George's situation."

"Of course, Monsieur Bluey, but first you will have breakfast with the family."

* * *

For Bluey, the weekend passed slowly and although Gilly and the girls did their best to cheer him up, he was inconsolable. It seemed everyone had accepted that George would be found guilty, and the only discussion concerned the punishment that would be handed down. Most people he talked to were predicting a death sentence and this added to Bluey's misery.

On Monday, he did his usual visits to Captain Solway, Lieutenant Whybrow, Sergeant King and the MP Headquarters on Monday. Everyone knew him and sympathized, but no one could give any reassurance about the court martial. All agreed that unless George could prove his innocence, he was going to be convicted of being involved in the deaths of Johnson and Bailey.

It was a disheartened Bluey who returned to the farm later that morning. After lunch, Bluey retired to write letters in what the group had called their recreation room. He heard the outside bell ring indicating visitors were at the front gate, but he took little notice. He looked up when Gilly appeared. "Monsieur Bluey, you have visitors," she announced. Then he saw but could not believe; "My God, Al. What are you doing here? You're supposed to be heading for home."

Al laughed. "I missed the boat Bluey, so thought I might come back to keep you out of trouble. And I have someone you might like to meet." A man stepped from behind, a man in a Scottish regiment uniform. "Bluey, this is Major Malcolm MacDonald, a very experienced barrister who's agreed to represent George. How about that?"

"Pleased to meet you Sir," Bluey stammered as he shook hands with the Major.

The Major stepped back and looked searchingly at Bluey. "So, this is the famous bushranger I've heard about?" he said with a broad Scottish accent.

Bluey looked to Al for help. "What's he talking about?"

"Relax Bluey. Remember the Highland Regiment we helped during the big push. Well, when we referred to you as a bushman, they became confused between a bushman and a bushranger and the name bushranger seemed to them to fit you better. Come to think of it, they were pretty close to the truth."

"What a lot of nonsense. But what does that Regiment have to do with the Major being here?"

Al turned to the hostess, "Gilly, would it be possible for us to have a cup of tea? We've had a busy and tiring day and there's still much to do."

"Of course Monsieur Al. How silly of me not to have offered you refreshments when you arrived. Tea and biscuits coming up."

"Well, you lads seem to have found yourselves a nice billet," observed the Major. "It certainly beats living under canvas, especially now the cold weather has arrived."

"We were very fortunate to find this place but that's a story for another day. Take a seat and I'll bring Bluey up to date."

"Please Al. Here I was thinking you were sunning yourself on the deck of a troopship and all the time you've been running around Scotland."

"Not quite Bluey. In fact, I haven't been all that far away. As mentioned, we did give some assistance to the Highland Regiment, and they were grateful. So much so that their CO, when we parted, offered to return the favour. Well, at the time, neither of us expected to see one another again. But I did remember his offer and when it became obvious that George wasn't going to get a fair trial, I got to wondering if the Regiment might have access to legal advice we could use. I didn't have a clue where the Regiment was camped. For all I knew they may have returned to Scotland. But things here are so desperate, I made up the story of getting my ticket home just so I could go looking for the Regiment. As it turns out, they were just outside Amiens and packing up to go home."

Al continued. "I met with the CO and he remembered me. He listened to my tale and told me the regiment legal officer was visiting and he arranged a meeting with Major MacDonald. After hearing my story, Major MacDonald agreed to come and see if he could help. I might add, the Major has a lot of experience in criminal law."

The kitchen door opened, and Gilly and Marie entered with a tray of steaming cups of tea and biscuits. "Gilly you're a real gem, thank you."

"It's no trouble Monsieur Al. We're all so happy to have you back. Even my mother-in-law is pleased, and it takes a lot to please her."

"That's good to hear Gilly. Tell her I'll be home for dinner and if she behaves, I'll play her a tune or two on the violin."

"She will be pleased to hear that."

After Gilly had left, Al exclaimed, "Oh bother! I forgot to ask Gilly if it'd be OK for you to join us for dinner."

"Sorry Corporal Wilson, but I have a mountain of research to do, and I want to circulate in the Officers' Mess to get a feel about the general attitude of the officers towards this trial. As you know, the court martial board will come from these officers, and it'll be interesting to see if they are discussing it among themselves. They shouldn't be but a few glasses of port can sometimes loosen tongues. But now down to business." The Major turned to Bluey. "As I understand it Sapper Dowson, you have been involved with Lieutenant Johnson from the very start. Take me through the story starting with your first encounter."

"It's a long story, sir. Goes way back to the recruitment camp in Melbourne."

"It doesn't matter how long it takes. What is important is that you don't miss any of the events where Lieutenant Johnson was involved."

WHO IS HE PROTECTING?

Major MacDonald drew a notebook from his pocket. "Right Sapper Dowson, when you're ready, let's hear the story. Take your time."

Bluey collected his thoughts. "It all started the day we entered recruitment camp at Broadmeadows just outside Melbourne. Each man was allocated to a tent. Johnson was allocated to the same tent as me. Also in that tent were Darkie Fleming and Eric Pettersen. Johnson started to throw his weight around, claiming he'd been put in charge of the tent. This didn't go down well, especially with Darkie. As the weeks went by, it was obvious that Johnson wasn't pulling his weight. His mother used to come and take him home in the evenings. He never took a turn at guard duty but would detail one of us to do his stint. He claimed he was in charge, and as we didn't know any better, we accepted that. A few weeks into our training we went to the rifle range, and I embarrassed him. Johnson shot a very poor score and claimed the rifle was defective. I swapped with him and proved it was not defective. He never forgave me."

Bluey paused. “It was all so stupid.”

Major MacDonald nodded. “Yes. But it’s also important. I must know the whole story, for Morbey’s sake.”

Bluey continued. “It became a stand-off between Johnson and the rest of us, and it came to head one night when Eric Pettersen and I were on guard duty. Johnson had volunteered us. Johnson went off with his mother and returned to camp late that night. Pettersen challenged him and demanded the password. Johnson had either forgotten the password or perhaps he wanted to torment Pettersen. He refused to give the password and teased Pettersen. Eric allowed Johnson to get too close to him and Johnson grabbed the rifle from Eric. He laughed at Eric and told him that he’d be reported for surrendering his weapon to an intruder. Eric responded by grabbing the rifle and punching Johnson in the face. It flattened him. Johnson screamed for the Sergeant of the Guard and demanded Eric be arrested for assault. Eric was put in the cells and next day he was charged. I was called as a witness. The Major dismissed the charges and Eric and I returned to camp. We never saw Johnson again until he turned up to join the Company at Hazebrouck, although we had heard he had been selected for officer training.”

Al spoke, “Perhaps I should continue the story. From Hazebrouck onwards I was involved with all the Johnson incidents.”

“By all means Corporal Wilson. Fire away.”

Al took up the story. “No.3 Section was heavily involved in fighting at Bullecourt and lost two men, Eric Pettersen and Max Walters. In time, they were replaced by George Morbey and Simon Young and so we were back to full strength. The Section moved to Belgium with the Brigade. We were settling in at Hazebrouck when we were joined by Sapper Bailey. At the time, I thought this was unusual as we were already up to strength and other Sections were short. Later I found Lieutenant Johnson and Sapper Bailey were friends and that Johnson had asked to be posted to No.3

Section and he also asked for Bailey to be similarly posted. Had I known about this unusual arrangement at the time, I might've asked why."

"It certainly was unusual," the Major said, scribbling in his notebook, "but then you didn't know about the events at recruitment camp."

"True, but when I saw the reaction of Darkie and Bluey to the news that Johnson was joining us, I demanded an explanation and they told me the story. I decided the differences of opinion were probably in the past and no one would be so stupid as to jeopardise operations by bringing such petty matters to the war. I told Fleming and Dowson to carry on as normal. I thought that if a problem did exist, I could sort it out. I was wrong."

Major MacDonald nodded, "Don't blame yourself Corporal. Please go on with the story."

"It soon became apparent that Johnson was out to punish the Section for what had happened in the recruitment camp. I found that puzzling as only Dowson, Fleming and Pettersen were involved during those early training days and of course Pettersen was no longer with us, having been killed at Bullecourt."

Al continued, "First there was the assault at Mezzines. This was Johnson's first taste of action - not that he got too close to the actual fighting. The Artillery got their figures wrong and Dowson and MacKenzie raced across open ground under fire to warn the gunners of their mistake. Dowson and MacKenzie were recommended for a bravery award but Johnson successfully opposed it. That didn't impress the other members of the Section nor the Artillery men who supported the recommendation. After Mezzines, the Brigade returned to the Corbie area and the Section was again billeted at this splendid farm."

The Major interrupted. "You must've been the envy of all in the area. It really is an impressive arrangement."

Al smiled. "Yes, it is. Life here was comfortable. Johnson saw this and volunteered the Section for two weeks duty at the front-line over Christmas. That was disappointing but we accepted that someone had to man the trenches. When we returned from the front, Johnson organized for the Section members to train on using new portable wirelesses. It was obvious this was an attempt to break up the Section, so the members deliberately failed the course. These results enraged Johnson and he arranged for the Section to be returned to Belgium."

"Excuse me Corporal, but how can a Lieutenant dictate where a unit should be or not be?"

"It's a question that initially puzzled me and I discussed it with Sergeant King. The orders to move came from Brigade HQ and we now know Johnson had the ear of his uncle, Colonel Payne. But more of that later."

Al continued. "By now the entire Section was anti-Johnson. Shortly after arriving in the Ypres area, the Section lost Lacey and O'Brien. They were running a line when a hidden sniper took them out. That had a big impact on us, but Johnson wasn't blamed."

"Winter set in and the fighting stopped. However, Johnson insisted the Section run a line named K5, in front of the trenches, for training purposes. Madness! Who exposes themselves to the enemy in a training exercise? It turned into a complete disaster and a hidden sniper took out MacKenzie and Fleming. That should've been the warning to cease running that particular line, but Johnson convinced a higher authority it was a vital part of our training, so the Section continued to run K5.

"Then the German sniper shot Ralston and Jackson. The Command decided to close down K5 but Dowson persuaded them to keep it open so he could have a shot at the sniper. This happened, and after Dowson had killed the sniper, the line was closed down. But the damage had been done. Four good men had been lost unnecessarily. That left us with a Section of four men, five if you count Bailey."

"Hardly an operational unit."

"No sir, but with the help of Sergeant King we managed to persuade Captain Solway we could operate as a mobile station with a wireless set in the back of a truck. Captain Solway agreed and it was while operating like this we encountered your Regiment."

"Yes Corporal, you did encounter my boys and saved most of them from death or becoming prisoners. They still tell stories about the Australian bushranger and his mates. But Sapper Bailey wasn't part of this group, was he? Perhaps now is a good time to tell me about the late Sapper Bailey."

"Right sir. Bailey joined us at the same time as Johnson. It was Bailey who brought us the news that Johnson was replacing Lieutenant Crowthers. I recall that at that time, Bailey did say he and Johnson had attended the same school but that didn't raise any red flags with me."

"Well, why should it?" commented the Major.

"No reason Sir. We all went to a school somewhere at some time, but later events suggest Johnson and Bailey were a little more than old school pals."

"I see. But tell me, how did Bailey fit in with the rest of the Section?'

Notebook poised; Major MacDonald waited for Al to continue.

"From the start, Bailey didn't fit in. Johnson more or less kept him away from the Section. He got Bailey detailed off as the batsman for Captain Solway and himself. We hardly ever saw Bailey unless he was in the company of Johnson. I realized Bailey was not a team player, so I wasn't fussed he didn't join in. He certainly didn't share this billet."

"An error on his part, I dare say," Major MacDonald smiled. "But Sapper Bailey was involved in a stunt right at the end of hostilities, was he not?

Al nodded. "On the night of the 10th, all the Section were involved in a raid by the Battalion troops. We acted as a reporting post. It was strange because for the first time Johnson and Bailey were there with me, Bluey and Morbey, in a frontline stunt. Sapper Young manned the phone in Battalion HQ. I managed to collect a piece of metal in the head and couldn't see, so Morbey led me back to our lines and got me to an aid post.

"The stunt was terminated, and Johnson and Bailey returned from the observation post to our lines. Johnson told Bluey he would send someone out to assist him to reel up the line. No one came and the telephone line was cut, so Bluey had no way of knowing what was going on. We suspect that either Johnson or Bailey cut the line.

"When the Armistice was announced, Sapper Young ran across no-man's land to take the good news to Bluey but a German sniper shot him. The Section believes either Johnson or Bailey were responsible for Simon's death. If the line had been operational, Simon Young wouldn't have made that trip."

Major MacDonald held up his hand. "I think that's enough for the moment. You've given me plenty to think about. I need to get back to the Officers' Mess for dinner. Tomorrow you won't see much of me, if at all. I must go over the statements collected by Lieutenant Whyborn and talk to others. I'm not happy with the timing of this court martial, and I'll try to get it postponed until I'm fully up to speed with my duties, although, after talking to the Brigadier, I suspect things will continue as scheduled. So, I'll take my leave but don't you two go wandering off as I may need you at short notice at any time."

Major MacDonald exited the room.

Al turned to Bluey. "So, my old friend, what do you think of the latest addition to the team?"

A large smile crossed Bluey's face. "Two hours ago I believed George was going to be shot. There was nothing, nobody, to save him. Now I have hope. I don't know how he can do it, but I hope and pray that Major MacDonald will pull it off."

Al nodded. "So do I Bluey. The officers at the Scots Regiment said he is one of the best barristers in Britain. How lucky are we?"

"No Al. How lucky is George. I only hope George will accept him and assist him. Up to now he's refused any offers of help. He won't talk to Captain Solway or Lieutenant Whybrow. I'm sure he's hiding something from us. I know he didn't kill those rats but at the same time I think he's protecting someone."

"Sorry Bluey, I can't agree with you. Who could he be protecting? You and I are his only friends here and we certainly don't need protecting. Anyhow let's leave it to the Major to sort out. Time we cleaned up for dinner."

* * *

As he predicted, the two sappers saw little of Major MacDonald over the next two days. They did occasionally see him and Lieutenant Whybrow driving past in the staff car. However, on Wednesday evening, the Major and Lieutenant Whybrow arrived at the farm. Once the four men had settled down at the table and had been served with a cup of tea, Al and Bluey started to speak. Major MacDonald held up his hand to stop the barrage of questions. "I'm sorry gentlemen but you'll have to be patient. Lieutenant Whybrow and I, have spent the last two days asking questions and not always getting satisfactory answers. It'll be a different story tomorrow when we're in court."

"Yes Major, but will you be able to get George acquitted?"

"A good question Sapper Dowson, but one that cannot be answered right now. We have done all we can, but I really do need more time to prepare the case. But I'm not confident extra time will be allowed. There appears to be a determination amongst some that the sooner this matter is settled, the better. Sapper Morbey seems to have accepted he'll be found guilty, and that is a worry. There seems little evidence to support the charge, but

I also don't think Sapper Morbey is telling me the whole story. Can either of you think of any reason he wouldn't tell us what happened?"

Bluey shook his head. "Strange Major that you should ask that question. I asked Al the very same question, but we couldn't come up with an answer. Why should he shield someone? And if he is, who?"

Major MacDonald stood up. "We still have work to do so we must go. Please thank Gilly for the tea. Perhaps Sapper Dowson we'll know the answers to your questions tomorrow." The two officers departed and left Al and Bluey to ponder what they'd heard.

HAVE FAITH

The Château ballroom had been furnished for the court-martial of Sapper George Morbey. A raised dais at one end with three chairs and a table served as the Bench. Facing this were the prosecution and defence tables, each with three chairs. A make-shift dock had been erected to the left of the Bench while a witness stand was on the right.

Next to the witness stand was the table and chair for the Judge- Advocate who was responsible for the conduct of the trial and was the legal adviser to the Court.

Seats were available for some fifty spectators, and all were occupied. The trial had aroused interest not just from within the Australian Army but also from the British Press.

The prosecution team was Captain Sampson and two assistants. But it was the Defence table that held the most interest. On one chair sat a young Australian soldier with several files on the table in front of him. Next sat Lieutenant Whyborn, the nominated Defence Counsel, and in the seat usually occupied by the team leader, was a Major dressed in the uniform of a Scottish

Regiment. His dress was in stark contrast to the Australians. On his chest were two medal ribbons, the Distinguished Service Cross and the Military Cross, proof that this particular Officer had been involved in serious frontline service.

The three members of the Court entered and took their places. The Judge-Advocate announced the Court was in session, Lieutenant Whyborn rose. “If it pleases the Court Mr President, I wish to make application for a change in the legal team for the Defence”. The President nodded, “Yes Lieutenant Whyborn, please approach the Bench and I suggest your learned friend accompany you.”

The President continued, “Before you start Lieutenant Whyborn, I must inform you I have been briefed by the General Staff about this unusual development. Why an officer from another country should become involved in what is a matter for resolution by the Australian Army is beyond me.”

Lieutenant Whyborn recognised the President was unhappy with the new arrangements and care should be taken. “Perhaps I could start by introducing Major Malcolm MacDonald, an experienced barrister who has been involved in a number of murder cases in England. I myself have no experience in criminal court matters. I am a country solicitor and as such am not really qualified to represent the defendant in this serious matter.”

“Perhaps Major MacDonald can enlighten us as to how and why he is here?”

“Certainly, Mr President.” The words were spoken quietly with a trace of a Scottish accent. “The defendant, Sapper George Morbey was, and probably still is, a member of an Australian Signal Section which rendered great service to my Regiment in the recent conflict. It is not an exaggeration to say they saved the Regiment. This placed the Regiment deeply in debt to these men, a debt which we never expected to be able to repay. However, when approached with a request for assistance for Sapper Morbey, my

Commanding Officer had no hesitation in ordering me to do all I could to help. I do have, as mentioned by Lieutenant Whyborn, considerable court experience. I believe I can be of help in the trial of Sapper Morbey."

"I expect Sapper Morbey can do with all the help he can get, and I accept you represent him. However, I wish to impress upon you Major MacDonald I will not allow any time-wasting tactics some legal people seem to indulge in. The war is over and those Australians who came over in the first convoy have been away from home for over four years. Lieutenant-Colonel Talbot, here on my right, and myself were in that first convoy and we are most anxious to start the journey home. It is most unfortunate this trial threatens to delay our departure so we will be looking for a speedy resolution. Do I make myself clear?"

"Perfectly clear Mr President and I believe Sapper Morbey is also hoping for a speedy resolution. However, although speed is one consideration, I believe justice must take precedence over all else."

The comment provoked the Colonel. "Justice! Of course justice is paramount. Why do you think we are here? This Court has been convened to hear the evidence and to administer justice. We don't need you to tell us our job."

Major MacDonald shook his head. "I'm sorry for any misunderstanding. I did not intend any criticism of the court and if my words have offended then I withdraw them unreservedly."

"Right." The Colonel was not completely placated but saw the wisdom in not pursuing the matter. "Let's get on with the business at hand."

It was the Major who now shook his head. "Sir, I must submit an application for an adjournment. I have had less than three days to acquaint myself with my brief and there remains a lot of interviewing and research to do before I am in a position to defend Sapper Morbey to the best of my ability."

The Colonel looked at his two companions for some sort of support, but none arose. "I do not understand your request Major MacDonald. Lieutenant Whyborn has been working on this case for the past week. He has all the facts and surely you only have to use his notes to conduct the defence?"

"No Sir. With all due respect to Lieutenant Whyborn, I do not believe he has all the information I require, and I must become intimately acquainted with all the facts if I am to provide the defendant with the defence he is entitled to. I do need time."

"All right Major MacDonald, but how much time is the question?"

"Thank you, Sir. I understand the Court is hoping for an early resolution of this matter so I will try to be ready to proceed in two weeks from today."

The Colonel's face went red. "Two weeks!" he spluttered. "Two weeks! You expect this court to sit around doing nothing for two weeks while you re-visit the ground already covered by Lieutenant Whyborn? Your request cannot be entertained. I warned you about wasting the Court's time, Major MacDonald. This Court will now adjourn and reconvene on Tuesday 26th of November 1918 at 9:00am."

The President held up his hand to indicate there would be no further discussion and rising from his chair he left the courtroom followed by the other members. The Advocate repeated the President's words and as George Morbey was led from the room the spectators began to disperse.

Al and Bluey hurried to the Defence table. "Bloody hell Sir" said an upset Bluey. "You're not going to let that windbag treat you like that are you?"

The Major smiled. "Calm down Sapper Dowson. This is his court and what he says goes. I didn't expect him to act any differently. What we must do is be sure that by Tuesday morning we're ready. So, there is much work to be done. For you and Corporal

Wilson I have several matters I want you to investigate. With some of them, I want you to involve a member of the prosecution team so the facts you provide are agreed by both defence and prosecution."

Bluey frowned. "I thought they were the enemy and now you want us to work with them?"

"Yes, Sapper Dowson, that is exactly want I want. Let me give you an example. I want to know how long it takes a man to run from Sapper Bailey's room to the front of the Château. And I want the prosecution to agree with the figure you produce. By doing this, when I produce the figures in court, they won't be challenged and so we'll save a lot of time and trouble. Now here is your list. I want to hold a council of war at the farm this evening at 6:00pm. Please try and have the information by then."

Al Wilson took the list. "Come on Bluey, we have work to do. See you back at the farm Major."

* * *

Major MacDonald was already at the farm when Al and Bluey arrived. He was seated at the table in talking with Gilly. The Major greeted them with a wave of his hand, "Ah, my helpers are on time and I hope they have good news to report."

"Yes Sir," replied Al. "We completed all tasks and have the results written on this sheet." He handed the Major the piece of paper.

"Splendid. Did you manage to get a member of the prosecution team to accompany you, and more importantly did he agree with your findings?"

"No problem there Sir," Bluey said. "Captain Sampson detailed off two of his men to accompany us and although we sometimes had to repeat the exercise to get agreement, in the long run everyone agreed with the figures on that sheet".

The Scot ran his eye over the list. "Well done. In fact, very well done. These are just what I had hoped for."

"Sir, can we be let into the secret of what these figures are for?" Bluey asked.

"Not just yet Sapper Dowson. All will be revealed in good time. Now even though Madame Pruvost has invited me to stay for dinner, and I have no doubt that her cooking is far superior to that of the Army, I must get to my office and plan for tomorrow. I will meet you two at the Château tomorrow at 9:00am. I will have some more errands for you. I think we now have most of the material I need just a few loose ends to tie up. I'll spend the day with witnesses going over their statements. We'll be ready by Tuesday and that'll make the Colonel happy."

The men rose from the table and stood to attention as the Major departed. As they resumed their seats, Al looked at Gilly and asked, "Well, what was all your talk about? You two looked as thick as thieves when we came in."

Gilly shook her head. "I don't know I am allowed to discuss it."

"Did the Major tell you not to?" asked Bluey.

"Well no, he didn't," Gilly replied.

"Well then, if Major MacDonald wanted you to keep it to yourself, he would have told you." Al was not certain the Major had an opportunity to swear Gilly to secrecy, but he was deeply curious. "Come on Gilly. We're family and we're all in this together."

The lady nodded. "You are right Al. We are family. But I must ask you keep this to yourselves."

"We have no problem with that Gilly. You have our word on that."

"I really don't know how to explain it. It seems Major MacDonald wants Yvette to testify in court, but George is adamant she is not to be called. Before she can be called, three things must happen. Because of her age I, as her mother, have to give my permission. Secondly, because George is on trial, he has to agree to any appearance of a witness for the defence, and finally

Yvette herself has to agree." Gilly paused as if she expected some questions but there were none.

She continued. "I have faith in Major MacDonald, and I know he would not call Yvette unless it was to help George. So, I am inclined to give my permission for Yvette to attend. I am sure Yvette would agree if she, in some way, could help George. However, the Major says George refuses to agree to her appearing. I don't know why."

Al nodded. "This is strange. Still, we must leave it to Major MacDonald to sort out. He knows what he is doing and I'm sure George will come around to the Major's way of thinking."

Gilly shook her head. "It's such a mess. I really don't know what to believe. Surely George didn't do those awful things?"

"No Gilly, he did not, and the Major will prove that. Mark my words."

"Well, I left the cooking of dinner to the girls and it should be ready so let us go and eat and try to forget our problems for a while."

"Easier said than done," muttered Bluey. "I feel so useless in how I might help George."

"Well, my friend," said Al, "if it's of any comfort to you, we all feel the same way. But have faith in the Major. It's his job and from all accounts he's good at it."

The two men followed Gilly into the kitchen where the rest of the family was waiting.

* * *

The next days passed quickly for the defence team. Major MacDonald had numerous tasks for Al and Bluey. Al once remarked he suspected the Major was giving them tasks to stop them pestering him while he interviewed witnesses. Whatever his motive, it was a relief for Al and Bluey, at the Monday evening gathering, to hear him declare that all was in readiness for the start of the trial the next day.

“Will we be allowed in the courtroom?” asked Bluey.

“I don’t see any reason why you would be barred,” replied Major MacDonald.

“But won’t we be required to give evidence about the cutting of the wire? That’s what this trial is all about,” asked Al.

“No Al. The cutting of the wire may be the trigger which started the chain of events, but it is irrelevant to the matter before the court. George is on trial for murder. That is what we must focus on and I must ensure that is what the court focuses on.”

The Major paused in case there was any argument, but there was none. “Right, get a good night’s rest and I’ll see you outside the courtroom at 8:40am tomorrow. And cheer up! By tomorrow night the trial will be over and done with, and we can have a celebratory drink.”

Bluey frowned. “But will George be here to share that drink?”

The Major shook his head. “Have faith Sapper Dowson. Have faith.” And with that he left the room.

“Tell me Al. Be honest. Can he get George off those charges? Everyone I have spoken to believes George killed Bailey. Can he get a fair trial?”

“Sorry, I can’t give you the answer you want. We’ll get the answer tomorrow, but if anyone can get George a fair trial, I believe the Major can. So why don’t we have faith and get some rest, although I doubt if either of us will be sleeping soundly tonight. Come on, let’s turn in.”

I DON'T BELIEVE HIM FRANKLY

By 8:40am on Tuesday 26th of November, the court room was full. The news that the eminent Major MacDonald was conducting the defence had aroused the interest of the Australian Army and the British Press.

The Defence team gathered outside the court room for final instructions from the Major. He addressed Al and Bluey: "I want you to sit in chairs directly behind me. If I pass a note asking you to do or check something, stand up, bow to the President, and then hot foot it out and get me what I ask. Speed may be vital. Are you clear?"

The two nodded and followed the Major into the court room. Lieutenant Whyborn and his assistant were already standing by the Defence table. "Well Lieutenant Whyborn, are we ready?" asked the Major. "Yes Sir, as ready as we will ever be."

"Good. Let's hope the Prosecution is also ready."

"I don't think there will be any doubt about that, Sir. My feeling, shared by many colleagues, is that nothing will stop the

Colonel proceeding today. I wouldn't like to be in Captain Sampson's boots if he is not ready."

The Major nodded. "The Colonel made it clear the trial will start today and I am sure Captain Sampson got the message. Ah! I see he and his team have arrived."

Sapper George Morbey was already seated in the dock.

Right on 9:00am, the side door opened and members of the court led by the President entered. After acknowledging the bows from the participating parties, they took their seats. The Judge-Advocate announced the court was in session.

"Gentlemen are we ready to proceed?" asked the President.

Captain Sampson stood. "The Prosecution is ready Sir."

Major MacDonald also came to his feet. "The Defence is ready Sir."

The President nodded, "Judge-Advocate, please get the proceedings under way."

The Judge-Advocate rose and in a stern voice instructed Sapper Morbey to rise.

"Sapper George Morbey of the Australian Imperial Force, you are charged with the murder of Lieutenant Ronald Johnson of the Australian Imperial Force, on the 11th November 1918. How do you plead?"

"Not guilty," responded George quietly.

"Speak up," ordered the President.

"Not guilty," George answered in a firm loud voice. Major MacDonald nodded his approval.

The Judge-Advocate continued. "Charge two. Sapper George Morbey of the Australian Imperial Force, you are charged with the murder of Sapper Colin Bailey of the Australian Imperial Force, on 11th November 1918. How do you plead?"

George answered in a strong voice, "Not guilty."

"Resume your seat," directed the Judge-Advocate.

The President looked at Captain Sampson. "Prosecutor, you may proceed."

Captain Sampson rose. "If it pleases the court, I would like to make a submission regarding a procedural matter. The Defence and I are of the opinion that the two cases before the court should be dealt with separately. Many of the witnesses to be called are involved in both cases and their evidence could become confusing unless we try one case at a time. I therefore submit to the court a request that the case against Sapper Morbey of the murder of Sapper Bailey be held first and as a separate issue from the case involving the death of Lieutenant Johnson."

The President spoke to his two fellow members. "The court can see merit in your request to treat the two cases separately but surely both cases are linked?"

"Yes Sir. But both the Defence and the Prosecution are concerned we will spend a lot of time and effort unravelling those links if the cases are heard concurrently."

The Colonel turned to the Defence table. "Perhaps the Defence would like to comment?"

Major MacDonald stood up: "The Defence agrees with the submission to try the two cases separately."

The President nodded. "Very well, that is how we shall handle the matter. The Court will now hear the charge of the murder of Sapper Bailey. Prosecutor, you may proceed."

Captain Sampson rose to his feet. "The Prosecution will produce evidence to show that on the afternoon of 11th November, Sapper Morbey had motive and opportunity to kill Sapper Bailey. The motive was one of revenge because Sapper Morbey believed Sapper Bailey was involved in the cutting of a telephone wire on the night of 10th November and as a result of that action, a series of events unfolded and ultimately resulted in the death of his good friend Sapper Young. The Prosecution will show Sapper Morbey was involved in a scuffle with Sapper Bailey just prior to Sapper Bailey's death. There may be some substance to the belief held by Sapper Morbey, that Sapper Bailey was in some way responsible for the death of Sapper Young but that should be determined by an independent enquiry. There is no excuse for the defendant taking the law into his own hands." Captain Sampson returned to his table and sat down.

The President called Major MacDonald.

"The Defence strongly disagrees with the claim that the defendant visited the Château to seek revenge on Sapper Bailey for the death of Sapper Young. The Defence will show that Sapper Morbey was trying to contact Sapper Bailey to try and ascertain exactly what did happen on the night of 10th November. To use the word 'revenge' is emotional, and untrue. Sapper Morbey could not be seeking revenge when he did not know what had actually taken place that night. His motive for visiting the Château was to try and find the truth. The Defence will also show that Sapper Morbey did not have the opportunity to kill Sapper Bailey as claimed by the Prosecution." The Major returned to his seat.

The President made some notes before speaking, "Captain Sampson, you may now call your first witness."

"Call Colonel Payne."

Colonel Payne entered the courtroom, walked to the witness box and took the Oath before sitting down.

The President spoke, "Colonel Payne. Everyone here knows you have a personal connection to Lieutenant Johnson and we offer our sincere condolences. It's a sorry mess and we will try our upmost to bring these proceedings to a quick and just conclusion."

"Thank you, Mr President. I hope I can provide a useful contribution to your deliberations."

"I am sure you can Colonel. Please proceed Captain Sampson."

The Prosecutor approached the witness box. "Colonel Payne, would you please describe your duties in the Brigade."

"I am the Chief of Staff for administrative matters. I try to ensure that things run smoothly in the various Brigade sections and cells. If there is an administration problem, I try to resolve it."

"Could you please tell the Court about your activities on the morning of 11th November?"

The Colonel settled back in his chair. "We at HQ already knew the Armistice was to come into force at 11:00am. The men in the field did not know. The Brigadier directed me to be at the frontline at 11:00am to receive a confirming message and then I could break the news to the men. So immediately after breakfast I was driven to the frontline.

"On arrival, I was greeted by Captain Solway who told me he had a problem. It seems he had two men from No.3 Signals Section stranded in no-man's land and he feared for their safety. I knew they were perfectly safe, but I couldn't say anything until the confirming message arrived."

Captain Sampson interrupted. "Did Captain Solway offer any explanation as to why these men were stranded in no-man's land?"

"Not at the time, but I learned later the telephone cable to recall them before daylight had been severed. Anyhow, it didn't matter as the long-awaited news arrived on time and I was able to tell the men they were out of a job."

"I can imagine what the mood was like Colonel. You would have been regarded as the messenger from heaven when the news was given. But something went wrong immediately after you broke the news. Please tell the Court what happened."

"Yes, it was a great pity, and it spoilt the celebrations. Sapper Young asked permission to run across to the two men stranded in no-man's land. There was no reason to refuse his request. The war was over. It should have been perfectly safe."

Again, Captain Sampson interrupted. "But it wasn't safe, was it Colonel?"

"Regrettably no. A rogue German sniper shot Sapper Young as he crossed no-man's land. It really upset the troops and I feared they would retaliate and cause an incident."

"Did they retaliate?" asked the Prosecutor.

"No, but Sapper Dowson took it upon himself to rush into the enemy trench. Dowson was armed and I have no doubt he intended to avenge Young's death." The Colonel shook his head. "He should not have had a rifle. I had made it very plain throughout the campaign that only infantrymen were to carry arms - men who knew how to use weapons."

"Please continue Colonel."

"Well, we heard a shot from the enemy lines and assumed Dowson had been killed but to our surprise he emerged from the enemy trench accompanied by a German officer. It turned out the Germans had executed the offending sniper and the German officer wished to discuss matters concerning the implementation of the ceasefire." Colonel Payne shook his head. "It was quite a relief to realise the matter of the shooting had been resolved."

"That is an interesting comment, Colonel." The Prosecutor was staring at Bluey seated behind Major MacDonald. "You say the matter had been successfully resolved. Were all who were present at the time satisfied with the outcome?"

"I don't think I can answer that question. I did not ask anyone for their opinion on the matter." The Colonel paused.

"But why would they not be satisfied? The sniper who fired the shot had been punished. Honour had been restored."

The Prosecutor shook his head. "No Colonel, I was not referring to the act of the shooting. Perhaps some people were not satisfied with the reason Sapper Young was crossing no-man's land at that particular time."

"I don't follow you. I gave Young permission to cross to where the two signalmen were hiding. The war was over. No one could have foreseen the action of the rogue sniper."

"I agree Sir." Captain Sampson was unsure if he should pursue this line of questioning. "But if the two sappers had not been stranded in no-man's land, then Sapper Young would not have needed to run across to them to deliver the news."

Colonel Payne nodded. "That is correct. However, they were there. Why were they there? Well, you will have to ask someone else that question."

"Yes Sir. Can we move on with your account of what happened after the German officer crossed to our lines?"

"Certainly. Major Manfried and I retired to the Battalion HQ to discuss how we could jointly implement the ceasefire. He was most cooperative. Then we heard a shot. It came from nearby, so we exited the HQ. Outside we saw a group of men standing around and it was obvious someone had discharged a weapon. I demanded to know what was going on. Sergeant Phillips explained how the Germans had left a round in Dowson's rifle when they removed the magazine. Dowson had accidentally fired the rifle giving everyone a horrible fright."

"What did you do then?"

Colonel Payne grimaced. "I gave Dowson a blast. He should not have been carrying a rifle. It was against my explicit orders. I ordered him to hand over the weapon to Sergeant Phillips. Then as my business with Major Manfried was completed, I returned to Brigade Headquarters at the Château. My nephew, Lieutenant Johnson, seemed very upset. I gather he had had a very trying night directing an assault on the enemy lines, so I offered him a ride back."

Captain Sampson consulted his notes, "Did you and Lieutenant Johnson discuss what had occurred?"

Colonel Payne frowned. "Do you mean what had happened the previous night or what had just occurred at the frontline?"

"The court is interested in both matters. There seems to be some sort of connection."

The Colonel nodded. “Ronald, I mean Lieutenant Johnson, had a lot to say on the return journey. He was extremely agitated. I put it down to the fact he had been closely involved in the fighting the previous night. He told me how Sapper Dowson had become stranded in no-man’s land. Someone had cut the telephone wire and the Signal Section blamed Ronald. He told me he had had a lot of trouble with Sapper Dowson stretching as far back as the initial training camp. He claimed that when Dowson fired his rifle that morning, he, that is Dowson, was trying to kill him.”

The Prosecutor looked up from his notes in surprise. “That is a very serious accusation to make Colonel. What was your reaction?”

“I didn’t want to further upset Ronald, so I ignored his statement.”

Captain Sampson shook his head. “I find that difficult to understand Colonel. An officer has just accused one of his men of trying to kill him and you chose to ignore the statement. You must have had a very good reason to take that course of action?”

“Yes, Captain Sampson. I had a couple of reasons for not pursuing what I considered an outlandish claim. Firstly, as I said earlier, Lieutenant Johnson was visibly upset. I have known the boy all his life and he has always been highly strung - prone to over-reaction and exaggeration. Secondly, why would a soldier try to shoot an officer in front of half a dozen witnesses? Heavens above, the war had just ended. As we all know, to have survived day after day, year after year, the daily threat of death, one’s survival feels like a miracle. So why come through all that fighting and danger and then try to kill one of your own in full view of so many people?”

“So, you didn’t report the conversation to higher authority?”

“No, I did not.” Colonel threw up his hands in a gesture of despair. “The war was over. We were all going home to live in peace.

Why start a witch-hunt based on the rantings of an exhausted and stressed young man?"

"I understand Colonel. Can you tell us what happened after you arrived at HQ?"

"Ronald and I had sandwiches for lunch and then we both went upstairs to have a bath and to dress for the celebrations. My last words to Ronald were 'I'll see you in the bar.' I never saw him alive again. I was in the ante room having a drink when Lieutenant Rogers came running in and said there had been an accident. I went outside with a number of officers and I saw Ronald's body on the ground. From the angle of his head, it was obvious he was dead."

"Did you at any time think there might be a connection with Lieutenant Johnson's death and the claim he had made earlier about Sapper Dowson threatening him?"

Colonel looked towards the court members. "I had such thoughts at that time and when I returned to the mess from the accident scene, I mentioned the matter to the Brigadier. I didn't mention the alleged death threat but I did tell the Brigadier there was bad blood between Ronald and Sapper Dowson. The Brigadier said he would have the matter investigated. Captain Solway, who was present, asked if he could conduct a preliminary investigation as No.3 Signal Section was his responsibility. The Brigadier told him to carry out the investigation immediately as it was a disturbing situation."

"Did Captain Solway investigate the matter?" asked the Prosecutor.

"Of course. Captain Solway is a fine officer. A group of us, including the Brigadier, were still at the bar when he returned, and he told those present that Corporal Wilson and Sapper Dowson had cast iron alibis and neither had been anywhere near the Château that afternoon."

“Ah,” said Captain Sampson, “Sapper Morbey wasn’t mentioned in his report?”

Colonel Payne gave the question some thought before replying. “Now you mention it, Captain Solway was quite specific in clearing Wilson and Dowson. Morbey’s name was not mentioned.”

The Prosecutor looked relieved at this piece of information. “So, do you know how Sapper Morbey came to be a suspect?”

Major MacDonald rose from his seat to object. “Mr President. I don’t think Colonel Payne is in a position to tell the court what the evidence is to support the allegations against my client.”

The President thought for a moment. “No, the court will allow the question. Colonel Payne was closely involved in the matter, and we would like to hear what he has to say. Colonel you may answer the question.”

“When I came down for breakfast on the morning of Tuesday 12th November, Sergeant Horne, the Mess Manager, told me he had seen Morbey and Bailey struggling in the passageway of the Château the previous afternoon. I asked him what he had done about this important piece of news, and he said he had referred it to the Military Police and they were investigating. Later that day I heard that Sapper Morbey had been arrested.”

“Thank you, Colonel,” Captain Sampson said. “I have no further question.”

The President spoke, “Does the Defence wish to cross examine the witness?”

Major MacDonald got to his feet. “Yes, Mr President. Colonel Payne, were you not a little worried when Lieutenant Johnson failed to join you in the mess for a drink as planned?”

Colonel Payne shook his head, “Not at all. I imagined he had decided to have a rest and had drifted off to sleep. It was obvious the party would be going on for a long time so there was no urgency for Ronald to join me. I guessed he would be down before dinner.”

"So, you didn't go upstairs to check on him?"

"No. The war was over. Ronald was safe and sound. He had survived like the rest of us. Why should I worry about him just because he was a little late in meeting me at the bar?"

Major MacDonald consulted his notes. "Only that morning, Lieutenant Johnson had told you there had been an attempt on his life by a member of No.3 Signal Section. Didn't that concern you?"

Colonel Payne frowned. "I have already told the Court I had dismissed Ronald's claim as over-reaction, exaggeration, mild hysteria - call it what you like. The claim came from a man who was very stressed having just returned from the frontline. To put it bluntly, I didn't believe him."

The Major laid his papers on the table. "Colonel Payne, you knew Lieutenant Johnson better than any other man in this court, so we must accept your assessment of the claim made by your nephew. I have no further questions."

The President looked toward the Prosecutor. "Do you wish to reexamine?" Captain Sampson shook his head.

"Very well Colonel Payne, you may step down."

Colonel Payne stood and looked at the President. He paused as if he were about to say something, but then nodded and departed the witness stand.

TREACHERY

The President raised his hand before the next witness could be called. "One moment Captain Sampson. There is a matter which concerns me. We have learned from the witness there was ill-feeling, call it a feud, between Lieutenant Johnson and No.3 Signal Section. There has also been reference to the stranding of a sapper in no man's land on the night of the 10th. It seems to the Court these matters lay at the heart of this trial but on examining the witness list I cannot see where any of Section No.3 are to be called. Can you enlighten the Court why this is so?"

"Certainly Sir. The Prosecution and Defence held a pre-trial conference and one of the topics discussed was how we could expedite the trial, knowing time is a major concern. Major MacDonald proposed we adopt a certain course of action and I agreed. As it was his initiative, I think Major MacDonald should explain our intentions."

"Very well." The President turned his gaze to the Defence table.

"Major MacDonald, would you please tell the Court why the animosity between the Signal Section and Lieutenant Johnson is not to be tested here and why the incident involving the cutting of the wire on the night of 10th is not relevant to our deliberations."

Major MacDonald came to his feet. "Sir, the animosity between Lieutenant Johnson and the Section and the cutting of the wire are relevant to this case. The Prosecution and Defence agreed on this and we agreed that Colonel Payne should be the person to bring them to the court's attention. The ill-feeling between Lieutenant Johnson and members of the Section dates back as far as recruit training. If we were to try and sort out who was in the right or wrong, we could be here for weeks. We might even have to get witnesses from Australia. What we propose is that the court accepts as a fact there was animosity between the two parties. No one is disputing that."

Major MacDonald paused in case there were any questions. The President addressed the Attorney-General. "I need guidance on this matter. Can the Court accept the proposition as put forward by the Defence?"

The Attorney-General nodded. "Yes Sir. If the Defence and Prosecution are agreed the matter is not in contention and does not need to be tested, the Court may accept that and proceed on that basis. However, if the Court considers the matter is in contention, then the matter must be tested in the courtroom."

The thought of spending time on the matter was foremost in the mind of the President. "Very well. The Court accepts the submission that there was a strong feeling of animosity between Lieutenant Johnson and the members of No.3 Signal Section going back over a long period. But that doesn't explain who was responsible for cutting the telephone wire on the night of 10th, and to me, that seems to be the cause of the matters we are investigating today."

"Again Sir, you have gone straight to the nub of the matter". Major MacDonald's remark seemed to please the President. "Who did cut the wire? We could start an investigation, but it would take time and we would have to call many witnesses. And then we may never find out the truth as the two men accused of cutting the wire are dead. So, what would we end up with? Wasting a lot of time away from the real reason we are here."

"So, Major, you don't think it important that we know who cut the wire."

"No Mr President, I don't. What is important and relevant to this case is that Sapper Morbey suspected that either Johnson or Bailey cut the wire. That, by his own admission in his statement, is why he went to the Château that afternoon. And that should be our starting point into the events that occurred at the Château on the afternoon of 11th of November."

The President now turned to the Prosecutor. "Captain Sampson do you agree with the claim made by the Defence that we would be wasting time if we tried to establish who cut the wire?"

Captain Sampson had a slight smile on his lips. "I agree with Major MacDonald. As just revealed by the Defence, Sapper Morbey went to the Château believing that either Johnson or Bailey had cut the wire and his intention was to wreak revenge. We now have his motive and all we need now is to prove that Morbey had opportunity."

Major MacDonald leapt to his feet. "I strongly object to the use of the word 'revenge'. I said no such thing. What I did say was that Sapper Morbey went to the Château suspecting that either Johnson or Morbey had cut the wire. He went, not for revenge, but to try and ascertain the truth of the matter."

The President spoke to his two associates and they nodded in agreement. "Gentlemen, the Court accepts there was a long and bitter feud between Lieutenant Johnson and the members of No.3 Signal Section. The Court also accepts Sapper Johnson went to the Château on the afternoon of the 11th of November with the intention of accosting Lieutenant Johnson or Sapper Bailey to resolve the matter of the severed wire. Do you both agree with the Court's ruling?"

Both Captain Sampson and Major MacDonald agreed.

"Let us proceed. Captain Sampson, call your next witness."

Private Duncan was called and sworn in.

Captain Sampson addressed the witness. "Private Duncan, will you tell the Court where you were and what you were doing on the afternoon of 11th of November."

"Sir, Eddie and I, that's Private Taylor, are grooms. We look after the officers' horses. We exercised the horses in the morning and cleaned the stables. After lunch, we groomed them ready for riding. By 3:00pm, as no officer had indicated he wanted to go riding, we stabled the animals and fed them. After that we returned to our room and opened a couple of bottles of beer."

Captain Sampson interrupted the witness. "Private Duncan, describe to the Court your living quarters."

"Eddie and I live in what is called 'the stable quarters'. Above the stable there is a row of nine rooms. Eddie and I are in number nine. Sapper Bailey lives, sorry, used to live, in room number eight. He lived on his own."

Again, the Captain interrupted. "How do you gain access to these rooms?"

"There is only one way in. The rooms are on the first floor along a north-south line. They've a window which overlooks the horse parade - that's where we exercise the horses. To get to the rooms you climb a stairway on the northern end of the stable. A corridor runs the length of the stable and the nine rooms are on the left. Number nine is the last room in the row."

"One moment, Private Duncan. It is important the court has a clear view of the layout. As I understand it, the only way in is via a staircase at the northern end. When you reach the top of the stairs you will see on your left a row of rooms, nine in number.

You and Private Taylor occupy number nine and Sapper Bailey occupied number eight. Am I correct?"

"Yes sir, that is correct."

"Now can we move to what happened after you and Private Taylor returned to your room to have a beer."

"It was our intention to go into town or to the canteen to celebrate but we thought we'd have a couple of quiet ones beforehand. We'd just opened the first bottle when we heard someone walking along the corridor. With the wooden floors, you can hear anyone moving to or from their room. You can also hear voices or snoring as the walls are thin. There isn't much privacy." Private Duncan paused. "But they're better than being in a tent, especially in this weather."

"Yes, Private Duncan. You said you heard someone enter the corridor. Do you recall what time this would have been?"

Private Duncan shook his head. "I couldn't say the time exactly, but it must've been around 5:00pm, give or take a few minutes."

The Prosecutor nodded. "You heard someone enter the corridor. What happened then?"

"At first, we thought it was two people as you could hear talking but as he got closer, we realised that Bailey was talking to himself in a loud voice. He seemed very upset."

"How did you know it was Sapper Bailey?"

"Oh, Bailey had a very distinctive voice. Sort of high pitched."

"Private Duncan, I want you to think very carefully before answering this question. Was it possible that Sapper Bailey was accompanied by a second person?"

Private Duncan gave the question some thought before answering. "I don't think there was anyone else. We heard only one set of footsteps. And no one spoke but Bailey. He was talking to himself. We didn't hear another voice."

"Right, let us move on." The Captain appeared displeased with the answer. "What happened then?"

"Bailey arrived at his room, he entered and slammed the door."

"He didn't lock the door?"

Private Duncan shook his head. "No Sir. The doors don't have locks. Bailey entered the room, slammed the door and then threw himself onto his bed. You could hear the bed rattle. He was still talking to himself. And then there was the sound of a gun going off. It rattled the whole building. It gave Eddie and me a horrible fright."

Captain Sampson nodded sympathetically. "I am sure it did. What did you do then?'

"Well, Eddie and I rushed into Bailey's room. It was awful. Bailey was lying on the bed with a revolver pointed at what remained of his head. A horrible mess."

"So, what did you do?"

"I said I would go and get Sergeant Horne, the Mess Manager. He would know what to do. I told Eddie, Private Taylor, to phone the military police. I took off and ran to the Officers' Mess. I ran into the mess through the western door, ran along the corridor and just outside the ante room I ran into a steward. I asked him where I could find Sergeant Horne and he said there'd been an accident at the front of the building and the Mess Manager would be there. I ran outside and spotted a group of officers gathered at the south-east corner of the Château. I ran over to them and saw Sergeant Horne. I told him there'd been a shooting accident."

Captain Sampson interrupted. "Tell me Private Duncan. Why did you go looking for the Mess Manager instead of a medical officer?"

Private Duncan shook his head. "There was nothing a medical officer could do for Bailey. I reckoned the Mess Manager would know what to do."

"So, you told Sergeant Horne there had been an accident. What did he do?"

"He spoke to the medical officer and the two of them accompanied me back to the stables. When we got there Eddie was still standing guard outside room eight. Sergeant Horne and the medical officer went into the room, but I stayed outside with Eddie." Private Duncan frowned as he tried to recall the next event. "Oh yes. We'd been there only a few minutes when Sergeant Morris arrived. He's a military policeman. He went into the room and spoke with the Mess Manager and the doctor. After a while the three of them came out and the Mess Manager and doctor left, and Sergeant Morris questioned Eddie and me about what had happened."

"What did you tell Sergeant Morris?"

"The same as I've told you here today. That's all I know."

"Very good Private Duncan. I have no further questions." Captain Sampson resumed his seat.

Major MacDonald rose. "You say Private Duncan that Sapper Bailey was talking to himself when he entered the building".

"Yes Sir."

"How can you be sure that he wasn't talking to someone else?"

"Because no one answered him. Anyhow, it wasn't like a normal conversation. He just kept repeating the same words in a high-pitched voice."

"The same words. Tell me Private Duncan, could you understand what he was saying?"

Private Duncan shook his head. "It's difficult to say. We could make out some words which he kept repeating. He kept saying something like: 'They're going to blame me and I didn't do it. They'll shoot me'."

Major MacDonald frowned. "'They are going to blame me.' What did you make of that?"

The witness shook his head. "I have no idea what he was talking about. None of it made sense to me or Eddie."

"But you are quite clear those were the words used?"

"Oh yes sir, he kept repeating them."

"Right Private Duncan, let us move on. Are you sure there was no one else in the stable quarters that afternoon?"

The witness thought for a moment. "Well, if there was someone there, surely they'd have come out of their room when they heard the gun go off."

Major MacDonald nodded. "Yes, you would expect that. But what if they didn't want to be seen? Perhaps Sapper Bailey didn't shoot himself. Perhaps someone else shot him."

"No Sir, that's not possible. Eddie and I were out in the corridor seconds after the gun went off. We would've seen anyone leaving the room."

"Now then Private Duncan, think carefully. You said that when you heard the shot, you and Private Taylor rushed out of your room and into room eight. Could there have been someone hiding in that room?"

"No Sir, there is nowhere to hide in our rooms."

"In a cupboard perhaps?"

"No Sir, we don't have cupboards. We hang our clothes on nails driven into the walls."

"Now soon after you discovered the body of Sapper Bailey, you ran to find the Mess Manager, leaving Private Taylor on guard outside room eight. How long would it have taken you to run from the stable quarters to the front of the Officers' Mess where the Mess Manager was?"

Private Duncan smiled. "Three minutes Sir."

"Really? You seem to be very precise with the time."

"Yes Sir, I am." Duncan nodded towards the seats where Al and Bluey were sitting. "Your two helpers made me run it three times before they were satisfied that three minutes was the correct time for the run."

"Very good Private Duncan, that will be all from me." Major MacDonald sat down and made some notes.

The President asked Captain Sampson if he wished to re-examine the witness. "No Sir, I have no further questions, but I would like to place on record the Prosecution agrees with the timings of Private Duncan's run from the stables to the front of the Château."

The President frowned. "I really don't see the relevance of the time it took Private Duncan to run to get help."

Major MacDonald rose to his feet. "The relevance will be revealed in good time, Sir. What is important is that the accuracy of the timing will not be contested by my learned friend at some future time."

"Very well. Captain Sampson, call your next witness."

The Judge-Advocate called Captain Gregory and swore him in.

"Captain Gregory, tell the court what your duties in the Australian Imperial Force are."

"I am a medical officer attached to the Divisional Staff."

"Now Captain Gregory, I know you were involved with two incidents at the Château on the afternoon of 11th November but at this time we are only concerned with the death of Sapper Bailey. Do you understand?"

"Yes, I have been briefed on what the Court is doing".

"Fine. Would you please tell the court how you came to be involved with the Bailey case on the afternoon of 11th November?"

The medical officer settled back in his chair. "It was around 5:00pm. I was in the Mess having a drink when Lieutenant Rogers came running in and said there had been an accident at the front of the building. Along with several other officers, I ran outside and could see a body on the ground near the south east corner. When I got closer, I could see it was Lieutenant Johnson. From the angle of his head, it was obvious he was deceased but I checked his pulse to confirm that impression. I had been there only a minute or two when a soldier came running up. He spoke to the Mess Manager, Sergeant Horne. Sergeant Horne then approached me and told me there had been a shooting accident in the stables. As there was nothing that I could do for Lieutenant Johnson I asked one of the officers standing by to contact the hospital and tell them to send an ambulance to collect the body. I then accompanied Sergeant Horne and the soldier to the stables."

Captain Gregory took a sip of water before continuing. "On arrival at the stables we went up the stairway to the living quarters. There was a soldier standing outside room eight. The door was open, and we entered. Lying on the bed was the body of a soldier whom I now know to be Sapper Bailey. Sapper Bailey was holding a revolver in his right hand with the weapon pointed at his right temple. There was a bullet hole entry in the right temple and a mass of bone, tissue and blood on the bed and wall. There was nothing to be done to assist Sapper Bailey. Shortly afterwards Sergeant Morris of the military police arrived. Sergeant Morris said he would have the body removed. As there was no reason for me to stay, I left the scene with the Mess Manager."

Captain Sampson asked, "Was there anything about the scene that you thought was unusual?"

The Doctor frowned. "I don't think I understand the question."

"Captain Gregory, you said Bailey was holding the revolver in his right hand. Is it possible someone put the gun there?"

Captain Gregory thought for a moment. "Are you suggesting someone shot Bailey and then put the gun in Bailey's hand? I am not a detective, but I would find it difficult to work out how someone got Bailey to lie down on his bed and then shoot him, place the gun in Bailey's hand and then depart unseen. But you should ask the police that question, I am here simply to confirm that Sapper Bailey died from a gunshot wound to the right side of his head."

"Thank you, Captain Gregory, I have no further questions."

The President spoke. "Your witness Major MacDonald."

The Defence lawyer got to his feet. "I do not have any questions for Captain Gregory. As he said, his task here today was to tell the court the cause of Bailey's death. But Captain Gregory did make a short statement to say it would be difficult to work out how someone got Bailey to lie down on his bed, shoot him, place the gun in Bailey's hand and depart unseen. I totally agree with Captain Gregory. It is difficult to work out."

EXTRACTING REVENGE

The next witness was Sergeant Morris of the AIF Provost Corps.

Captain Sampson began: “Sergeant Morris, please tell the Court of your involvement with the Sapper Bailey case on the morning of the 12th of November.”

“Sir, about 8:30am I received a phone call from Sergeant Horne, the Mess Manager at the Officers’ Mess. He told me he had seen Sapper Morbey and Sapper Bailey fighting in the passageway of the Mess the previous afternoon. As I had been actively involved with investigating the death of Bailey on the afternoon of the 11th, I made a connection between the two incidents.”

“What do you mean by ‘two incidents’?”

“Well Sir, I had a witness who saw the two sappers fighting in the passageway in the Officers’ Mess and a short time later Sapper Bailey was found shot in his room. You don’t have to be Sherlock Holmes to know there might possibly be a connection between the two incidents - the fight and the shooting.”

"I suppose a policeman's mind would work that way," Captain Sampson smiled. "Having made the connection, what did you do then?"

"I spoke with my Commanding Officer. He agreed the matter needed to be followed up. I took two men and went to the billet where Morbey was living and arrested him."

"Did he put up a struggle? Did he protest in any way?"

"No Sir, he did not resist but he did protest that he didn't know anything about Bailey's death. But you would expect him to say that."

"You may be right, Sergeant Morris. Was Morbey questioned and charged at the Police HQ?"

"Yes Sir." The Sergeant was on the defensive. "We have strict rules for the conduct of an investigation, and we stuck to those rules, despite what others may say."

The Prosecutor was quick to put the witness at ease. "I am not aware, Sergeant Morris, of any criticism of the manner in which this investigation has been handled. Let us move on. Has Morbey at any time admitted involvement in the death of Sapper Bailey?"

The Sergeant shook his head. "No Sir, he has always maintained his innocence."

"Right. Let us go back to the afternoon of the 11th.What can you tell us about your involvement with the death of Sapper Bailey?"

Sergeant Morris consulted his notes. "Shortly after 5:00pm on the 11th November, I received a phone call informing me there had been a shooting in the stable quarters at the Château. I proceeded to the quarters and on arrival saw two soldiers standing outside room eight. I entered room eight and was greeted by Captain Gregory and Sergeant Horne. On the bed was a body which I was told was Sapper Bailey. There was nothing that could be done for the victim so I told Captain Gregory and Sergeant Morgan, I would arrange for the body to be transferred to the hospital. They left and I then questioned Privates Duncan and Taylor and took a statement from each of them. I then returned to my office and made the necessary arrangements for the body to be moved."

Captain Sampson paused for a moment. "Sergeant Morris, you are a policeman of considerable experience. Having viewed the scene of the crime and questioned witnesses, what conclusion have you come to in relation to the death of Sapper Bailey?"

Sergeant Morris gave the question some thought before replying. "I believe there is only one explanation for the death of Sapper Bailey and that is he took his own life."

Captain Sampson frowned. "Why do you exclude the possibility of someone else shooting Bailey and then putting the gun in his hand before fleeing the scene?"

"Sir, from all the evidence presented to me plus my own observations, I cannot see how a second person could have been present in Bailey's room at the time of the shooting and escaped unobserved. Privates Duncan and Taylor both claim they heard only one set of footsteps when Bailey entered the building. They heard only Bailey's voice. They rushed to Bailey's room immediately they heard the shot. They saw no one leaving the room. There is nowhere in the room for someone to hide."

Captain Sampson interrupted the witness. "Perhaps he made his escape through the window?"

"No Sir." Sergeant Morris was adamant. "The window is a fixed pane of glass. It doesn't open and close, and it wasn't broken. The only way a second person could have left the room is via the hallway, and no one did."

"Thank you, Sergeant Morris." Captain Sampson wasn't at all happy with the way the trial was going. "I have no further questions."

Major MacDonald was quick to his feet without waiting to be called.

"Sergeant Morris, the Prosecutor has described you as a policeman of considerable experience and I agree with his character reference. You have given the court a number of reasons why you believe Sapper Bailey took his own life, but you are the person who charged Sapper Morbey with murder. Can you explain that to the court?"

Sergeant Morris looked at the Prosecutor. "Sir, I do as I am told by higher authority, and I was told to charge Sapper Morbey with the murder of Sapper Bailey, and so I did."

"I see. No one can put any blame on you for any wrong action taken regarding Sapper Morbey."

Captain Sampson leapt to his feet. "Mr President, I object to the words used by the Defence. It is the Court who will decide whether or not Sapper Morbey murdered Sapper Bailey, not Sergeant Morris nor Major MacDonald."

The President raised his hand to calm the Prosecutor down. "You are correct Captain Sampson, and the Court will make a finding on the matter in due course, but Sergeant Morris is entitled to his opinion. I find the evidence given by Sergeant Morris to be of considerable interest. You may proceed Major MacDonald."

"Thank you, Mr President." The Major turned to the witness. "Sergeant Morris, it is very important we eliminate any possibility there was a second person in room eight at the time of the shooting. You have already given several reasons why you believe there was no other person present. Can you elaborate further for the Court?"

"Yes Sir. I believe we can accept that Bailey entered the building unaccompanied. Privates Duncan and Taylor are adamant there was only one set of footsteps along the hallway and no one spoke other than Bailey. So that leaves us with the scenario that the killer was waiting in Bailey's room. I totally reject the suggestion that someone was lying in wait in room eight." The Sergeant gave court members a long, hard stare.

"You seem very sure of that Sergeant Morris."

Sergeant Morris turned his gaze to Major MacDonald. "Yes Sir, I am sure of myself. If someone was waiting in the room for Bailey, I would expect Bailey to say, 'Who are you?' If he knew the person, I would expect him to say, 'What are you doing here?' But Bailey didn't say anything like that. All Duncan and Taylor heard were his ravings about being set up for some crime which he claimed he didn't do. And then consider the gun. I understand that a witness, perhaps two, saw Bailey take Lieutenant Johnson's revolver from the coat rack in the Officer's Mess. Later I took the gun to the armoury, and they confirmed that it was the gun issued to Lieutenant Johnson. Now the phantom killer has to wrest the gun off Bailey and then get him to lie on the bed so he can shoot him. There were no signs of a struggle. There was no second person in that room. Bailey shot himself."

Major MacDonald smiled. "Thank you, Sergeant Morris, you have been most helpful. I have no further questions."

The president addressed the Prosecutor. "Do you wish to re-examine the witness Captain Sampson?"

"No Sir. I would like to call my final witness, Sergeant Horne."

"Very well, but first I would like to ask Major MacDonald a question." The President looked down at the notes he had been taking. "Major MacDonald, the court members believe you have, with the assistance of the Prosecution witnesses, established the fact there was no second person involved in the shooting of Sapper Bailey. Do you wish at this time to make a submission to the court?"

Major MacDonald shook his head, "No Sir. I look forward to hearing what the next witness has to say. Sergeant Horne was involved in this case from the very beginning. His testimony may be very important."

"Very well, call Sergeant Horne."

Sergeant Horne took the Oath and sat down.

Captain Sampson addressed the witness. "Sergeant Horne, please tell the Court your current position and duties."

"I am the Officers' Mess Manager. I am responsible for running the mess. Catering, supervision of staff, administration, in fact anything that impinges on the orderly and smooth running of the Mess is my responsibility."

"Before you start telling us what you know about this case, perhaps it would help the Court if you described the layout of the Château. It would help us visualise where people were and what they were doing as events unfolded."

"Sir, the Château faces east so the main entrance is sometimes referred to as the east door, but most people call it the main door or sometimes the front door. When you enter through this door you find yourself in a long corridor which runs all the way through to the western entrance, or back door. On entering the building through the main door, you find the dining room on the right and the ante room on the left. Moving along the corridor you come to a door on your right - it opens into the kitchen.

"Opposite that door is the sweeping staircase which leads to the first floor sleeping accommodation. Under the staircase is a door leading to the toilets. Along the corridor, just past the toilet door, we have a row of coat hooks, and each has a number. Officers are allocated a number and they use that hook to hang their coat and cap. Sometimes if they are wearing webbing, they also hang that on the hook, webbing not being allowed in the ante room or dining room."

Sergeant Horne paused to see if there any questions. "Further along the passageway there are a number of rooms. I have my office there and there is a dining room and recreation room for the staff, staff toilets and some storerooms."

"Thank you, Sergeant Horne. Now I want you to tell the court what happened in the mess at about 5:00pm on 11th of November."

Sergeant Horne consulted his notes. "Sir, at about 5:00pm on the 11th of November, I was in the dining room and heard loud voices. I stepped into the corridor and saw two soldiers struggling and shouting. They were standing at the foot of the staircase that leads to the first-floor accommodation area. I called to them, and they immediately ceased struggling and yelling. Sapper Bailey, whom I recognised, turned and ran towards the rear entrance to the Château. I called on him to stop but he kept running."

Captain Sampson interrupted, "So he just took off and ran from the building?"

"Well Sir, he took off down the corridor but on the way, he ran to the row of coat hooks on the left side of the corridor and grabbed some webbing from a hook before racing down the corridor and out of the building. I investigated what he had seized and found it was Lieutenant Johnson's webbing which contained Lieutenant Johnson's revolver."

Captain Sampson again interrupted, "You didn't pursue him?"

"There was no reason to chase him. I knew who he was, and I could question him later when I wasn't so busy. As I didn't recognise the second soldier, I asked his name. He identified himself as Sapper Morbey. I asked him what he was doing in the Officers' Mess and he said he had come to find Sapper Bailey. I should also mention that one of the local girls who we employ on domestic duties, Mademoiselle Yvette Pruvost, was also present."

"Why would Mademoiselle Pruvost be in the corridor?"

"When officers enter the Mess and do not wish to go upstairs to their room before entering the ante room, they leave their coat and cap on the hooks in the hallway. Sometimes they also leave their webbing and sometimes there is a revolver attached to the webbing. There is always a member of the staff present to take their gear to make sure it is hung on the correct hook. Sometimes that member of the staff is a steward and sometimes it is one of the local staff we employ. In this case, Mademoiselle Pruvost was carrying out that duty."

"Right Sergeant Horne. Let us return to the events of 11th of November. You have told the court you saw two soldiers struggling and shouting in loud voices. You have identified the two soldiers as Sappers Bailey and Morbey. Bailey ran off. What did you do then?"

Sergeant consulted his notes. "I didn't want to carry on a conversation with a soldier in the Officers' Mess, so I told him to follow me, and we went into the kitchen and exited via the kitchen door on the north side of the building."

"A moment please, Sergeant Horne, what about Mademoiselle Pruvost? Did she accompany you?"

"No Sir. She remained at the bottom of the stairs and carried on with her duties."

"Right. Now you and Sapper Morbey are outside the Château. What happened then?"

"I reprimanded Morbey for being in the Officers' Mess and pointed out that under normal circumstances I would have had him put on a charge but seeing it was such a special day, I would let him off with a caution. He replied he was sorry but all he wanted to do was question Bailey about an incident which had happened earlier in the day. I told him if he wanted to see Sapper Bailey then he should seek him out in his quarters, not in the Officers' Mess."

Captain Sampson quickly looked up from his notes. "Tell me Sergeant Horne, did you tell Sapper Morbey where Sapper Bailey's quarters were located?"

"Yes I did Sir. There was no reason not to tell him. It's common knowledge the staff quarters are over the stables. I told him that's where he should talk to Bailey, not in the Officers' Mess."

"Do you know if Morbey went to the stable quarters?"

"I don't know where he went afterwards. We had been talking for only a short period when Lieutenant Rogers came through the kitchen door and told me there had been an accident at the southeast corner of the Château. He said Lieutenant Johnson had fallen from his room and was badly injured. I told Morbey to be on his way and I accompanied Lieutenant Rogers to the front of the building. Lieutenant Rogers told me he had alerted Captain Gregory and when we reached the scene of the accident, I saw Captain Gregory bending over a Lieutenant Johnson's body."

Captain Sampson spoke. "So, you don't know where Sapper Morbey went after you left him outside the kitchen door?"

"No Sir. When I left with Lieutenant Rogers, Sapper Morbey was standing outside the kitchen door."

"So, he could easily have gone to the stable quarters?"

Sergeant Horne gestured with his hands. "He could have gone anywhere Sir. I didn't see him again after we parted company."

"But he could have gone to the stable quarters?" Captain Sampson persisted.

"As I have already said Sir, he could have gone anywhere."

"Thank you, Sergeant Horne. Now let us return to the scene of Lieutenant Johnson's accident. What happened after you arrived there?"

Sergeant Horne again consulted his notes. "I had hardly arrived at the scene when Private Duncan came running up and told me there had been a shooting accident in the stable quarters. Captain Gregory heard Duncan's report and he stood up and said, there was nothing he could do for Lieutenant Johnson so he had better have a look at the shooting incident. Captain Gregory then asked Lieutenant Rogers to phone the hospital and ask for an ambulance to collect Lieutenant Johnson's body. Captain Gregory and I then accompanied Private Duncan to the stable quarters where we found Private Taylor on guard outside room eight. Inside the room we found the body of Sapper Bailey. It was an awful mess."

Captain Sampson nodded. "I'm sure it was. Can you describe the scene?"

Sergeant Horne took his time before answering. "The body was lying on the bed. He was on his back and his right hand was holding a revolver to his right temple. The left side of his head was shattered and there was blood, bone and tissue over the wall, a horrible sight. There was nothing for the doctor to do, and shortly after our arrival Sergeant Morris appeared and he took charge of the situation. Captain Gregory and I then left and returned to the mess."

"I imagine that was a very busy night in the mess?"

"It was Sir. Everyone there had a lot to be thankful for and a good reason to celebrate. It was a pity the celebrations were somewhat spoiled by the two events."

"Yes, Sergeant Horne, most unfortunate. From the evidence of a previous witness, we learned it was you who reported the altercation between Morbey and Bailey to the Provost Office."

Sergeant Horne nodded, "Yes Sir. I was very busy on the night of 11th and it wasn't until the next morning that it occurred to me that there might be a connection between the struggle between Morbey and Bailey, and Bailey's death. I felt it was my duty to bring the matter to the attention of Sergeant Morris."

"Quite right Sergeant Horne, thank you. I have no further questions Mr President."

MINUTE ZERO

The President turned to Major MacDonald, "Do you wish to ask Sergeant Horne any questions?"

Major Macdonald stood, "Mr President, yes and no. Not really questions but I do want Sergeant Horne to help me in a brief review of the matter before the Court. Sergeant Horne, I want you to give careful attention to what I am about to put to you. I would like you to construct a time chart of the events starting with the moment you stepped into the corridor and saw Sappers Morbey and Bailey arguing. We will call that moment Minute Zero. That is when we start the clock. Now when you called to them, Sapper Morbey let go of Sapper Bailey, and Bailey ran down the corridor."

Sergeant Horne was puzzled by this new line of thinking. "Yes Sir, that is what happened."

"Good. Now you approached Morbey and Mademoiselle Pruvost and spoke to them for a short time before leading Sapper Morbey through the kitchen and out the north side door. Let us allow half a minute for you to approach the couple. Now, how long were you talking to the couple and how long did it take you and Morbey to get outside the Château?"

Sergeant Horne gave the question some thought. "Well Sir, I didn't waste much time talking to Morbey inside the Mess. I simply asked, 'Who are you and what are you doing here?' He answered my questions and I then said follow me and I led him through the kitchen to the north door. So, I would say we were talking for a minute and then it took half a minute to walk outside."

"Splendid. Half a minute to approach the couple, one minute talking to them and then another half minute to exit the building." Major MacDonald smiled. "So you and Morbey arrive outside the kitchen door at Minute Two?

"Yes Sir."

"Then you remained talking to Morbey until Lieutenant Rogers appeared. How long was that?"

"I have given the matter a lot of thought and discussed it with your associates. We even tried to re-enact the discussion and we came to the conclusion that Morbey and I were standing outside the kitchen door for two, perhaps three, minutes before Lieutenant Rogers appeared."

"That's fine Sergeant Horne. Let's call it three minutes. If we accept that you and Morbey were talking for three minutes, then Lieutenant Rogers arrived at Minute Five. Please continue."

"Lieutenant Rogers told me there had been an accident at the south east corner of the Château."

"Did he say what sort of an accident?"

"Yes Sir. He said Lieutenant Johnson had fallen from his room and it looked very bad. I asked him if he had informed the doctor and he said 'affirmative'. He said Captain Gregory had gone to the scene of the accident. I then told Morbey to be on his way. I left with Lieutenant Rogers and we hurried to the front of the Château."

"Right Sergeant Horne. Now let us bring our timeline up to date. We have established that Lieutenant Rogers arrived at Minute Five. Now how long did you talk and how long did it take you and the Lieutenant to reach the scene of the accident?"

"Again, Sir I have gone over the events, and I think it's fair to say Lieutenant Rogers and I spoke for about three minutes and then I spent another half minute telling Morbey to thank his lucky stars that he wasn't on report and to be on his way. It then took Lieutenant Rogers and myself about half a minute to reach the scene of the accident."

"Very good Sergeant Horne. So, let's again bring the timeline up to date. Minute Five Lieutenant Rogers appears. You and he talk for three minutes. You talk to Morbey for half a minute and then it takes you and Rogers half a minute a to reach the scene of the accident. That's four minutes to add onto Minute Five. Are we agreed that, give or take a few seconds, you arrived at the scene of Johnson's accident at Minute Nine?"

"Yes Sir, that would seem to be correct."

"Splendid Sergeant Horne. Now we need to identify the moment that Private Duncan arrived with the news of the shooting of Sapper Bailey."

"Well Sir, as I recall, it was soon after I arrived at the southeast corner that Private Duncan came running along the front of the building and told me about Bailey's accident. I would say Duncan arrived two minutes after me."

"Very good Sergeant Horne. By my calculations, Private Duncan arrived with the news of Bailey's death at Minute Eleven. Do you agree?"

"Yes Sir."

"Thank you Sergeant Horne, I have no further questions."

The President looked to the Prosecution table. "Captain Sampson, do you agree with this so-called timeline put forward by the Defence?"

"Yes Sir. The Prosecution was involved in the re-enactments carried out by the Defence and does not challenge the timings."

"Very well, the witness may stand down. Does the Prosecution wish to call any further witnesses?"

"No Sir."

"Major MacDonald, do you wish to make a submission to the court or do you wish to call witnesses for the Defence?"

Major MacDonald re-arranged the papers he held in his hand. "No witnesses Mr President, but I do wish to make a submission to the Court. We have heard the evidence of Private Duncan and Sergeant Morris that clearly supports my claim that there was no second person involved in the shooting of Sapper Bailey. Bailey was alone in his room and took his own life. I submit the evidence given by Private Duncan and Sergeant Morris should be sufficient to acquit Sapper Morbey of the charge of murdering Sapper Bailey. However, in addition to the evidence given by Duncan and Morris, I wish to bring to the attention of the Court the evidence given by Sergeant Horne."

The Major looked at his papers. "What I want to do now is to complete the timeline, going through the crucial points, that I have constructed with the help of Sergeant Horne. Firstly, that the timeline starts at zero with Sergeant Horne challenging Morbey and Bailey in the passageway of the Château. Bailey runs off. Now at minute five, Sergeant Horne and Morbey are outside the northern kitchen door when Lieutenant Rogers arrives with news of Lieutenant Johnson's accident. Sergeant Horne and Lieutenant Rogers arrive at the scene of Johnson's accident at minute nine. Two minutes later, at minute eleven, Private Duncan arrived with the news of Bailey's death."

"Now, let us back track Duncan's movements. It took him three minutes to run from the stable rooms to the south east corner of the Château. That means he departed the stables at minute eight. Let us allow Privates Duncan and Taylor three minutes to recover from the shock of seeing the body of Bailey and to make the decision for Duncan to go for help. That means that Bailey was shot just prior to minute five. Remember both soldiers ran from their room to the room next door as soon as they heard the shot. Bailey was in the Château at minute zero and he ran from there to his room. Perhaps he wasn't as fast as Duncan and perhaps he may have even walked part of the way. But allowing Bailey four minutes to reach his room and a further half minute to rant and rave before shooting himself, the actual act would have taken place between minute four and minute five."

"Mr President, we know that at minute four, Morbey was in the company of Sergeant Horne. Sapper Morbey was nowhere near the stable quarters when Sapper Bailey died. I ask the Court to find my client not guilty as charged."

The three members of the Court conferred briefly before the President addressed the court. "The Defendant will rise." George Morbey got to his feet. The President continued: "Sapper Morbey, the Court has heard the evidence both for and against you in relation to this case. It is the decision of the court that Sapper Bailey died by his own hand. The court finds you not guilty of the charge of murdering Sapper Bailey."

A murmur ran around the courtroom but ceased immediately when the President raised his hand. He glanced at his watch. "Observing the time it would seem appropriate to adjourn for lunch rather than commence proceeding with the second case. The court will adjourn and re-convene at 2:00pm."

All rose to their feet as the three members of the Court departed. Sapper Morbey with his escort followed.

* * *

Al Wilson and Bluey pushed forward to the Defence table.

"Congratulations Sir, you did it. You were brilliant," exclaimed Bluey.

Major MacDonald shook his head. “Thank you Dowson, but remember it was a team effort. You all helped. And it wasn’t really a difficult case to win. Morbey should never have been charged in the first place. The Prosecution didn’t have a case. The whole matter was triggered by emotion without facts to support the accusation. Captain Sampson knew that and so did Sergeant Morris. However, this afternoon is a different matter. I must talk to Sapper Morbey. What are you men going to do about lunch?”

“No problem, Sir,” replied Al, “the kitchen staff have invited us to eat with them. Marie and Nicole Pruvost are on duty and I suspect they had something to do with the invitation. No doubt they want to hear what has happened.”

“And where are Gilly and Yvette?”

Bluey spoke. “They’re at the farm. Gilly wouldn’t let Yvette attend the trial. She said it would upset her and I agreed.”

Major MacDonald frowned. “Oh, I expected Yvette to be here today.”

He thought for a moment. “That’s all right. You two go off and have your lunch. I’m off to talk to George Morbey. Meet me outside the Château at 1:45pm. There is still work to be done.” With that the Major moved towards the door leading to the rear of the courtroom.

Bluey scratched his head. “What does he mean, ‘there is still work to be done’? We won’t have much time to run errands if we meet him only fifteen minutes before the trial starts.”

“Bluey, you worry too much. We both know the Major is running this show. The others are there to make up the numbers, only they don’t know it. Come on, let’s get some tucker. I’m ready for some food from the Officers’ kitchen.”

FIFTEEN FEET IS NOT ENOUGH

Al and Bluey were at the entrance to the Château when a staff car came along the sweeping driveway. It stopped at the entrance and Major MacDonald, Gilly and Yvette emerged.

Bluey laughed. "Travelling in style these days, ladies?"

Gilly shook her head. "Major MacDonald offered us a ride and we thought it would have been rude to refuse."

"And if we had walked, we wouldn't have been here on time," Yvette added.

Major MacDonald was in a hurry. "We don't have time for chatter. Dowson, you are to stay in the outer anteroom with the two ladies. I don't know if Yvette will be called to the stand but if she is, the Court Orderly will come to escort her to the Court. You will then accompany Gilly to her seat behind my table. Wilson, you come with me and reserve four seats behind me for yourself, the two ladies and Dowson. Yvette will join you after she has given her evidence. Are we all clear on what is to happen?"

The two soldiers nodded, and the group entered the building. Bluey and the two ladies found seats outside the courtroom. The

Major and Al entered and had just settled in their seats when the Judge- Advocate called the room to stand. The three members of the Court entered and took their places. “This Court is now in session.”

The President raised his hand. “Please advise me Judge-Advocate. Do we need to restate the charge against the defendant?”

“No Sir. The charge as read out to the defendant this morning remains extant.”

“Thank you. Captain Sampson, are you ready to proceed?”

The Prosecutor rose to his feet. “Yes Sir. The Prosecution will provide evidence to show the defendant came to the Château on the afternoon of the 11th of November with the intention of finding out who cut a telephone wire on the previous night, an action that ultimately resulted in the death of one of his companions. Sapper Morbey was convinced that either Lieutenant Johnson or Sapper Bailey had cut the wire and it was his intention to extract revenge. That was the motive for this crime. The Prosecution will produce evidence that Sapper Morbey was in the Château at the time of Lieutenant Johnson’s death - motive and opportunity.” He sat down.

Immediately Major MacDonald was on his feet. “The Defence totally rejects these allegations. Sapper Morbey was at the Château on the afternoon of 11th of November to try and find answers to the events of the previous night. But how could he be contemplating revenge when he didn’t know how the line had been cut or by whom, or if a person was involved? As to the question of opportunity, the Defence will show he did not have the opportunity to harm Lieutenant Johnson that afternoon. Thank you, Sir.” The Major sat down.

Captain Sampson rose, “Call Lieutenant Rogers.”

Lieutenant Rogers entered, took the stand and was sworn in.

"Lieutenant Rogers, I understand you and Lieutenant Sharpe found the body of Lieutenant Johnson on the afternoon of 11th of November? Would you please tell the Court the circumstances of the discovery?"

"Sir, Lieutenant Sharpe and I were returning to the Château from a stroll in the South Garden when we heard the sound of breaking glass. We didn't pay much attention to it as there was quite a lot of windows broken that day. When we reached the southeast corner of the building, we saw a body on the ground. It was Lieutenant Johnson. From the angle of the head, it was obvious he had a broken neck. He certainly was dead."

"What did you do then?"

"I said to Peter, sorry, Lieutenant Sharpe, I would go for help, and he should remain with the body. I ran to the Officer's Mess and when I reached the anteroom, I saw Captain Gregory and some other officers at the bar. I told them about Lieutenant Johnson and a group of them left the room and went outside."

The Prosecutor interrupted, "Did you accompany them?"

"No Sir. They knew where the body was. I went looking for the Mess Manager, Sergeant Horne. I hurried down the hallway. There was a girl, one of the staff, standing at the foot of the stairs and I asked her if she had seen the Mess Manager. She pointed at the kitchen door. I entered the kitchen and asked another staff member if she had seen Sergeant Horne and she pointed to the outside door. I went outside and found Sergeant Horne talking to a soldier.

Captain Sampson interrupted, "Did you recognise the soldier?"

"No Sir, not then, but I now know the soldier was Sapper Morbey. I told Sergeant Horne about Johnson and he and I went to the scene of the accident."

"Did Sapper Morbey accompany you?"

"No Sir. Sergeant Horne told him to be gone."

"Did Sapper Morbey leave the area as instructed?"

Lieutenant Rogers shook his head. "I wouldn't know Sir. Sergeant Horne and I left him standing outside the kitchen door. I didn't look back, so I don't know if he left or stayed."

"Please tell the court about your arrival back at the scene of the accident."

"Well Sir, when Sergeant Horne and I arrived there was a small group of officers standing around the body and Captain Gregory was kneeling by the body. Nobody was talking. Shortly after we arrived, a soldier came running up to Sergeant Horne and told him there had been a shooting accident in the stable quarters. Sergeant Horne spoke to Captain Gregory. I don't know what was said but Captain Gregory, Sergeant Horne and the soldier left the scene. As they were departing Captain Gregory instructed me to call for an ambulance which I did. A little while later an ambulance arrived and collected Johnson's body. Lieutenant Sharpe and I then retired to the bar for a drink."

"Thank you, Lieutenant Rogers. I have no further questions." Captain Sampson sat down, and Major MacDonald rose to his feet.

"Lieutenant Rogers, I know you have been assisting my support staff in timing your activities on the morning of the 11th and I would now like to go over the results. Let us start with the sound of breaking glass. We will call that start time or Minute Zero."

"Yes Sir."

"Now following that noise how long did it take you and Lieutenant Sharpe to reach the body?"

"I estimate it took about a minute."

The Major made a note on the file he was carrying. "Now, how long did you stay at the scene?"

"Not long Sir. Although we both believed Lieutenant Johnson was dead, we felt we must get a doctor to check as soon as possible. I reckon I was only there for a minute, perhaps a little less, and I then ran to the Officers' Mess."

"Now take us through what you did next and try to put a time on your actions."

"Well Sir, I have been working with your staff to try and get the timings right. I would say it took me half a minute to reach the anteroom. I would have spent a minute explaining the situation to Captain Gregory. I then took half a minute to run down the passageway and through the kitchen to the north door where Sergeant Horne was."

"Thank you, Lieutenant Rogers. If my arithmetic is correct, the time lapse between you hearing the glass breaking and your arrival at the north door was four minutes. Do you agree?"

"I do Sir. The time scale might be out by a minute or so, but I reckon that four minutes is close to the right number."

"Thank you, Lieutenant Rogers, I have no further questions."

Captain Sampson was already on his feet as Lieutenant Rogers left the witness stand. "Call Captain Gregory."

The medical officer entered the courtroom, took the stand and was sworn in.

"Captain Gregory. I understand you were in the anteroom of the Officers' Mess around 5:00pm on 11th of November."

"Correct. I was having a celebratory drink with other officers when Lieutenant Rogers came running into the room. He approached me and said that there had been an accident and Lieutenant Johnson had fallen from his room on the southeast corner. He said it looked bad. I immediately left the anteroom accompanied by several officers and went to the southeast corner. On arrival, I saw Lieutenant Johnson lying on the ground. I checked for a pulse and there was none. Just from looking at the position of his head I knew he hadn't survived the fall. There was nothing to be done except arrange for the body to be transferred to the hospital."

"Tell me Captain Gregory - was there any possibility that Lieutenant Johnson died before he fell from the window?"

The doctor shook his head. “Sergeant Morris of the Military Police asked the same question later in the day, so I carried out a thorough examination of the body on the morning of 12th November. I found no trace of any injuries other than those that would have been caused by the fall. There were numerous cuts caused by coming into contact with the glass in the window but none of those were very serious. Lieutenant Johnson was an unlucky man.”

Captain Sampson frowned. “Unlucky? Of course, he was unlucky - he was killed by the fall from his room.”

“Yes, Captain Sampson, but I would guess the windowsill is about fifteen feet from the ground. Normally if someone fell that distance they might end up with a broken arm or leg, perhaps some rib damage. Lieutenant Johnson was unlucky in that he landed headfirst on a rock in the garden.”

Captain Sampson shook his head. “I suppose it comes down to how you look at it. Thank you, Captain Gregory, I have no further questions.”

Major MacDonald got to his feet. “That is an interesting observation you just made Captain Gregory. Fifteen feet is not a great height. Now if someone was contemplating suicide, surely they would select a greater height from which to jump?”

“I agree Major. If Lieutenant Johnson was thinking of suicide, I would have thought he would have climbed to the roof to jump or selected another means of ending his life. There are many ways a man can kill himself. Corporal Bailey is an example. What really is important is the mindset of the man - how determined he is to carry the act through to a successful conclusion.”

“If I am following you correctly Doctor, you are suggesting Johnson was not attempting suicide when he fell from the window.”

"That is my opinion, and I stress it is simply my opinion. To jump from a window fifteen feet above ground level suggests to me he was doing something to draw attention to himself."

Major MacDonald paused. "Yes Doctor, that might be one possibility but there is also the possibility that Lieutenant Johnson didn't jump. The exit through the window may not have been instigated by Johnson - a second person may have thrown or pushed him through the window."

"Yes Major, that may be a possibility, but I have no medical evidence to support that theory. That is something for the police to work out."

"Of course, thank you Captain Gregory. I have no further questions."

ONE FINAL WITNESS

Captain Sampson spoke, "Call Sergeant Morris." The military policeman moved to the witness box and was sworn in.

Captain Sampson: "Sergeant Morris, on the afternoon of 11th of November, were you called to the scene of a death at the Château?"

"Yes Sir, I was attending the scene of the death of Sapper Bailey with Captain Gregory and Sergeant Horne, the mess manager. They told me there had been a death at the Château. They told me Lieutenant Johnson had fallen from the window in his room and had died at the scene."

"What did you do?"

The Sergeant looked at his notebook. "After I had arranged for the body of Sapper Bailey to be collected, I went to Lieutenant Johnson's room in the Château. On entering the room, I saw the window had been broken. I looked out of the window. Lieutenant Johnson's body had been removed but I could see broken glass on the lawn and could judge where he landed."

"Was there any sign of a struggle in the room?"

"No, not that I could detect. The bed was made up. The sheets were not turned back but I think that someone had been resting on top of the blankets. Everything else seemed to be in place."

"Nothing to suggest foul play?"

"No Sir. No broken furniture, no blood, nothing out of place - everything looked normal."

"Thank you, Sergeant Morris. I have no further questions."

Major MacDonald took his time in rising to his feet. "Sergeant Morris, in your experience, would you say that jumping from a window, fifteen feet above the ground, a good way to commit suicide?"

"I'm sorry Sir, but I don't believe there is such a thing as 'a good way to commit suicide.'"

Major MacDonald nodded. "You are quite right, that was an unfortunate choice of words on my part. Let me rephrase the question. If someone was contemplating suicide, do you think they would attempt it by jumping from a window, fifteen feet above the ground?"

"It's impossible to say Sir. A person about to commit suicide is not thinking rationally or logically, and who knows what they are thinking. If this incident is a suicide, then I believe we are entitled to wonder about the choice of height. And there is another unusual aspect. I have some experience with cases of suicide and there is a strange irony in most cases where jumping from a window is involved. Usually, and I stress the word usually, the person opens the window and then throws themselves out. It is thought the person opens the window as they are afraid of getting cut by the glass if they jump through the pane. It's ironic to say the least. They are trying to kill themselves but are afraid they might be cut by the glass."

Major MacDonald interrupted the Sergeant. "Please let me make sure I am following you correctly. You are saying that fifteen feet is not a height that would normally be selected for a suicide attempt. And you are also suggesting that in most suicide cases involving jumping from a window, the victim usually opens the window before jumping to avoid being cut by the glass - strange though that may sound."

Sergeant Morris nodded. "Yes Sir. If you research cases of suicide resulting from jumping from a window, you will find the majority jumped from a height well in in excess of fifteen feet. And you would also find in the majority of cases the victim opened the window before jumping. These are hard recorded facts."

"Interesting indeed, Sergeant Morris. You hold the view that Lieutenant Johnson did not commit suicide but there was a second person involved in his death?"

Sergeant Morris shook his head. "No Sir. I do not hold that view because there are no facts to support that. What I am saying is that this case is different to what one might call typical. We do not know Lieutenant Johnson's state of mind at the time. Perhaps he was suffering from delayed shock from his war experiences, maybe he had mental problems we are not aware of. All I can say is that it is not a normal case but without any evidence to show a second person was involved, I assume Lieutenant Johnson acted on his own and jumped from his window. Perhaps he didn't mean to kill himself. We will never know."

"Thank you, Sergeant Morris." The President looked at Captain Sampson. "Do you wish to call further witnesses?"

Captain Sampson stood up. "One final witness sir. Call Sergeant Horne." The mess manager walked to the stand and was sworn in.

"Sergeant Horne, would you tell the court what you saw and heard in the Château passageway around 5:00pm on 11th November."

Sergeant Horne frowned. "Sir, I told my story this morning, I have nothing to add."

"Sergeant Horne, this is a different case so we need to hear your account of events again."

The mess manager looked embarrassed. "Sorry Sir, I was confused. On the afternoon of 11th November around 5:00, I was in the dining room when I heard loud voices. I went into the hallway and saw two soldiers arguing. One I recognised as Sapper Bailey, the other I didn't know although I know now, was Sapper Morbey.

"Morbey had hold of Bailey's arm and Bailey was trying to break free. I shouted at them and Morbey let go of Bailey's arm. Bailey then ran off down the passageway. I shouted to him to stop but he ran to the coat rail, took something from the rail and then ran along the passage and out of the back door. I approached Morbey and asked his name and why was he arguing with Bailey. He said he had come to the Château to ask Bailey some questions about a stunt that had gone wrong the previous night.

"I ordered him to follow me and we entered the kitchen. I led him to the northern door. When we got outside I demanded to know what was going on. Morbey said he wanted to talk to Bailey to clear up some unanswered questions about a wire being cut. We were talking for a short time when Lieutenant Rogers came out of the kitchen. He told me there had been a serious accident involving Lieutenant Johnson. I told Morbey to be on his way and to count himself lucky he was not on a charge. Lieutenant Rogers and I then went around the building to the body of Lieutenant Johnson."

"Did Morbey depart from the area?"

"I don't know Sir. I left him standing there. I don't know what he did after we left."

Captain Sampson nodded. "Thank you Sergeant Horne. I have no further questions."

The President inclined his head towards the Defence table and Major MacDonald rose to his feet. "Sergeant Horne, I know we spent some time this morning working out a timeline for events but I'm afraid we must do it again. I will read from the timeline I have noted down and ask you to agree or disagree with the timings. Is that clear?"

"Perfectly clear Sir."

"Now, we agreed to start the timeline at the moment you saw Sappers Bailey and Morbey arguing in the passageway."

"Correct Sir."

"Now, it took you half a minute to approach the group and you spoke to Morbey. We allowed a minute for your conversation and then another half minute for you and Morbey to walk through the kitchen. That means you and Morbey arrived outside the kitchen door at Minute Two."

Sergeant Horne had taken a note book from his pocket and was studying it. "Yes Sir, that is what I have recorded."

"Good. Now, we estimated you and Morbey were talking for about three minutes before being joined by Lieutenant Rogers. So Lieutenant Rogers joined you at Minute Five."

The Sergeant nodded. "Yes Sir, that is my understanding."

"And finally, after a brief conversation, you and Lieutenant Rogers went to the scene of Lieutenant Johnson's accident, arriving there at Zero plus Eight."

"Yes Sir, that is correct."

Major MacDonald put down his papers. "Sergeant Horne, the crucial point in this examination is where was Sapper Morbey when Lieutenant Rogers heard the breaking glass? We agree Lieutenant Rogers arrived at the kitchen door at Minute Five on your timeline. That was Minute Four on Lieutenant Roger's timeline. We know Lieutenant Rogers heard the glass breaking four minutes prior to him arriving at the kitchen door. So now we track back four minutes on your timeline and find you talking to Sapper Morbey in the passageway. Is that your understanding of the timelines? The Sergeant looked up from the notebook he had been studying. “Yes Sir, I agree with those the numbers. Sapper Morbey must have been with me when the window was broken.”

“Thank you Sergeant Horne. I have no further questions.”

The President looked at Captain Sampson who shook his head.

“Right Sergeant Horne, you may stand down.” As the witness left the room, the President conferred with the other court members.

“Major MacDonald, we have all been doing our maths using the timings you and the Sergeant discussed. We believe the conclusion is clear and on that basis I imagine you now wish to make a formal submission to the court.”

“Mr President, I do wish to call one witness for the Defence.”

The President looked surprised. “Another witness? To me and my fellow court members your presentation of the case for the Defence has been most persuasive and conclusive. I cannot understand what possible evidence another witness could contribute to the case.”

“I understand your concern Sir. However, in my experience in cases such as this one, if we leave matters where they now stand, we leave the case in limbo. I can, and will argue that Sapper Morbey did not kill Lieutenant Johnson. But we are left with the unanswered question - ‘what happened?’ From my experience, Morbey’s name will never be completely cleared while that question is being posed. People will gossip and some uninformed persons will say that Morbey got off only because he had a smart lawyer.”

“And you are a smart lawyer Major MacDonald?”

“I will take that as a compliment Mr President.” Major MacDonald continued, “Until we know the truth about Lieutenant Johnson’s death, Sapper Morbey will, in some people’s mind, be guilty even though the Court found otherwise. Now I have a suspicion of what might have occurred in Lieutenant Johnson’s room. I don't know if I can here, in this Court, find the truth of the matter but I would like to try. I have a feeling, which may or may not be correct, but nevertheless I would like to test it."

The President conferred with the other court members. After a brief discussion it was obvious from the nodding of heads they agreed. The President addressed Major MacDonald. "The Court is very interested to hear just what your hunch is Major MacDonald, so please call your witness."

MADEMOISELLE

Major MacDonald paused. The room tension increased. "Call Mademoiselle Yvette Pruvost." Surprise ran through the Court. Yvette entered the courtroom and was escorted to the witness stand.

The President recovered from his surprise and asked: "Judge-Advocate, is this civilian allowed to appear before this court?"

"Yes Mr President. Civilians may take the stand in a court-martial."

"Very well. Major MacDonald, do we require an interpreter?"

"No Mr President, Mademoiselle Pruvost is fluent in English."

The Judge-Advocate advanced and administered the Oath. The President then addressed Yvette. "Tell me Mademoiselle Pruvost, do you understand the oath you have just taken?"

"Yes Mr President, I understand but it was always my intention to tell the truth."

Major MacDonald moved close to the witness stand. "Mademoiselle Pruvost, the court has heard you were present in the

Château passageway on the afternoon of 11th of November. Is that correct?"

"Yes Sir, I was there."

"Will you please tell the Court why you were there and if there were any other persons with you?"

Yvette nodded. "I was there as the coat and cap attendant. When officers enter the Château and don't want to go upstairs to their room, they leave their coat and cap on a hook in the passageway. I take the coat and cap and put them on the correct hook. Everyone has their own special hook. That afternoon Monsieur George was with me."

"Monsieur George?"

Yvette pointed towards the dock. "That is Monsieur George."

"Very good Mademoiselle. It would seem you know Sapper Morbey?"

"Yes, I do Sir, he is one of the soldiers billeted at our farm."

"So please tell the court why Sapper Morbey was with you in the Château that afternoon?"

"Monsieur George arrived at the Château that afternoon looking for Monsieur Bailey."

Major MacDonald interrupted. "How do you know Sapper Morbey was looking for Sapper Bailey?"

Yvette smiled for the first time. "Because he told me. Monsieur George came to the kitchen door and my sister Marie saw him. Marie asked what did he want and he told her he wanted to see Monsieur Bailey. Marie had no idea where Monsieur Bailey might be so she brought Monsieur George to the passageway to ask me if I knew. I didn't know but told Monsieur George that sometimes the officers' servants went to the officers' rooms via the stairway. Monsieur George said he would wait with me in case Monsieur Bailey came along. Marie then left us. We talked for a while. I was trying to find out exactly what had happened to my Simon that morning. Monsieur George told me a telephone wire linking Monsieur Bluey to the Australian trenches had been cut."

Major MacDonald held up his hand. "Let the court records show the name 'Monsieur Bluey' as Sapper Dowson and when Mademoiselle Yvette refers to 'my Simon' she is referring to Sapper Simon Young."

The President nodded. "Major MacDonald, we keep coming back to this cut in the telephone wire."

"Yes Sir, we do, and it is at the very heart of the matter. Please Mademoiselle, what did Sapper Morbey tell you about the cut in the telephone wire?"

Yvette reached for a handkerchief and wiped her eyes. "Monsieur George said Monsieur Bluey was in an observation post in no-man's land. He should have been recalled but he couldn't be contacted because of a break in the telephone line. When peace was announced, my Simon ran to tell Monsieur Bluey the good news, and as he ran a German sniper shot him. They shot my Simon after the war was over."

Yvette was visibly upset. "Now take your time, Mademoiselle. Perhaps a sip of water. We know this is difficult for you. When you feel ready, please continue but in your own time."

"I'm all right Major, I can go on. Monsieur George told me the members of the signal section suspected the line was cut by either Monsieur Johnson or Monsieur Bailey. He wanted to find out who cut the wire and why."

Major MacDonald again interrupted. "Now Mademoiselle, I want you to think very carefully about this question. Can you recall the exact words Sapper Morbey used when telling you why he was at the Château?"

Yvette gave the question some thought. "Yes Sir, he said 'I want to know who did it and why.' Those were the words he used."

"Thank you Mademoiselle, you have been most helpful. Now how long were you and Sapper Morbey talking, and what happened next?"

"I really don't know how long we were talking. Perhaps ten minutes. Maybe not that long. We had just agreed there was no point in Monsieur George staying in the passageway as we had no idea where Monsieur Bailey was. But just then Monsieur Bailey came running down the stairs. He was crying and talking in a very loud voice. He kept saying 'I didn't do it and they are going to blame me. They'll shoot me.' Monsieur George grabbed his arm and told him to settle down. Monsieur Bailey wouldn't stop crying out and struggled to get away. Then there was a shout and Sergeant Horne came out of the dining room. Monsieur George let go of Monsieur Bailey, and Monsieur Bailey ran down the passageway. Sergeant Horne called out to him to stop."

"And did he stop?"

"No, he first ran to where the coats where hanging and I saw him take a revolver from the Monsieur Johnson's hook. I know which hook belongs to who. After he grabbed the revolver, he ran down the passageway and out the back door."

"And no one tried to follow and stop him?"

Yvette frowned. "Who would run after a man with a gun?"

"A very sensible answer, Mademoiselle. Now I want you to think very carefully about the words Sapper Bailey was calling out. Can you be sure of what he was saying?"

"Yes Major MacDonald. I am very sure because he kept repeating them. He said, 'I didn't do it and they are going to blame it on me. They will shoot me'."

"You are sure he used the word 'they'?"

"Yes Sir, he said 'they'."

"So, what happened then?"

"Sergeant Horne was very angry. He wanted to know Monsieur George's name and what was he doing in the Officers' Mess.

Monsieur George told him why he was there. Sergeant Horne told me to stay where I was and told Monsieur George to follow him into the kitchen."

"So now you are on your own in the passageway?"

Yvette hesitated. "Yes, I was on my own but I still didn't know whom was responsible for the death of my Simon. I was angry and upset. Monsieur Bailey had run away so I would not be able to ask him. Monsieur George had gone and I still had no answers. I decided that the only person remaining who could give me the answers was Monsieur Johnson. I didn't know if he was in his room but I did know which room was his as I had at times been employed on room care duties. So I decided to go to Monsieur Johnson's room and if he was there ask him for some answers."

A murmur swept through the courtroom. "Mademoiselle Yvette, have I got this right? You decided to go, on your own, upstairs and question Lieutenant Johnson in his room?"

"Yes Sir, that is right."

"Was that a wise decision?"

"Wise! It probably wasn't wise but I was desperate to find answers. I was very angry. I am still very angry. Simon should not have died."

"So you went upstairs to Lieutenant Johnson's room. Was he there?"

"Well, I started to go upstairs but I had only gone three or four steps when an officer came rushing down the stairs. He was in a dreadful hurry. He knocked me aside and I bumped into the banister. It hurt me and took my breath away."

"Did the Officer apologise?"

"No he didn't. I don't think he saw me. He was in such a hurry and probably didn't even know he had hit me."

Major MacDonald frowned to show his displeasure. "After you recovered your breath, what did you do?"

"I sat down on the stairs and cried. Everything was so wrong. I didn't know what to do. Then an officer came running along the passageway. I think he came from the ante room. He asked me if I knew where the Mess Manager was. I pointed to the kitchen door and he went through there."

"Did you recognise the Officer?"

Yvette shook her head. "He was a junior officer and I have seen him before but I do not know his name."

"So you are sitting on the stairs and are very upset. What did you do then?"

Yvette wiped her eyes. "I decided to go home. There was nothing I could do at the Château. I was too upset. So, I went into the kitchen to get my coat and ran into my sister Marie. I told her I was going home, and she said I should wait for her and my other sister Nicole. But I had had enough and left. When I came out of the building, Monsieur George was standing there. I ran to him and he gave me a hug - just what I needed. We talked for a few minutes and he told me an officer had told Sergeant Horne that Monsieur Johnson had fallen from his room and it looked very bad. I don't know if I was sad or happy to hear the news. Monsieur George said he would walk me home and that is what happened. When we reached the farm, Monsieur George said he was going into Corbie to have a drink. That is when we parted."

"Major MacDonald consulted his notes. "Thank you Mademoiselle Yvette. Your evidence has been most useful. I have one final question. The Officer who so rudely pushed you aside as he ran down the stairs - do you know him?"

"Yes sir, I do. That is him sitting over there." She pointed. All eyes in the room looked at the Officer.

Major MacDonald spoke. "Let the record show that Mademoiselle Pruvost has indicated that Colonel Payne is the officer who pushed past her on the stairs. Thank you Mademoiselle, I have no further questions."

Like everyone else in the courtroom, the President was surprised by the turn of events. Quickly regaining his composure he asked: "Does the Prosecution have any questions for this witness?"

Captain Sampson got to his feet slowly. "Just one, Mr President. Mademoiselle Pruvost, you have given your evidence in a most commendable manner. However, like all here, I have been surprised by your identification of Colonel Payne as the officer who pushed past you on the stairs. Are you completely sure Colonel Payne was that person?"

Yvette nodded. "Yes sir, it was Colonel Payne. Whenever I received from him his cap and coat or when giving them to him, he always had a nice word to say. He was a real gentleman. I don't know all the officers in the Mess, but I do know Colonel Payne."

Captain Sampson turned to the President. "I have no further questions."

The President turned to Yvette. "Thank you Mademoiselle Pruvost. Your evidence has been most enlightening. You may leave the witness stand."

Yvette nodded to the President and walked to sit beside her mother. All eyes were now on Major MacDonald.

REPREHENSIBLE

The President spoke, "Well Major MacDonald, do you have any more tricks up your sleeve?"

Major MacDonald was quick to his feet. "Mr President, those remarks are offensive. Mademoiselle Pruvost was not a trick, as you put it. She was an important material witness to what happened in the passageway that day."

The President raised his hand. "Major MacDonald, I apologise for the use of the word 'trick' - it was an error on my part. The Court recognises the value of the evidence given by Mademoiselle Pruvost. It was just that we, the Court, were not expecting any further witnesses after Sergeant Horne and were taken by surprise when you called the young lady. Please accept my apology."

"Thank you, Sir. I accept the apology. We all make mistakes and I trust my next move will not be a serious error in judgement on my part or a breach of court protocol. Normally at this juncture, I would summarise the evidence to show clearly that Sapper Morbey was nowhere near Lieutenant Johnson's room at the time the Officer fell from his window."

Major MacDonald paused. "You may recall, Mr President, that earlier I spoke of the need to try and finalise our understanding of just what did occur to Lieutenant Johnson. I wish to call Colonel Payne to the stand, but first the Court needs to decide if that course of action is legally permissible. Colonel Payne has been in the court throughout the entire proceedings and has therefore heard all evidence. And I am not sure whether I have the right to call Colonel Payne. The Court must consider that, should Colonel Payne take the stand, my proposed line of questioning may impinge on his rights. These are complex questions that need to be addressed."

The President looked towards the Judge-Advocate. "You have heard what Major MacDonald is proposing. Can you give the Court a ruling on this proposal?"

The Judge-Advocate closed the manual he had been consulting and rose to his feet.

"Major MacDonald can call anyone as a witness in this case. However, the matter of calling Colonel Payne as a witness is rather complex. Colonel Payne can be called to take the stand and should that occur the Colonel could be sworn in. However, in view of the point made by Major MacDonald that some of his questions could impinge on Colonel Payne's rights I advise that should a question arise that Colonel Payne does not wish to answer, then the Court must decide whether the question has to be answered. After swearing in Colonel Payne, I would advise him of his rights in this matter."

The President turned his colleagues. After a brief consultation, the President addressed the courtroom. "The Court has decided to follow the course of action proposed by the Judge-Advocate. Call Colonel Payne."

As soon as his name was called, Colonel Payne strode to the witness stand and took the oath. The Judge-Advocate started to explain his rights but Colonel Payne waved him aside. "My hearing is perfectly good and I fully understand my rights. Can we get on with the business?"

The President nodded to Major MacDonald who rose to his feet.

"Colonel Payne, on a previous appearance in the witness box you stated that on the afternoon of 11th of November you did not leave the bar to check on the whereabouts of Lieutenant Johnson although he had not joined you as arranged."

Colonel Payne nodded in agreement. "It is true I made such a statement, but that was not the truth. I am well aware of the seriousness of lying to the Court, and I sincerely regret doing so."

"Did you see Lieutenant Johnson at any time after you had lunch with him on 11th of November?"

Colonel Payne paused before replying.

The President intervened. "Colonel Payne. Are you declining to answer the question?"

Colonel Payne shook his head, "No Mr President, I am prepared to truthfully answer any question put to me. What I am trying to decide is what is the best way to sort out this awful mess and I think the best and quickest way is for me to make a full statement now. That will save a lot of time and trouble for all."

The President looked at Major MacDonald, "Well Major, are you agreeable to the proposal made by Colonel Payne?"

"I certainly am, Mr President. This is an unusual course of action but then this is an unusual case. I anticipate it will save me asking a lot of questions."

"Very good. Colonel Payne, you may make your statement."

Colonel Payne took a long drink of water. "After Lieutenant Johnson and I returned from the front, we had lunch in the mess and agreed to meet later in the bar for a celebratory drink. I arrived at the bar around 4:00pm. I had been there for about an hour and Ronald, Lieutenant Johnson, had not appeared. I thought he had probably dropped off to sleep so I excused myself to the group I was drinking with. I indicated I was going to the toilet. I went upstairs. The door to Ronald's room was not locked so I went in. To my surprise and horror, Ronald and his batman, Sapper Bailey, were both sitting on the bed in a state of undress. They both stood up. I didn't know what to say. Finally, I found my voice and shouted at them to get dressed, which they did."

A strange silence had come over the courtroom. All eyes were riveted on the Colonel. He continued: "While they were dressing I tried to regain my composure. I didn't know how to handle the matter. I was disgusted and extremely angry. I looked out the window so I didn't have to look at them. I then said to Ronald that perhaps there was some truth in the accusations made by No.3 Signal Section that he did cut that wire last night. Ronald replied he did not cut the wire, but Sapper Bailey had."

"On hearing that, Sapper Bailey screamed out that Ronald was a liar and that he, Ronald, had cut the wire. Ronald just laughed at Bailey and said 'Who is going to believe you? I am an Officer, and they will take my word before they listen to you. You are in big trouble Bailey. They will shoot you.' Sapper Bailey went to pieces. He was crying and yelling out 'It's not fair, I am innocent, you can't blame me'. The whole thing was getting out of hand. I ordered Sapper Bailey to return to his quarters and wait for the military police. He ran from the room still crying and shouting. I am surprised no one heard him."

Colonel Payne took another sip of water. The room remained quiet.

"Once Sapper Bailey had left, I started to speak to Ronald. I was now in control of myself. I told him what a failure he had been. I told him how disappointed I was in his behaviour. He just laughed. He was treating the whole thing as some sort of joke. Then I said 'just wait until your mother hears about this.' As soon as I said this, his whole attitude changed. He yelled at me 'don't you dare tell my mother anything, you great oaf.' He became hysterical. I replied I would be telling his mother everything, and with that he ran at me and threw back his right arm. He then swung his arm in a round-arm punch. It was easy to avoid and I grabbed his arm and swung him around. It was my intention to throw him against the wall but as he swung round he hit the window and went through it."

Colonel Payne shook his head. "It was a nightmare. The whole thing. I looked out of the window and could see Ronald lying on the ground below. The angle of his head made it obvious he was dead. I didn't know what to do. I panicked. I ran from the room along the passage and down the stairs. I don't remember seeing that young lady on the stairs and if I harmed her as I rushed past, I am truly sorry. I got to the bottom of the stairs and collected my thoughts. I then walked back to the bar. No one seemed to have noticed my absence. I was only there for a short time before Lieutenant Rogers entered and informed the group that Ronald was lying on the ground and looked to be in a bad way. We all rushed to the scene of the accident. There was nothing to connect me with the event."

Major MacDonald held up his hand to stop Colonel Payne, "What about Sapper Bailey? He could place you at the scene of the crime, if indeed it was a crime."

"Yes Major, he could say I was there, but at the time I wasn't thinking straight. Later when I heard that Bailey was dead, I felt relieved as now no one could connect me to Ronald's accident. Of course I wasn't aware of pushing past the young lady on the stairs." He paused.

Major MacDonald spoke. "Colonel Payne. There are some people who might feel sorry for you as it was a most difficult and harrowing situation that you faced. However, I have little sympathy for you. This Court is sitting here today to try Sapper Morbey for the crime of murdering Lieutenant Johnson, and you have sat here in this court room, and allowed the trial to proceed knowing that Morbey was innocent. I find that reprehensible."

Colonel Payne interrupted Major MacDonald. "No, I would never have allowed Sapper Morbey to be found guilty. My hope was that he would be acquitted and then the circumstances of Ronald's death would become a mystery, soon to be forgotten."

"I do not see how you could have overturned a guilty verdict but that is not my concern." Major MacDonald turned to face the President. "Sir, I do not want to pursue this matter any further. I think justice has reigned in the court room today, and for that we should all be grateful." Major MacDonald sat.

The President spoke to the fellow members of the Court before addressing the court room. "Colonel Payne, we are unsure of the correct procedures to be followed here so I am directing you to return to your quarters and await instructions from higher authority." Colonel Payne rose and, watched by everyone present, made a slow exit from the court room.

The President continued. "I believe the matters before this Court have been completed in a most satisfactory manner. I would like to make special mention of the contribution made by Major MacDonald. Thank you Major. There being no further business..."

Major Macdonald rose to his feet. "Before you dissolve the Court, Mr President, there is one important matter to be resolved."

The Judge-Advocate was also on his feet. "Sir, you have not delivered the verdict on the charges against the accused."

"Good point and a glaring error on my part. Sapper Morbey, stand."

George got to his feet.

The President continued: "Sapper Morbey, this Court finds you not guilty of the charge of the murder of Lieutenant Johnson. You are free to go." A burst of clapping broke out.

The court members stood up as the Judge-Advocate declared, "This Court is now dissolved."

* * *

Gilly and the girls went to great lengths to arrange a party at the farm that evening. There was an ample supply of alcoholic drinks available but only a few of the guests indulged. It was quite early in the evening that Major MacDonald announced that he would be leaving as he had other commitments back at his Regiment. Al and Bluey tried to dissuade him but he could not be persuaded to change his mind. Bluey accompanied the Major to his car.

"You have all been very generous with your kind remarks Sapper Dowson but I do have other matters that require my attention and other persons who require my help. This sojourn with the Australian Army has been most enjoyable especially as we got the result we all hoped for."

"Yes Sir. And all thanks to you. You were magnificent."

The Major shook his head and laughed, "That's going a bit too far Dowson. It really was an easy case to defend as the prosecution didn't believe that Sapper Morbey was guilty. There really wasn't a case for Morbey to answer. No evidence at all. Just a lot of people in a hurry to get the matter settled. I think any barrister worth his salt would have convinced the Court of Morbey's innocence."

"Well if they didn't have a case why charge George, why go to all that trouble?"

"Egos come into the equation Dowson. Someone had to be held responsible or the higher echelon would lose face. Remember Colonel Payne was pushing hard for a trial and we know what his motives were. But Morbey can owe his survival to his best friends, yourself and Wilson. Without your help who knows what might have happened. It doesn't bear thinking about." The Major held out his hand. "Time I was moving on. I've said my farewells to the others so I can slip away. It's been a pleasure to meet the famous bushranger after hearing all those stories about you. If you ever get to Scotland I can assure you of a very warm welcome." With those words Major MacDonald entered his car and departed.

DINNER AT SEVEN

Al and Bluey were sitting at the table after breakfast the next morning when Gilly entered the room. "Gilly, a lovely party last night! George doesn't seem to have learned his lesson as far as having the odd drink or two but we'll let him sleep."

"I agree Monsieur Al. He has earned a rest. Fancy him thinking that Yvette had killed Lieutenant Johnson and he being prepared to take the blame."

Al smiled. "All the Section loved your family Gilly, and George as a parent, felt a very special responsibility towards the girls. It wasn't until Major MacDonald sat down with him and convinced him that Yvette was innocent that George relented and agreed to Yvette giving evidence. As things turned out, the Major could already prove George's innocence before Yvette took the stand but it was her evidence that finally brought out the truth. She deserves a medal."

"Oh, I don't think she wants a medal, Monsieur Al. What she wants, and in fact what all the Pruvost family wants, is for you and Monsieur Bluey to stay longer. Of course, I include Monsieur George."

"That's very kind of you Gilly, and there is nothing we would like more than to stay in this lovely home but we have to be realistic. We came to help defeat the Germans. That has come to past and now we must return home. We shall miss you but home is home, and Australia is a wonderful country. Perhaps we can persuade you and the girls to migrate to Australia. This country is in a mess. What about it?"

"A lovely thought, Monsieur Al. Several times members of the Section have asked us if we would consider moving to your country. We have heard so much about Australia but to go there isn't really possible or practical at the moment. My mother-in-law, Madame Pruvost, would never leave this home and while she stays, I stay. You are right, this country is in a mess and I feel we must help to tidy up that mess, and that will probably take some time. I would love to visit Australia and so would the girls. Perhaps at some time in the future we will be in a position to accept your kind invitation."

"I fully understand Gilly, but know that the invitation to visit will always be there."

"Something for us to dream about Monsieur Al. You will be here tomorrow?"

"Yes Gilly." The two men stood up and Al continued: "Captain Solway has told me that we, that is, the first contingent to come overseas, will be moved to depots in England very soon to be ready go home. Other troops like Bluey here will be moved to camps in various parts of France and Belgium to dig graves in formal war cemeteries. I feel sorry for you Bluey."

"Not looking forward to it myself Al. But you never know, I might get lucky and get posted to a camp nearby and then I can visit the farm."

Gilly smiled. "That would be just wonderful, Monsieur Bluey."

"Well, we'll see you both tonight. Dinner at seven." Gilly left the room.

"We'd better get moving Bluey. I told Captain Solway we'd report in this morning to see what surprises the Army has in store for us. What's the time?"

Bluey went through his well-established routine for consulting his precious watch. He carefully removed the watch from its case, opened the cover and gazed at the dial. Then with a flourish he snapped shut the cover and returned the watch to its case. Only then did he pronounce his findings. "Time we were going to Captain Solway's office."

Al shook his head. "One day you'll actually tell me the time in hours and minutes but I won't hold my breath."

"Be satisfied Al. You've been given all the information you require. Let's go."

With that, the men set off to walk to Corbie.

TOZ DADSWELL

"Commodore Dadswell grew up in Red Cliffs, a soldier settlement in North-West Victoria. He entered the Royal Australian Naval College in 1946 and on graduation in 1949 was awarded the Kings Medal. He specialized in Naval Aviation and was awarded his wings in 1956. In 1964 while joining the carrier's landing circuit he witnessed the collision between the carrier HMAS MELBOURNE and the destroyer HMAS VOYAGER.

Among the number of senior postings he held in the Royal Australian Navy, were Commanding Officer HMAS MELBOURNE and Commanding Officer HMAS ALBATROSS, the RAN's Naval Air Station. In 1981 he was made a Member of the Order of Australia.

After retiring from the RAN in 1986 Commodore Dadswell was recalled to active service to design a scheme for the employment of the tall ship YOUNG ENDEAVOUR, a bicentennial gift from the British Government. The outcome of this exercise was the creation of the Young Endeavour Youth Scheme a most successful project which is still operating today."

ACKNOWLEDGEMENTS

I wish to thank my three daughters for their support and encouragement in the writing of this book.

I would also like to thank Ms Marlene Knight for applying her artistic, literary and administrative skills to the production of this book. It is because of her devotion and determination this book had been published.

Lightning Source UK Ltd.
Milton Keynes UK
UKHW010309081222
413533UK00004B/139